PUCKSTRUCK

PUCK

Distracted, Delighted

STRUCK

and Distressed by Canada's Hockey Obsession

Stephen Smith

GREYSTONE BOOKS

VANCOUVER/BERKELEY

14 15 16 17 18   5 4 3 2 1

Greystone Books Ltd.
www.greystonebooks.com

Cataloguing data available from Library and Archives Canada
ISBN 978-1-77164-048-0 (cloth)
ISBN 978-1-77164-091-6 (epub)

Editing by Jan Walter
Copy editing by Lesley Cameron
Jacket design by Jessica Sullivan and Nayeli Jimenez
Text design by Ingrid Paulson
Jacket photograph courtesy of the Glenbow Archives, NC-6-11932b
Printed and bound in Canada by Friesens
Distributed in the U.S. by Publishers Group West

Every attempt has been made to trace ownership of copyrighted material. Information
that will allow the publisher to rectify any credit or reference is welcome.

We gratefully acknowledge the financial support of the Canada Council for the Arts,
the British Columbia Arts Council, the Province of British Columbia through the Book
Publishing Tax Credit, and the Government of Canada through the Canada
Book Fund for our publishing activities.

Greystone Books is committed to reducing the consumption of old-growth forests
in the books it publishes. This book is one step towards that goal.

Puckstruck
\\'pək-strək\\

(adjective)
hit by a puck; bewitched and bewildered
by the game that ails us

The boys at Olney have likewise a very
entertaining sport, which commences annually upon this day
[5th Nov.]: they call it Hockey; and it consists in
dashing each other with mud, and the windows also.
— William Cowper, in a letter (1785)

Is it important? Am I missing something?
Is there something else here?
— Rick Salutin, *Les Canadiens* (1977)

Sarah

[Contents]

[Preamble]

Stan Fischler: Do you read books by ex-hockey players?
Mike Palmateer: I've been there; I've played the game.
I don't care what John and Joe did ten years ago.
I often wonder how much is real and how much is bullshit they're
writing to make the story sound good. I stay away from that.

GOALIES (1995)

THIS IS A book about what I found out when I read all the hockey books.

I started this project in 1970 or so, though in those early years it's fair to say that I was mainly looking at the pictures, some of which I may or may not have been colouring. The first book was likely Chip Young's *The Wild Canadians*, in which rats, otters, bears, and bobcats skate and score in the winter woods of Tennessee. Another early and beloved title, complete with murky photographs, was *The Hockey Encyclopedia* by Gary Ronberg. That's where I learned about Aurèle Joliat, Busher Jackson, and Gump Worsley, names that were as everyday to me as those of the kids in my class at school. I read Scott Young's stories of boy hockey players, hockey biographies, coaching manuals, the backs of hockey cards, all the good and all the bad, and always the runic rhymes of newspaper scores: Who got the second assist on Pierre Larouche's goal? How many shots did Ken Dryden stop in the second period? At hockey-reading, I was a natural.

Five or six years ago, I became more systematic in my reading, seeking answers to specific questions, many of them to do with why I remain so consumed and excited by this game that also so regularly puzzles and exasperates me. Why were hockey players still punching each other in the head, and why hadn't I stopped watching in protest? The longer I watch hockey, the less plausible it seems. This game that takes the place of reason in a man's brain—as the poet Al Purdy wrote—it *used* to make more sense, didn't it? I expected to ache more, playing the game on Friday mornings as I continue to do, and I've known for years that my backhand, never mighty, is a lost cause. But I never really doubted my faith in hockey until recently.

Disclaimer: I didn't read *all* the hockey books, because there are just too many, and more appear every year. Hundreds, though, did figure into this project, and they piled up at home in Toronto to such an extent that the moon began to shift them like tides. They flooded a weekend place, too, two hours to the north, not far from the pond where I'd eventually conjure up a rink. I carried Dave Bidini's *Tropic of Hockey* to Dingle in Ireland, and through Asturias in Spain the puckish novel *Amazons*, which Don DeLillo pretends he didn't write. (He did.)

I read *Hockey Town* and *Hockey Towns*, *Hockey in My Blood* and *All Roads Lead to Hockey*. I read the book where eight-year-old Stanislas Gvoth got on a train in Prague and ended up in St. Catharines, Ontario, where he turned into Stan Mikita. I read about Camille Henry's skate when it cut up through Bobby Baun's throat and missed his jugular but reached the underside of his tongue. The doctor who stitched him up wore a handgun in a belt-holster, and then Baun went out and played the third period of the game, and afterwards he nearly died from hemorrhaging and not being able to breathe, and then a week later he played for the Leafs in Detroit.

Some books I read on a sailboat, many others on trains. A few of those I left behind on purpose, to continue the journey without me.

Discovering that a man called Dick Smith may have been (probably) one of the first to write down formal hockey rules in 1878, I may have allowed my unearned pride to justify a tendency to be easily and righteously miffed when I see the game straying into havoc.

I read that the puck is a metaphoric penis, and while the resemblance of the back of the net to a woman's buttocks may be unintentional, are you seriously trying to tell me that out in front, with the crease, it isn't plainly labial in form? This I learned from *Scoring: The Art of Hockey*, the remarkable 1979 collaboration between the novelist Hugh Hood and the artist Seymour Segal. Hood, who also wrote a memorable biography of Jean Béliveau, said elsewhere that making love is better than skating, but skating is a close second.

Although I didn't make it through all the hockey Harlequins available, I can recite titles (*Her Man Advantage, The Penalty Box*) and do recall the exact moment that Marissa knew that she loved Kyle: right after she watched a big Pittsburgh defenceman plant a fist in his nose. One of the scientific studies I pondered used hockey to consider the relationship between face shape and aggression. The truth about *How Hockey Saved the World* is that I skipped right to the final page to see if everything turned out okay. Parts of *From Rattlesnake Hunt to Hockey* I read, other parts I left alone.

From the chapter titles of hockey books, I assembled a poem:

Born to Play Hockey
The Five Truths of Shovelling
Techniques of Mayhem

Woodchopping Galore
Hospitals and Hockey Can Mix
Greatest Thing Since Penicillin

Facing Four Hundred Saracens on His Own
When Hull Shoots, I Must Not Blink
A Piece of Rubber Unites an Entire People

with this coda just from Soviet-era books:

Hockey and Astronauts
Think Up and Try
Gretzky Is Really Powerful!

I scoured Alice Munro, because although she doesn't write hockey novels per se, the glances she gives the game in her stories make the point, again, that her perception is rarely anything but lucent. In the story "Train," for instance, she writes about the people in a small Munro-country town:

> They did not have much to do with each other, unless it was for games run off in the ballpark or the hockey arena, where all was a fervent made-up sort of hostility.

On my list of hockey odours was

- Dennis Hull's autobiographical observation that post-expansion, the new NHL smelled of shampoo and hairspray and hairdryer heat, which was never the case before.
- a fictional journeyman defenceman's impression of facing Bobby Orr from Roy MacGregor's *The Last Season*: "I smelled him, not skunky the way I got myself, but the smell of Juicy Fruit chewing gum."

I copied out appalling sentences:

- "Once, when we were playing the Buffalo Bisons, Zeidel sliced Gordie Hannigan so badly that the blood was flowing out of his head to the beat of his heart."

- "I lived in constant fear that someday I was going to murder someone with that stick."

Maybe you've noticed, as I did, the unsettlingly jocular and even jolly tone with which a lot of the worst of hockey horror is depicted. I thought a lot about the language we use—or don't use—to talk about the game. I collected words that should have long since gone into the hockey dictionary, including:

- shog: v. to upset or discompose, and also to shake, jerk, or jolt. *Bill Nyrop has been after Bobby Schmautz all night, shogging and galling him.*
- frangible: adj. capable of being broken. *Have you ever seen the Gumper so frangible?*
- Pokemouche: n. 1. town in New Brunswick, on the Pokemouche River. 2. a homegrown Donnybrook. *Looks like Colton Orr is on his way to the box after that Pokemouche in front of the Vancouver net.*

I grew fond of the frank talk some older hockey books offer about conditioning (shun liquor, says Rocket Richard, but a beer after the game is okay), smoking (not harmful if you stick to cigarettes, according to Sid Abel), and pies and pickles (turn your back on both, Black Jack Stewart mandates).

I confess I didn't expect so many books by fathers of hockey players, all the Murray Drydens and Réjean Lafleurs, Walter Gretzkys, Viacheslav Kovalevs, and Michel Roys who felt the need to explain their sons.

Sometimes it seemed like the books were talking among themselves: not long after I finished *If They Played Hockey in Heaven,* I came across *They Don't Play Hockey in Heaven.* And is it just me, or is *Bobby Orr: My Game* spoiling for a fight with Bobby Hull's *Hockey Is My Game*?

I read the libretto of what may be the sole hockey opera, which Jaroslav Dušek wrote with composer Martin Smolka. As you may recall, the Czechs won the gold medal at the 1998 Olympics in Japan, beating Canada and Russia in succession. The operatic version is called *Nagano*. It premiered in 2004 in Prague, where it's possible that in song, in the original Czech, it didn't sound as stilted as it reads on the English page. For example, when Ice Rink, performed by a women's chorus, serenades tenor-Jaromir Jagr:

ICE RINK: You're mine, I'm yours, mine, yours.

JAGR: You can be treacherous, treacherous, oh plain of ice!

I will reveal that my nominee for best hockey image from a hockey poem is in John B. Lee's "Lucky Life":

they quarrel with a skatelace
that sets porridged in an eyelet
too snug for moving either way.

I read Borje Salming's memoir in English, though I continue to favour the Swedish title, *Blod, svett och hockey*. Old Russian books I wish I had the Cyrillic to navigate in their original editions would have to include *The Hot Ice, I Am the Same as Each, The Real Men of Hockey*, and *Get Ready to Offence, Get Ready to Defence*.

If there was a work of hockey art I kept going back to, it was *Hockey Fights/Fruit Bowls* by Chris Hanson and Hendrika Sonnenberg because really, what better, more beautiful sense is there to be made of hockey fighters than to inundate them with fresh grapefruits and oranges and lemons?

Historian Bill Fitsell lent me one of the three remaining original copies of the first proper hockey book, *Hockey: Canada's Royal*

Winter Game, and I read it gently (it's very frail), with the particular pleasure of knowing that its author, Arthur Farrell, was elevated to hockey's Hall of Fame mainly on the strength of this literary achievement. That's not to say he wasn't a magician of pucks when he played for the Montreal Shamrocks and won three Stanley Cups, it's just that the record suggests his case wouldn't have been as strong without his landmark 1899 book to support it.

Farrell was the first one to cite hockey's rules in a book, along with lots of solid practical guidance, such as if you intend to play, get your heart checked. I thought he was talking about taking stock of your own mettle, a gut check, but no, he literally means you should go for an actual medical examination. As for violence, Farrell didn't think at that early date that it was a concern. The fans, he wrote, would keep the game clean — anything else they'd be sure to jeer out of existence.

I WATCHED MANY hockey movies that weren't very good. Compared to hockey's books, not to mention hockey itself, the movies have more barrel-jumping, bribery, and helicopters crashing down at centre ice. The movies aren't all terrible all of the time, but movie-hockey is consistently, unrelievedly awful. That started me on a search for a hockey movie where the hockey was authentic-looking, without a well-lit Rob Lowe bursting past congealed defencemen to score on a goalie who waves his glove at the puck as if to say, *So long*. *Idol of the Crowds*, from 1937, tries to smudge it the way hockey movies sometimes do, by laying in actual NHL footage, which is great to see, even if it is enlivened by a very unNHL-like but nonetheless jaunty flight of jazzy clarinet. The problem is the movie's hero, Johnny Hanson, portrayed as the best player ever in New York Crusher history. He's played by John Wayne who, when he steps onto the ice, can barely stand up. Other than an ankle-turning Wayne, *Idol* *of the Crowds* is notable for its examination of the question of whether a responsible adult should in good conscience pursue a hockey career when he could be running a chicken farm north of the city. "I'd feel kind of foolish going clear down there just to play hockey," Wayne's character drawls at one point. "Seems like a man ought to have a regular job. I want to build something and see it grow."

I read the novel *Slap Shot*, I confess, without (somehow) ever getting around to watching the movie. Many hockey movies I could only read about, the older ones especially, because they're almost impossible to find. Many of these are from the 1930s, when Hollywood was crazy for hockey and its awfully interesting gambling problem. No, I didn't know about that either, but it seems hockey games rigged by dastardly bad guys were a big draw for a while. I didn't watch *Hell's Kitchen*, *Times Square Lady*, *King of Hockey*, *Gay Blades*, or *Manhattan Melodrama*, starring Clark Gable. The bankrobber John Dillinger went to see that one in 1934. When he strolled out of the cinema after the movie, a policeman shot him dead. *The Game That Kills* I also didn't find, though I'm hoping someone gets around to resurrecting that one.

I'm sorry that none of us will ever see *The Great Canadian*, with Gable and Mae West. Even before you know the plot, it sounds like a movie that would be brimming with insights into national character and how the game we claim as our own is played. The first time it showed up in the industry papers, it was all about wheat farming on the wide-open prairies. By 1937, though, MGM had switched natural resources and wheat was replaced by hockey in a script by Anita Loos. The studio had Phil Watson from the New York Rangers lined up to grow his moustache and double for Gable on the ice, but then West backed out and Gable needed a break and the movie was never made. "I can't see myself horsing around with hockey players in a business way," West said. "It would make me feel unappealing."

I READ *CRUNCH* and *Grapes* and also *Shootin' and Smilin'*. There was *Blood on the Ice*, *Fire on Ice*, *Power on Ice*, *Cowboy on Ice*, *Heaven on Ice*, *Level Ice*, and *Steel on Ice*. I confess to browsing Eldridge Cleaver's Black Power manifesto *Soul on Ice*, just in case.

I was unprepared to discover how much baking there is in hockey books. And not just in the NHL cookbooks, of which there are piles. May I recommend *Favorite Recipes of the St. Louis Blues*? That's the one with Brendan Shanahan's Surprise Spread. Goalie Gump Worsley boldly includes his straightforward recipe for Pineapple Squares in his autobiography. Separated eggs, baking powder, shredded coconut, it's all there. "Bake at 350° about 30 minutes," he concludes. "Cool and cut into squares."

I read about teams called Imperoyals and Sudbury Frood Miners and Atlantic City Boardwalk Bullies. There were Buckaroos, Sabercats, Jackalopes, Salmonbellies, and Silverbacks. I came across Saskatoon Hoo-Hoos and Sheiks, and Winnipeg Vimys and Sommes. Zephyrs skate in the pages of hockey history with Pests and Porkies, Estacades and Saugueneens. The Toronto Research Colonels may be my favourite team name, unless it's the Toronto Dentals. I don't think the Whitehorse Men of the Apocalypse is an actual team; I believe somebody made that one up. I know that if I had a team of my own in north-central Maine I'd call it the Bangor Bebanged.

Like everybody, I had my favourite players when I was younger, many of whom played centre for the Montreal Canadiens in the 1970s, and I read about them eagerly. That leads me to a further disclaimer: there's more looking back here than ahead, lots of historical hockey, not so much of the present day.

The names of baseball players, Don DeLillo has said, make a poetry all their own. Hockey's stanzas include Fido Purpur and Sprague Cleghorn, Flat Walsh and Mud Bruneteau, Radek Bonk and Per Djoos,

Steve Smith and Zarley Zalapski, names I couldn't have made up if I'd tried. Hockey fiction's Hurry Bertons and Felix Batterinskis, Rupe McMasters and Bucky Crydermans can't really match them.

Hockey, of course, has many instructional volumes offering five-point plans for prospective players, the second of which is sometimes *Take man first, puck second* and also *Keep yourself in condition* or *Maintain your concentration* or *No touch football or skiing in the pre-season in case of ankle injuries.* Another golden rule, courtesy of Johnny Bucyk: *Don't get disgusted with your performance.*

With *Blue Line Murder* I got as far as page 15, which is where Cowboy Brandt winds up to take a shot in the warm-up and *ptchoo!* a sniper in the stands puts a bullet through his head. Hockey players often get murdered in the middle of big games in the hockey mysteries. Either they take a cold tablet that turns out to be cyanide (Billy Siragusa in Emma Lathen's *Murder Without Icing*) or like poor Gaston Lemaire in *Crimson Ice*, they're both stabbed *and* poisoned while sitting in the penalty box. When the ante's been upped that high, is it any wonder that a murder that takes place on the way out of the rink—I'm thinking here of G.B. Joyce's *The Code*—feels like a letdown?

HOCKEY IS FAMOUS for not having a literature. Lots of people who can't name a single hockey novel can chat about this deficiency, often invoking comparisons to the towering achievements of baseball's writers. I'm no ball fan, which is maybe why this kind of talk has always annoyed me, but it's the fear that it might be true that nags me more. Tetchy dread can't be the best fuel for a project like this, but I confess that at least some of my readerly determination came from the need to prove definitively that hockey's prose was just shy, a fugitive who only needed chasing.

In light of the hard times that hockey has been in recently, a search for its literary soul may not seem like the most pressing priority facing the game. I don't know if it's the worst time in the sport's hundred-and-thirtyish years of formal history, but let's see how it looks on the page: There has been no worse time for hockey ever, than now.

It did go through a pretty terrible time in the 1970s, you may remember: right after Paul Henderson scored his famous goal in Moscow to win the 1972 Summit Series, and then on through the decade. It was as though, despite the glorious victory in the Soviet Union, hockey caught a bad cold that just kept getting worse. If you were willing to put a metaphorical slant on things, maybe this was a punishment for the way we'd won, a lesson to be learned. And actually, some of the Canadian players did come home with an ailment that dogged them for years afterwards. By all accounts, it was as unpleasant an affliction in the flesh as it was an elegantly useful analogy in print. Think of Montezuma's Revenge, the sportswriter Jim Proudfoot wrote, or better yet, the Sovietsky Parasite. The blame was on Moscow's sanitation, and the medical explanation was—well, Proudfoot didn't travel too far into the technicalities, preferring the lay terms *varmints, microscopic passengers, wee brutes*. It was 1974 before doctors figured it out and put those who were suffering on pills and a strict diet and told them to hold up on the alcohol for a bit. Henderson's was the worst case, and Pete Mahovlich was pretty bad, as were some of the players' wives. It was part of the reason, Henderson said, that he went into a slump after the series: the virus made him mediocre.

But here's the thing with the 1970s: hockey got through its bad bout. With the trouble hockey is in now, I wonder whether it has finally strayed beyond hope, too far for anyone to rescue. Is hockey worth it?

This is a serious question. We know what hockey means to us. The unique expression of our authentic selves, says Andrew Coyne, realer than queen or flag. "An outstanding agency of Canadianization," a Montreal editorialist wrote in 1943 when NHL president Frank Calder died. Poet Richard Harrison says it's our id. The truest

Canadian currency according to—forgotten who. Bruce Kidd and John Macfarlane: it's the dance of life. Peter Gzowski: hockey is us.

Today, if you had to locate them in the body, hockey's troubles wouldn't be intestinal. You'd have to look to the head, perhaps between the ears of Boston Bruins centreman Marc Savard, who early in 2011, having suffered his second concussion in a year, was reported to be experiencing symptoms that exactly matched hockey's own, including "headaches, irritability, and memory lapses." Within a few months, at the age of thirty-four, Savard was out of the game for good.

It can seem some days as though hockey is an exercise designed expressly to daze and injure as many of its players as possible without quite killing them, though that also happens. Recently, much more of the talk around hockey has focused on the tolls of speed and contact, and on brain lesions resulting from men punching one another too much in the head. None of which is new, in fact: hockey long ago decleared war on the human head. The evidence has been piling up for years. When you sift through the history, it's all there: having figured out that the biggest threat to its ongoing survival is rational thought, hockey has systematically laid siege to the enemy's redoubt—the brain.

Several times, reading the many, many hockey books, I came to a standstill. My notes from these halted times ask why we revere a game that bleeds and breaks us and our children, interferes with their education, stokes everybody's anger, sneers at Swedes, feeds our jingoism, distracts our Saturday nights all the way through to June, wrecks downtown Montreal in 1955 and again in 1986, makes a mess of Vancouver circa 2011, encourages Don Cherry, and expends so much of our energy on downplaying, not worrying too much about, making light of, and/or apologizing for the worst of its excesses and outrages.

Then I'd get reading again, and my enthusiasm for roaming hockey's library would return. The game's geography would work its power on me, and I'd begin to hope that it might just be possible to surprise some sense out of it, decode some of its ciphers.

It's not just any story we want from hockey, of course; we want it to tell us *our* story, the one about what it means to be Canadian, and how we fit into the world we live in. I've never really been able to decide whether hockey knows any better than the rest of us, but I can declare how much I've enjoyed the journey, spreading out the map without worrying whether I'm going to be able to fold it up properly again.

[First]

I've seen the game escape its limits,
and leap the width and breadth of things,
become a mad chase going nowhere
AL PURDY, "TIME OF YOUR LIFE" (1973)

CAN'T REMEMBER THE first proper hockey game I went to. It may have been when I was five years old, at the Memorial Centre in Peterborough, Ontario, where I'm from. There was a big portrait of Queen Elizabeth II hanging on the wall at one end. That's something I remember—the young queen, presiding over the hometown Petes, who wore maroon and white, as they still do. (At the time, I thought you had to be named Peter to play for them.) Sometimes the queen's eyes followed you when you left your seat, but not always. I never saw her lower her gaze to the ice, which always made me wonder whether the hockey beneath her was just that. I went back not long ago and did my best to catch her eye, but she wasn't having any of that. She hasn't aged a day. She still looks demure and dutiful. Her smile is thin.

"I never knew that hockey originated," King Leary says in Paul Quarrington's great novel, also named *King Leary* (1987). "I figured it was just always there, like the moon." That's how it was in Peterborough, too. Which is why it doesn't really matter whether or not I remember the first time I saw a slapshot or an offside or a fight. In an old hockey novel that you may not have read, the captain of the school team is explaining to somebody the way of the world, and he says some chaps—"chaps" is what he says—are born with hockey sticks in their mouths. If that expression never really caught on, there's a similar metaphor that did: now we speak of *hockey in the blood.*

The phrase sounds a little dangerous when you put it down on paper: a medical complication, possibly negligence on the part of the neonatal ward at Civic Hospital in Peterborough, in my case. But it's very common. Hockey in the blood is a naturally occurring Canadian condition. If it seems like a colourful way of talking about our devotion to the game, well, yes, it is. Harry Sinden says: "Hockey never leaves the blood of a Canadian." A poet describes Bobby Orr's blood as "roaring." Don Gillmor says—and this is great—hockey "sings in our blood." It's how we claim the game as our own. Without it, we'd die.

I'm not boasting of any kind of special status here. I do admit to being someone for whom, during hockey season, news stories reconstitute themselves involuntarily in my brain. When scientists found evidence of ice on Mars, for example, fairly pure ice no more than 10 per cent dust, the obvious speculations were all about the existence of other-planetary life. The scientists exulted: "The early results from the gamma ray spectrometer team are better than we ever expected." But I thought: How long until the NHL starts thinking about expansion up there? Same thing with books. Browsing through Dante, I came across the startling news that the deepest circle of the Inferno has no flames because it's frozen. Hockey in Hell!

Peterborough isn't the only place you can contract a case of viral hockey. You can get it in Hamilton and in Mitchell, Ontario, in Montreal and Fort Qu'Appelle, Saskatchewan. It's a problem abroad, too, in places called Örnsköldsvik, Voskresensk, and Warroad. Hockey will be there, always, and if you don't get around to playing the game professionally, or even paying attention to it, hockey will nevertheless be as normal to you as the snow. That's the critical factor, not remembering your first game.

Icebound: Charlie Conacher tromps the way, leading the Leafs to meet the Bruins in Boston, 1936.

Some people who do remember their first hockey game are lucky enough to come to it as adults, which means they can concentrate on what they're seeing, analyze it, articulate their feelings. Lots of famous people who attend their first game enjoy the added advantage of having other people on hand, including writers, to watch them watch their first game, after which they (the writers) will often record their (the famous people's) reactions. Studying the experiences of Babe Ruth and Roland Barthes and William Faulkner, and also the population of Sweden, to find out what they saw and how quickly they fell in love with the game—how could they not fall in love?—was instructive but unnerving. I'd feel a rising anxious responsibility, as if I personally had something to do with whether or not they were going to like it. Was there somebody there to explain it to them properly so that they understood?

Lord Tweedsmuir, fifteenth governor general and bestselling novelist in his spare time, admitted (shyly) to having played hockey in Scotland as a boy. When he saw his first Canadian game in Ottawa in 1936, he was reported to be (1) hatless and (2) the happiest man in the rink. Before the first period was out, he was planning a trip to Montreal to see a game there.

The Dionne Quintuplets' first game was in 1948, in North Bay, an exhibition between the Kansas City Pla-Mors and the Chicago Black Hawks (as they were then, before the nominal merge into Blackhawks). The quints, who were fourteen at the time, got autographed hockey sticks (only two, for some reason) and candied apples and popcorn, but the game didn't really do much for them. They were reported to have watched with expressions that didn't change. Fine, no problem. They were still young.

Adolf Hitler's first hockey game was in Berlin, probably in 1933, and it involved the Grosvenor House Canadians, expatriates visiting from London, where their home rink occupied one of the ballrooms of a Park Lane hotel.

The *New Yorker* joined Jonathan Miller at the second hockey game he ever attended. This was in the mid-1990s, and the British author, doctor, and director went with a friend to watch thirteen-year-olds and their parents, who fascinated him. "All these American games," he said, "full of parental testosterone." As the game went on, he joined in the shouting: "Very good!" A kerfuffle reminded him of the movie *Dr. Strangelove*. He witnessed a breakaway. "This is really very beautiful," he said, and that's where the story ended.

A LOT OF the time in the hockey books, it's worth noting, you're reading about the game that underlies the game: the elusive organic ideal of hockey, the pure stuff, the true solid maple spirit of hockey, hockey the way it's supposed to be played. No one owns it, because everyone does; let no single league, let alone any individual player, diminish or tarnish it. This immutable metaphysical game never ends, it's sacred and it's unalloyed, and we should distinguish it in some special way, not to embarrass it, of course, or overstate the case, just to keep it clear. Nothing too ornate: **The game.** A little shouty? **The game.** Too 1970s, probably. *The Game.* That's better.

It's there in every hockey novel, *The Game*, but elsewhere it can be hard to locate. What you see on NHL ice at the Scotiabank Saddledome or the BankAtlantic Center (formerly the National Car Rental Center), is a hockey game as opposed to *The Game*, because the latter isn't sullied by advertising or any kind of commercialism or even professionalism. This is the higher hockey we're talking about, with no fighting or high-sticking or—does it have any penalties at all? It's the one that John Macfarlane and Bruce Kidd are talking about when they dedicate their book *The Death of Hockey* (1972) to the rightful owners of *The Game*: "the Canadian people." I'm pretty sure *The Game* is always played outdoors, on a frozen pond, when it's snowing, preferably with mountains in the background. That's why the NHL stages its fresh-air Winter Classic every year, hoping to summon hockey from a time before it lost its innocence, the hockey we all dream of, the one we're bound to protect because that's our birthright. Beware, you who would taint, besmirch, dilute, or disparage *The Game*, because we will work to keep it forever free of—but this is where it gets complicated. What exactly constitutes a taint to *The Game*? If NHL hockey is hockey after the fall, a degraded brand of *The Game*, when did the tumble from grace occur, and who did the shoving?

Would we recognize *The Game* if we saw it? We know only a bit about its specifications, thanks to Bobby Hull. "*The Game*," he said, "will never be bigger than a small boy's dreams." Theo Fleury backs him up: "We're all just kids in this business, and we always will be kids as long as we get to play *The Game*." It's in poems, wrapped in faith and love and nostalgia—for example, when Richard Harrison skates in Côte d'Ivoire: "I touched the ice and I could be any boy in love." Childhood often seems to be involved, and men remembering when they were boys. *The Game* is eternal, cold and boreal, fast and simple, fun and endless. Anyone keeping time? Any referees? Does it matter what the score is at the end? Does anyone have to lose?

Sometimes, we know, *The Game* is offended, which is to say its defenders, called *purists*, are offended on its behalf. They have variously expressed their disgust with Fox TV pucks, too many teams in Florida and not enough in Quebec City, third jerseys, composite sticks, cheerleaders, and the shootout. During the 2005 NHL lockout, when plucky citizens demanded that the Stanley Cup be freed from the grasp of the NHL, it was for the good of *The Game*.

The Game is Doug Beardsley's subject in *Country on Ice* (1988), also Ken Dryden's in *The Game* (1983) and Peter Gzowski's in *The Game of Our Lives* (1981). In *The Death of Hockey*, NHL games go on while a corpse lies with its feet sticking from under the hedge: *The Game*'s. The murder was so obvious and ugly that another book of the same title had to be published in 1998, this one by two American journalists named Jeff Z. Klein and Karl-Eric Reif. Loving *The Game*, they just about pop an elbow pad detailing how much they hate what's happening to it, framing their indictment with words like *wrong, insular, fritter, boring, bloated, stink, graceless, buffoonish, tacky, troglodyte, laughingstock, bush league,* and *ferrchrissake!*

It's sobering to ponder on the enemies of *The Game*. Once in a while there's honour involved: according to Beardsley, it was *The Game* that triumphed when Edmonton was winning a string of Stanley Cups during the 1980s. But why, more often, is *The Game* under attack—and by its own players? It's hard to watch the indignities it's subjected to. In the 1992 Stanley Cup finals, Chicago coach Mike Keenan accused Pittsburgh's Mario Lemieux of diving. "The best player in the game is embarrassing himself and embarrassing *The Game*." Coaches are often the ones to notice infractions of this sort; sometimes entire teams manage it. After a humiliating 2002 loss to Detroit, L.A.'s Andy Murray put his Kings on notice:

> It's an insult to every parent who has taken their kids to minor hockey at 5:30 in the morning...just like their parents had done for them. You probably had a lot of kids come over from Canada tonight who had a game or practice at seven in the morning and came down to watch tonight. That's an embarrassment to *The Game*...to come out and play like that.

ALL HOCKEY PLAYERS have more or less the same background, wrote W.C. Heinz in 1959, "only the names and the places and the dates are different." He was writing about Gordie Howe, trying to explain him to a wider American audience at a time when nearly every one of the NHL's players was Canadian and needed explaining.

The literature tells us that hockey players are born at home, or at least they used to be. Howie Morenz debuted on a Sunday — September 21, 1902 — the sixth of six children. His father grew prize-winning vegetables and had a china store in Mitchell, Ontario, until it went bust. His mother couldn't be a nurse because of a habit she had of fainting in operating rooms. As a boy, Howie knocked over a pot of boiling potatoes and scalded his legs. He recovered.

Gump Worsley was born in his parents' bedroom in the flat on Congregation Street in Montreal, Dr. Allen attending. Homemade soup was a staple of the Worsley table, and fish and chips, except that the fish was actually potato fried to resemble fish, a trick of his mother's in hard times.

Eric Lindros was a Wednesday child, emerging at 8:10 PM, two weeks late. The attending obstetrician was a great guy. Eric didn't cry but he blinked, according to his mother. He was a tiny, pink thing. Lindros weighed seven pounds, one and a half ounces—a little less than Howie Meeker's eight pounds. "I entered this world on the plains of Saskatchewan at a hefty ten pounds plus," says Bobby Baun.

In 1959, Kevin Lowe's birth was a labour, for his mother, of twenty-four hours. The family business in Lachute, Quebec, was a dairy, and his mother fed the future defenceman from a bottle, not a breast. "But each time she fed me with it, I vomited," Lowe later confided. I wish I could say he said this on *Hockey Night in Canada* after winning the Stanley Cup, but the truth is, he saved his vomit for his autobiography.

Bernie Parent: "They tell me that I used to cry and cry. No wonder! I was starving! That's true. I wasn't getting enough to eat."

Detailed accounts of infant feeding are sorely lacking, as far as I'm concerned, from more recent biographies of hockey players. Did Mark Messier latch on? What about Dale Hawerchuk? Most of the books get their subjects born, out of the crib, and onto skates all within a single paragraph. As another American, Gary Ronberg, explained, "Canada's young are introduced to skates at age three, stitches at ten and dentures at fifteen."

Paul Henderson walked at nine months, having never crawled. Mario Lemieux was holding a hockey stick before he could walk. This sounds at least as risky as hot potatoes, not to mention, have you ever asked an infant to try to get a grip on a Koho? Still, by the time he was three, Mario was playing the game on skates. His first recorded deke came at four.

Mike Ricci patrolled the house with his skates on at age two. Billy Burch, the first captain of the New York Americans and an alleged hothead until he decided to change his ways, is supposed to have taken his skates to bed at age four so often that—his sheets were sliced to shreds? Child welfare agents got wind and took him into custody? Maybe so, but the story is simply that it became a tradition. The first time Sean Burke, all of five, stepped onto the ice, he was hit in the forehead by a puck and had to get stitches. Right then, he decided to be a goaltender.

Fred Sasakamoose received bob skates from his grandfather when he was six; the grandfather used to clear the snow from the slough with a team of horses. Gaye Stewart and friends were out every day after school on the Neebing River until dark. They kept a shovel stuck in the snow that no one ever stole and harboured a hole off to the side, for occasional floods with a bucket. Stan Mikita wore screw-on skates, the old-fashioned kind with a turned-up toe like a ram's horn that later on he wished he'd saved. Mrs. Morenz hoped Howie would be musical, but he'd skip out of piano lessons to play hockey on the Thames River with homemade sticks and chunks of coal.

Rivers amble through hockey's childhoods: the Nith (Wayne Gretzky) and the Seguin (Bobby Orr), the Magnetawan (Gary Sabourin), and Patterson's Creek (Syd Howe), too. Buddy O'Connor, the first man to win the Hart and Lady Byng Trophies in the same season, learned to stickhandle while dodging rocks on the frozen St. Lawrence. On a weekend in Kitchener, Howie Meeker was in the middle of four hundred kids playing forty different games at once on the Grand River.

Cyclone Taylor's boyhood rink was a pond called the Piggery that smelled of the neighbouring slaughterhouse. Busher Jackson skated on Toronto's Grenadier Pond. There was also a slough near the Mahovliches' home in Timmins, Ontario. Frank's mom would give him red and blue ribbons, and with a kettle of hot water in hand, he'd lay the lines.

Pavel Bure's father—Valeri's, too—didn't know anything about hockey, so it was news to him that skates need sharpening, which is why Pavel went out his first day with dull blades. He couldn't move; he had to hold on to the boards.

It's the memory of ice that hockey players seem to retain, that and the earliest skates they wore. Red Dutton was NHL president after his playing days ended. In 1938, he affirmed that "just about every game a boy or girl plays in the Dominion is done on skates." Those are the fundamentals, the vital point of contact between players and their game; only rarely do you see mentions of any other gear in these reminiscences, including sticks. When it comes to recalling hockey childhoods, hockey nostalgia struggles to rise above the ankles.

So basic is the backyard rink to the landscape of Canadian childhood that it's only a matter of time before Historic Sites and Monuments gets around to erecting a plaque behind Walter Gretzky's house in Brantford, Ontario, right beside the swimming pool put in after Wayne went to the NHL. In Montreal, Mike's dad flooded the yard behind the Bossy apartment on St. Urbain. ("Dad made pretty good ice," the son reported later.) A rink in the yard was all about self-preservation, Walter Gretzky claimed. Pouring his own from a hose meant that he could sit inside while Wayne skated, instead of freezing by the boards over at the outdoor public rink.

There were backyard rinks before the Gretzkys', of course, but in a lot of cases, if you read the biographies and memoirs and the oral histories, what we had in this country was a whole lot more ice and a good deal more time. This is the way childhood works: magnifying time and place, stretching out the past at the margins to make everything bigger, longer, clearer.

Bill Goldsworthy, his biographers say, was like many Canadian boys: "he played hockey morning until night." Bill Gutman, harkening back to Bobby Clarke's hometown of Flin Flon, Manitoba, reports that hockey was constant on lakes, ponds, streams, brooks, rivulets, swashes, freshets, and arroyos, "and sometimes right on the frozen streets." In Montreal, for Rod Gilbert, it was a case of skate or be stranded—maybe for the entire winter: "Skating was something you did almost in self defense if you grew up in my neighbourhood," he writes in *Goal!*, his 1968 autobiography. "There was so much ice around that unless you could skate it was tough getting from one place to another."

HOCKEY HAS A long history of struggling to express itself. When the pro game first got to New York City in 1925, the Americans assigned spare (Canadian) goaltenders to sit with the local sportswriters to explain what was going on. It's not that the game is especially complex, just that it's so fast and frantic. Punch Imlach called it the most deceptive of all sports. "It looks disorganized and unplanned; tactics, at least positive tactics that have a beginning and an end, seem completely lacking."

The speed and the clash and the chaos make it difficult for TV cameras to keep up, let alone the broadcasters who have to narrate the blur before them. No time for filigree or long words while the puck's in play, and even with the swiftest tongue, you're missing more than you're telling. "Score!" Foster Hewitt was just able to blurt in 1972, before it was already over and he was reporting history: "Henderson has scored for Canada!"

It's no easier to commit the game to the page. Ideally, the hockey players themselves would be writing down what they'd seen and felt and done as soon as possible after they'd seen and felt and done it. Practising with the Boston Bruins in the 1970s, George Plimpton tucked a notebook and pen in behind his goalie pad, the spirit of which I have to admire even as I recognize, practically speaking, how suicidal it was. The hard truth is that hockey players have better things to do than write. If there's a time for writing, it's later, after the hockey's over, in retirement, with a ghostwriter sitting by and a book contract in hand.

There are those who haven't waited, preferring the immediacy of journalism. When Montreal's teams met in the playoffs in the spring of 1928, the Maroons ended the Canadiens' season, directly following which Howie Morenz and Aurèle Joliat both filed their columns for the next morning's *La Patrie*.

"I must tell you that in this game," Morenz advised his fans, "I lost six pounds and two teeth. Joliat my friend had gone to 134 pounds, the lowest weight of his hockey career. All other players are exhausted and do not blame anyone for the defeat. Poor George Hainsworth, who cried after the game, was solid and brilliant."

Charlie Conacher was a *Globe and Mail* columnist in the 1930s, and an outspoken one at that. In the mid-1950s, Boom-Boom (Boum-Boum, to Quebeckers) Geoffrion had a writing gig at *Parlons Sport* around the same time that his fellow scribe and teammate Rocket Richard was using his column at *Samedi-Dimanche* as a platform to blast away at NHL president Clarence Campbell.

And if you followed the syndicated column that Gordie Howe wrote in the 1960s, you'd know that the reason the ice improved in the old Boston Garden around 1964 was because (in Gordie's opinion) they'd reduced railway traffic at the North Station a level below. "They had little ripples in the ice from the vibrations caused by the trains," Howe wrote. "The shaking also brought down dust filaments."

Wayne Gretzky wrote for the *National Post* in the 1990s, although that was after he'd retired from the ice. I'm not sure that *wrote* is the right word, either; he helped Roy MacGregor write a column is maybe what we'll say.

I'm not forgetting the literary lesson learned by left winger Harry Watson, but I've left it until the last. That particular Watson never played in the NHL, though that didn't keep him from the Hockey Hall of Fame, from which he received an invitation in 1963. Born in St. John's, he flew fighters for the Royal Flying Corps in the First World War. After the war, he skated for the Toronto Dentals. As a member of the Toronto Granites, he won successive Allan Cups in the early 1920s. And when the Granites went to the 1924 Winter Olympics in Chamonix, France, Watson was their scoring star. He chalked up eleven goals when Canada shellacked Czechoslovakia 30–0, and a further six when they plastered Sweden 22–0. He scored thirteen in the 33–0 drywalling of Switzerland. In the final, he could only manage a meagre hat trick in the 6–1 win over the United States.

But: the lesson. Depending on how you look at it; the moral could be something in an Olympic vein, about humility and sportsman-ship, or just plainly practical, a simple matter of self-preservation. From Chamonix, Watson sent back dispatches for the *Toronto Telegram*. Ahead of the final, he predicted that Canada would beat the U.S. by a score of 10 or 12 to zip. Understandably, this perturbed the Americans, resulting, according to the *Toronto Daily Star*, in "an exceedingly rough match."

Bad feeling due to a remark that [Canada] would show up the Americans was shown from the start of the match and it increased in each period.

Watson was cross-checked in the face in the first minute of play, "but played a sensational game with a bleeding mouth."

The Canadians had "science, skill and team work" on their side, said the *Daily Star*, and they duly won the gold.

The *Globe* reported it was Watson's nose that bled.

HOCKEY FATHERS ARE titans, like characters from folklore. They have bear-paw hands[1] and their strength earns them the nickname Magilla Gorilla.[2] If they felt like it, they could trace their ancestry back to the Duke of Rutland.[3] They sail from Liverpool on the ss *Lake Manitoba*, then travel by train and wagon to Saskatchewan, where they settle a town with four brothers who name the town after themselves: Delisle.[4] They're five-foot-one butchers and house painters.[5] They're tinsmiths with the MacDonald Sheet Metal Company in Winnipeg, as strong as oxen, and one day they knock a man down, one punch, at the corner of Selkirk and MacGregor, and then the man's pal comes along, name of China Pete, and studies the downed man and says it's Harry Dillon, the light heavyweight boxing champion.[6] Or else another day, in wintertime, in Lucknow, Ontario, they single-handedly lift back onto the road a car that has skidded off it. Once, on a dare, they hoist a six-hundred-pound salt barrel onto a scale.[7] They're excellent swimmers, and compete in three Olympics: 1968, 1972, 1976.[8] At one point they own a Coca-Cola franchise and then a Kuntz's Brewery franchise out of Waterloo, Ontario. They have two big Geoffesson trucks.[9]

They're pleasant-looking men with brown hair and grey eyes, head tilted at a jaunty angle to the right. Nobody wants to embarrass them, so they're never asked the reason for the jaunty tilt.[10] They have no affinity for Americans. If they're driving from Ontario to Saskatchewan in the summertime, even though it would make for a shorter trip, they refuse to travel through the United States.[11] One

Tools of the trade: CPR machinist Joseph Kneeshaw and family, in Calgary, 1905–06.

of their hobbies is mice.[12] They're maintenance men at a textile factory in Ruzomberok.[13] They're machinists in the Angus Shops of the Canadian Pacific Railway in the east end of Montreal,[14] and also bakers in Chicoutimi.[15] During the years when their son George is captain of the Maple Leafs, they work in Sudbury's mines for Falconbridge and if a co-worker abuses Toronto, the fathers of hockey players piss on the heads of the abusers as they come up in a cage from underground.[16]

At fifteen, they leave home to become lumberjacks.[17] They think oatmeal is the key to life.[18] In 1883, they play lacrosse in England to show what a great place Canada is for settlers and capitalists alike.[19]

They're Winnipeg Blue Bombers.[20] Eagle-eyed, white-haired, tanned, they resemble the baseball manager Sparky Anderson.[21] Their sons resemble them the way a terrier resembles a Great Dane.[22] After stints as air force navigators in the war, they refuse to fly, so they never see their sons play on Long Island.[23] Here's what they do when they go hunting in Saskatchewan at a time when they're too broke to buy shotgun shells: run a coyote down on horseback, swoop out of the saddle to hobble it by slashing its hind leg with a knife, then smack it on the skull with a rock or a fencepost.

Ab Howe, Gordie's dad, was the coyote killer, which makes some sense. One other particular hockey father I would have liked to see in action is Wilfred Paiement. Two of his sons played in the NHL, Wilf and Rosaire. There's a photo of him in lumberjack garb, posing in a studio. He's wearing a tie. At twelve years old, Wilfred arm-wrestled all comers, up to and including men weighing 250 pounds. In 1933, aged twenty-four, he crushed the hand of Paul LaTour, the northern Quebec champion. Wilfred went to Quebec City in 1939. Eighteen thousand people gathered in the Coliseum there, and that's where they watched him wrestle a seven-hundred-pound brown bear until the bear was sprawled out with its dead tongue gone blue.

There have been plenty of sons of hockey players in the NHL in recent years, Hulls and Steens and Folignos, but mostly it's a verity of hockey history that fathers went to work without their skates, packing explosives (Doug Orr) or fighting Germans (Garnet Henderson) or rising through Quebec's civil service (Michel Roy). Is it so very surprising that having sired all those Brents and Darryls and Rons and Duanes, Louie Sutter never learned to skate? The man had a farm to run.

Viacheslav Kovalev writes in his book that he decided in the maternity ward that he would make his son, Alexei, a hockey player.

The Road to Success (1994), his book is called. As an infant, Alexei was covered with what you and I might call boils; his father prefers the word *furuncles*. Alexei skated at four. He loved it so much that once he put his skates on and tried to walk down the five flights from his family's apartment. He also liked to ski. He never complained. He was small. In photos from kindergarten he wears shorts and dances under the gaze of a portrait of V.I. Lenin. When he started playing hockey, his father traded a box of candies for a real stick. He skated with children two and three years older than him, which some doctors thought would be dangerous. He practised for two hours a day. His father loved his independence. Above all, his father says, what he wanted to teach his boy was kindness.

HOCKEY FATHERS WHO write books do so (they say) with open hearts (Viacheslav Kovalev) and to help other parents who are raising children in parlous times (Murray Dryden). I wish hockey's mothers would write more books, if only to prove out my theory that they, more than most of us, understand that as much as hockey might look like life, it's only ever hockey.

Mostly the mothers of hockey players *don't* write books—other than Colleen Howe, who perhaps deserves a bright asterisk for having published both as a hockey mother and as a wife. It may be worth noting, as an aside, that Mrs. Gordie Howe's book has more to say about sex than all the hockey fathers in all their books combined. Among other things, *My Three Hockey Players* (1975) reports that Detroit coach Jack Adams believed sex "had a direct, injurious effect on a player's performance" and each year mandated his players "to keep it in your pants."

Things she learned about the Soviet Union in 1974 when another Team Canada went over include:

- Russians are not thin and have no deodorant;
- They are crybabies;
- Russian hotels have no Bibles and, while the beds are clean enough, "they were not conducive to lovemaking."

Phyllis Gretzky is a more typical literary model in that however mountainous her love for and support of her eldest son, she only shows up in the Gretzky annals at the edge of the frame. That's how it goes, mostly, for the mothers. As fully involved as they might be in person, they tend to be slight figures in the memoirs and autobiographies.

We do know that Babe Dye's mum, Essie, was the one who flooded the backyard rink, tied her son's skates, and taught him the game. Others taught their sons how to knit (Jacques Plante); washed floors and made gallons of soup (Gump Worsley); or always seemed to be sitting in the parlour sewing somebody's pair of pants, as well as attending church every morning at 6:30 (Boom-Boom Geoffrion).

"Mothers worry about injuries," Billy Harris confides, "and whether their sons are taking their proper vitamins." Both Chicago goalie Charlie Gardiner's and Boston centre Milt Schmidt's wouldn't let them play football when they were at school: too rough. In Leamington, Ontario, Winnie Hillman never fretted too much about her NHL-employed sons, Larry and Wayne. "I just hoped nothing happened to their eyes, which wouldn't be very handy to replace."

In the middle of Ken Dryden's career—"many years after she had wanted to say it," as he put it—his mother asked whether it was all right if she stopped coming to games. Any enjoyment was cancelled out by anxiety. "She would watch until the puck came into our zone," Dryden wrote, "then look at her feet until it had left again."

When Bobby Orr was growing up in Parry Sound, his mother worked part-time as a waitress at the coffee shop at the Brunswick

Motor Hotel. The story's told that after one of his boyhood games for the local team, she took him aside to give him her notes. "What's happened to you?" she is supposed to have asked. "You played like an old lady."

IN HOCKEY MOVIES, when the protagonist suffers a crisis, such as after punching a referee (*It's a Pleasure*, 1945) or having steadfastly refused to drop the gloves (*Youngblood*, 1986), he either holes up in his apartment with his butler until the champagne runs out and the girl he loves comes to save him, or he leaves his team in a snit, bids his girlfriend goodbye, and drives home to the farm, where his brother, who had his own hockey dreams until they were ended by a stick in his eye, wants to fight him for being so stupid. Which the protagonist doesn't want to do, even though he's still in his snit. He'd prefer not to fight his brother, because what does fighting solve? But then he realizes there's nothing worse than leaving hockey behind and so he returns to the team and scores the winning goal in the big game while also finally fighting a goon who's not his brother, proving he's no wuss, which seems to please everybody, including the girlfriend.

In real life, for the everyday reader of innumerable hockey books, the crises come in all sizes, and few of them can be resolved with champagne or a quick scoring/fighting cure. It's easy to talk, as Steve Yzerman did in a bank commercial not long ago, about "the simple love of the game." For me, that's just not complicated enough. There's a Russian word for fans of sports—*bolelchiki*—that has loaded into it a sense of the suffering spectators endure watching the sport they adore. Out on the pond or following the team Yzerman took to the Sochi Olympics, you experience the euphoria the game can generate. Watching Carey Price fall to injury and take down Montreal's playoff hopes, you remember the frustrations. And then there are those other times when you understand that if hockey were a country, Foreign Affairs in Ottawa would advise you to stay away, while in Washington there would be murmurs from maverick senators about the need for regime change.

The whole country felt the shock in January of 2009 when a twenty-one-year-old defenceman named Don Sanderson died from injuries he'd sustained in a Senior-league game in Brantford, Ontario. The story of how it began was as familiar a winter's tale as we have in this country. Two young men let go of their gloves, freed their fists, started to throw them. Sanderson lost his helmet and fell, his head hitting the ice. He was angry at first, when they got him to the bench: he wanted to go back out and finish the fight. Then he was in the ambulance, unconscious, then in hospital, comatose, then dead.

A terrible, awful thing. Dumbfounding. Nobody wanted to raise a voice too loud in the bleak thereafter, out of respect. There were things to be said, though, weren't there? For one: Why is fighting part of the game when it's not? Hockey addresses those circum-stances in which two players end up repeatedly punching each other's head, with no other purpose but to injure. Rule 21 in hockey's rule book prohibits such behaviour. Surely that, on its own, would be reason enough for broad action, for change?

It didn't come. Ontario's Major Junior league took steps, but small ones. Otherwise, nothing. What seemed urgent that January across hockey's frozen front simply wafted away. The game went on. The other guy in the fight wasn't the same afterwards: Corey Fulton was shattered by grief and remorse, though of course nobody blamed him. It was a long time before he was back playing hockey, far away, in the U.S. The next time he shed his gloves, he took precautions. "The kid I fought fell," he said, "and I put my hand under his head. Now when I fight I'm always trying to hold the other guy up."

Watching this from a distance, like everybody, I was numbed. Did somebody actually utter the words *That's hockey,* or did the phrase only prevail over the whole episode because it's what someone always says when a fight goes bad and the stretcher-bearers take to the ice? Other verbal shrugs offered: *It's part of the game* and *He knew what he signed up for,* as if hockey were a snowstorm that keeps hitting us, a polar vortex, beyond any human agency to alter its progress.

I did wonder about giving it up, walking away. If the game can't learn, what can it possibly have to teach? It's not the most compelling of existential struggles, I realize, and poor grist for headlines: *Middle-Aged Man Considers Paying Less Attention to Sport He's Loved Since He Was a Kid.* It dogged me, though.

Unlike my brother, who's never had any interest. For all the songs that his blood sings, hockey was never one of them. And I've seen my dad's octogenarian love for the game dwindle. He'll watch the playoffs (my mother, too), but there's nothing necessary about it now. Perhaps there's a waiting-it-out option, just letting it fade away naturally, like energy, like patience. Somewhere in there I riddled myself this: Is it possible for a hockey-blooded person to disenthrall himself from the game?

I wondered about this over a period of summer weeks that flowed into fall, during which one answer that emerged was: Yes, maybe so, though probably not while you're reading all the hockey picture books. These were Bobby Clarke picture books mostly, a surprising abundance of them, that I picked up and put down as part of my comprehensive investigation into how, as an author, you might explain that time in 1972 when Clarke broke Valeri Kharlamov's ankle in a way that would make sense to children.

Fred McFadden's *Bobby Clarke* (1976), from the Super People Series, has good information on diabetes and how Clarke was able to manage his, which is one of the reasons there are such a lot of

Clarke books for kids: his story is the inspirational tale of not letting disease stop you on your journey from Flin Flon to Philadelphia where, as a super person who's also a super player, you too can win successive Stanley Cups. No mention of the slash.

I was well into Julian May's book about Clarke when I came up with a compromise that reconciles my thinking about how to quit the game by *not* quitting the game. If small steps are the ones to start with, then how about this: a new reading program, one that concentrates on distilling the goods of the game, its graces and joys. Let hockey do what it has to do—punch away! Ignore the consequences! That's hockey! But I can make my own difference, if only to me.

Not that May's book is a great place to start. It's called *Hockey with a Grin* (1975). Given its Kharlamov content, that title is both cruel and just about right. Clarke: *Not proud of what I did, not ashamed, either.* Okay, then. What else have I got on the shelf? Lower down when I look it's *Violence au Hockey* (1977), *Tough Guy* (2010), and *Blood on the Ice* (1974) that scowl out. But then there's no single book that plies only the positive side of the puck; if there were, you'd have no choice but to indict it for willful denial. "Hockey," David Adams Richards affirms in his hockey memoir, *Hockey Dreams* (1996), "is where we've gotten it right." Doug Beardsley in *Country on Ice*: "It represents the very best of Canadians." But neither book pretends that there isn't an ugly underside to the game.

And *The Hockey Sweater*? It's true that as I'm reaching for Roch Carrier's 1979 classic the thought does radiate through my mind that here is the game's innocent exuberance distilled into a form of pure refreshment, no nasty additives or aftertaste. But have you re-read it lately? It's a very disturbing story. I don't just mean the catalogue mail-order tragedy that young Roch suffers as a young consumer— that's the least of it. The bullying he undergoes is unprecedented in Canadian literature. It's not just the kids, either: his own mother turns her back on him and the priest is a tyrant. Not even God can help poor Roch in his pariah's Leaf-blue.

What is it about hockey that seems to pull it towards apocalypse? All those sudden-death overtimes and annulling NHL lockouts can't have helped. On a Wednesday in October of 2010, I began to wonder whether a dire sufficiency of small, disparate events might be enough to do the job of seeing hockey snuff itself out altogether, like a degenerate star.

Patrice Cormier had pleaded guilty to assault causing bodily harm. That was the first thing in the newspaper that caught my attention. A Junior star, Cormier's adjectives include *mature* and *ultra-aggressive*. He'd elbowed a rival named Mikael Tam in the head. *Vicious* and *ugly* were words describing the play in the press, and, referring to Tam, *convulsing on the ice* and *a night in hospital*. Now a court had discharged Cormier absolutely. He'd have no criminal record, so no problems travelling to the United States when the time came for him to star in the NHL.

Meanwhile, from the rarefied heights of the big league's headquarters in New York came the story that a Vancouver player named Rick Rypien (adjectives: *gritty*, *hard-nosed*) had been suspended for attacking a fan during a game in Minnesota.

Also: the Mayo Clinic happened to be convening a conference discussing head trauma in hockey. Helmets are not the answer to bringing down concussion rates, attendees were told, it's going to take a ban on head checks. Asked the head of the Canadian Standards Association's committee on hockey equipment: "Can anyone leave this room without demanding, loud and clear, a ban on head checking?"

The last piece of news—I admit, I stopped looking after this one— came from Alberta. Parents of Minor-hockey-playing children were being required to take anger management courses when they signed up their kids up for the season.

I didn't know what to make of all these stories, other than to spend a few further hours of the afternoon wondering what *more* it might take for a sport to supernova, and what the aftermath might look like. I kept reading. If nothing else, what the welter of the hockey books suggests is that the game's calendar has survived so many days of miscellaneous strife—brawls, riots, and stick-swingings; damning reports and public denunciations; even deaths—that there could be no doubt it would see this one out too. Wednesday wasn't the day that hockey attained terminal stupidity.

WHEN THE MOON was full, you could play all night, Duane Sutter recalls. This was on the pond north of Viking, Alberta, where winter's thermometer could drop to −40° Fahrenheit. There were nine Sutters at home in those years, living in four rooms with no lights, no running water. "We'd keep feeding coal and wood into the stove," said Brian, "but it was always cold."

With his four brothers, Mush March used to skate the frozen streets of Silton, Saskatchewan—that's where he was said to have picked up his trademark *dogged determination.* Gordie Howe says that when it fell to 50 below in Floral, Saskatchewan, you could hear a person walking blocks away. It was a mile from his house to the rink, and when he was young and playing goalie, he used to skate there with his pads held up in front of him to shut out the wind.

Dave Schultz, the Hammer, wrote a 1981 memoir of the same title in which he says a Saskatchewan outhouse at 20 below is an experience he wouldn't wish on the worst of his enemies. The snow was so deep where he grew up that his father had to haul in his grandparents' car on a horse-drawn sleigh when they came to visit the farm. Bernie Parent was a boy who dreamed of a heater in his hockey bag for practice in Rosemont, Quebec. The skaters, at least, could skate; the goalies just had to stand there, worrying about frostbite.

Bullet Joe Simpson recalled outdoor games at rinks in Edmonton and Saskatoon when the temperature fell to minus 45. "We used to have snow shovelled into the dressing room to warm our feet when we came off the ice," he said. "We'd tramp around in the snow in our stockings. Thaw out gradually that way and avoid frozen feet. Sometimes a fellow would have to sit with his feet in a pail of snow for twenty or thirty minutes."

In 1925, when Tex Rickard built Madison Square Garden in New York and hatched a team, the Americans, to play there, Simpson was one of the players he recruited from Canada. Billy Burch and Shorty Green were two others. The team wore stars and stripes, reds and whites and blues. When they struggled to win at home that first winter, the players complained that the rink was too warm. Burch couldn't get through a first period without swooning; in a game against Toronto's St. Patricks, he sweated off seven pounds. The players wanted the thermostat dialed down to 40, and their Canadian coach, Tommy Gorman, was with them. Rickard, a legendary boxing promoter, worried that his paying customers would catch a chill: 70 was as low as he'd go.

They finished fourth of seven NHL teams at the end of the hockey year, out of the playoffs, having won just four tepid home games out of seventeen. By the winter of the following season, Gorman was asking Judge Crain of the New York Supreme Court to legislate the temperature to 40. His affidavit argued that it wasn't possible for players to play at their best in a too-warm rink, it sapped and slowed them, ruined the game. Rickard was alleged to have told him he didn't care about the players, it was all about the money coming in. While the judge mulled, the Madison Square management released a statement to announce a truce. The players accepted that the best compromise fast hockey could make with healthy spectators came in between 53° and 55° Fahrenheit.

IN AN ICE BOOK, I read about the stuff they call *brash*, which sounds like the ice that hockey should be played on. As it is, when it comes to hockey ice vocabulary, *good* and *bad* or *hard* and *soft* is about as far as it goes—nothing at all when you compare it to the ice of glaciers or Arctic oceans. Which is as it should be, some might say. What's to talk about, ice-wise? But let's allow for a little imaginative climate changing, a fast thaw: If the ice wasn't important, wouldn't we love field hockey more? I think we take it too much for granted. Who votes for a wider descriptive spectrum for hockey ice?

Brash is the ice you get when you (or Nature) conglomerate smaller cakes and chunks, which you then coalesce and refreeze into irregularly shaped elements, often with sharp projections. Science has *fast* ice and *grey* ice, *polynyas*, *ice rind*, and *nilas*, which is the fragile young ice that swells on cold winter waves like watered silk, as the American non-hockey writer Barry Lopez describes it. Then there's *rafted* ice and *skim* ice, *grease* ice and *shuga*. The more specific we can be the better. *Looks like Pierre Mondou may have hit some frazil ice in the neutral zone.*

In Roy MacGregor's *The Last Season* (1983), Felix Batterinski recalls the ugliest arena of his life, the ice "like black cellophane." You forget that they blanch the ice. Before they did, the ice at New York's Madison Square Garden was, depending on your outlook, either a dirty, disturbing brown or the colour of coffee. A writer watching a game in 1925 noted that it looked like a big cake of maple sugar scratched by mice. A year later they started painting the ice white— froze a half-inch of water, painted, froze another inch on top—though the rumour went around that they were mixing in milk. Toronto didn't get painted ice until 1949.

At Montreal's old Forum, Hugh MacLennan recognized that it wasn't just players and puck that made the spectacle, "for the ice itself is a part of the drama of the game." Ice time is what you crave as a player—that's the only way you're going to prove yourself, score, show the coach that you deserve to play.

The ice in poems glistens wet and bluish, like the white of an eye. In novels, sometimes it's "blue-silver." "The creamy ice," says Peter Gzowski, which sounds desserty. "Ice lacks a forgiving texture," says Pat LaFontaine, once of the Sabres and Islanders. "You land and you hurt." In 1905, Ottawa is said to have done their best to slow down Nibs Phillips and his Rat Portage Thistles by powdering the ice with salt and crushed glass.

Lionel Conacher's dad, Ben, a teamster, used to walk out across Toronto Bay in the wintertime to cut ice by the slab, for which he earned $7.50 a week. Nights he earned an extra dollar clearing the snow off the rink at Jesse Ketchum Park, not far from where I'm sitting now.

"Some mornings," Scott Young remembered of his boyhood in Glenboro, Manitoba, the rink ice "was so brittle from cold that when a train passed, vibrations in the frozen ground would splinter the ice like glass."

The world's first artificial rink was the Glaciarium, built in Chelsea in London, England, and opened in January of 1876, under a tent. Professor John Gamgee was the man behind it, veterinarian, author of *Yellow Fever, a Nautical Disease: Its Origin and Prevention*, not to mention "a physicist of no small merit." Moved to permanent premises, his rink measured forty feet by twenty-four, and it featured murals of Swiss Alps and Arctic regions on the walls. Skating was by subscription, with a target clientele of "noblemen and gentlemen under certain conditions." Gamgee laid down four inches of loose earth on six inches of concrete. Six inches of cow hair covered the earth, then two-inch wooden planks, overspread by a half-inch of tarred hair. Copper pipes lay atop the layer of the upper toupee, with water covering the pipes. A steam engine in the machine room kept sulphuric acid pumping through the pipes, which condensed to a liquid, which expanded in a vacuum, which generated an abiding cold to freeze the water. This is not something you should try at home, even if you have the cow hair: the process involves several other steps containing the phrases *copper casing, solution of glycerine*, and *flowed by gravity*.

Two modern-day experts in the field are Shorty Jenkins and Dan Craig, and they have nicknames like Doctor Ice and Cubes. "I think it's just in our blood," says Craig, the NHL's director of facilities, summoning the familiar phrase: "All the good ice makers seem to come from Canada. Next best is the northern states." To flood the old New York Garden in the 1970s took six thousand gallons of water. NHL ice was five-eighths of an inch thick at that time; today it's up to a little more than an inch, without any *rind* or *shuga* to it. The guy in charge of the Vancouver ice on which Canada won its 2010 Olympic gold medal likes the building at about 57° Fahrenheit and the ice at 21° Fahrenheit. Hockey players want hard ice for fast passing and no bouncing from the puck. Dan Craig says, "It has to be just right. The players know the difference."

Indoor hockey has a pause built in that I've always savoured, standing there by the door in the boards, watching the Zamboni scumble its circuit. In Matt Robinson's poem "Zamboni Driver's Lament,"

> . . . the ice,
> it seems, will always be there: a constant wound
> to dress, a scar i run myself along and over.

Batterinski loves to watch "the water spreading wet and glimmering behind him, the steam rising from the spread rag and the taps." He always wants to be first on new ice because, truly, is there any cleaner sheet of possibility than a freshly Zambonied rink? "I love skating in circles before each game," muses a character of Mark Jarman's, "because anything is possible coasting the ice in that breeze." For Ken Dryden, the ice is the page on which you step out, after the flood, to write your story.

THE MEASURES OF a nation's values are many, and that's how we know how well we're doing in the world. Canada rated third on the 2013 Prosperity Index (assessing global wealth and well-being). Sixth on the UN's World Happiness Report that same year. Seventh on the 2014 Global Peace Index. Eleventh on the UN Human Development Report (2013).

Norway is doing better, you can't deny that. Switzerland, too. Otherwise though, by any gauge that doesn't factor in bad hockey behaviour, we have to be proud. What we lack, maybe, is the audacity to distill our national essence into law. Turkey, for instance, is a nation so sure of itself that in 2005, the government enshrined it in Article 301 of the national penal code, which makes denigrating Turkishness in public a crime. Not only that, but if you do your denigrating in a foreign country, the term of imprisonment can be increased by one-third. The sole problem being that nowhere in the law is Turkishness explicitly defined.

Or what about Iceland? In 2009, after all their banks collapsed and the government fell over and the whole place nearly went under with a hiss of seismic steam, Icelanders convened a national assembly of fifteen hundred citizens from every corner of the country to chart the nation's way forward. One of the first things they did was to sit down at 162 tables of nine. Next, they voted to determine the value that's most important to Icelanders. It wasn't hard. The consensus was quick and overwhelming: they chose *heiðarleika*, honesty.

I don't know enough about how international value systems work to be able to say whether, with Iceland decided, honesty is off the table for all the rest of us. I do wonder, though, what would be the value we'd vote ourselves if we sat down at 162 Canadian tables of nine. Courtesy? Respect? Saying sorry?

In 1948, if I can detour back that far, Vincent Massey published a book called *On Being Canadian* that grappled with the same question, though without all the tables. Before he was governor general, during the Second World War, Massey was high commissioner in London, which is where he starts a chapter called, promisingly, "The Canadian Pattern." He's talking about wartime London, where all the soldiers from all the Allied nations are gathered. Englishmen upon Scots mixed in with Poles and New Zealanders, followed closely by Americans, all those Gurkhas, Australians, Free French, Norwegians. Lots of soldiers in lots of different uniforms, all walking around. And here's the thing: you don't have to see a uniform or a badge, Massey says, to know a Canadian:

> Something in their bearing told the story—a combination of qualities—on the one hand a naturalness and freedom of movement, a touch of breeziness and an alertness which suggested the new world. They also showed self-control, an air of discipline and good manners, and they had generally taken some trouble about their appearance. They were rarely found lounging; they seemed always to have some purpose in mind.

Impressive. Doesn't sound like hockey, though. Wouldn't hockey, our de facto national game, have to reflect those proud traits in some serious way, or at least aspire to them?

THE GAME, KEN DRYDEN'S sagacious more-than-a-memoir that frames the week he decided to leave hockey, has often been called the sport's best book. "Nobody would ever argue for another," declares Bill Simmons, the sportswriter and Grantland.com editor, in his foreword to the thirtieth anniversary edition, published in 2013. Maybe, maybe not. Let's just say for now that Ken Dryden is the best hockey player to have written a great hockey book. Who, then, is the greatest writer to have played the best hockey?

We'd know by now if Robertson Davies had been hiding any hockey adjectives under a bushel. David Adams Richards has a severe love for the game, but the disabled left arm that's hindered his participation all his life is right there in the subtitle of his *Hockey Dreams: Memories of a Man Who Couldn't Play*. I don't know if Mark Jarman skates at all, but *Salvage King, Ya!* (1997) is one of the funniest novels on my shelf, hockey or no. Bill Gaston's *Good Body* (2000) is another—and he could play, and did, professionally in France, as he tells in a keen memoir, *Midnight Hockey: All About Beer, the Boys and the Real Canadian Game* (2006).

Hugh Hood loved to play, and when he wrote *Strength Down Centre*, his 1970 account of Jean Béliveau, he did something no other hockey biographer had done before: he spent an afternoon skating with his subject. Béliveau was still playing, if not at the top of his talent, at a very high level. It was a fairly informal skate, no equipment, but a rare opportunity. As Hood writes: "You don't get the same view

At the ready: Bruins and Maroons prepare to do battle in Boston, 1929–30.

of Jean, even from a seat at rinkside, that you do when you're playing with him—it's a totally different impression."

Hood is granted a fascinating, granular tutorial, and the reader with him. Béliveau is an articulate, interested guide, and there's a communion between the two men, not only talking about hockey but doing it. The passage ends with a telling exchange in which the writer and hockey player work out together why Béliveau's left skate is half a size larger than his right. It's because the left is the one, most of the time, that he puts his weight on to shoot.

Peter Gzowski once borrowed equipment when he embedded with the Edmonton Oilers to write *The Game of Our Lives,* but he found it hard to stay upright once he got on the ice. Everybody laughed, fondly. The same can't be said, I don't think, for the bishop of Montana who, funny and fusty and entirely unself-aware, signed on to infiltrate the Chicago Black Hawks in the early 1970s.

Former bishop, I should say. Chandler W. Sterling's Episcopalian bishopric was over when he decided that it was time he spent a year in the company of hockey players. He was by then rector of the Good Shepherd Church in Hilltown, Pennsylvania. I'm still not sure what he's up to in *The Icehouse Gang* (1972), the book he wrote chronicling that year. He'd played shinny as a boy in Illinois, "with a putty-filled salmon can" for a puck, no less. He spends his preface warning anyone who might dare to skate with professional hockey players to think very carefully. You would have to be a fool to do it. Even an angel would fear to tread on NHL ice—an undrafted angel, I take it he means. Here he is meeting the moist Black Hawk players for the first time:

> I nerved myself to go into the locker room where the men were dress-ing. Whenever a player emerged from the shower room I would follow him to his stall and introduce myself. Without exception I was received in a friendly way with what I believe was a minimum of reservation.

He calls himself an Armchair Albert, which is his way of admit-ting he doesn't skate anymore. His motives are pure, he says, and his naïveté indubitable. He's full of glad cheer and strange fancies. He natters and belabours. He reports that hockey ice is the hardest on the planet, it makes glaciers look like slush. He's enthralled by the food at training camp: "There were scrambled eggs to order and all kinds of cheeses, fruits and jellos. There were canisters of broth."

As for the hockey, he asks you to pretend you've bought a car. Then when you're driving home, some guy sideswipes you. That's hockey—or at least that's the bishop's tortured analogy.

Which brings us, not a moment too soon, to George Plimpton. He wanted several things from hockey, one of them being the loss of a tooth. That, he thought, would prove him a true hockey player. On a larger scale, I think what he was after, what he needed to know, was just how lifelike hockey is. Why else would a fifty-year-old New Yorker barely able to skate arrange to suit up—and as a goalie—for Boston's Bruins? Other than for comic effect, I mean. Which is what Plimpton did, and beautifully well. By the 1980s his participatory schtick was well established. He'd already been punched by boxer Archie Moore, squandered ten yards for the Detroit Lions offence while standing in as quarterback, pitched to Major League batters, and played a Bedouin in *Lawrence of Arabia*. A naïf, too, but no fool: *Open Net* (1985) is sharp and sophisticated, a thorough unlocking of hockey as well as a pure pleasure.

ADVICE:

Don't smoke. If you do smoke, what that tells Gordie Howe is, you don't want to be a hockey player. Keep your head up, of course: everybody knows that. Also, stick on the ice. A priest once told Howe that you can have two of three things and here they are: hockey, social life, or education. Up to you.

"Let's face it," says Ken Hodge, "you'll never be a good hockey player unless you are a good skater."

Syl Apps: "You'll find that to be a hockey star, you have to give up a lot of pleasures that would keep you from playing."

Long before *Outliers*, where Malcolm Gladwell wrote about the ten thousand hours you need to succeed in any given pursuit, the ten-year-old hero of Pete McCormack's novel *Understanding Ken* (1992) was hearing it at home: "Dad says you gotta play three hours a day if you want to make pro. That's what Bobby Orr said, too."

Be born in January, Gladwell suggests, by the way: that's when the really good hockey players originate.

Ralph Henry Barbour's *Guarding His Goal* (1917) is one of the earliest hockey novels, but that's not all: it's a veritable catalogue of hockey counsel. "You don't need the frills in hockey. What you need is to be able to stay on your feet and skate hard and—and be a bit tricky."

"I didn't learn the game in a book," growls Brian Sutter. "I learned it by playing in the league for twelve years."

Frank Mahovlich: "Many youngsters (and even men) think there is some secret way to avoid bodychecks or the less punishing stick-checks." Wrong.

Loneliness is a theme in *Phil Esposito's Winning Hockey for Beginners* (1976). For example, when you're hurt, you're all alone, not even a doctor can tell you if you can get back on the ice, which is why Esposito feels it's paramount that you know this: "Basically, if you can skate and can walk, you can play."

"You can't take any fudge from anybody and be a hockey player in Canada," according to Derek Sanderson.

Don't fret about injuries, says Rod Gilbert. "Worrying about getting hurt is the surest way to cramp your style and get yourself injured in the process."

Hockey's books, especially the autobiographies, spend a lot of time on pre-game routines: to shave or not, steak or eggs?

Stan Mikita left his razor in the cabinet the morning of a game: "the sweat and cold air hitting my face will irritate it." He liked to rub Vaseline on his face, to guard against the cold. Although goalie Lorne Chabot always shaved: "I stitch better," he said, "when my skin is smooth."

Mikita drank black coffee and watched *The Andy Griffith Show* with the kids before heading out to the rink for the regular 11:00 AM team meeting. Steak for lunch, a 2:00 PM nap. Last thing before stepping on the ice: dry heaves.

In Scott Young's novel *A Boy at the Leafs' Camp* (1963), the players sit down for their steaks at 2:00 PM, though his hero, Bill Spunska, makes do with a peach and an apple. Jean Béliveau was another 2:00 PM beef man, though Howie Morenz usually held off until 5:00. When Boston visited Montreal, Derek Sanderson would eat fast (steak medium-well, baked potato) then scoot down to Place Ville Marie. "The female scene there is fantastic," was his opinion. "I just sit there at the little eating spots and watch the girls walk by."

Sometimes Morenz skipped the steak altogether. If he'd had eggs, for instance, and then played well, the next game would demand eggs again. Either way, he always had a side of Limburger cheese. Gordie Howe's pre-game meal, circa 1959: steak, peas, lettuce, fruit gelatin, tea.

Don't tell John Bucyk any of this: "It's important to a hockey player's performance that he plays on an empty stomach." A cup of coffee was enough: "The sugar in the coffee gives me that extra little strength I need in the game."

Keith Magnuson confided the care the Black Hawks took: "Before a game we all pay a visit to the dressing room commode to make ourselves as light as possible."

For an eight o'clock game, Bobby Orr used to get to the rink by 3:00, settling in to read a book or the mail. Howe was still at home at that hour. At 3:55 he'd put on his pajamas and sleep for two hours. At 6:20 he shaved. His suit was brown and his shirt was white and he carried a topcoat over his left arm, and on the way to the rink he drove the cleaning lady home. At 6:55 he walked into the dressing room and hung up his coat and jacket and sat down to play gin rummy with Gus Mortson.

Brad Park needed a Coke after his nap. "I have a big, thick, sticky taste in my mouth and the Coke clears that away." Nerves he channelled into fixing up sticks, taping and retaping. He took fifteen minutes to get dressed, after which he'd sit taking deep breaths. Just before heading out he'd comb his hair.

Magnuson wore no socks. "I like to feel every part of the ice." Red Dutton noted that some players spent as much as an hour and a quarter "putting on their boots." Not him: "I used to get mine on in a little less than an hour. And I never thought this was a great deal of time to spend—for the skates were my tools."

Dave Schultz passed the hours before a game visualizing himself in a fight. George Plimpton describes Keith Magnuson working himself into a "jungle mentality" in the dressing room: his voice went down and his shoulders came up, you could stand and watch "all aspects of his civilized behaviour slackening."

Phil Esposito and his wife, Donna, made love "all afternoon" in Montreal on September 2, 1972, until it was time to go to the rink and play the Soviets. When Pierre Trudeau dropped the ceremonial puck to open the Summit Series, Esposito prevailed in the friendly faceoff because it seemed important not to, quote, let that Red bastard win it. Esposito scored a goal in the game's first thirty seconds, and Paul Henderson added another, right before the Soviets started to score and everything changed. "We were shocked," Esposito wrote later. "It scared the shit out of us."

IT'S EASY, ONCE you get up a little momentum, to ply the game's positive side, where it reflects brightest on us. Though, again, it takes a measure of strategic avoidance. If this were TV, maybe you'd want to start with some restorative footage of a glorious goal from history. A quick confetti of book-borne hockey-joy, affirmations of pleasure and happiness and fulfillment might include Ken Dryden talking about the best part of his Montreal career. Above everything else, the Stanley Cups and the money and the adulation, was the *fun* he had: "We just loved to play hockey."

As an outsider looking in, George Plimpton saw some of this. Few sports, he noted, seem to be enjoyed as much by their players as hockey. Doug Harvey once told his coach, Dick Irvin, "You may think I'm kidding, but I love that puck."

There were times, on the ice, at the height of a game, when Guy Lafleur would get so excited that he'd burst out laughing. He would have been in trouble if Rocket Richard had caught him. "I never did like to see anybody laughing, making a farce out of something," Richard said in his day. Also, it should be said that Lafleur could go the other way, too. In 1978, after the game in which the Canadiens had won their twentieth Stanley Cup, he felt empty and unable to celebrate, locking himself away in a tiny room in the Montreal Forum, where teammate Pete Mahovlich finally found him. As designated bon vivant, Mahovlich took it upon himself to shake Lafleur, as Georges-Hébert Germain describes it, "like a rag doll, trying to get him to be happy."

When Vladislav Tretiak was asked whether he took pleasure from his performances on the ice, he said, "It sometimes happens that I catch a really difficult puck, a dead-on goal shot, and I feel such a thrill it gives me goose pimples to know I stopped it! It's a feeling that's impossible to describe."

When he played in the 1970s for the New York Rangers, Swedish centreman Ulf Nilsson had no such difficulty expressing his feelings: "I get a hard-on when I score a goal," he said. He had 197 of each, a quick check of his career statistics shows.

For Eric Nesterenko, it was skating. When Studs Terkel asked what was his most joyous moment on the ice, he said it wasn't in the NHL, but after he'd retired, out driving in his car somewhere one winter. There was a pond, he pulled over, and he had his skates. In a minute he was skating, just skating—pure joy.

In Roy MacGregor's *The Last Season*, Felix Batterinski finishes up a fight: "I knew it wasn't right, but it felt great."

So maybe that's enough of that, for now.

HOCKEY BEFUDDLED THE French semiotician Roland Barthes the first time he saw it in Montreal in 1961. Hubert Aquin was making a documentary for the CBC, and Barthes was brought in to cogitate on the meanings of bullfights and bicycle races, and what makes us pursue pucks. He was confused by the offside rule, which to him "dominated" the game. Children who seemed to be fighting, he observed, were merely learning how to inhabit their country.

William Faulkner's first game was Rangers and Canadiens at the old Madison Square Garden in 1955. Babe Ruth saw the same two teams play as early as 1926. He'd even played a bit before that, in Baltimore. And? Loved it. It looked hard and fast. In baseball, you knew where the ball was coming from. "Here," he told a reporter at Madison Square in 1930, "they fire at you from all directions, jab you with sticks, trip you up, knock you down—boy, this is real rough. Did you see that goalie get kicked in the face by a skate?" Still, if he tried it again, goal would be his preferred position. "But I'd play behind the net instead of in front of it." Okay, great, Babe. Anything else? Just that fighting is, quote, apple pie to hockey. He wanted to mention that, too.

Faulkner can be excused for ignoring hockey in 1918. That was the year he joined the Royal Canadian Air Force, which was so new at the time that it wasn't Royal yet, or formally called the Air Force. It was summer when he arrived in Toronto, and on into the fall he was busy with training, so there wouldn't have been time for hockey even if they'd been playing. By November the war was over and Faulkner was demobilized, and while he was waiting to leave, a lot of the city was in quarantine, trying to avoid the Spanish flu, and anyway, that was a year of disarray for the fledgling NHL.

Another Nobel Prize winner, Ernest Hemingway, is truly problematic, given how much he would have had to disfavour hockey to avoid it so entirely when he was in Toronto two years later. Hemingway was working as a reporter at the *Toronto Star*, where his good friends included Morley Callaghan and Greg Clark. Are you telling me they never took him to a St. Pats game at the Arena Gardens on Mutual Street, barely a mile's walk from the *Star*'s offices on King Street West? This was in 1920 and into 1921, when the Ruthian Babe Dye was playing for the St. Pats, leading the league in scoring, and the defenceman Harry Cameron, about whom I knew nothing at all until I looked him up, was his teammate. *The man who curved his shot*, let the record show, *before anyone was curving a shot*. And Sprague Cleghorn! Sorry, but if you know anything about the man, you know that the exclamation mark is automatic. Apart from how great his name is to say aloud, Cleghorn! was one of hockey's best players and also, truly, one of its worst.

Just the name in and of itself sounds like two hockey words, *sprague cleghorn*, maybe a serious though seldom-called penalty, or else a medical condition occasioned by a stick hitting your skull. When you read about the man himself, many times it's in association with words like *melee* and (truly a hockey adjective) *fistic*, and also the phrase *he'd kick your balls off*. Sentences that begin with *Sprague Cleghorn* sometimes go on to report that *on February 1, he almost wiped out the Ottawa team single-handedly*. A fearsome, fascinating character. I can't believe that Hemingway could have resisted writing about him, if he'd seen him. Grace under pressure? The great Spanish bullfighter Manolete, whom Hemingway met and championed and hung around and wrote about in *Death in the Afternoon*—I'm sorry, no disrespect, but Hemingway would have had exactly no use for Manolete if he'd come across Cleghorn. All I'm saying is, if Hemingway had discovered Cleghorn! in Toronto, I think he would have stayed, and if he'd stayed, soon enough he would have run into Eddie Shore and the rest would be history, except that it isn't. Since I can't believe that Hemingway didn't go to a hockey game, the alternative might be that he went and it left him cold. Hemingway saw hockey in Toronto and turned his back on it.

Faulkner had it almost as good. In January of 1955 he was commissioned to write a hockey essay for *Sports Illustrated*. Maybe you know it. Certainly it's one of the most anthologized pieces of hockey prose, which isn't surprising, given how rarely Nobel Prize winners write about hockey. Looking at a hundred years of laureates leading up to Alice Munro, it may in fact be one of the unwritten Nobel codes that in order to be considered for recognition from Stockholm you have to have avoided the game entirely. Faulkner ignored the ban; of course, he already had his Nobel, and what were they going to do, grab it back?

"An Innocent at Rinkside," the essay is called. For all its anthologification, I'd never read it. I guess I expected big things, though if I'd thought about a bit more, I could have worked it out. If the result of Faulkner's exposure to Rocket Richard and the rest of the powerful Habs of the 1950s had been enchantment—well, we'd all know that, wouldn't we? Faulkner would have hurried home bearing the seed for a hockey trilogy in which he'd chronicle the up-and-down exploits of the Yoknapatawpha Unvanquished, their changeable fortunes in the old Southern Broiler League, and that's how hockey would have filled his last years before his death in 1962 with late-blooming joy. Faulkner's eighth novel, *Pylon*, sounds like it should have some hockey in it (nope). Same with *The Sound and the Fury* (zilch). Best of all, though, would have to be *Go Down, Moses*, which might be the greatest goalie novel never written, the story of a stand-up netminder grown weary of watching the low shots sneak by. Whereas, in fact, nothing of the sort. If I was looking for a model of hockey disenthrallment, I found him in Faulkner.

His piece starts promisingly enough. "The vacant ice looked tired." That's not bad. Then the game starts and Faulkner gets the hell out of there. Unwilling to implicate himself, he hands the narrative to the third-person:

> To the innocent, who had never seen it before, it seemed discorded and inconsequent, bizarre and paradoxical like the frantic darting of the weightless bugs which run on the surface of stagnant pools.

Did you catch that? The dismissal followed by the sneer capped off with the kick? You're still dealing with *discorded* when you hit the word that really hurts—*inconsequent*—and then he lays on *bizarre*. And he hasn't even reached the insects yet. *The weightless bugs*. The bugs of no weight whose outlandish skitterings have no significance. And that pool of theirs, also? A brackish pool like that is nothing to be proud of.

There's a specific hockey word for what Faulkner's doing and here it is: *deking*. Because as soon as he swerves at you, right away he's swerving the other way and then, before you can think too much, Faulkner's gone around you. Forget about ugly Nature. Hockey speaks to him, it's urgent and important. It's a dizzying turnaround, but that's what we like about hockey, isn't it, one of its virtues. Actually, no. Faulkner starts to discern meaning, but just like that, it's gone. He catches a pattern, a design "which was trying to tell him something, say something to him urgent and important and true in that second before, already bulging with the motion and the speed, it began to disintegrate and dissolve." He doesn't appear to mind too much. Easy come, easy go. This is the moment in which hockey loses Faulkner. Truth and importance are right before him, playing hard to get, but he doesn't care to play.

Maurice Richard catches his notice. That's the next thing. But only briefly the Rocket holds him and here's what he says—get ready, because it's his high note, the best thing Faulkner will write when it comes to hockey, all in a fragment of a sentence:

> Richard with something of the passionate glittering fatal alien quality of snakes.

And that's it, done. Geoffrion gets a mention after this, and so does Edgar Laprade from the Rangers, but really, though Faulkner has another eight hundred words to work through, as far as the hockey goes, he's lost, as they say, the plot. Doug Harvey is playing in this game, Jean Béliveau, Jacques Plante. These are Dick Irvin's Canadiens Faulkner is watching, and later on in the year they'll play the Detroit Red Wings for the Stanley Cup. I didn't even mention Mosdell or Olmstead. Not that Faulkner does, either.

Who's to blame? Faulkner himself might have claimed it was the cigarette smoke that ruined the game for him. He certainly has a lot to say about this. His innocent eye follows the tiers of seats up and up until they vanish into the pall of tobacco smoke trapped by the roof. To Faulkner, the haze that fills the rink represents more than the promise of future cancers. While the hockey plays out in front of him, Faulkner worries about exhaust, not just of air but of violence being stirred up on the ice. This is hard to follow, but after many re-readings I think I've got it. It seems that the attention of New York fans is, to Faulkner, as palpable as the smoke of their cigarettes. Faulkner sees it: "All that intent and tense watching," he writes, blending with the smoke. The resulting brew rises to the roof and then, trapped, drops back down iceward where it comes in contact with—stay with me, now—the violence. The violence, which Faulkner identifies as a byproduct of hockey's speed and motion, has nowhere to go. Without the roof, the smoke and the watching would float free, apparently. And this, as it turns out, is Faulkner's whole point. He brings in sloops and lions and little Norwegian boys after this, and then (no kidding) there's a beauty pageant and Miss Sewage Disposal takes a turn while the hockey fades out of focus.

I was worried that the blow that Faulkner was getting ready to deliver was that hockey isn't worthy of anybody's notice, let alone a Nobel laureate's. But Faulkner was never interested in hockey, not in Toronto in 1918, and not in distractingly smoky New York thirty-odd years later. *Sports Illustrated* would have done better to hire T.S. Eliot, the 1948 Nobel winner in literature, or better yet, Sir Winston Churchill, who won in 1953.

It wasn't all Faulkner's fault, I guess. Hockey does have to shoulder some of the blame, the hometown Rangers in particular. They were awful that whole year, in fact. Asked what he needed to help the team, coach Muzz Patrick replied, "A pistol." They'd won just one of their previous eighteen games, and with the crowds dwindling away, management had come up with an answer: start the losing earlier. At Faulkner's game, instead of 8:30, the puck fell at 7:00. It worked, too, in its way. Instead of their usual six or seven thousand, the Rangers that night had 13,607 smokers and intent watchers in the stands. With Montreal winning 7–1, the masses began to boo and stamp their feet—and laugh. It was a shame that so many youngsters were there, a columnist commented next day in the *World Telegram*. "Judged by what they saw," he wrote, "they will not become the customers of tomorrow."

IF FAULKNER HAD been invited to the first game they arranged for Princess Elizabeth, who knows? Maybe then we'd be looking through the mirror at a world where you couldn't win a Nobel *without* having written a hockey novel. As it is, we're backing up four years to October of 1951, when the princess and her husband, Prince Philip, were in Toronto. She wasn't queen yet, but it was important that she see a hockey game while she was in town, if only to give Her Future Majesty a look at the spectacle her portrait would be slenderly smiling down on into the next century. She didn't have time in her schedule to attend the Saturday night season-opener at Maple Leaf Gardens, so for her benefit the Leafs and the visiting Black Hawks put on an afternoon demonstration match. Fourteen thousand fans packed into the Gardens for the three o'clock game, after which, at precisely 3:15, the royal party was supposed to leave to visit Riverdale Park. Originally the park was going to have her for fifteen minutes more than the arena, but in the end she stayed with the hockey for a full half-hour.

I'm willing to take at face value the fact that the royal schedule was the reason for truncating the game and that it didn't have to do with hockey people, in a cold flash of self-abnegation, realizing that there was only so much hockey a first-timer could be expected to endure. Because if not, of course, I'd have to face the essential Shakespearean question of whether hockey is hockey which alters when it alteration finds.

The *Globe* reported the next day on the festivities. The royal couple was "introduced to a new phase of Canadian life" and heard a sound "that must certainly have been unique in their experience." The scream of an aggrieved Howie Meeker? Joe Klukay baiting Rags Raglan? No. "The roar of a hockey crowd as a home player sweeps in on goal is different from any other sound in any other game. It builds up quickly to a crescendo and explodes when the shot is made."

The royals sat in Box 50, west side of the Gardens. A large Union Jack adorned the front. The regular seats had been removed, replaced with chairs. Princess Elizabeth had a better view than her husband. Their faces were animated. They asked many questions. "Big time hockey is a thrilling game," said the *Globe*, "and the Royal couple seemed to enjoy their first taste of it."

The Hawks had the better of the play. "Body contact was hard but no fights broke out." The prince was relaxed. His laughter was hearty. He slapped his thigh to see such hard bodychecks. "The Princess betrayed her emotions by a wide-eyed look and an automatic jump of the royal shoulders when a player was hit hard." Several times she asked Conn Smythe to explain what they were seeing. The crowd divided its attention between the game and the royal couple. No goals were scored. For those, the commoners would have to return for the evening game, in which the Black Hawks beat the Leafs 3–1.

As it turned out, the demo pleased the princess and prince so much that two weeks later in Montreal, they took in a full game at the Forum. Surrounded by eleven Mounties, they watched the Canadiens beat New York 6–1. The princess wore *a three-quarter-length mink coat over a brown taffeta dress and a cloche brown hat with gold sequins and a veil.* The prince was *hatless.* The royal couple showed considerable interest in the ice sprinklers. The prince put on a pair of dark glasses near the end of the second period. When Jersey Joe Walcott, world heavyweight champion, appeared on the ice between periods, the royal couple clapped. Despite all the goals, it was a dull game, spotty. Maybe because the NHL had asked the players to behave: no fighting, no arguing. Maurice Richard, for one, decided he'd comply. The story goes that he almost got into it with New York's Steve Kraftcheck, but turned his cheek. Prince Philip is supposed to have walked along the boards to the scene of the squabble, calling out to the Rocket as he went: *What's the matter, don't you want to fight?*

HARD TO BELIEVE that I'd never tried to make a rink before but true enough, I never had. I wasn't organized enough in the city. Or else I was organized and the winter let me down. In 2007, I was readier than I'd ever been, but January in Ontario was green as golf courses, which were all open for business, with everybody riding their bikes in downtown Toronto. The whole country was waiting on winter, according to the CBC. If you turned on your radio, that's what the news was, hour after hour, a tremor of uncertainty crossing the country, where's the winter, what's happening, why isn't the government doing anything? Not acceptable, Shelagh Rogers said. "It's eating away at our national identity."

Winter itself wasn't saying much, but then winter was never much of a talker. It's the silent, stubborn type, as Margaret Atwood says, and even when it's not killing us outright, it reminds us of what death might be like, still and blank and cold. Although Bernard Mergen says in *Snow in America* that snow's moral teachings include purity, the cumulative effects of seemingly unimportant actions, and the existence of life *after* death.

When it does come, as it finally did in 2007, the verbs of winter are hockey verbs: winter *wallops* and *blasts* and *socks* and *pounds*. The referee misses it all. So we push back. Toronto spends $65 million a year struggling against snow and slush, *shoving* and *plowing* it, more hockey words. Sometimes, when the onslaught gets to be too much, Toronto calls in the army. In 1999 this happened, and the nation laughed. Why? Because the nation enjoys laughing at Toronto and does it snow or no. But also, because we're Canadians, winter is not supposed to make us panic. *My country*, Gilles Vigneault sings in his song, *my country isn't a country, it's the winter*. It's the same message with which the 2014 Olympic Team branded itself for Russia: #WeAreWinter. This is where we live, it's what we do, the whole history of Canada is about coping with wintertime, about *not* calling in the army.

Atwood's book about this was called, obviously, *Survival*. It happens to have been published in 1972, probably just by coincidence. Resistance to winter is, as she points out, futile. Hate it if you will, fight it if you have to. "You can also make houses in it," she says. After that, it's a question of dignity. You could stay in your house, hibernate, wait for the thaw to come. But could we look ourselves in the national eye if we stayed indoors? Was there ever really any doubt that we'd get out and flood the yard, or in my case, head out over the bridge to the pond?

Voltaire used our winter to mock us ("a few acres of snow"), and so did Rudyard Kipling ("Our Lady of the Snows," he chuckled). And it's true, winter has a way of making us amusing, with our waggish snowblowers, the rich absurdity of our negative temperatures (in 1947, Snag, Yukon, hilariously bottomed out at –81.04° Fahrenheit). Not to mention the droll winter wardrobes we affect, funny clothes with funny names: *mukluks, mittens, dickies, earmuffs*. When Sidney Crosby first went to Pittsburgh, kids he met there didn't know what a *toque* was.

Hockey is our argument against all that. When people see how seriously we take it, they have no choice but to take us seriously. Nobody laughs at hockey—or at least, not to hockey's face.

HOCKEY'S FIRST GAME: now that way lies some treacherous territory. Those who ask the question *Where did hockey begin?* must be answered by a series of other questions, including *Who's asking?*

What do you mean by hockey? *Who have you been talking to?* as well as—very important—*What's your postal code?* Claimants from Montreal, Kingston, Niagara Falls, Halifax-Dartmouth, Pictou, and Windsor, Nova Scotia, all have their fortified camps. Some even have commemorative ballcaps, among other merchandise. Délı̨ne, Northwest Territories, the latest to step up, offers for sale a full line of T-shirts and mini-sticks. If you read all the hockey books, one of the useful tasks you may imagine might be yours is to solve, for once and for all, the question of where hockey started. Good luck. Because in the matter of origins, hockey is riven by dispute. At times the riving has been rancorous. If it were a road we were talking about, it would be a riven, rutted, rancorous road. Its shoulders would be narrow. Its corners would be blind. Never on any road would you have seen so much heaving, or roadkill.

It's puzzling, because for a long time the facts of the case seemed to be more or less settled. And yet, for every careful, credible report that's been commissioned and delivered, there's a book, a website, a big sign at the edge of a pond in Nova Scotia, to discredit, debunk, roundly drub the experts, so-called, and their findings. In hockey terms, the history of the history of hockey has been marked by many offsides, much hooking, assorted subtle elbowing, and plenty of trash-talking. Most civilians are confused by the whole ruckus.

For those still curious, we can carry it as far back as you wish, all the way to *pagnica*. We can look at *kaslo, yula, lunki*, all the peasant games of old Russia. We can touch on *kolf*, but we shouldn't spend too long on it. Two Swedish historians, Carl Gidén and Patrick Houda, have written the book on all these, five-hundred pages thick. *Pukku-mikku* is worth investigating, and maybe *keritizin*, from Greece. *Knattleikr, beikou, cumbok*, no problem. We can discuss the shades of difference that make *hurley* hurley and not *rickets*—which, can we just say, sounds very uncomfortable.

You can read the histories. The ones that aren't fooling around start 100 million years ago, with the formation of the continents, which made hockey possible in the first place. Others will tell you that boys who played *hurley* in Nova Scotia in the early nineteenth century could go home and read in the newspaper about Napoleon's invasion of Russia. A few will tell you exactly when the game was first declared not only *annoying* but *dangerous*.

Arthur Farrell, author of *Hockey: Canada's Royal Winter Game* (1899), says that the beginnings of the game are lost in a background of Egyptian darkness. Someone else: by 1864, all the boys in Canada who used to be seen throwing rocks had given that up for hockey.

Red Dutton says young men in eastern Canada invented the game to fill the winter months when it was too cold for baseball or rugby. In 1941, a man named Fox explained about his father having played hockey in Montreal in 1836, on Dorchester Street, when a bunch of Irishmen put on skates and grabbed their hurling sticks and off they went. One of them, Jim Gleason, invented the puck.

That's not a story that carries too much historical ballast. We do know that soldiers were playing in Kingston in 1843. We can talk too about the shift in value systems and how the British amateur ideal fell away as winning became more important. Another thing worth discussing is the crisis in Canadian masculinity that struck the nation just after we became a nation, in 1867, a case of national jitters that only got worse when the British Army withdrew its imperial garrisons in 1871. Who was going to defend us now?

Gordon Green says that stubbornness was in the very soul of the game.

Jack Tremblay: "It is a Canadian game conceived by Canadians through their love of skating on the abundant ice of their frozen lakes and rivers."

Clarence Campbell said hockey didn't exist until the first rules were written up and a game played. "As such, ice hockey has to be regarded as Canadian."

F.G. Gnaedinger, who claimed he was there at that first organized rule-governed game in Montreal but may have been confused about his dates, says that all the skaters were football players and that the sticks were heavy. Having said that, we've gone far enough without mentioning the name of James Creighton from Halifax, an engineer in his later life and law clerk of the Senate, who studied at Montreal's McGill University. He was the one to arrange that first public game, which took place at the Victoria Skating Rink on March 3, 1875. He never called himself the Godfather of Hockey, but others did, and after a delay even lengthier than mine in introducing him here, he's beginning to be more widely recognized for his role. Prime Minister Stephen Harper attended the unveiling of a monument in Ottawa in 2009, and there's an ongoing effort to see Creighton's name elevated to Hockey's Hall of Fame.

We do know when hockey arrived in Toronto and who brought it: 1887, T.L. Paton, a goalie from Montreal and a friend of Arthur Farrell's. In his book, Farrell creates a scene that might be straight out of some ancient legend of Camelot, crying the names of the intrepid knights errant who set out to spread the good word and the game: Tom Paton to Toronto; Mr. C. Shearer to the U.S.; George Meagher to Europe. Although a later chronicler, Henry Roxborough, says it was John Massey who first brought sticks and rules to Toronto. Maybe he and Paton rode in on the same train?

Vince Leah's *Manitoba Hockey: A History* (1970) tells us that P.A. Macdonald carried the first hockey stick to Western Canada, arriving by rail in Winnipeg at some point in the 1880s. The rest of his baggage remains a matter of purest speculation, along with his looks and his business. He could have been travelling with a trunk filled with pumpkins. Give him a ginger moustache and sloe eyes, it doesn't matter, he's distilled now to a single item of his luggage. What happened next? How did one stick beget enough for a game? Was it checked luggage or did he sit in the carriage holding it upright between his knees? Wherever hockey started, this is the part that I treasure, the idea of the game being delivered by hand to all the corners of the map.

Oh, and about my namesake, Dick Smith, who claimed to have co-written the game's first rules in 1878: Iain Fyffe's new book, *On His Own Side of the Puck* (2014), confirms that his story doesn't stand up. He was a big Montreal liar.

A VITAL DOCUMENT for anyone pointing a compass in search of hockey's birthplace is the 2001 *Origins of Hockey* report put out by the Society for International Hockey Research. Full disclosure: I am a paid-up member of the Society, known as SIHR, the august international institution that might be likened to NASA in matters of hockey history and statistics and arcana, a mission control overseeing the whole cosmos.

Or maybe not NASA. A better model might be—I was going to say the Vatican, but then the NHL probably is the Vatican, with its unflappable belief in its own infallibility and an undying determination to protect its brand and its business largely by pretending it can't hear any word of dissent that it doesn't want to listen to. So the SIHR would have to be a small chivalrous order, like the Knights Templar. Based in Toronto, the Society's membership reaches as far as hockey itself. It's a covey of hockey historians, writers, freelance researchers, statisticians, anecdotalists, other sundry partisans, and the prime minister. It's true: Stephen Harper is a member. I'm a poor acolyte, never having contributed to the newsletter or annual, glancing only occasionally at the online discussion of whether Leo Labine was credited with a goal he scored on his own net while playing for the Red Wings. I'm no help when it comes to inputting stats, and I almost never make it to the Toronto chapter meetings. I do cheer when SIHR fights the good fight to right a wrong of public hockey perception or recognize James Creighton or get behind the worthy effort to raise a statue of Lord Stanley in downtown Ottawa.

Does it matter where hockey started? Maybe not. Certainly with boxing, Pierce Egan held that to trace back the high art of punching men to its origins was not worth the time, because who knew? Also, why would you concentrate on such a speck of a detail when the real issue is something else entirely? This is in Egan's book *Boxiana*, published in 1812. Whether you care for boxing or not, it spins a beguiling argument. Did Adam uppercut in Eden? Don't worry about it. It would be sheer gammon, that's what it would be, to worry about such a niggling tiny detail as how it began. Wherever boxing originated, Britons need never apologize for the very natural pursuit of punching someone in a scientific way. All you need to know is that once upon a time, when hurt feeling produced resentment, the very reasonableness of the British race saved the day. "Coolness, checking fiery passion and rage, reduced it to a perfect science." Boxing adds "generosity to their disposition," "humanity to their conduct," and "courage to their national character." Britons don't carry knives, Egan says; petty disputes don't lead to stabbings where he's from, and whatever revenges they do like to practise, murder isn't one of them. "Boxing removes these dreadful calamities; a contest is soon decided, and scarcely ever the frame sustains any material injury."

Egan says that boxing is in "perfect unison" with the "feelings of Englishmen." Also, consider the good it does releasing social pressures. "A dispassionate review of those countries where Pugilism is unknown, we find, that upon the most trifling misunderstanding, the life of the individual is in danger." Boxing is a kind of anti-venom, infusing "that true heroic courage, blended with humanity, into the hearts of Britons, which has made them so renowned, terrific, and triumphant, in all parts of the world."

Not bad. That works: wherever hockey came from is irrelevant so long as you understand its true value. And yes, if you flip it around, Eganeer the logic, it is true that so many of the benighted nations in the world, the ones that cause the most trouble, your North Koreas and Zimbabwes, Syrias—none of them has ever known the calming social influence of hockey. Coincidence? Either way, it's outlandish enough to sound almost true.

THE ORIGINS OF HOCKEY sub-committee was struck in 2001 to respond to claims out of Windsor, Nova Scotia, to the effect that hockey started there and nowhere else. In their conclusion—it's very respectful and even encouraging—the sub-committee uses words like *no* and *failed* and *no* again, and *skeptical* and also (right after *failed*) *to offer credible evidence*. As for the sub-committee itself, it makes certain to plead no opinion. If anything, it stands *with* Dr. Garth Vaughn, the Windsor claimant, who was (he died in 2012) of the school that hockey was not invented *per se* and did not start on any particular day in any exact year. They didn't like that answer elsewhere in Nova Scotia, and still don't, from what I can tell. In Windsor, the sign down by Howard Dill's pond says what the website says: The Cradle of Hockey.

Over in Halifax-Dartmouth (and at Hockey's Home online), they're not too sure about that. Lawyer Martin Jones says they're all amateurs at the SIHR, not to mention self-appointed, and mostly from Ontario and Quebec, and maybe what those initials stand for, really, is the Society for Ignoring Halifax's Records.

SONAHHR is the New York–based Society of North American Hockey Historians and Researchers. (I'm not a member there, though

I'd gladly apply if I could figure out how to do it.) What they say is that fen hockey in England was the first organized game of ice hockey. *Organized* and *standardized* are important words when it comes to tracking the true history of hockey. Regarding North American roots, SONAHHR comes down firmly in Dartmouth.

Did Sir John Franklin play futile hockey on the great Northwest Passage of a rink that trapped his ships *Terror* and *Erebus* even as they served as convenient goals for the opposing teams? Probably not. On an earlier, slightly less disastrous expedition, Franklin's men did play hockey in the Northwest Territories, which is where Déline enters with what I'd have to call the most gleeful of birthplace claims. No rancour up there, just lots of pride and energy and quick action: in 2006 the town got a motion passed in the NWT Legislative Assembly staking the claim on hockey's ancestry.

The biggest development yet to hit the hockey nativity scene came on a shining spring day this past May when SIHR convened its annual congress in Penetanguishene, Ontario. It was almost the end of the day. Much business had been completed, many informative papers delivered. Hall of Fame defenceman Pierre Pilote was there in the Brian Orser Room at the North Simcoe rink, telling Chicago stories about why he always passed to Hull and not Mikita (more assists).

I was sitting near the back of the room, and I have to admit, it took me a moment to realize just what we were hearing from SIHR's outgoing president, Montreal researcher Jean-Patrice Martel. His co-authors were the respected Swedish historians Gidén and Houda, who'd made the journey from Stockholm. If anyone suspected that their research was motivated by revenge—well, no, of course not. Revenge for what?

Any air of triumph, and there was some, was earned.

They were launching a new book, *On the Origin of Hockey* (2014), but it was more than that, too. This was an official notice. We here today, we few, would carry the message out to the wider world, let it be known that the road that leads to hockey's source is not being just repaved but ripped up entirely, for export to England, where it properly belongs. Although really the point of their bravura presentation was: there's no road. Never was a road.

Step-by-step that late afternoon in Huronia, Martel marched us away from the obsolete confidence that our game started here, among us. Microphone in hand, PowerPoint in play, he laid out the book's clear conclusions. The (voluminous) research showed that by the definitions set out by SIHR's Origins sub-committee, the case was now clear that many games on ice, some called hockey, some not, had been played in England as far back as 1820, which we know because Charles Darwin witnessed them. Doesn't matter how much it speeds our blood: hockey started elsewhere.

I left just before the end of the presentation, so I can't report how much wailing or keening the membership mounted on our nation's behalf. In the week that followed, the news that our birthright had been seized and proven to belong to other parents rippled in and out of the media. I don't know exactly how much uproar I was expecting: some. To be fair, with the long, hard winter we'd had, it may be that we were more willing this spring than we might be in others to forgive hockey its sudden betrayal of our devotion. Maybe just this once we'd be willing to forget the whole thing.

PUCK. IS THERE a better hockey word? And then the actual item: Is there anything more pleasing than a puck? Anything so superbly plain and perfectly weighted and fun to slide around with your stick and also so essential to hockey, not to mention the great noises it summons out of goalposts and rinkboards? Peter LaSalle, in a short story from his collection *Hockey sur Glace* (1999), has the puck knocking scuffed boards "with echoes like somebody hammering in the country." Rod Gilbert says that Boom-Boom Geoffrion and Rocket Richard both used to smash pucks off boards so hard that you'd want to cover your ears.

Coming cold to the game, Roland Barthes concluded that nothing was as important as the (evil?) puck: "It is as if the men were sucked up less by the opposing goal than by the malicious object that leads them to it."

It's easy to overstate the importance of the puck, as in: sometimes in history there's a leap of innovation, a burst of brilliant light, a flourish of hacksaw that changes everything. Nonetheless, that's the story of the hockey puck right there. Without it, there would be no hockey, simple as that. Before the puck, there was the ball, and that's why all those games we squint at in old wintry paintings aren't hockey. Kolf and shinny and rickets and hurley and lacrosse, they used a ball, and are welcome to it. In bandy the ball was called a *cat* or sometimes a *kit*, although at times it wasn't a ball at all, but a *bung* of cork or wood that did service, not to be confused with *dung*, which has, at least in legend, fulfilled its own hockey purpose, hence the Canadianism *horse puck*, which is not to be mixed up with *horse hockey*, which means *nonsense* or just plain *horseshit*. Best quality *horse buns*, as far as Frank Selke remembered from his childhood, would last a whole period before blowing apart. Lumps of coal, potatoes, apples, blocks of wood, they're all part of puck folklore. And then at some point, somebody sliced a rubber ball—cut the round right off—maybe at Montreal's Victoria Rink, where the arena manager wielded his saw when he'd seen too many windows broken.

Are pucks female? Because the soccer ball is. Like ships and motorcycles, according to the novelist Eduardo Galeano, soccer balls are feminine. So: pucks? The French language answers *yes* (*la rondelle*) but Italian and Spanish (*il* and *el disco*) disagree. In Swedish, the *tomte* is a mythical creature in folklore, taking the form of a bearded old man. He looks after a farmer's home and family, especially at night, while everybody's asleep. This isn't far, as Shakespeare knew, from one of the English meanings of the word *puck,* though in English the sprite has a mischievous if not outright malicious cast to him. There are those who'll say that hockey's puck was given its name by early players who'd been reading *A Midsummer's Night Dream*—Puck is always vanishing without warning.

Ebbie Goodfellow speaks of carving his own hardwood pucks as a boy. And King Clancy's sister recalls her bustling brother, always on the go, a whole hockey industry unto himself, taping up sticks, building boxes in which to store shin pads, and "making pucks in the oven." In Toronto's *Star*, on Saturday, February 4, 1905, it's referred to as *the gypsum*: "Blanchard bent his back to save himself from the impact of the gypsum." Funny anecdotes from this era often involve pucks lost in rink rafters and goalies' pockets or, in Montreal, the puck breaking in two and before anyone could realize it, "there were two games in progress at the same time and finally goals scored simultaneously at both ends of the rink."

In London, the *Times* reported on the composition of the puck in December of 1908: "a circular piece of compressed india rubber measuring 4 in. in diameter and 1 in. in depth, in the interior of which is a piece of lead to give it the necessary weight of 1 ¼ lb." (NHL pucks are smaller, three inches in diameter, and lead-free.)

The puck recipe followed by Toronto's Viceroy Reliable Group calls for

- natural rubber
- synthetic rubber
- filler (usually coal dust)

- sulphur
- and an antioxidant, to make the puck healthier—no, that's not so; it's to help the rubber to cure.

Viceroy sells about 2.5 million pucks a year. Boston Bruins goalie Jim Pettie had family who worked there. He told George Plimpton, "My mother makes pucks, my sister sells pucks, and I eat pucks."

I once went for a wander through the Viceroy factory in Toronto. Gone today, it was then a dim, grim experience in a place that looked like no one had visited for a hundred years, all the ancient machinery churning away on autopilot, with maybe a few diligent Beatrix Potter mice taking care of packing and shipping. I have to admit that the extruders were satisfying to watch, the long ooze of molten pucks. There's satisfaction, too, in puck-making terminology: *extrude*, *Banbury* (a mixer), *knurling* (the process that dimples the puck's edges), and *flash* (excess rubber that needs to be trimmed). Viceroy used to feed the NHL most of its pucks, until the Slovaks undercut the market. I remember reading about this back in the 1990s, tasting the gall of it, wincing at the extreme irony, the shameful symbolism of having become a country that has surrendered its own secure puck supply. Are we blind? Isn't this exactly what happened with the United States and their oil and Iraq? There were stories at the time about failures of foreign quality control and the dangers of malignant Eastern Europe and even Chinese pucks, too heavy (smashing Plexiglas, maiming goalies) or uncooked (splintering into lethal shrap at the slightest slap).

Not true, apparently. Viceroy did lose the NHL contract, but it only strayed as far as Sherbrooke, Quebec, where InGlasCo now handles the account, using liquefied rubber and an expensive injection process.

Bobby Hull wrote a whole chapter, "You and the Puck," which includes a reminder: "It is the man with the puck the crowd watches." Brad Park's dad told him, "Never give it away. Make sure you know where it's going before you pass." When Ken Morrow was six, his dad cut the hearts out of pucks so they weren't too heavy for him. When Alexei Kovalev was twelve, his father drilled out the middle of pucks and filled them with lead. Vladislav Tretiak says you have to watch yourself. If a person ceases to develop intellectually, if his curiosity is dulled and the circle of his interests shrinks to the size of a puck, then inevitably his mastery of the sport will also be diminished.

The Afghan sport of *buzkashi* is played on horseback, a wild sort of polo with an important technical difference: instead of a ball, players propel the corpse of a headless calf around the field. You'd think that this kind of thing would be natural grist for a hockey novel, maybe a murder mystery, but no. Roch Carrier—this is in *La Guerre, Yes Sir!* (1968) rather than the lesserly gruesome *Hockey Sweater*—does have a street-hockey game where a man's severed hand stands in as a puck, but that's about it.

I'm fonder of the notion of the puck as a living creature rather than a dismembered limb. In 1927, a writer for the *New Yorker* watched one fly "like a violent, heavy bird." Sometimes it seems like some kind of brutal vole, as in this player's lament from a Mark Jarman story: "My nose is still broken from a puck running up my stick on its mission."

The puck has eyes, it's said, which means it finds a tiny breach in a goalie's ramparts where no human eye sees one. Pucks can confer intelligence on a player ("He's a genius when he has the puck," Billy Harris said of Bryan Trottier) and coax out deep-set character (Gordie Howe told son Mark, "The puck brings out so much in you, it's the damnedest thing in the world"). But they can also unman. Here's Harry Sinden on Philadelphia gendarme Dave Schultz: "When the puck came to him it looked like it was alive and something to beat to death. Bang it! Cut it!" But of course there's only one way to kill the puck and that's to get it across the other team's goal line, where it lies, as Andrew Podnieks says, "lifeless."

At Sochi's 2014 Olympics, organizers had 3,500 pucks at the ready for the men's competition, which was enough to provide for a truly Putinesque extravagance of 116 for each of the thirty games played. (One that served in the gold medal game sold at auction four months later for more than Cdn$4,000.)

As of the end of the twenty-third year of Martin Brodeur's ongoing NHL career, he'd faced 36,798 pucks, 33,606 of which he parried. This doesn't count those directed his way in warm-up or practice, or tossed domestically, in jest, by his children or house guests.

You can see where the term *puck-shy* comes from. Jack Adams thought this was Glenn Hall's trouble in the 1950s. He'd returned from an injury and seemed to be flinching at incoming shots. Hall might have called this *puck-sense*, although that's usually an attribute reserved for intelligence in non-goalies. *Puck-shyness*, I guess, can lead to *puck-shock*. Other puck compounds include *puck-handler* (which by rights ought to be *puck-stickler*), *puck-carrier* (sounds like a naval vessel), *puck-chaser* (a beer?), *puck-pusher* (a civil servant who's traded in his pencil).

Pucks can seem *as solid as a bullet head* and they can be launched, says Stan Fischler, *like a torpedo on a string. Scalding disks*, John B. Lee calls them in his poem "Falstaff as a Hockey Goalie: Taking the Edge Off." Goalies would know about that. Glenn Hall saw so many pucks in his career that, forty years later, he was still reciting what they used to have written on the label: Art Ross patent no. 2226516.

Vladislav Tretiak believes he reached his peak in 1976. How did he know? "The puck 'listened to me,' as if it was trained. I felt great." This was something he'd noticed years before, working with his mentor, the great Konovalenko, who'd exercised "a command over pucks."

For Guy Lafleur, it was vice versa. In 1975, New Year's Eve, Montreal and Moscow's CSKA met in an exhibition game that's come to be known as one of the best ever played. Though not for Lafleur. He was having a hard time handling the stardom that had befallen him, and that night he carried his crisis out to the ice. As Claude Larochelle writes,

> the puck was what he truly feared, because it symbolized such heavy responsibilities. He was so anxious to do well that he was terrified to do anything. His teammates had quickly understood and stopped passing the puck to him.

George Plimpton felt that his lack of success as a goalie was a problem of acquaintance: he'd never really gotten to know the puck.

> One would appear with the abruptness of a bee over a picnic basket, and then hum away, all so quickly that rather than corporeal it could well have been an apparition of some sort. A swarm of them would collect in the back of the net during the shooting drills without my being sure how they got there.

From the veterans he learned that you never bother with a puck that's in your net after a goal. A bee no more, it's your mess and your shame—"like dogshit on a carpet."

Wayne Johnston's novel *The Divine Ryans* (1990), which is all about pucks, offers up a whole charming cosmology, based on Draper Ryan's father's notion that a star is a hole that's created when a puck is punched out of the night's sky. All pucks come from the sky, he says, and that's how we know when the world will end: all the pucks will have fallen and there'll be no sky left. Which means, of course, that every puck lost is a step closer to oblivion for us. And that goalies are the ones charged with saving the world. It's a lovely notion, this idea that if not for hockey, the world would last forever, and as purely Canadian as any you'll find. Though maybe only here, in Canada, does its particular poetry make sense.

A dream of Draper's has pucks raining on St. John's and all the windows of the cars parked along Fleming Street are smashed and he gets into his goalie equipment and goes out, despite the fear that—worst possible fate for a goalie—he'll be buried under pucks. And what else could that be called but the *Apuckalypse*?

IF ICE AND pucks are constants of the game, hockey has seen its changes, too. It's added forward passing and a red line, magnetic nets, goalie masks, helmets, visors. There used to be an extra player on the ice, until hockey decided to subtract him, along with (a partial catalogue) the requirement that goalies stay standing; rinks clouded over with cigarette smoke; a whole dictionary of words that have long since disappeared from the game. *Stickfight* is one; *kitty-bar-the-door* is four more. Today the *hook-check* is hardly mentioned.

The hook-check era might be designated, more generally, as hockey's *scientific age*. That's an expression you don't hear anymore, hockey-wise, though one does catch references to hockey's *golden age*. Let's bring up the lights and see what the room thinks. Was hockey's scientific age also its golden age? Anybody? It's tempting to imagine the single day when hockey was perfect. The rink would have to be cold. The skill would have to be balanced, exquisitely, with the toughness. You think you've got the game's golden age nailed down at the edges and then someone else comes along to curl a lip. I think of the 1970s, when Montreal was winning all those Stanley Cups, as being the hockey I'd like to see again. But that's when Bobby Clarke and the Philadelphia Flyers were bullying the NHL. That's when my dad says he started to lose his enthusiasm for hockey.

Pop Bentley believed it was the emphasis on playing the man instead of the puck that was ruining the game, circa 1951. The same year, his son Max ended up third in NHL scoring, just behind rivals named Gordie and Maurice. Art Ross felt that all the free-spirited personalities were gone from the game by 1953. King Clancy: "The days when I played hockey," he said, "were gay and carefree and rollicking." That takes us back to the years 1923 to 1937. Frank Selke pinpoints the years 1927 through to 1934 as the *gilded age* of tough, entertaining, skillful hockey—what Andy O'Brien called "one of the slambangest eras of hockey." Nobody was bodychecking by 1962, said Selke: that's when the golden age faded for good. "Sadly we watched it pass away."

The arenas changed, that was part of the problem, for players and fans both. The new rinks pushed the fans farther away from the ice and made them throw their toe-rubbers from way back, and the players felt this and wished for the up-close, noisy days. (Babe Pratt, on seeing New York's new Madison Square Garden for the first time: "I looked around and thought, 'Jesus, this is a cold-looking joint.'") In the 1974 Clark Blaise short story "I'm Dreaming of Rocket Richard," the love of the game is all about immediacy. "It had to do with the intimacy of old-time hockey," the narrator hymns, "how close you were to the gods on the ice; you could read their lips and hear them grunt as they slammed the boards."

The game was simple, once. That's when it was better. The books of hockey are filled with sighs for the good old days, the steady plainchant of regret, a chorus of loss. Stan Fischler has a whole book organized around laments for bygone hockey: *Those Were the Days* (1976). Ebbie Goodfellow is in there, shaking his head in 1976. "Personally, I wouldn't want to play today because hockey is all a big business, whereas we seemed to have more fun."

Frank Boucher starred for the New York Rangers in the 1920s and 1930s, and he went on to coach and manage the team into the 1950s. He was someone who looked around in 1952 and said, "Hockey's fine. There's nothing wrong with it." In the brutal 1970s, one of the NHL's bloodier epochs, Gary Ronberg argued that players had, in fact, come a long way since the olden days. "They are more intelligent and better balanced emotionally—in short, less crazy."

But the norm for looking back is regret. This has been the case at every stage of hockey's development. And it's not just the fun that's gone out of the game. The game is less skilled. No one holds on to the puck nowadays, and does anybody hit? Along with your pension, what you earn when you retire from the NHL is the undying right to carp, carp, carp. If you listen closely, Ebbie Goodfellow is still muttering: "We had a hell of a lot more beautiful goals, nice passing, and good stickhandling."

The problem runs deeper than we might have thought. Goodfellow isn't alone in his nostalgia for the winters that were and the hockey players they forged. "The winters seemed to be much more severe then, too, than they are now, and even in forty below zero we'd be out on the rink." Rod Gilbert and Maurice Richard thought so, too. How could hockey not suffer? For Richard, mild winters were only at the top of a whole shopping list delineating the depreciation of hockey. In *The Flying Frenchmen* (1971), the book he did with Fischler, he has an entire chapter whose meaning is hard to mistake: "Hockey Was a Better Game in My Day." He was also convinced there used to be less traffic on the streets of Montreal, which allowed the kids to play more hockey, which made them better stickhandlers.

Hugh MacLennan fondly remembered Montreal's years on the natural ice at the Mount Royal Arena before they moved to the man-made stuff of the Montreal Forum. (The Forum, to him, was too chilly.) Brian Kilrea, all-but-eternal coach of the Junior Ottawa 67s, has complained that nowadays there's no such thing as walking. Also, "back then," if you wanted to play hockey "you didn't need the high-falutin' education that you've got to have now."

Former Bruin Myles Lane wondered: Where's the wily stickwork of yore? "Now it's a game of shove and push, hoping to score with blind shots," he said in 1976. "I think possibly half the goals scored today are because the goalie is screened and doesn't see the puck."

The shooting used to be more accurate, the passing smarter. Richard again: "There was much more individuality." Babe Pratt: "It was a different kind of game then. Today, they stress board-checking and checking from behind, both unheard of when we played. We'd hit a man standing right up and now the players don't seem to want to take that kind of check. The only check they want is on the first and 15th of the month."

This is a standard line, of course, you hear it often, how tough the old hockey was. Conn Smythe used to give his head a rueful shake in the 1950s: Sprague Cleghorn could have broken any of the modern tough guys in two pieces. Don Cherry has been known to ask that when people talk about rough hockey today, they recognize that what they're seeing is fun child's play compared to the game that was waged in the AHL during the same mid-century period.

Of course, Cleghorn was saying much the same thing himself as early as 1934. "Everything about the old game was tougher than it is today," he told Maclean's. "Players were tougher, rules were tougher, playing conditions were tougher, spectators were tougher, officials were tougher."

Gordie Howe felt that it had to do with a hostility deficit. "Hockey's different today, isn't it?" he asked novelist Mordecai Richler in 1980. "The animosity is gone. I mean, we didn't play golf with referees and linesmen." His old teammate Bill Gadsby tended to agree that the enmity was spread so much thicker in the old days. Do the math: six teams, seventy games, fourteen games played against each team, possibly another seven in the playoffs. "Grudges built up quickly and lasted longer."

Standards continue to slip. By 2007 Marty McSorley was complaining about the loss of honour among goons. McSorley recalled the incident seven years before, when he whacked Donald Brashear on the head with his stick, that ended his career and sent him to court. McSorley had challenged Brashear to a fight with twenty seconds left in the game, and when Brashear turned him down, what choice did he have? "The game has changed," McSorley moaned. "The penalties are more severe, and so-called tough guys duck and cover their heads to get the other guy penalized."

SID ABEL WAS seething for many when he said in 1952, "The new rules have turned hockey sissy. Girls could play this game now." (As, of course, they already were.) One that may have riled him in particular could have been a 1939 change that gave referees the power to fine players who attacked them. Also, no doubt, he was upset by the red line that was drawn across the ice in 1943. That's when, says Emile Francis, "puck control was sacrificed for pure scoring."

Indeed, prior to 1943, an insidious defensive system had bogged down the game to the point of stagnation. *Kitty bar the door*, they called it, with a capital Kitty, though who she was, exactly, nobody wants to say. *A Concise Dictionary of Canadianisms* (1973) insists on hyphens and no capital, *kitty-bar-the-door*, like a panicky order given to an able-pawed cat. Whichever it is, it means once you go ahead by a goal or two, you forget about trying to score any more. Everyone is behind the puck, defending for all they're worth. *Parking the bus* is soccer parlance. The early Ottawa Senators were said to have been masters of the art, but then the question came: Who wants stifled hockey?

Nobody did, including Art Ross, who knew stifling hockey, since as a player he'd been one of the inventors of the kittying and barring of hockey doors. Now, in the early 1940s, as manager of the Boston Bruins, he was of the opinion that the more goals teams scored, the more exciting the game for the fans. As chairman of the NHL's rules committee, he was in a position to do something about this, and he did. Ahead of the 1943–44 season, the league added the centre red line, allowing a defending team to make longer passes without going offside. Eliminated in 2005 for the purposes of two-line passes (again to up scoring), the centre line is enshrined to this day in *The NHL Rulebook*, right down to the proper shade of red to pick up at the Home Depot. Paint code PMS 186 is the rightful one for hockey lines, same as you'd use if you were stitching up a Union Jack, though not the Canadian flag (PMS 032) or the Stars and Stripes (PMS 193).

The red line worked in 1943, reducing offsides, quickening pace, provoking scoring. "It was by far and away a different hockey game," Boston's Milt Schmidt said. Sportswriter Andy O'Brien approved. "It's plain nonsense for so many old-timers to argue that the game hasn't speeded up and improved many hundred per cent from the old days when replacements were few and speed lagged at the end when players 'ragged' the puck in mid-ice to kill off penalties."

Francis wasn't the only one complaining. The ice now looked like, quote, a surrealist's idea of a geometrical problem. The *Toronto Star*'s Andy Lytle railed that the line of red completely disrupted the game "by making it impossible for an observer to distinguish between a champion player and a boy off the minor or the juvenile streets." Already the NHL had slimmed down the goalie's crease, allowing as a legal goal any puck that got in "by any means short of being accompanied into the nets by the scorer's girl friend." They could be "jostled, kicked, putted or convoyed in off the chest of a rival." And now with the red line, it was all a *scramble*, a *higgelty pigglety*, nothing but "continuous ganging plays," which he found, well, *annoying*.

Tommy Gorman was there when the NHL started, recruiting players, coaching Ottawa's original Senators. By 1949 he was declaring a desire to take the game back twenty years "to the days of the great stickhandlers." If he was boss he'd eliminate the forward pass and ban boarding "and have persistent offenders banished from the game for life." And, "Although I wouldn't go so far as to say hockey's going to the dogs," he bayed, "it certainly could be improved."

MASTERS OF THE hook-check: Hooley Smith, Frank Nighbor, Pit Lepine. You never hear about their exploits nowadays, because it's an art that's dropped right out of the game. Due to how hard it is to write about? Stephen Harper compiled a whole book about the age of the hook-checkers without mentioning it once, but where others might condemn the omission, I understand. Scoring goals has its own lingo: *five-holes* and *sniping, roofing, top shelf*. Tending goal you *stack the pads, flash the leather*. Hook-checking is a bit of blind spot in comparison. People think it has to do with hooking, which, of course, it doesn't at all—that's a penalty. Or they think hook-check = poke-check, which would be hilarious if it weren't so wrong. The mysteries surrounding hook-checking are many. The big one: Is it really fair that it disappeared while fighting hung on?

Everything I've read points to Nighbor as being the virtuoso of all hook-checkers. Peerless Frank, they called him, and the Pembroke Peach. He was *crafty* and *unselfish*, according to the adjectives stored in the Hockey Hall of Fame next to Nighbor's name. The Gliding Ghost is another of his monikers. King Clancy said nobody could handle a stick like him. He could do it all, and did, including goal scoring.

Nighbor didn't invent the hook-check, though. For that we have to follow him up to Port Arthur, Ontario, today's Thunder Bay, on Lake Superior. In 1911, Harry Cameron from the Pembroke Debaters was invited to join the local team but wouldn't go without his friend Nighbor, and when they arrived, one of their new teammates was Jack Walker, who doesn't seem to have had a nickname but whose adjectives are *thoughtful* and *brainy*. No surprise when you think about the hook-check, which is by far the most contemplative of hockey checks. Anyway, Walker had been hook-checking for a while when Nighbor got to Port Arthur, and didn't mind passing on his expertise.

Walker is sometimes said to have invented the poke-check, too. My feeling is that he didn't. I think it's another case of people who are lazy assuming that there's no difference between the two. The hook-check takes reach and timing, a delicate touch, a quart of courage, execution. The poke-check is an act of clumsy desperation and chaos. Who gets the puck when you poke it? Anyone might. A poke-checker is left as he was before he poked—puckless—whereas the puck you hook is yours. In both practice and spirit, the hook-check is a good of the game.

It's also one of the few hockey skills that are transferable to real life. People talk about the advantages to be gained from playing—lessons of teamwork and toughness, sportsmanship, pain tolerance—but as far as practical mechanical skills, what can you take away? Blocking shots has no real place in the everyday world. Same with penalty killing, winning faceoffs, losing faceoffs, changing on the fly, pulling the goalie, staying onside, icing pucks. Punching other people in the face, I guess, has its workaday applications. But more than the hook-check? Why else do you keep a Koho in the broom closet if not to be ready for the inevitable household rescues demanded by TV remotes under couches and cat toys beneath fridges?

As a hook-checker on the ice, it's true you run the risk of tripping your opponent by virtue of your not being a genius at it, and when the fellow goes down and the referee who doesn't care for craft blows his whistle—well, so then you've taken a penalty. Better to be a genius, then.

In 1912, Cameron, Nighbor, and Walker all went down to Toronto to play for the Blueshirts. Nighbor stayed only a year before heading off to join Ottawa's Senators, which is where he truly came into his own. There he refined the hook-check in some unspecified way, making it even more effective than it was before. If only we knew how! In any case, it's hard to believe that hockey has seen better times than during those halcyon hook-checking days. In a 1914 game, Jack Walker stopped opposing forwards "nine times out of ten with his peculiar check." Over to the east, Nighbor, who was tall and thin, maintained a poker face; at times he was said to become "almost a team in himself." King Clancy: "Instead of poking the puck off somebody's stick, he had a knack of trapping it with a hook-check and bringing it back to his own stick as if the puck were on a string. It was a magician's touch." One night, Nighbor is supposed to have hook-checked Howie Morenz so often and so effectively that the Montreal star never passed centre ice, finally bursting into tears from the frustration. (Another version features Nels Stewart instead of Morenz. Stewart's nickname was Old Poison; his adjectives included *fiery* and *willing to use his stick*. Instead of crying, he shot the puck at Nighbor.)

In 1926, on their way to winning the Stanley Cup, the Montreal Maroons recognized Nighbor as Ottawa's "main threat." Maroons coach Eddie Gerard instructed his players not to take the puck anywhere near him. When they got close they were supposed to shoot it by him, off the boards.

Was this the beginning of the end, the thoughtful hook-check overthrown by the crass dump-in? I don't know. It's not as if there weren't hook-checkers post-Nighbor, after he retired in 1930. Pit Lepine's hook-check was described as being *rink-wide*. And Hooley Smith: his was *devastating*. There would be those who'd say the game got too fast. Or else the hook-check's end came when defenders shifted from playing the puck to taking out the man. By 1936, still (*sic*) *rolicsome as a kitten*, Nighbor was coaching Minor-leaguers in New York, telling anyone who'd listen that there was a yet a place in the game for the hookers and the pokers. In *Hot Ice*, a government propaganda film from 1940, he skates out to teach the hook to shinnying kids on a frozen river, a desperate rearguard action. Hook-checking was definitely on the run by the time Smith finished up in 1941. Who was there to keep it going after that? Other than the brothers Bentley, I mean: Scoop was called the *hook-checking little defenceman* in 1948, while Max was known to be persisting with the hook for the New York Rangers as late as 1953.

The evidence seems to show that you have to be of good character to hook-check. There never was a more sporting player than Nighbor, according to the literature. Jack Walker was *clean-living* and *a credit to the game*. There's no question that his standards were high: when Toronto won the Stanley Cup in 1914, Walker accused the people of the city of not saying thank-you. Though he acknowledged that some of her citizens did treat a few of the champions to a plate of oysters.

MAYBE IT'S NOT the calendar of years we need to be studying so much as the arc of a lifetime. Childhood was when hockey was better. In books, it's the prospect of Christmas pond hockey in Roy MacGregor's *Forever* (2005) or the shining snowy morning that opens Roch Carrier's *The Hockey Sweater* (just before everything goes so terribly wrong).

In my case it was 1971, when I was six. Wayne Gretzky was eleven that year, the year he scored 378 goals. That same winter, my first in organized hockey, I toiled on defence for the All Saints Anglican Novices. When I say toiled, what I really mean is tottered in place: it would be a couple of seasons still before I had a command of any skills past collapsing in a heap and looking pleadingly towards the bench.

At All Saints our colours were without colour, black and white. Our hair was long and our teeth were babies and our dads kneeled before us in the dressing room to yank at our laces and ask, "Too tight?" They taped our sticks and talked to each other and when we tugged on their coats they kneeled again and tied our skates a second time, a little looser. On the ice, we dropped our sticks and had to get down on our knees to pick them up again. We burned our ankles, skating on them. In the first team photo we all look wide-eyed and doubtful, wary primitives wondering if it's true that Nikons steal your soul and your wrist-shot. The promise scrolled across our chests, ALL SAINTS, could only have increased our unease: we just weren't sure this was something we'd be able to deliver on. I don't remember scoring any goals in Peterborough. It's entirely possible that I scored not a single one before we left town and moved north to Lakefield in 1976.

PETERBOROUGH IS A hockey word. For me, it's one of the defining nouns, hockey or otherwise, because it's where I was born, in the spring, a quick hour or so northeast of Toronto, just at the corner of Weller Street and Wallis Drive, within the walls of Civic Hospital. If it's hard for outsiders to understand what the game means to Peterbruins, we don't mind too much: one of the things that we treasure most about our special relationship to hockey is just how ineffable it is. That, to us, is a big plus.

Saints all: Standing tall at the back among Peterborough Minor Atom team-mates in the early 1970s.

Is it our hardscrabble pioneer roots that make those of us who hail from the banks of the Otonabee River such an historically quiet, mumbly people with tongues so easily tied? It's said that in days gone by, our forebears would nod and shrug rather than speak three sentences in a row. Even today, Peterboroughers much prefer to text or email or poke you on Facebook than speak to you face-to-face. It's nothing personal; it's just the way we are.

As Fort McMurray is to bitumen, as Waterloo is to formerly market-dominant smartphones—that's how we Peterbrogonians think of our town, hockey-wise. If our superiority seems familiar, that's because it's a pared-down version of what we as Canadians feel about the game in the larger world beyond our borders. Wherever hockey may have been born, at a young age it moved up Highway 28 and settled in Peterborough. That's not my line: it's from *Hockey Town*, Ed Arnold's 2004 book about how all the other towns that think they have more hockey running in their municipal blood are mistaken and should give it up. Kamloops? Ha. Red Deer? Fuh. Oshawa? Whoop-de-doop. As for Detroit, so what if they've copyrighted the word Hockeytown°? Hockey Town, we have no problem telling ourselves, is more words.

The intensity of our hockeyness is not, to be clear, paternal: Peterborough has never been and never will be one of those feisty strivers—hey there, Délįne, NWT—trying to convince itself that the game was conceived there. And it's not as though Peterboroovians can claim any statistical advantage in terms of how many home-grown players we've sent to the NHL: Sudbury has sent more, and Kingston, too. All we know is that while the number of hockey greats who've played for our hometown Petes would be enough to embarrass most towns—Stan Jonathan, Doug Jarvis, Steve Yzerman, Larry Murphy, Chris Pronger, the Plager and Larmer boys, the Redmonds, even Gretzky—we've learned not to let it get us down.

I have a clear memory, certainly false, possibly profane, that the All Saints rink lay within the church walls on Rubidge Street, just back from the altar, in a regulation-sized space amid pushed-aside pews. How would they have kept it cold enough? Not to mention the theological implications. I can't find anything about hockey at all when I go to the All Saints website. A fire gutted the building in 1983, and it had to be rebuilt. Scroll down and there is, finally, a mention of the hockey team in a list of church-sponsored programs. No archive of how many games I played, or whether I did score a goal, ever.

The mouthguards we wore made us look like we were pilots who needed them to breathe. My helmet was the same brand Paul Henderson wore, smaller but the same, and sometimes, because it was the 1970s, bits of my hair stuck out through the holes in the helmet, which seemed necessary at the time. Not all of us had Henderson CCMs, some of us made do with Dave Dunns. I don't know about the protection they afforded, but in design they were monstrous. Stan

Mikita's helmet was also not cool, everybody understood that, and if that's the helmet you had, well, too bad, we felt sorry for you. You couldn't get a Jofa helmet, like the Swedes wore, at the local sporting good store, Borje Salming, Anders Hedberg, and Ulf Nilsson. I wept when a neighbour's Labrador retriever ate my Henderson helmet, though by nightfall I had a brand new one.

As for team gear, my dad expected that in matters of sweater and socks, All Saints would provide. And they did—a black sweater with a blocky white A on it, black socks banded red and white—but not until well into the season. Did my parents mean to afflict and shame me with the uniform they improvised until we got our real ones? I have to trust that they didn't. But let the record show that for the first three games of my hockey career, I skated the wing wearing an oiled Irish fisherman's sweater with the green stockings my mom used for cross-country skiing. The green, as I remember, was lambent, alien bright, a pioneer trick to guard against wandering off and getting lost in blizzards. The sweater was patterned the way Irish sweaters are, except more so. It was a museum of wool, a hall of woven woollen fame, row on row of plaits, textured twirls, inlaid columns, the whole rig as heavy as chainmail.

Teammates. I remember the coach's son. Craig was his name, or maybe Dean. I can't shake the idea that he was unemployed at the time, though of course, this is unlikely since he couldn't have been more than seven or eight when I knew him that first Novice season. He dropped his gloves in practice once, while we were skating laps, and threw a punch at a winger who'd crossed in front of him. My partner on defence was named Hector. He was prim and bemused, a seven-year-old with a middle-aged soul. If I had to guess, I'd say he went into the civil service. Never at home on the ice, he concentrated by biting his tongue. A mean bone in his body? All of his bones were kind. He liked to consult me before he passed the puck, which sometimes meant skating over so he wouldn't have to raise his voice. This called for more time than we had, as defencemen, and it usually ended with Hector being pushed to the ice and the puck taken away.

When I study the team pictures now, even when a name doesn't come, I know what kind of player each of these guys was. Harvey with the wilderness of blond hair had a bit of a Mario Tremblay spirit. We had two scorers: Jeff, who did his work in a quiet Steve Shutt sort of a way, and Sean, who affected a bit of a Guy Lafleur flourish, though in the end, he was really no more than an Yvon Lambert. I tried to get the goalie—Mike, I think—to try Ken Dryden's signature resting stance, stick planted in his crease, arms folded on top. I tried it myself, but it wasn't easy for a defenceman. You rarely get an opportunity for that kind of repose as a skater, and even when you do, there's always going to be a linesman at the faceoff to tell you, *Hey, number eleven.*

After Dryden, my favourite Canadien was Bob Gainey. He was from Peterborough, born and bred and mentioned (the only hockey player to feature) in the city's official historical timeline, our very own Hab. You had to overlook the fact that he'd played his home-town hockey for Immaculate Conception, a sworn enemy of ours over at All Saints. I admired Gainey's solemn demeanour, his steady hard work. The Canadiens had a breed of hard-worker that no one else could match. Dougs Jarvis and Riseborough were two; later, it was Brian Skrudland and Guy Carbonneau. Gainey was the original and the exemplar, and he had something more, grit and grace, a dedication that didn't depend, as Guy Lafleur's game seemed to, on being noticed and celebrated. "It is a great temptation to say too much about Bob Gainey," Dryden wrote in *The Game*, just before he launched into the quite-a-lot he had to say about Gainey's place as a player on those sublime Montreal teams of the 1970s. Soviet coach Viktor Tikhonov called Gainey the best all-around player in the world. Even if it was true, you weren't supposed to say so, that just didn't fit with Gainey. I was horrified on his behalf, and for a while I did what seemed to be the proper thing: I averted my admiration.

At All Saints, I remember losing a lot—to St. John's, Sacred Heart, St. Luke's, and especially Immaculate Conception. Their sweaters were a rich papal purple, and they regularly smoked us. I remember hearing one of our coaches say to the other, "Well, Immaculate Conception really beat the hell out us." I remember them laughing. Sometimes it was *bejesus*.

It would be crazy to blame that early trauma for my subsequent lack of hockey success and long-term bonus-laden NHL contracts. The fact is, I'm just not that good. You've heard talk on *Hockey Night in Canada* of *soft hands, great wheels, puck sense*? I have *palms of stone, missing spokes*, and a *headache*, respectively. If there's anything I bring to the table, the hockey table, it's reach, and even that only goes so far.

THE POND HAD no name. It was fine without one. It used to be a farm field and before that, probably a forest. The trees on the far shore were young pines in straight ranks. Five hundred years ago the Petun lived here. Before them, it was all cold proglacial Lake Algonquin. Cousins to the Huron, the Petun grew tobacco. Maybe they were the ones who first discovered the delight of maple syrup. Champlain may have come by to visit around 1616. They were all gone by 1649-ish, driven out by the Iroquois. We don't know what their games were.

I took my stick, the pucks, and a shovel, the dog was with me, too, and we headed out over the snow and across the barrel-backed bridge, up the berm to where, halfway hidden in the woods, winter had (to borrow from the poet Richard Harrison) stunned the mouth of the creek. The snow was deep and it kicked up as light as ashes.

The dog stood on the dock and looked at the ice. She wouldn't take the first step. She wanted me to go first.

It was a pretty sight, a pond with a serene and secluded feel to it, despite the nearby highway and ski hill, with no lurking murk during summer swimming season and a freeze-up two weeks before Christmas. I saw that the deer had blazed a trail that wasn't there a couple of days ago, which seemed encouraging.

Long piers of pine-tree shadows reached out from the far shore. Over there was the creek, and beyond that the skiers skimmed. I bit the cold and swallowed it, and felt the corners in my throat going down. I cleared a patch near the dock, and where I whapped the ice with my stick, it didn't crack or chip. It turned a whiter white.

This is where hockey started, before it found our blood. You don't have to read a single hockey book to know this. When it comes to hockey's origins, the geological model makes perfect sense to us: with all this ice under us, it was only a matter of a few thousand years before the trees forced their crooked branches into our hands and we were out in the slot, waiting for someone to pass us the puck, just as soon as they'd invented it. Is there any greater glory than the ice? "The subtle substance," as Quebec's *Chronicle* put it in 1895. Shovelling aside more snow, I found the rink waiting underneath.

Maybe the dog would play goalie. Maybe that was something she could learn. I don't know why I'd even brought my stick with me; the shovelling would take an hour or more before I'd be ready to skate. I called to the dog down at the far end of the pond where she was nosing the shore. She looked up, but that's all. There's not much in hockey for dogs. Not compared to what's in woodland animals, as long as they can be caught.

In England, the people used to play for a leg of mutton. Bury Fen, 1827. After it was over, they'd all get together, the two teams, to drink and forget. That was an important part of it, you had to forget your, quote, hard luck. They had a word for the drinking and the forgetting session: *the randy*. Everybody drank, everybody forgot, half the people went home with a victor's share of mutton. In 1827, the game had a clear reward that you could put in your sandwich: a good of the game that anyone could get behind, man or dog.

I tried a slapshot off the dock and watched it fly. It's hard to resist slapping a puck off a dock when it's just you and all that clean winter spread out in front, waiting to be marred. I saw where the puck hit, too, and got over there promptly. There was a perfect slot in the snow. I dug carefully, but the puck was gone to wherever pucks go.

The second one I dropped and scooped up skyward. Technically it was a backhand, but I put too much hoist into it and up it went with a puff of snow. You couldn't call it a hockey shot, there was nothing hockey about it. Two shots, snap and scoop, and where the scoopshot landed was the far end of my rink.

The dog had maybe snagged something. I watched her as I shovelled. Snow had started to shake down, softly erasing the work I was doing as I went. "You never catch anything," I told the dog. But she did seem to have something, a muskrat maybe. It must have come out with paws in the air. Sticks the dog would toss and bow down to, and she was going with what she knew, playing with her food, harrying it, prancing and tail-wagging. She was pleased with herself. She wanted me to come and see her unfortunate prey.

Bears love hockey, at least the ones I'd been reading about. Show a bear a rink and he'll be out there in a second, no need to ask him twice. You will have to help him on with his skates, I suppose, and lend him a stick. The Moscow Circus has been doing this for years. At home, coached by Anatoli Mayorov—brother perhaps to the great Boris and the almost-as-great Evgeny?—they played on a circular rink. In 1970, while the circus was in Toronto, amid many Boston Bruin jokes, Maple Leaf players Jim Dorey and Jacques Plante scrimmaged with Mashka, a Himalayan black bear. The *Star*'s take on the bears: "They stickhandle and shoot and at times look no more disorganized than the Leafs on a bad night." Be careful how much you advertise your hockey-bear, though. In recent times, people have tended to protest the cruelty. (The bears may be protesting, too: in 2009, a Russian hockey-bear killed the director of his circus and was shot dead.) "A sick joke," is what the people sometimes say. The Moscow Circus has been accused of bear-exploitation. One question: Is it the hockey in particular that bothers people? Is that the barbarity, or would it be just as bad if it were tennis the bears were being compelled to play? Also, it's never Canadian bears you hear about. What do they have against hockey?

I could have done more research on the rink. It wasn't like me to skip the research. Normally I wouldn't just eyeball it like this, though a pond does allow and even encourage the eyeballer. You don't need the liners and boards on a pond that you need in your backyard rink. Nature does most of the foundation work, leaving you to do the shovelling. South then east, turn and turn again, and I was back where I started.

This was as fundamental a hockey moment as there is, of course, even without a stick or a puck. On the scale of hockey purity, a backyard rink has a limited capacity that is surpassed by a pond. The more human agency that goes into making your rink, the more hoses and squeegees and snowblowers you bring to bear on its construction, the more you have to subtract something from the equation, some imperial measure of authenticity.

The purest hockey is played on a big lake that froze all on its own, swept clean as a wineglass by the wind, and you just happened to be driving by like Eric Nesterenko and found it, and fortunately you had your stuff with you. Even better, Gordie Howe was already there, playing with Gretzky and Mario Lemieux... That must have been a

TV commercial, now that I think about it. An ESPN commercial from 2000, now that I look it up. The one with Gretzky, Howe, and Lemieux wandering in the woods until they come across a perfect rink, and Pavel Bure, Eric Lindros, Paul Kariya, and Jaromir Jagr are skating aimlessly around trying to remember their lines and their cues. "Yup," says Gretzky, "this is what it's all about." The rink is roughly 150 times bigger than mine. Howe et al. never get on the ice—no stuff. No one's even brought any beer.

Paul Henderson has said that nothing compares to playing pond hockey with your friends as a small boy, not even scoring the goal of all goals in 1972. Is that true, though, or just one of the pieties of hockey that seems like it's true because we've been repeating it for so long, over and over, until MasterCard or Molson had no choice but to take over the job for us?

THE LIST THAT the *Literary Review of Canada* compiled in 2007 to anoint Our Most Important Books of All the Ages includes several titles—*Roughing It in The Bush, The Unconscious Civilization*—that seem to hanker for puckstricken stories to tell. Only one actual hockey book made the grade, in fact, and it wasn't Dryden's *The Game.* The author himself professed shock that his modest 1973 paperback could be mingling in the company of books by Jacques Cartier, Robertson Davies, and Lucy Maud Montgomery. "You're kidding," Howie Meeker said when he heard the news.

Strictly speaking, Meeker's *Hockey Basics* makes the grade as a cultural artifact insofar as it crystallizes an era in which we (some of us) started to wonder whether our national game was rotten at the roots. Having seen the NHLers almost fail in 1972, Meeker believed he had the map with which we could turn ourselves around. Back we go, he said, to the game's fundamentals, make sure the kids start out by holding their sticks properly, passing the puck the way it's meant to be passed, and—most important—having fun.

It is a classic among hockey how-tos. Once the genre got its start with Arthur Farrell in 1899, it picked up momentum until it reached a peak in the mid-1970s, and by then the roster of helpful authors sharing their secrets between covers included Plantes and Parks, Howes and Hulls, and Orrs.

It goes without saying how pleased I am by the notion of learning to play by the book, even if it really never worked out for me. Meeker, too, discovered the challenges, which he writes about. One: hockey how-tos never taught *him* a single thing. Plus, as he acknowledges at the very front of his own book, "instructional books are not the easiest to read."

What to do? Tommy Gorman's 1935 booklet "How to Become a Hockey Star" tries a sprint: everything you need for the job in just thirty-two pages, including the greatest trick in all of hockey (how to carry the puck without looking at it) and why you really can't do without Crown Brand Corn Syrup (how else are you going to replenish your energy?). Over at the other end of the spectrum is the solid, earnest mass of Lloyd Percival's *Hockey Handbook* (1951), the Dead Sea Scrolls of hockey's literature: much revered, little read.

Behind Meeker's brisk *Basics* (140 pages) lies a biography befitting a national icon. Serving as a soldier in 1944, he was blown over a high fence in a grenade accident. Three years later, he won the Calder Trophy as the NHL's superior rookie while helping the Maple Leafs win the Stanley Cup. He'd win three more in his career with Toronto, during which time he also sat as a federal MP. He coached and managed Toronto before upping skates for Newfoundland. Premier Joey Smallwood wanted him to come and help develop the province's youth hockey program. So he did that.

His adjectives as a player: *speedy* and *pugnacious*. If you're of age, you might remember his fervent years at the Telestrator as a broadcaster on CBC's *Hockey Night in Canada*. Where Don Cherry bullies from his between-periods pulpit, Meeker was fuelled by high enthusiasm and barky sermonizing.

His literary style echoes that. He says he only started to learn how to play hockey in 1958 — four years *after* he finished his Hall of Fame career. He did it with the help of the thousands of Newfoundland kids who came to the clinics he convened over his nineteen years there; later, he spread his gospel west. He realized children's skates were ill-fitting junk. Their sticks? Too long. Why weren't they taught proper balance? No one ever taught him how to pass; he only managed "by guess and by God." All of this made him mad, doggone it. That's in the book, too: his books and his films, Meeker confesses, allow for "a controlled release" of his anger at how we've squandered our hockey riches.

As a ten-year-old, I remember finding him funny and terrifying at the same time. I'm not in the book, but in 1976, I did go to one of Meeker's summer camps, which is how I ended up in a later series of the TV tutorials he filmed for CBC. *Starring* isn't the word. Having watched some of the footage recently, what I can say is that I was just one more grinning pre-adolescent extra on the ice — the very tall one in the too-small hockey pants.

I could have attended Bobby Orr's hockey camp that summer, or Mike Pelyk's. Both were close to home. Maybe because they were defencemen and I was a forward now, my parents saw the choice as obvious. Also, Meeker's ads promised to improve my skating by 50 per cent. I could have used that. Not to mention that if ever there was a ten-year-old who could do with some light Meekerizing, I was shy and bookish him. Packing up my hockey pants that didn't fit, my dad's old Oxford gloves that smelled like the 1950s, and the rest of my gear, I travelled south from Peterborough with my parents until we hit Port Hope, where they left me.

I don't remember a whole lot about those two summer weeks. The food was good. My roommate didn't talk to me, or perhaps I didn't talk to him. I was homesick and then I wasn't. The cameras came for an afternoon, maybe two. I recall the drills that the films show—the Squat, Toe In, Kick Three Times—though none of the scrimmages. When the cameras weren't there, Howie mostly left the coaching to his staff, though I do recall him presiding one day from the penalty box. He called me over to show me why my grip was all wrong. He applied a smidge of black tape to my stick to remind me how (uncomfortably) far down my lower hand belonged.

Seeing my preserved hockey past, I am a little disappointed by— what, exactly? That there's no doubt how the story unfolds from here and that it ends up nowhere near the NHL ice of the Montreal Forum? I'm still not entirely convinced that it's me in the films, though the height and the helmet and general ungainliness are all about right. I have no way of gauging how much fun I had, or to what extent the Meeker cure upgraded my skating or skills. My church-league career continued the next winter, and the way I'm going to tell this is that I was happy to be playing as the player I was. Was there talk, when it was time again for summer planning, of my needing to take the next step? I don't think so. Anyway, there was no hockey at my next camp, just J-strokes and portages and one-match fires—everything a boy needs to prepare him for life as a woodsman.

TO READ THE hockey books, you'd think that the whole country was rinked over, one big piece of national ice, at least in winter, forcing us to skate, which of course led to hockey. It is easy, not to say enticing, to think and even act as though the Laurentide Ice Sheet never retreated one inch and still covers the continent and that's why we deserve to win Olympic gold medals every four years. Down there by the muskrat death scene, where the ice stops and the woods begin? Imagine the ice just carrying on up the slopey section and into the pine trees and spreading out into the distance, up over the mountain with the skiers on it, then down the other side, spilling south, opening like wings to the east, wings of ice filling out the geography, just like one of those movies from the 1930s with their map animations that scroll out until the whole country is ice-covered, right to the 49th parallel. In which case, we *had* to skate. If it had been up to us, maybe we'd have chosen stilts, but it wasn't up to us, as explained in an 1852 book, *The Art of Skating*, by a Scottish enthusiast by the name of George Anderson:

> In more Northern countries, where the roads are blocked up for months
> with deep snows, the frozen surface of the lakes and rivers forms their
> only roadway; skating and sleighing their only means of travelling and
> communication between pretty distant places. In this way, the inhabit-
> ants, men and women alike, are skaters, and can travel their fifteen
> miles an hour with ease, keeping up the pace for several hours.

Obviously I checked the ice. Before any of the shovelling, I went for an auger in the shed, and when I found there was none, settled for the big spike of a steel crowbar. I dragged it out and over the bridge. It was way too heavy, like hauling a railway tie. The dog wasn't sure. She sniffed the spike and tilted her head and gave her quizzical ears-up look. Hunting a muskrat makes sense across the species, whereas hockey is one of those narrow human endeavours that must seem so arbitrary to dogs. She gave me a little shrug and headed back down to check again on the wildlife.

YOW! A 1949 comic book investigates why thin ice is the worst of all the ices.

I put on a life jacket. Even if you haven't read all the hockey books, you probably know that thin ice is the worst of all the ices, malicious, murderous, child-swallowing. Black ice seems almost humorous in comparison. If you have read all the hockey books, then you know that hockey's novels would be in big trouble without it. It's such a constant of hockey literature that you begin to discount novels that leave it out as being half-formed, incomplete. As early as 1917, characters were going through the ice (Barbour's *Guarding His Goal*), and they were still at it in 2005 in MacGregor's *Forever*. This could be exhibit A for the prosecution's case that hockey fiction lacks imagination, though it's also possible that it's we as readers who are at fault: somewhere it's been determined that this is a cautionary tale we just haven't heeded and so will go on being repeated until we're deemed to have learned the lesson.

Sounds associated with falling through ice while trying to play hockey:

- ominous creaking, anguished cry, crash (*Lightning On Ice*, Philip Harkins, 1946)
- silence (*Pass That Puck!* Richard T. Flood, 1948)
- "YOW!" "CRASH!" "CRACK, CRACKLE!" (New Heroic Comics, 1949)
- gentle splashing, shouts of people running (*Brother of the Hero*, Lev Kassil, 1968)
- "HELLLPPPPP!" (*Forever*, Roy MacGregor)

In fiction, it's a bit of a rite of passage for young players. If you're going to learn the game, then you're going to have to take a swim, losing if not your life then at least a boot. What often happens is that your brother Joe comes by with his hockey stick and lies down on his stomach and says, "That's a brave boy" and "Wrap your arms around it and hold hard," and so you do that, and he fishes you out and makes you skate to shore to get your circulation going instead of carrying you, which is smart. That's what happens in *Skating Today* (1945), possibly one of the worst titled hockey novels of all, though still compelling as a story in its own hokey way.

With the spike in hand, I set up on the summer swim raft, standing right on it so that if the ice proved to be lethal at least I'd be safely afloat. It didn't take much: two good slams and I was through into black water. The ice looked thick, four inches, five. The water wasn't warm but it wasn't exactly icy, either. You can drive a Sherman tank across five inches of ice, though you probably shouldn't. I think that's right, unless it's ten inches you need and a Panzer. A nuclear sub can surface through three feet of ice. Where did I read that?

Prince Albert almost died skating on his pond at Buckingham Palace in 1841. It was January, the day before his first-born daughter's christening, and he went through the ice and the lady-in-waiting screamed and Queen Victoria was the only person with the presence of mind to help. Whether that was to drag him to shore or reassure him until he could rescue himself, I don't know. Am I the only one to wish the queen had fished him out Joe-style, with a hockey stick? "The shock from the cold was extremely painful," the prince wrote later, "and I cannot thank Heaven enough that I escaped with nothing more than a severe cold."

I worried that the ice was weakest at the far end where the creek fed in. I certainly didn't want to fall through and freeze and drown, floundering around in icy water like the guy in George Saunders's 2011 short story "Tenth of December": "He wanted the shore. He knew that was the right place for him. But the pond kept saying no."

It's in all the books—the struggle to pull yourself out, the ice breaking at the edges. This is the futility that's going to undo you until you have no choice but to die. Or else you go right under and can't find the original hole and keep bumping up against the unyielding ice-ceiling and that's how you end. People might say, well, it's what he loved. He loved it, and he was doing it, and he died. How appropriate, they'd say; yes, this is what he would have wanted. And I wouldn't be there to say, no, not at all. I love hockey, but not enough to die for it in cold water.

THE HISTORY OF hockey requires a certain amount of squinting and even then, when the squinting's done, you can't quite be sure what you've seen. If you've spent any time looking into the game's origins, you'll have gazed into the deep background of late-sixteenth-century

European paintings to spy out the hockey that's being played. So much the better if you have a superior jeweller's loupe. In dim weather, under smoky January skies, the hockey's there, it's just that it's in the middle distance at best, through the trees, behind the vendors of vegetables, beyond the gambolling children, off past the birds of distraction. In the painted past, hockey seems to be approaching from a great distance, skating hard to make it out of the background and never quite getting there.

But is it hockey? The Flemish painter Pieter Bruegel the Elder worked up two winter scenes in 1565, *Winter Landscape with Skaters and a Bird Trap* and *Hunters in the Snow*. The latter has such a familiar feel that it could be Magog or Jasper. The snow makes it seem so local, that and the rinks. This is where the deep peering is required, the leaning in to gaze past the nominal hunters headed home with their dogs, into the dimming distance where two sizeable rinks have been scraped clear of snow so they can be filled with skaters. But *are* they skating? Anyone see a hockey stick down there? It's almost impossible to tell. A passel of poets has been moved to verse by this painting—Walter de la Mare, Joseph Langland, William Carlos Williams—but none of them refers to the possibility of hockey. The poems don't help.

Winter Landscape with Skaters and a Bird Trap rewards closer scrutiny. It brings us nearer the ice—a bend of frozen river, in this case—as well as to the birds oblivious to the trap that stands ready to crush them. The trap looks like a big door balanced on a big stick, baited with seed perhaps, and with a line tied to the stick that trails up between the houses. Somebody's on the end of that line, ready to tug and crush the hungry coots, wigeons, buffleheads, koet, or smient. They have no idea, the birds. After the drama of the bird trap, the stored energy about to be unleashed, the trembling anticipation of crushed birds, the ice is a bit of a disappointment. People are skating (if those *are* skates), people are curling, or maybe that's shuffleboard, and there's the guy with the other guy who's winding up to take a shot on the third, crouched guy. It's hard to see their skates; they may not have had their stuff.

In the art world, critics have lots to say about these skaters and birds. I've read about how Bruegel is moralizing here on the subject of man's perilous journey and skating on thin ice, or possibly it's the perilous journey of birds. Some say that the bird trap is a warning to the skaters. Unless the skaters are a warning to the coots and buffleheads.

Dutch painter Hendrick Avercamp has a bird trap too, though smaller. *Winter Landscape with Iceskaters* (c. 1608) is a busy canvas indeed, full of what the Rijksmuseum calls "daring details," including men urinating and a copulating couple. I can't, myself, spy any hockey players, but there are some definite ice-golfers in his *Winter Scene on a Canal,* and also in *Winter Landscape on the River Ijssel near Kampen,* while *A Scene on the Ice Near a Town* has a Jacques Lemaire look-alike in the near-middle distance who may or may not be working on his faceoffs. Avercamp loved the ice. He couldn't stop painting it. An essay about him and his seventeenth- and eighteenth-century Dutch colleagues speaks of ice representing the slippery nature of the human condition. Aert van der Neer, Adam Silo, they both catch winter's haze, the thin light of a frigid sun, even while they had to stay indoors to do their actual work to keep their paints from freezing.

That crouching figure in Silo's *A Dutch Whaler and Other Vessels in the Ice* really does look like a goalie at the ready if you get your eye up close enough.

MY DAD HAS a theory about hockey-playing Smiths that he first presented to the world when my son, Zac, was christened. It was a funny speech, and also true. Here's the theory: starting with my grandfather, each succeeding generation has gotten a little worse, hockey-wise. Bit by bit, we Smiths have been losing hockey talent. We didn't have a whole lot to begin with, but nobody says we did. Zac was asleep for most of the time my dad was theorizing. I didn't wake him up.

I remember my grandfather, but only fadingly: he died in 1984. He was a lawyer in Edmonton and later a judge. There's a school named after him, in recognition of his judging and general contributions to the community. We never played hockey together, though I used to send him drawings of Oilers. Hockey for him was the road not taken. Maybe he'd still have a school in his name if he'd followed the hockey road; possibly it would be a rink. I looked up the school: its motto is "Strive to Be Your Best," and it has a resident dog, named Crush, who is hypoallergenic and calm and helps the school counsellor.

In an email, my dad wrote:

Your grandfather played for the University of Alberta in the years 1918–1921 or 1922. I think he played centre, and the story I grew up with was that he was a very good player. When the NHL was created, several Western Canada Hockey League teams were moved to the original NHL cities, and one became the Chicago Black Hawks. My memory is that Chicago wanted Dad to join them, and at that point he made his decision to practice law instead. I don't know of any written record of this. By the time I came along in 1932 I think he had stopped playing, though I certainly skated with him, at first on bob skates in, perhaps, 1935 or 1936. Mom and Dad skated with me from then on, for a few years. Later I skated with pals on local rinks, and especially at the 111th Street rink on Friday nights, which had a big surface and music.

Eventually I found a hockey photograph of my grandfather, along with a bit of hockey biography. He was a defenceman on the U of A team, it turns out. Scottie McAllister was his partner. Their *blocking tactics* were famous. Billy Esdale was the captain, a left winger. He was *modest* and *unassuming* and he had *worlds of speed*. At centre was Harry Morris. He had *weight, speed,* and *a wicked shot.* My grandfather was one of *the prettiest stick handlers* on the team and his *dazzling cork-screw rushes* led to many goals.

WHEN MY FATHER travelled to Oxford for the first time in 1953, he carried his hockey equipment with him on the ship from Montreal. I like to think of him at the rail of either the *Empress of France* or the *Empress of Canada*, two of the ships that carried him across in those Oxford years. I don't mind putting his hockey stick into his hands as he stands there on deck, either, and having him turn the blade in the salt wind, as though calling for a pass from somewhere out in the Atlantic.

He'd been at McGill in Montreal, though he didn't play much hockey there. At an interview for a Rhodes scholarship, he was asked what he'd do if he didn't win it and he said he'd find a way to get Oxford somehow. His friend told the interviewer that he'd have to stay home and go to work. The friend won the Rhodes.

The history of Oxford's hockey has a few clouds drifting over it, obscuring finer detail, imposing a low-pressure range of dispute. There has been hockey at Oxford since at least 1885, when they played Cambridge in the first inter-varsity match—which wasn't *at* Oxford. They actually played the game in Switzerland at St. Moritz. Oxford won, 6–0, unless the game never took place at all (as some say) and assuming that (defying some others) it wasn't bandy they were playing.

The early Oxford players were Englishmen. The captain in 1900, for instance, was Bernard Bosanquet, later a famous cricketer and the inventor of the *googly*, which could have been a good hockey word if it hadn't already been taken. The advent of Cecil Rhodes's scholarships in 1904 brought an influx of Canadians to Oxford, which strengthened the team, though soon enough the Canadians were banned from the varsity match as a gesture of mercy towards Cambridge. So they started their own team, the Oxford Canadians, sometimes called the Rhodies. They played in the English League (they topped that in 1907) and later took part in the European Championships (which they won in 1910). Accounts of Oxford hockey inevitably mention the great Canadians who played there. Talbot Papineau was one, grandson of Louis-Joseph and a man many people thought could have been prime minister if he hadn't been killed at Passchendaele. The historian and Dominion archivist Gustave Lanctôt was an early goalie. After the First World War, when Canadians were welcomed back to the team, Lester Pearson and Roland Michener played together. Clarence Campbell was a captain in the 1920s.

In photos, my dad is tallish and angular, mostly black-and-white, smiling, waiting for a pass by the side of the net. In Kitzbühel, at a restaurant table, he's sitting out of focus, down at the far end. He looks like me. He looks *at* me, looking like him. He appears happy back there, in his blur. My favourite photos might be a pair that show him standing alongside his defence partner at the stadium in Garmisch-Partenkirchen, Germany, where the 1936 Winter Olympics played out. In the colour version, he and Guy MacLean are squinting in the sunlight. In its monochrome companion, they've taken classic tripod hockey-card poses, leaning down on their sticks and looking up brightly at the camera.

He was listed as a left winger, but he also played defence. In case you're browsing any old British hockey histories and/or scrapbooks, be careful not to mistake him for the other Smiths who were skating at the time, including Icy and Biff, two famous names from the 1950s. The nickname my dad would eventually acquire in Britain was Smoothy.

Smoothy and Sinbin: My dad and his Oxford defence partner, Guy MacLean, on the ice at Garmisch's Olympic stadium in 1954.

I asked him what kind of a player he was. "They used to shoot it in from the blueline and I'd be there and I'd slap it in," he said. "I was the peacemaker. The referees wouldn't do anything." Did he ever fight? "Scuffled a bit, perhaps; but normally my role at Oxford was to intervene to hold off Alex McIntyre when he began fights."

They played the Southampton Vikings, whose uniforms were royal blue and gold, on Saturday, November 14, 1953, at 6:15 in the evening at the Southampton Ice Rink Sports Arena on Archers Road. Otto Lang was the Oxford goalie, a future minister of Justice in Pierre Trudeau's cabinet, but a loser on this night, 11–3. A little while later they lost 16–12 to the Grimsby Redwings and 10–4 to Southampton again.

Next they crossed the Channel for a tour of Europe over Christmas and into January of 1954, the *Englische Universitätsmannschaft Oxford*, as the Mannheim paper called them in an article I can't read, other than the score—5–2 for Oxford—and the byline—Peter Puck. They went on to Bolzano in Italy, where they were announced as *the Oxford University Icehockey Touring-Tema*. They lost 19–2. That might seem to suggest the goals were hard to come by, but they had some prodigious scorers. Ian Macdonald was one, and my dad's great friend David Harley another, and they had borrowed a couple of Canadian ringers from Cambridge for the tour, Tom Lawson and John Pettigrew (a goalie), more friends of my dad's. On January 10, they beat Zell Am See 10–1. On a return to Mannheim for a rematch they lost 5–4. The first game had attracted a crowd of three thousand, and it was double that for the second. The Germans had added three international players, my dad recalls. Also, he says, Tom Lawson never passed the puck.

Switzerland next. At Grindelwald they lost 7–5. Queen Juliana of the Netherlands came to the game, and somehow she was assigned a seat on the Oxford bench. She'd spent the war exiled in Ottawa, so it could have been simply that she felt most comfortable close to Canadians, but nobody recognized her and it was reported that "an Oxford undergraduate" (my dad doesn't recall who it was) asked her to leave.

Due to poor ice conditions, they played the next four games in twenty-four hours, winning all four and carrying away the Leysin Challenge Trophy. Some of the games were played in blinding snowstorms. Overall, the team travelled some four thousand miles through four countries in nineteen days, winning seven games, losing six. Their first game back, in Grimsby, they lost 13–4.

Nine of Cambridge's fourteen players for the big varsity match that year were Canadians; Oxford had nine, to go with two Americans and an English goalie. The Oxford *machine*, *Isis* reported, set mercilessly to work from the word go. The *Oxford Mail*: "Both MacDonald [*sic*], the captain, who was hardly ever off the ice, and Maclean [*sic*] were giants in both defence and attack, and Harley produced some sparkling solo runs." Final score: Oxford 7, Cambridge 4.

The following year, 1955, my dad was captain. On the way back to England from Edmonton, he dropped by the NHL offices in the Sun Life Building in Montreal, where NHL president Clarence Campbell donated $200 worth of new equipment which my dad and a friend shipped over to Oxford in their steamer trunks, shrewdly dividing the loot between them to confuse British customs officers.

If they'd followed precedent, Oxford would have abandoned the 1955 varsity game after two periods, which is what Lester Pearson's 1922 team did, having racked up a score of 27–0. But in 1955, Oxford was only ahead by 17 goals after forty minutes, so you can under-stand why they kept going all the way to the end. Final tally: 29–0. The Cambridge goalie was John Pettigrew from Montreal, which could be why my dad held himself to four goals and four assists.

WITH NO BENCH at the pond, I sat on my boot to put on my skates. There had to be lawnchairs I could drag over that would be better to sit on than my boot.

My ankle gave a little twinge, which it does whenever I pull on skates. I was sixteen when I broke it—which is to say, the endboards at the Dummer Township Arena broke it for me when I fell and slid and slammed against them. Those old boards had no give in them. It aches at night, sometimes, especially just before the Montreal Canadiens lose a game on the road. I was lying there for a long time on the Dummer ice. It was a rink with its own portrait of the queen, and she was watch-ing as my teammates kept shooting pucks at the net and errant slapshots pocked the boards around me. Maybe they thought I was napping. At the hospital in Peterborough they put on the biggest cast they could build without removing my hockey equipment first and then my mum came and took me home, and for the next two months I had no choice but to live in my hockey equipment. That's how I remember it.

Ebbie Goodfellow paid twenty-five cents for his first pair of spring skates in 1919. Joe Primeau wore his uncle's skates—way too big, so he had to wear bedroom slippers to make them fit. Rod Gilbert was three when he first put on skates, and twenty years later, thinking of that younger self reminded him of a little drunken urchin. He eventually inherited his brother Jean-Marie's skates, so oversized that he kept his shoes on when he played. Later he graduated to new twelve-dollar skates, which he took to bed with him at night.

Jack Adams bought his first skates with money earned wandering from saloon to saloon in Fort William, hawking newspapers in temperatures of –25° to –30° Fahrenheit—I'm assuming that's outside the saloons. Denis Potvin's father almost made it to the NHL, but he broke his back at the Red Wings' training camp. The skates he'd worn as a Junior were passed down through the family, which meant that Denis didn't get them until his two older brothers had finished with them. The trick to keeping his feet warm in those antiques? "I'd sprinkle a lot of pepper inside the boot. That would last for hours, and it always worked."

The most famous first skates in hockey have to be Gordie Howe's. The tale has been told over and over again, though mostly by people other than Howe himself. Six years old and a neighbour comes by the house—this is 1930s Saskatchewan we're talking about, so the words *dirt* and *poor* are usually invoked. The neighbour's at the end of her twine. Her husband's in hospital and she's selling what she can—a sack of stuff—for whatever she can get. Mrs. Howe gives her $1.50 while the children, Gordie and his sister, Edna, go for the sack. Inside are the skates. Gordie grabs one. Edna eventually surrenders the second. They're monster-sized: he has to pack on six pairs of socks to even come close to a fit. Howe himself passes the whole story by in his authorized biography, but he does say this: it was hard to skate well "without tight-fitting good" skates. "That's why they called me awkward."

In the book that Howe's wife, Colleen, wrote, she doesn't mind taking up the story: Gordie was six at the time. "A lady came to the door selling a bag of used clothes for fifty cents. His mother traded milk stamps for it . . ." Over to Roy MacSkimming. Howe didn't authorize the biography he wrote, but MacSkimming went ahead all the same. He quotes a *Globe and Mail* article by Jim Vipond on the subject of the skates, in which Mrs. Howe recalls the day no one will allow her to forget. The neighbour lady comes by with a *grain sack* filled with *oddments*. What if there had been no skates in there? But there were, two of them, men's size sixes. She paid $1.50 from her milk money. Later she traded a pack of her husband's cigarettes for Gordie's second pair.

There's another version that puts it all in perspective, and that's in the comic book biography, a personal favourite of mine. The story of the skates rates two-thirds of a page, and it holds pretty closely to the story we know, except that a couple of kids from Normandy seem to have replaced Gordie and Edna outside of Saskatoon. I'm judging by their berets. The neighbour is depicted as an itinerant witch.

After skates came the rest of the gear, and often it had to be improvised. Stan Mikita recalls strapping on double-runner skates in his native Czechoslovakia and heading out to the pond to, quote, push a cork with a tree branch. Maybe a couple of copies of *Slovak Geographic* would have served for shin pads, unless periodical protection is a specifically Canadian usage. *Life* magazines were what Eric Nesterenko used in Flin Flon. Frank Selke wore department-store catalogues,

Eaton's on one leg, Simpson's on the other. Garters were shoelace, binder twine, or strips of rubber cut from a Model T's inner tube. *Maclean's* was the right size for shoulder pads, he says.

One day a kid at school gave Mikita a stick, a Northland; it was like nothing he'd seen before. He knew he had to hit the puck. He took a golfer's swing and smacked the kid instead. "He was a nice guy, he didn't hit me," Mikita recalled. "He just took me by the hand and with sign language showed me the right way to shoot the puck. Then he taught me my first words of English—stick, puck, shoot, and goal."

I SPENT SOME time *thwacking* the puck into the snow net I made. Overnight, the ice had dried out. It was as gritty as toast. The surface may have suffered a thaw late in the day before, then fresh snow overnight stuck in the meltwater and refroze with these breakfast results. It was skateable, but not pretty. It wasn't the ice of hockey-poems that sparkles like a February silver dollar. In Paul Quarrington's *King Leary*, it's "blue-silver," hard as marble. I was still after that on the pond. Or "blue with a pearlish tint," a description of Moscow ice.

I practiced my hook-check—not easy to do solo. You really need someone there to try to keep the puck away from you to feel like you're accomplishing anything. Never having executed a successful hook-check is one of the regrets of my hockey career. I didn't have the dexterity to get down, snag the puck, skate away.

I *tooled* around for a while. Though that's not a verb I love so much for skating. I tried *swirling*, which is a better word. Though I'm not much of a swirler, either, so for a while I just skated, puckless. Then I did pick up the puck, stickhandling around the cracks and lumps in the ice. *Carrying* the puck I never liked too much as a verb—there's no carrying to it. Hugh Hood has a line about Jean Béliveau when he had the puck: he could navigate his way around the ice *like a lunch-room pro balancing his peas on a knife*. I tried to think what that would look like and tried to do it, but no. Another hockey word that never made sense to me is *dangle,* for stickhandling: it seems a little too loose for something that's supposed to describe guile and control. Never had much of those on the ice, either.

It was a good net, though if I *thwacked* too hard the puck kept on going into the snowbank behind, so mostly I limited myself to sliding my goals along the ice, with only the occasional full wind-up *thwop*. I skated and I *thwopped*, and I got up some speed and came around again and this time I gave the puck more of an unrestricted *rap*. The stick made good contact and the puck took off. I got it back and *swooped* through centre and *smited* the puck at the net, and went around again and *whapped* in a high shot. I was out there for another hour, *winging, firing, blasting, poking, lashing, slinging, steaming, arrowing, airmailing, smashing*, and *peppering* pucks. I must have lost twenty of them in the snow before I ran out of hockey verbs and headed in.

When it comes to explaining my shortcomings as a player, the poor skating, weak arms, lack of killer instinct, and watery eyes only go so far. The real problem, a perpetual drag on my progress as a hockey player, has always been narrative. Reading all the hockey books certainly hasn't helped with this. What it boils down to is that whenever I'm playing, rather than just playing, I'm seized by the compulsive need to describe to myself what's happening as it happens. This includes finding just the right words for hockey actions and also sound effects, up to and including those for which no words exist. This naturally lends itself to dreamy behaviour rather than puck control, and involves more murmuring than effective forechecking. The problem is one that Bill Gaston writes about in *The Good Body*. Out on the ice you're churned in "the lightning-fast flux of friends and enemies, the blending of opportunity and threat." No time for thinking let alone talking, telling yourself stories. "Words didn't stand a chance here."

I don't have specific memories relating to those early murmurous years in Peterborough, but I'm pretty sure I was fully infected by the time we moved to Lakefield and I was playing in the village league. Eventually I followed my brother up the hill to Lakefield College School, the Grove, where in Grade 8 I played for Fifth Hockey. This sounds like an entry in a bartender's recipe book—two parts Jim Beam, a fifth of hockey, and a dash of angostura bitters—when in fact it was the lowest tier of competitive hockey at the school. We had the same red sweaters as the Firsts. That was something. And it was the period during which I was most attentively scouted. If this suggests a wily old bird dog in the stands, monitoring my wrist-shot, no, wrong. In our report cards at the end of each term, along with the marks for Geography and Math and English, there would always be a comment from the coaches of the sports teams you'd played on. "It has been a good season for Stephen," Coach Thompson wrote that first year. "He has adjusted well to his position and has been eager to develop his skills." Nothing too specific, but positive.

The next year I tried out for the Fourths. I was an early cut in the first week. Then—trauma—the Fifths had no place for me. A year older, a year more adjusted, as eager as ever, but the team had decided to go in a different direction. It was a rebuilding year, a numbers game; they already had too many ponderous left wingers who could only skate clockwise around the net without losing an edge. They didn't have to say why they were waiving me. I was a free agent. I played in the school's rec league that year—haughtily—and the year after that, in what looks in retrospect like a pressure tactic, I moved to Spain. There was no pressure in Spain—and no hockey. I was once again following my parents, who either didn't want me in the country to witness the 1981 Canada Cup or were on sabbaticals. The year after that, when I returned for Grade 11, I made Third Hockey. I got mixed reviews when the Christmas report cards went out: an A in Typing;

in Geography, I was mapping well. My term in the Physics lab was rated "reasonable." Over in History, Mr. Jones had his concerns: "The research assignment was a little below expectations." I would have flipped the pages expectantly to see what Mr. Milligan had to say about my progress on the ice. "Steve's size and weight always made it difficult for him to develop the mobility and dexterity some smaller players have," he wrote. "In spite of this, he played a fearless, albeit somewhat reckless, style of hockey. I continue to encourage him to be careful not to hurt himself."

I've always known my limitations. As Phil Esposito said, "I wouldn't walk across the street to see myself play." Still, in Grade 12 I thought I had a fair chance of making Firsts, especially in the case of a dropsy epidemic clearing out the roster of veterans. At the tryouts, during a deflection drill a guy in my class, a big defenceman we called Bobo, took a slapshot from the point, and instead of tipping it past the goalie, I took it in the skate blade, which exploded to smithereens. That was it for me, and I was sent down to Seconds. Of all the school teams, Seconds sounds the worst, like faulty factory-reject shoes, but the hockey was fine and better suited to my skills. It was a pretty good team, except for all the penalties and spotty goaltending. Coach Harris used to shake his head and laugh at us. There was an incident in Buffalo where a defenceman of ours, in goonish tribute to Mike Milbury and the 1979 Boston Bruins, clambered out of the penalty box into the stands to swat at someone who'd yelled at him. Mr. Harris used to bring a big red golfing umbrella to the games. Sometimes we didn't even have to be losing; he'd just pop it open to shelter himself.

Often in hockey stories, the heroes cultivate trick manoeuvres to bedevil goalies. I wish I'd known sooner about the *whirlygig* with which Quarrington's King Leary makes his name; things could have been so very different for me. In Charles Muller's *Puck Chasers Incorporated* (1927), Russell Quick only ever shoots backhanded, very sly, while Sharpshooter Bigley, from the Reeds, has a cunning *long-range shot* that involves lofting pucks from afar. In a 1932 Harold Sherman story, Frederick Baker is a former figure skater/accused coward who ends up wowing everybody/scoring the winning goal with his amazing *airplane dive*. To celebrate, he etches his name in the ice with Salchows before folding himself into a big bow.

Trying out for Firsts, I had to work with what I had, and that's when I decided to bring my hook-check to bear. There were some great players on that team, classmates whose hockey skills fetched far beyond mine—Chris Palmer being one of them. He went on to play in the New Jersey Devils' farm system and then in Britain, where, in successive single seasons, he scored 96 and 114 goals. Hammer was his nickname. He played with Tony Hand, the first British-born player to be drafted to the NHL, well enough to get into Hand's 2007 autobiography, *A Life in British Ice Hockey*. Hammer's adjectives there are *solid* and, as a goal scorer, *out-and-out*.

Compared to Hammer—well, the comparison is pointless. The only possible superiority I could claim was my reach. He was tall, but I was taller, and I could surprise him with my long arm and longer stick. This remains a solace, and today, even if only theoretically, I could, if I had to, outreach, say, Jarome Iginla. Iginla may outgun me in skating, wrist-shot, hockey sense, playoff experience, clutch goal scoring, regular non-clutch scoring, breakaway speed, upper-body strength, softer hands and mightier will, and superior acumen; have a solider frame, a wealth of poise, a poise of wealth, playmaking skills, a howitzer of a shot, a mortar of a bodycheck, a crazy work ethic; possess the puck with an authority I have trouble even imagining; excel at the little things; dominate down low; take good penalties; keep his head in the game; be a natural leader and willing to pay the price—is there a cliché he doesn't deliver?—be defensively sound, with plenty of two-way savvy, slot-moxie, just enough hash-mark sass, and a cool head; and his decision-making, I have no doubt, would make mine weep—and yet... He's just six-one while I'm six-seven.

I decided my best chance for making Firsts lay in hook-checking Hammer in a scrimmage. Maybe it would work and I'd be brought on as a specialist. But instead of Hammer, I somehow hook-checked Coach Armstrong. He went down. My timing was terrible. It looked like a trip; it was a trip. I never saw the puck. I saw Mr. Armstrong sprawled out and sliding. He must have forgiven me—I'd remember his wrath if he'd thought I'd done it on purpose. He was great guy, coach of the Firsts, and he also taught us History and Economics. Big Bob, we called him, except when he was within a rink-length of possibly hearing us. We loved and respected and feared him, and if we were smart, we never tripped him.

Once he'd been Bob Armstrong of the Boston Bruins. He'd worn number 4 for five years before Bobby Orr arrived on the scene. Twelve seasons he played in the NHL, 542 games, a big, solid front-porch defenceman, which is to say *stay-at-home*. His partner was often Bill Quackenbush. *Bruising* is the word that's attached to Mr. Armstrong, which could very easily speak to his own sensitive skin, but more often in hockey points to the punishment of others. Players who never fought—Jean Béliveau, Max Bentley—somehow ended up in fights with Mr. Armstrong. When you look him up, the records testify that *He never rushed the puck* and *Horvath was struck in the jaw with a slapshot off the stick of teammate Bob Armstrong, and had to be taken to nearby Massachusetts General Hospital.* Rod Gilbert has a story about Mr. Armstrong pairing off with the Rangers' Wally Hergesheimer, who was small. "Watch out, Army," Hergesheimer piped up, "or I'll bleed all over you." Don Cherry has one where he punches Mr. Armstrong in the eye as if he's "throwing a baseball." This is in the Minors, after Big Bob's years as a Bruin and before Cherry's. In a game the following night, Mr. Armstrong jams his stick into the back of Cherry's head, but then Cherry jumps up and hits Mr. Armstrong over the head with *his* stick and piles on him until a linesman intervenes, allowing Mr. Armstrong to kick Don Cherry right in the chest with his skates.

Mr. Armstrong, who died in 1990, didn't talk about his NHL years, not that I heard. Maybe he discussed them with the Firsts, in the dressing room between periods. I doubt it, though, that doesn't seem like him. He won no Stanley Cups. He played with Milt Schmidt and Hal Laycoe, Sugar Jim Henry, and Johnny Bucyk. He was nineteen when he was first called up, still in high school in Toronto, and then a year later he was on the Bruin blueline during the 1952 Stanley Cup, seventh game in Montreal, when Rocket Richard scored what lots of people at the time said was the best goal they'd ever seen scored. Lynn Patrick thought it was the most sensational goal in the history of the NHL.

It's in the movie *The Rocket* (2005). Remember where Mrs. Richard is at the Forum, up in the stands, watching the game, looking worried in the way that wives and girlfriends at hockey games in hockey movies always look? (The gold standard for worried women watching spouses play hockey has to be Meryl Streep in *The Deadliest Season* [1977]. She brings a level of bewilderment to her worry that Trudy Young comes close to matching in the 1971 movie *When Winter Comes Early*, but not quite.)

Early on in the actual game, Boston's Leo Labine checked Richard down to the ice, and as he fell, his head hit Labine's knee. Could be that he was knocked out before he hit the ice; in any event, he was already bleeding. Richard didn't remember being carried out to the Forum clinic. Today, with concussion protocols, he'd be out of the game, just like Paul Henderson in 1972—*he* was concussed, we now know, when he scored series-winningly for Canada. As it was, and in the movie, Richard gathered himself. The camera looks out through his eyes. Everything's slow and woozy. In the dressing room, the perspective zooms out of Richard's head so as not to stint on the stitching. The camera gets right in there on the gash over Richard's eye, blood and ooze and the pull of the needle doing its work in skin. The cut is more convincingly authentic than the hockey.

Nobody in real life thought he'd return; anybody who's ever seen a movie knows that the plot demands it. Onscreen, he clumps back to the bench for the third period. Mrs. Richard is more worried than before. What happened next in the actual game is open to interpretation. The plainest version has Richard surging in on Bill Quackenbush and Mr. Armstrong. Quackenbush tries to staple him to the boards, but he twitches past. Mr. Armstrong comes at him. Richard goes around Big Bob like he's turned to salt, the old Lot's-wife problem, a real liability for a defenceman. The Rocket has only the goalie, Sugar Jim Henry, to beat. He shoots, he scores.

That's one version, at least, from Andy O'Brien's Richard biography. Later, O'Brien changed his story: Big Bob is bowled over trying to administer a bodycheck. The *Sports Illustrated* account puts Mr. Armstrong first: Richard fends him off with his left hand, controlling the puck with the stick in his right. Richard himself makes no mention of any Mr. Armstrong at all in his book. In the paper the next day, Montreal coach Dick Irvin subtracts Big Bob and multiplies Bill Quackenbush by two. First, though, it's Woody Dumart. At centre, Dumart spins Richard "like an apple in taffy." Richard keeps going. Crosses the blueline. Quackenbush! Richard passes him by, skating all the way to the backboards, according to Irvin, passing the net—he *is* concussed, remember. Out he comes, only to be re-Quackenbushed. Spins away. Swoops. Henry dives as Richard shoots, but it's no use. There's a photo of this moment, just as the puck goes in. Richard doesn't look too wounded. Quackenbush is cruising in the background. Big Bob has his stick in behind the Rocket's skate, as though to scrape him feet-first out of the goalmouth in the way you'd back-hand the road-killed wet remains of a squirrel off your driveway—with quick disgust, into the ditch. Fans littered the ice with pencils and popcorn. Nine sweepers swept up the mess.

In a famous photo, Henry and Richard shake hands after the game's all over. Sugar Jim has a big raccoon's eye and a broken nose, and he's bowing to Richard. Richard's eye is bandaged, and there's blood on his cheek.

The greatest goal? The seventh-game significance adds a few degrees of greatness, but I think it has more to do with the concussion. The movie doesn't really do it justice. It's the old hockey-movie problem: even with actual players taking part, Sean Avery and Vincent Lecavalier, the hockey looks hopelessly faked. In this case, when movie-Quackenbush takes movie-Richard to the boards, he just seems to let him go. I know, that's what the scene calls for. Richard has to keep going. In real life there was the chance that Quackenbush would stop him.

The goal signfies more in the movie than in real life, which is to say it's freighted with meaning beyond simply the beating of Bruins and the propulsion of Canadiens into the finals. Which is understandable. Movies need to build narrative. The scene ends on screen as it did at the time: after the game, when the president of the Canadiens, Senator Donat Raymond, appears to congratulate the goal scorer, Richard breaks down in tears. To RocketRichardologist Benoît Melançon, this signifies that it's just a man there under the weight of all that myth.

ONE OF THE best parts of reading all the hockey books? All the hockey words. A lot of them are hockey sounds:

- *RRRRRR!* (sound of Gordie Howe's dad sharpening skates in the 1930s using a belt on a flywheel hooked up to the washing machine; a noise so loud you had to get the heck out of there when you heard him start up)
- *thump, thump, thump* (sound of Rod Gilbert's own heart as he wakes from a nap, pre-game in Montreal before his Rangers meet the Canadiens circa 1968)
- *foom!* (sound Maurice Richard uses to describe rearing back and hitting Bill Juzda and knocking him flat on his back with a good one after he, Juzda, said something unpleasant, 1971)
- *ponk!* (puck shot wide of the New York Rangers' net hitting the glass, cited by Roger Angell in the *New Yorker*, 1967)
- *Caribou, Maine* (sound the body seems to make hitting the boards, according to Don DeLillo in *Amazons*, 1980)

Poets like to put hockey to music: they evoke "the swift hiss of skatesong" (Brian Richardson) and report that "the river sings of shinny" (Alix Vance). I don't know that those allow for the game's full percussion, though. Hockey likes to keep its words simple and ono-matopoeic. That's why *bash* is a premium hockey verb, as are many of its several rhymes: *crash, smash, trash, lash, thrash, slash,* as well as (the important hockey compound noun) *skin rash*. Hockey is as taciturn as a Ray Carver story, its style flinty and plain-spoken. Or maybe I mean Hemingway, who liked to think that 90 per cent of the story is iceberged under the surface. It's a practical matter, too: at the most basic literary level of the word, hockey is too fast, too slick, too kinetic. There's no time when you're skating to build a sentence. It's not that it *can't* be expressed, just that it doesn't need to be. The form in which hockey best expresses itself is hockey.

It does have the advantage of being the only major sport that pro-vides players whose own names are complete descriptive sentences.

Zarley Zalapski sounds like he's writing out a detailed description of a goal he scored every time he signs a cheque. Radek Bonk announces a bodycheck that didn't quite work. Paul Shmyr sounds like one that did.

Clomp is a hockey verb. "To walk as with clogs," says the dictionary, although in this case, of course, the clogs are blades. Goalies in particular *clomp*, in part because of the size of their skates, which won't allow for lighter-footed verbs (*patter, flounce*). You can't *trudge* in skates, or *plod, scuttle,* or even *skulk*—something to do with the sharpness, I think. Though it sounds more like a kitty-litter word, *clumping* is close to *clomping,* walking or treading clumsily. *Tromp* is another word for *clomp,* a variation on but not really a satisfactory backup for *tramp,* which isn't a hockey word at all. The New York Rangers *tromp,* according to Brad Park, or at least they did in the early 1970s. Careful, though: all three words are mainly reserved for situations in which your team (a) is losing the game or (b) has already lost. Winning teams *head* to the locker room or simply walk, but *tromping, clumping,* and *clomping* are all disconsolate gaits, reserved for occasions (as in John Craig's 1968 novel *Power Play*) when the Nationals steal the fifth game of the Stanley Cup semifinals in overtime and the defeated Falcons have no choice in the matter: they "clumped in on their skates, dropped their sticks, and dispersed along the U-shaped bench." Sometimes allowances are made, for instance, if your team wins 4–3 but you yourself let in a couple of gift goals. In that case, according to Ed Fitkin's *Turk Broda of the Leafs* (1953), "the usually happy-go-lucky Broda was bluer than a housewife on a Monday morning when he clomped into the Toronto dressing room."

Hockey has never coined words with the alacrity that baseball has. *Deke* is an exception, from decoy, with alternate spellings. It's said to be the only word that hockey can claim to have given the language. Can that be right? According to *A Concise Dictionary of Canadianisms,*

Dickie Moore seems to claim the credit, circa 1960: "I've developed a little play of my own. It's kind of a fake shot—we call them 'deeks' for decoys."

Fistic is an antique word you used to see, another one borrowed from boxing. It comes with great-sounding accessories: *fistical*, *fistiana*, especially *fistify*. Hockey's words, a lot of them, have a limited shelf-life. Some will never die (*face-wash*, or how about Danny Gallivan's *spin-o-rama*), but others rise up and fade all in one motion. You have to wonder about particular waxes and wanings. *Dipsy-doodle:* that has to be a hockey original, doesn't it? No: it's from a 1930s song, borrowed to describe fine stickhandlers like Max Bentley (see Ed Fitkin's *Hockey's Dipsy-Doodle Dandy,* 1951) and heard nowadays only in wry usage.

Why isn't *dash* more of a hockey verb? It used to be. Howie Morenz did a lot of dashing in Eric Zweig's novel *Hockey Night in the Dominion of Canada* (1992); that's how you know it's a period piece, because of all the dashing.

Puck is a Four-Letter Word, as Frank Orr reminds us on the cover of his 1983 novel. Inside he adds an obvious rhyming other, *fuck*, "the hockey player's general reaction to everything." Mark Jarman, in *Salvage King, Ya!*, lends an example to show how effective it can be in helping describe the chaos of play:

> I'm working hard in the corners and in front of our goal, but the fucking wingers keep losing the fucking puck on the fucking boards one fucking inch from the fucking blue line and it stays in our fucking end: JESUS this drives me crazy.

Dogpile is a rare hockey word meaning to heap wingers and schnauzers on somebody. It's surprising, really, that you don't see it more in hockey descriptions, like this one from Bishop Chandler

Sterling: "The aim of the confusion is to dogpile the goalie and sneak the puck into the net."

Slick is a terrible verb to use on someone:

When Chico [Maki] slicked Tom [Johnson] in the back of the legs with his skates and severed a nerve, that was the end of Tom's career. (Ted Green, *High Stick,* 1971)

Lose is a hockey word, but if you played for Harvard at the same time as Tod Hartje, it's one you weren't supposed to utter out loud. If the coach heard it, you were on the floor for fifty push-ups. To his credit, if *he* slipped up and used it himself, he'd get down and do fifty.

The Hockey Phrase Book (1987) organizes itself thematically, one of the themes being "Wrong Moves," which include *coughing up the puck* and (a fall-down-goalie word) *flopper.* If the defenceman you pass by looks bewildered and/or falls down, it may be reported that you *undressed* him and maybe even *deked him out of his jockstrap.* Mike Bossy reports that coach Al Arbour had his own coinage for this: *rabidoux,* maybe named for a player he'd once embarrassed, as in *I rabidouxed Lepage and slipped the puck behind him.*

Bossy, of course, was a *top-six* winger, also a *sniper,* one of the best ever, as opposed to a *playmaker* or a *power-forward,* all of whom come in several levels above the *mucker,* the *plugger,* and the *energy guy* (not to be confused with your *glue guy*) in hockey pecking order. Phil Esposito was called a *garbage collector.* A player who gives everything might be *an absolute horse,* or maybe, if you're goalie Niklas Backstrom and *standing on your head,* you'll be deemed to be an honorary postal worker because of your work *carrying the mail for Minny.* Paul Henderson confesses to having wondered whether he would have to be a *charger-arounder* (also known, in a Butch Goring context, as a *buzzsaw*) in order to stay in the NHL. As it turned out, of course, he was a *situation-riser*, a phrase first applied to Charlie Conacher.

Hockey can't really contend with baseball and its spectrum of pitches, but it can try. *Pepper* is one of the words that hockey didn't coin so much as kidnap from the language at large. It's a fine, expressive hockey word in the sense of *to pelt with small missiles; to bombard*, which should never be confused with the word's other meanings, including *to infect with venereal disease*.

Beyond the basics, the *wrist, snap, slap*, and *backhand*, a Beaufort scale measuring the catalytic action of pucks might look like this. For a force-one shot, down at the lesser end of the spectrum, hockey borrows from repartee: "I had only the briefest peek at the puck...a zinger" (Plimpton). Next up, evil: "He rang a wicked one off our goalie's mask; out cold" (Jarman). Then small arms (Mike Leonetti: "he focussed on being at the right spot just as the shooter unleashed a blast"), graduating to artillery in its many forms (Jarman: "a cannon blasting by my gonads"; Fischler: "Mahovlich could... fire the puck with the fury of a howitzer"; and of course, Danny Gallivan's beloved "cannonading drive"). If you need to go right to the top of the scale, you want a hybrid of interstellar and maritime travel: "Bullock launches a rocket that sails over my left shoulder" (Ken Baker).

If you're a defenceman, the vocabulary that concerns you most is all about getting in the way, blocking shots, taking the man, rubbing him out on the boards (Pierre McGuire called Luke Schenn "the human eraser"). *Stand him up, shut him down, ride him off*. If you're Bryan McCabe, you used to get your stick in between an opponent's skates and give a twist, a *can-opener* that's called, except nowadays it's a penalty.

Slather is a great hockey word (from Scott Young) for what a defenceman wants to do to Pie Mackenzie behind the Leafs' net.

Sparkling is a goalie adjective, applicable to saves, the puckstopping equivalent of the stickhandler's *dazzling*. (Unless you're Gallivan, in

which case the word is *scintillating*.) *Save* is a powerful word, loaded
with rescue and redemption (see all those funny jokes regarding Jesus
and saves and Orr scoring on the rebound). *To preserve from injury,
destruction, to rescue from eternal death*, my old Webster's dictionary
advises, *to spare, to salve*. Does it seem overqualified for the job of
describing such a modest act as keeping a puck from crossing a line?
Goalie verbs include *smother, stonewall, turn back, repel, reject, rob,
stop, stump, stone, deny,* and *stymie*, but you rarely hear *confound, non-
plus, suffocate* or *suppress*. For those who excel, the praise is mostly
nugatory: you *blank* the other team, *pitch a shutout*. Although not
always: you can also *lay a goose-egg* or be, simply, *perfect*. At the other
end of the rink, you run the risk of falling in among the pots and pans,
as a lowly *sieve*. If you play in Montreal and your name isn't Plante or
Roy or Price, then it may be Andre Racicot, and (God help you) your
fate may be to wear for all time the nickname *Red Light*.

George Plimpton suggested that a goalie needs just a single word,
the one he was considering painting in big red letters on the mask
he wore when he suited up for the Bruins: NO.

Taking to the ice at the Boston training camp in 1977, Plimpton
describes himself as *maidenly*, not an adverb heard much in hockey
circles. This was right after he signed the waiver releasing the NHL
from liability with respect to the usual on-the-job risks of the rink:
"injuries, suffering, or death which may occur." Otherwise, his discovery of hockey begins with lessons in the language of the game. A
key part of the lingo has to do with the parts of the body that stand
to suffer the most hurts, which is to say the head (*melon, puss, pump-
kin, coconut*) and due south, the testicles. Haunted by stories from
his roommate, a goalie nicknamed Seaweed, Plimpton stuffed his
cup with pages from the local newspaper.

There's a long index of euphemism down there, of course, though
Andrew Podnieks's *The Complete Hockey Dictionary* (2007) is strangely

silent on the subject, lacking *pills* and *agates* alike. You don't have to be a hockey player to wince at the thought of the potential for damage below, but if you're questioning a man's testosterone, the technical term for what you've done is *instigate*. (A dire put-down, Plimpton notes, is to say of a rival, "He got no *seeds*.")

Instigate is undeniably a hockey word, maybe the longest one you'll commonly find in a hockey player's vocabulary, according to Fred Stenson's *Teeth* (1994). An *agitator* can be an *instigator*, though usually those guys (a.k.a. *pests*, a.k.a Sean Avery, Ken Linseman, Esa Tikkanen) are annoyers more than they're fighters. In a 1975 taxonomy that's a hockey rival to Roger Tory Peterson's *Field Guide to the Birds*, John Gibson calls them *antagonizers*, noting that their penchant for talk over walk means that they often need the assistance of *policemen*, unlike the *stickman or hatchetman*, who's on his own—no one respects him. Schooling Plimpton in battler terminology, Seaweed starts with *cement heads* and—but let's leave them for later. The indeterminate future, after all, is hockey's preferred place for discussion of its violent tendencies.

SPEAKING CANADIAN ENGLISH doesn't think much of hockey. I went to it having read H.L. Mencken on baseballish—a whole summer riot of *fungos* and *soup-bones*, *humpies* and *twirly-thumbs*. What has hockey got by comparison in the way of words that started on the ice and subsequently deked out into the larger language? Hardly enough to fill two paragraphs, that's what. Mark Orkin's 1970 look at the language has a bit of a creak to it now, but still, hockey makes a poor showing. Canadian wartime jargon rates whole pages, a few words of which—*shellwacky* being one— hockey should grab.

It's a sport that's never worried too much about the size of its vocabulary. Estimates vary when it comes to how many active words there are in the whole of the English language, but this we know: the twenty volumes of the latest *Oxford English Dictionary* (1989) house about 228,000 of them. The Bible apparently does its mighty work with fewer than twenty thousand distinct words, which isn't as many as Alexander Pushkin commands in his collected works (21,197), or Shakespeare, who comes in at 24,000, an impressive 1,700 of which he coined himself.

Can hockey's twelve thousand words and phrases really be enough to get its message across? That's the number *The Complete Hockey Dictionary* proffers, and since it's *Complete*, I don't know why we'd doubt it. With all due respect, I say it's time for an infusion, a doors-open immigration policy. If we have to go poaching, fine. Donnybrook is an Irish town with a famously boisterous fair, which is how *Donnybrook* (and, soon enough, *donnybrook*) came to be a standby word for a hockey *tussle*, even if today, other than in archives, you see it used only ironically. Start there, maybe, with local geography. Why not a *Squamish* to describe what happens when Clayton Stoner starts whaling on Luke Gazdic, and vice-versa? Industry has contributions to make, whether new (*fracking*: a penalty that Boston's Brad Marchand might take) or older (there's no good reason hockey can't farm the fishery for words like *sockeye* and *codswallop*).

The lexicon does grow on its own, but whatever hockey's natural rate for linguistic inflation might be, it's too slow. That's not to say there haven't been important recent additions. *Pansification*, from 2009, would be one of those: Mike Milbury's word on *Hockey Night in Canada* for what would happen to hockey if fighting were to be banned. In 2010 we got the interjection *Iggy!!!* (I!-gh!-EEEE!!!), a good one to have in your pocket in case, like Sidney Crosby at 7:38 of overtime at the Vancouver Olympics, you find Jarome Iginla nearby and need him to pass the puck so you can score while at the same time coining a term that sums up the urgency and exuberance of a gold medal won at home.

The year 2011 found its defining moment on its very first day when Crosby dropped to the ice in the outdoor Winter Classic after a hit from Washington centre Dave Steckel that he never saw coming. We all know the rest of the story and how little hockey Crosby played for a year while he rested his head. The phrase *Crosby's concussion* is meaningful to this day, or should be, given how many of number 87's symptoms—confusion, fear, lack of focus, uncertainty for the future— afflicted the sport as whole during the months of his absence.

Boogaard, Rypien, and *Belak* became all too readily familiar as hockey words at about the same time, each one with its own painful and poignant associations. *Boogaard* is the one that lingers, haunting the game and how it conducts itself even now, years after the man himself died. That's thanks in large part to a devastating series of articles that John Branch published in the *New York Times.* No one with a stake in the game or a love for it—whether player, fan, owner, or executive—should be allowed to see another puck until they've read Branch's "Punched Out: The Life and Death of a Hockey Enforcer," or the book that it's become, *Boy on Ice* (2014). At least then we'll all be caught up on the implications of *chronic traumatic encephalopathy,* commonly known as CTE, another fearful lexical item that has forced its way into hockey's dictionary in a way that the sport isn't going to be able to go on ignoring.

WHEN FOUR OF US flew to New Brunswick in a February freeze, I brought along a Max Bentley biography I thought we could all share. Fred from the Tobique Lions Club was waiting for us with his big white van at the airport in Fredericton, and once we'd collected our sticks and our gear, we were on the road north to Plaster Rock.

I'd heard the organizer of the World Pond Hockey Championships, Danny Braun, talking on the radio about what it was all about: "It's carving skates, sticks and pucks and laughter," he said. That sounded like fun, so we'd signed up, paid our money, made arrangements. Our sweaters were red and white, with a big exclamation mark on the front to intimidate people who are scared of punctuation. We were in our 30s, veterans all of many men's-league campaigns who took the game just seriously enough but no more than that.

Nick, Mike, and Evan are all better hockey players than me, but they also arrived in Fredericton knowing not as much about Max Bentley. *Hockey's Dipsy-Doodle Dandy* isn't my favourite Bentley book, but Ed Fitkin's biography tells such a blithely cheerful tale of the wily Saskatchewan centreman that just by bringing it with me, I thought I was boosting our team's karma.

There are pond-hockey tournaments everywhere now, but Plaster Rock's was one of the earliest to organize and it's still the most venerable. As of 2013, it has a novel, too: Brian Kennedy's *Pond Hockey*. No one—yet—has made the journey from Plaster Rock to the NHL. A thousand people live there, amid forests and ferns. (If you didn't know that it's the fiddlehead capital of Canada, you must have missed the giant fronded statue that guards the town limits.)

They dropped a puck out of a helicopter to get the tournament started. We missed that, but Fred got us to town and down to Lake Roulston in time to take the ice for the first of our Friday night games. Snow was blowing through the glare from big lights. There were twenty-four rinks cleared on the lake and games underway on most of them when we skated out to face the team from the Moosehead brewery in Saint John's. The whole lake was hockey, and if you closed your eyes to listen, you could hear it quoting the works of hockey writers like Betsy Struthers ("the shush of skates") and Peter Gzowski ("the thwock and clack of the puck") and R.J. Childerhose ("the shoo-oonk! of skate blades as someone stops"). I may have fallen into a reverie. I could hear myself muttering notes, as I do, annotating the action at the expense of helping it happen.

We were down quickly, 3–0. There were no goalies here. The nets were low and wide-mouthed, mailboxes for posting pucks. All this way we'd come without any real thought of how we wanted to play or what the conditions might demand. We were slow and bunched-up. We tried to learn from the beer-making boys as they were whomping us, but it was hard to learn and be losing at the same time. I didn't know what Max Bentley would have done in this situation, but I wondered. The game went fast. I was trying to think of the right word to describe Nick's dogged checking when the game ended. *Terrier-ish*? Lacking vocabulary and goals, we lost 15–6.

Next game, we tried sending Mike forward on his own while the rest of us stayed back. That worked for a while: we took the lead. Then we got tired and maybe nervous—it was a hometown squad, with lots of fans by the snowbank. New plan: one man back, everybody else to the attack. That worked to the extent that we lost Game 2 only 14–6. We ate our suppers with our skates on, perched on hay bales in the big rinkside tent where the beer was.

Firemen flooded the rinks with the town truck while we slept that Friday night. On Saturday morning, we sat on our beds in the suite at the Settler's Inn & Motel, taped our sticks, tied our skates, and when the time came, we clomped through the snow in the woods to find the firemen were back out, giving the ice a final spritz with potato sprayers. It was, we all agreed, *fucking* cold: there was a sense that just by showing up you were consenting to a cryogenic future.

In the brisk and the bright, we played a team with a mixed Montreal/Corner Brook lineage and managed to tie them, the

Quebec Newfoundlanders, 19–19. Then we started to win. *Squaloid* might be the word for the way Nick was hunting the puck, a good hockey word right up there with *temerarious*, which describes Evan's burst of enthusiasm in the final few minutes. All Mike did was score, with swagger. We were finding our adjectives now, and we used them to beat another Plaster Rock team, 14–6, followed by teachers from Oakville, 18–7. At the dance that night, at the high school, we found out that we'd made the playoffs, though we were too sore to do more than nod before we went limping back to the Settler's Inn.

Sunday morning's thermometer made Saturday's cold seem like a joke. We had to keep checking to see if our hands were still there in our hockey gloves, because we couldn't feel them. The team from Washington was not just fast, these guys were serious. No fooling around with them. They made our makeshift attack look like a skit for clowns. They had different plans, at least four of them, all elegant and effective, which they switched up with subtle nods. A small, dense mass of extra-cold had settled in the slot in front of our net, a micro-climate that we may have briefly hoped might reinforce our defensive structure, but it didn't faze the Americans. They were good guys, I have to say, even as they went on smoking us: 21–7 was the final score. We cheered for them in the final later that polar afternoon, but they lost to an even younger, faster, quicker-nodding team from Boston.

Nobody read about Max Bentley on the flight home, not even me. We'd come and lost and frozen and lost again and learned a little, enough to manage a few wins before we lost one last time. Now we ached.

I did arrive at an idea about why prose can't seem to contain hockey, but that was later, when I was thinking back to Plaster Rock. I'd been pulling down poems from the hockey shelf, Lorna Crozier ("fly us into the skate-blade brightness of the winter stars") and John B. Lee ("snow-boot goals"), and thinking about what Ken Dryden said about why you can't, as a hockey team, play as anything other than individuals:

[A game is] hundreds of tiny fragments, some leading somewhere, most going nowhere. Only one thing is clear. A fragmented game must be played in fragments. Grand designs do not work.

Browsing Stephen Scriver ("feel the body burst again") and Al Purdy ("swift and skilled delight of speed"), I thought that if I kept borrowing from the poets, eventually I could reconstitute the whole New Brunswick experience, line by line; it was only a matter of time.

I DON'T KNOW if Howie Morenz was the best who ever played. People who saw him in action say he was, probably. Films of him in flight seem to have trouble keeping him in frame, as though he were fleeing the camera. Having read all the hockey books, I'm ready to declare that no NHLer has more adjectives than Morenz: he comes in with approximately 10 per cent more than Bobby Orr.

Darryl Sittler is someone who's said that there was no one better than Orr. According to Elmer Ferguson, Orr used up four pairs of skates a year thanks to his skating power. Gump Worsley said that even people in Auckland, New Zealand, knew that Orr was the greatest defenceman who ever lived.

Jean Béliveau. Lots of votes for him. Hugh Hood: "Nobody will deny that for sheer beauty of style Jean is the greatest of them all, style in all respects, and not just on the ice either." Babe Pratt:

He was a polished performer who did everything—stickhandle, shoot, the works! Some of these fellows I see now couldn't even stickhandle past their mother without losing the puck—and some couldn't pass it to their mother if she were starving to death and it was a piece of bread they were handing her.

Béliveau himself said Marcel Bonin had as much spirit as anybody ever.

To Frank Selke, Newsy Lalonde was the ultimate, no greater battler on the Canadian sporting scene. Though Harvey Jackson was the *classiest* ever. Neither Aurèle Joliat nor Ted Lindsay could carry his stick when it came to, quote, superlative class. And good-looking? Are you kidding me? Jackson moved like a dancer, and his backhand was the best Selke ever witnessed. Though only Maurice Richard was greater than Charlie Conacher. And Joe Malone was the handsomest man in the old Trolley League.

Duke Keats was supposed to have been pretty great, too. No one could knock him around. He almost had a nail on the end of his stick to carry the puck around—that's how good he was. (Sprague Cleghorn had his stick examined for a nail once, but he wasn't using it as a stickhandling aid.)

Dick Beddoes offended the Gretzkys once by claiming that Wayne would have been the fourth-line centre on the 1947–48 Leafs, behind Max Bentley, Syl Apps, and Teeder Kennedy.

King Clancy: "Plain and simple, there weren't any better hockey players than Punch Broadbent."

Sweeney Schriner was the best left winger Conn Smythe ever saw: "That includes everybody." Also according to Smythe, Baldy Cotton put on "a death act" like no one else. Which I would like to have seen.

Toe Blake said that Jacques Plante was the best goalie ever; and that when he coached him in Montreal, he never said a word to him for seven years.

Derek Sanderson said, "There's no question in my mind that I'm the best faceoff man in the league."

Gordie Howe? Lots of people speak up for Howe, including Johnny Bucyk. When Howe was on the ice, he said, everybody tried harder. He was awesome, unstoppable. And scary. "Nobody wanted to tangle with him," Bucyk said, "absolutely nobody."

But Howie Morenz. Joe Primeau called him "that near-perfect human hockey machine," which you have to admit, is hard to beat adjectivally. He was (a partial list) *classy, hard as nails, confident, great* (as a player and man), *devastating* (his shot), *unsurpassed* (his heart), *cool, helpful* (a rare one, for hockey), *warm, sterling, seemingly reckless, terrific, stocky, electric, compelling, outstanding, blinding* (his speed), *unvengeful, most feared, not easy to spill, swift, keen, once-iron* (his legs), *unquestioned* (his offensive ability), *highest paid, good* (his golfing), *easy* (his grace), *grand, dynamic* (his rushes), *enough for two men* (his speed again), *bullet* and *blasting* (the shot), *beautiful* (his stickhandling), *uncanny, worth a cover story, matchless, spinning* (his dash), *jovial,* and *chuckling.* Also, children adored him.

What Morenz had more of than any hockey player in history was joy. Boom-Boom Geoffrion might be a close runner-up: "He was one who smiled the most," said a mourner in Montreal at his funeral in 2006. But given that he married Morenz's daughter, isn't it likely that at least some of that joy was handed down from his father-in-law? There's so much I'd like to know about Morenz, but this is already decided: it was his blend of skill and speed and tirelessness and joy that made him so great.

Morenz was small, five foot nine, 165 pounds. His skates were small, one of his teammates remembered later, and so too were his wingers. His wingers, in fact, were smaller than him: Aurèle Joliat, five-seven, 136 pounds, on the left, while to the right it was Johnny Gagnon, the Black Cat, five-five, 140 pounds. This miniature man, with his tiny skates, his micro sidekicks—just thinking about the three of them, you start to squint.

The joy is what makes the tragedy of Howie Morenz all the more poignant. Or how about this? A man so small, a heart so big, so full of joy—how else could this story have ended? When someone gets around to writing the first Canadian hockey opera, they'll have to take a good long look at Morenz. Wayne Johnston writes that his very name was "full of death."

Growing up, he wanted to play goalie. He back-checked like a demon. Skating through centre, he's said to have had the habit of hopping every few strides so that he seemed to skip over the sticks of his opponents. "Peerless Howie," the papers called him, and "Hurtling Howie," "the comet of centre ice." Howie Morenz "of the mercury-dipped skates," trilled the *Windsor Star*. (Although to be fair, Hec Kilrea and Babe Siebert are both supposed to have beaten him in races.)

He always got up when you knocked him down. He had a hot temper and a good opinion of himself. When he played in New York, he and Bill Cook used to bicker over who was the greater player. "Slope-faced, round-shouldered," *Time* magazine called him in 1931, which seems uncalled for. In July of that year there was a car accident near Cornwall, Ontario, and for a day or two the rumour wafted around that he'd been killed. Not true, he phoned in to report, though both Canadiens goalie George Hainsworth and Toronto centre Andy Blair were slightly hurt in the wreck.

In photos there always seems to be a fleck of amusement in his eye. This is the lasting visual trace of the joy he took in life, it's what you notice first, right before you look at his legs. In the hockey poses, he looks look a poorly designed bird, some kind of spindly sandpiper. Of course those haphazard legs were going to break. Did nobody say anything?

He spoke with a Scotch burr. He loved fun. In the summer he played golf just about every day. He also played a ukulele, and as Joliat remembered, "He was always singing."

Before a game he ate Limburger cheese and onions, unless there were no onions available, in which case he'd eat garlic. *Staggering quantities* is a phrase linked to the amount of Limburger Morenz ate. "First I breathe on the goalkeeper," he's supposed to have said, "then I shoot 'er in."

He was a Stratford Midget and also a Stratford Indian plus a Black Hawk and even a bit of a Ranger, but most of all he was a Montreal Canadien. Leo Dandurand signed him up in 1923, famously paying a forty-five dollar tailor's bill as part of the deal. Morenz tried to shrug out of it; the people of Stratford offered him $1,000 to stay amateur, but he loved Montreal once he got there, the city, the people, their hockey. He sobbed when Dandurand traded him, in 1934, to Chicago. He was supposed to be slowing, slipping. He wasn't playing with Joliat and Gagnon. Fans were booing, and Dandurand couldn't bear to hear that.

He was pretty good in Chicago, but he didn't get along with the owner. At about this time, in March of 1935, he turned to freelance journalism. In Montreal he had contributed columns to *La Patrie*, but now he addressed a bigger, manlier audience by way of *Esquire*. We'll accept that Morenz was moved to write the piece himself, that no collaborators were brought in to mediate his positively chipper tone, and that when he talks about himself in the third person, he means it. The big news he has to deliver is a surprise: having lost all three fights he started the year before, Morenz has decided to give up fighting. "Yes, from now on I'm a pacifist, a hold-backer." By the way, for those of you out there who thought that the fighting was a fake, "part of the show, fancy embroidery," well, hold on just one minute, buster. He makes it all sound so jolly, so much fun, even the scene when the fleet winger meets the defenceman's "solid, unlovely hip" and "the forward's breath leaves his body with a 'woof,' as he goes buckety-buck-buck and crashes into the boards." On he prattles, tickled as can be to be talking hockey, even when it's to acknowledge that "Father Time easily overhauls the fastest mortals."

I TOOK THE train from Toronto to Ottawa to hear an honoured, elder Montreal Canadien talk about his career and also, possibly, to meet the prime minister. The train was good for reading and would be, I later realized, a perfect conveyance for my whole hypothesis that there was never a better time for hockey than when it rode the rails. En route, I read hockey books the whole way, except for a break I took to eat a cheese plate and some intermittent pauses for long-range gazing at fast-moving countryside. From what I could see, most of barns on the north side of the tracks between Oshawa and Kingston were in good repair. They had a lot to do with how good the snow looked, too: without the barns it wouldn't have been as beautiful a day out there.

The Hab I was going to hear, Leo Gravelle, was the featured speaker at the annual meeting of the Society for International Hockey Research, the first one I'd attended. Going in, I didn't know that Howie Morenz's son was going to drop by with *his* son—Howies II and III, right there at the next table over, near the wonderful hockey artist Mac McDiarmid, who had also worked as a goal judge for the Montreal Canadiens, and not far from the man who knows more about Minor-league hockey than anyone in the whole world. A lot of the members talked to the Morenzes, but I was feeling a little shy. I did know about Stephen Harper being a member, and the word beforehand was that he might be dropping by. I was saving my pluck for him. If the chance presented itself, I was going to try to ask him a question.

By Port Hope I was dipping into my luggage of old hockey novels. I was having troubling reading them one at a time. Having read no more than a chapter of *The Chums of Scranton High at Ice Hockey* (1919), I'd lay it aside to pick up *Pass that Puck!*, which I'd stay with for a chapter before moving over to *Captain of the Ice* (1953). The fact is that a lot of the early hockey novels tell pretty much the same story, over and over again, which means that if you read them the way I was reading them as we passed by Cobourg, you don't miss a thing.

Long before Faulkner and Hemingway ignored it, hockey took its time catching the attention of novelists. We should get that out of the way before we go any further. Hockey chronicler Craig Bowlsby makes the point that the game's slow and gradual rise, along with the informality of its rules, made it as easy for writers or historians to overlook as snowball fights.

Nikolai Gogol does have hockey in an 1835 short story—unless it's bandy. Edith Wharton took some notice in 1907 in *The Fruit of the Tree*, a novel of euthanasia, abject labour conditions, and the whole question of what's a good profession for a woman. It features spinal injuries, morphine addicts, and infant deaths. And then:

> His last Saturday had now come: a shining afternoon of late February, with a red sunset bending above frozen river and slopes of unruffled snow. For an hour or more he had led the usual sports, coasting down the steep descent from the house to the edge of the woods, and skating and playing hockey on the rough river-ice which eager hands kept clear after every snow-storm. He always felt the contagion of these sports: the glow of movement, the tumult of young voices, the sting of the winter air, roused all the boyhood in his blood.

Not bad, as far as it goes. *All the boyhood in his blood.* But that's as far as it does go; hockey remains incidental, background colour, as we move on to the morphine and the infants.

The first proper hockey fiction started to appear just after 1900, although when I say proper, I mean full-length, because the novels in question were big, bold, wholesome adventure stories for boys rather than anything approaching literary fiction. These were dime novels streaming out of New York mostly, hearty yarns all, and their authors were only too happy to add hockey to the roster of sports they were already mining for heroic tales, from baseball to football to baseball again. They had titles like *Frank Merriwell's College Chums; Or a Stand for Clean Living* (1898) and *Frank Merriwell in Peru* (1910), and if it appears as though there's a theme developing here, that's because Frank Merriwell was something of a prototype character as far as early juvenile pulp fiction goes. Gilbert Patten was the original author, writing under the name Burt L. Standish to the tune of some eight hundred short stories, which first appeared in 1896, as well as dozens of novels.

He was Lionel Conacher's favourite author, which makes sense: Conacher was a bit of a Frank Merriwell himself, conqueror of all frontiers he turned to face. A character from a latter-day hockey novel, Paul Quarrington's *King Leary*, remembers reading about Frank: "He was a handsome do-gooder and always won the ball games with a grand-slam homer." In the illustrations from the books it's sometimes hard to see exactly how handsome Frank is, due to the train station ruffians attacking him and/or the distressed maiden clinging to his side in the prow of the lifeboat, but we'll say, for argument's sake, that he was Hardy Boys-handsome. As well as solving mysteries and smacking grand-slams, Frank did eventually play some hockey, too, though it was never his forte.

Ralph Henry Barbour's oeuvre includes *The Arrival of Jimpson and Other Stories for Boys about Boys* (1904), not to mention *Double Play* (1909), *The Secret Play* (1915), *The Play That Won* (1919), and (inevitably) *The Last Play* (1926). *The Crimson Sweater* seems to have been Barbour's first foray into hockey, in 1906. Eleven years later, he got around to *Guarding His Goal*, a novel of intrigue, laundry, monkeyshines, goalies, and reading. Like the novels I was reading on the train to Ottawa, it's a winter's tale set in New England among schoolboys named Toby Tucker or Thad Stevens or maybe Nat Collier or Frenchy Beaumont. Their heroes, like the plots, are hard to distinguish in memory. There's usually a funny sidekick, who's often a goalie. Sidekicks or not, the goalies are fat enough to be called, well, Fatso. There are hot tempers—but don't worry, there are cooler heads, too, that prevail. There aren't really many girls around. Sometimes the villain is just a jerk, like Jimmy Powell in *Captain of the Ice*. Once in a while the stakes are a little higher. Donald Ferguson's *The Chums of Scranton High at Ice Hockey* has Nick, just an all-round terrible person. He's tricky and he's low-down mean. His nature is warped. The chief of police can't wait to lock him up. If this were a story set in the present day, he'd be stealing cars, dealing meth, and parcelling up toxic subprime mortgages to sell to unsuspecting investors. Because it's 1919, he's just a bully and a petty thief and a "good-for-nothing scapegrace."

Maybe you can see where this is going. Thad and his chum Hugh want to help Nick. They think he can be rebuilt—*reconstructed* is the word they use. They're interested in redemption, the chums. Hugh's been reading *Les Misérables*. Maybe a revelation will alight on Nick the way it did on Jean Valjean. Thad laughs. But guess what: Nick isn't all bad. Hugh knows this because he's a great skater and wants to play hockey, and also he's quite a proficient blacksmith, another proof of good character, apparently. And so at the rink and at the forge the chums, of course—spoiler alert—redeem him.

That's pretty much it for the early hockey novels, and it would be for a lot of years. Even when the plots became more sophisticated, the novels went on being about making the team against the odds. The quality of the writing improved once the Hardy Boys' own Leslie

McFarlane and (especially) Scott Young got into the game in the 1950s, but the story remained the same: boy tries to make team, confronts obstacles, overcomes them, still has to prove self, does so, usually by scoring big goal. In the early hockey novels, heroes always triumph, and in the end, so does hockey. Jerks fall by the way, their violence is overthrown, and every now and again *The Game* (with an assist from the local smithy) wins out.

I DON'T HAVE too much to say about my Via Rail cheese plate. It was passable. I'm talking here about soft triangles of generic bloomy-rinded French cheese and of cheddar in shrinkwrap. (No Limburger, I'm sorry to say.) The cheese got me as far as Kingston where, as we stood in the station, I gave a small Camembert salute to the game's early roots. As we went on and the track turned north, I thought about a question I might want to ask the prime minister.

Stephen Harper isn't the best hockey player ever to have held the office. I believe that even he would have to cross party lines on this one and admit that Lester Pearson was by far the most skilled of our forechecking PMs. That's not to say you wouldn't take Harper if the sticks were thrown down and you were picking teams. He says he's no great skater, but I've seen him play the road game, and both his readily acknowledged love of the sport and his publishing record have to count for something, too.

As for the rest of them, the scouting reports are few and far between. Did Sir John A. Macdonald stay with his winger? What about Mackenzie Bowell? Did he tie up his man on defensive-zone faceoffs? Mostly we're left to extrapolate hockey possibilities from the recorded facts of prime ministerial biographies. Sir Wilfrid Laurier has a bit of a Jean Béliveau air to him, but he suffered chronic bronchitis from an early age, which kept him in his bed. "At heart he was an intellectual with little inclination to physical exercise but a passion for political action," says historian Réal Bélanger, as though intellecting must somehow be opposed to exercising. Bowell, now that I look him up, is said to have been diligent and scrupulous—so maybe a bit of a penalty killer? R.B. Bennett's mother was a steadfast Wesleyan Methodist, emphasizing hard work and self-denial. If he skated as a boy, it would have been on the Miramichi River—though John Wesley didn't like the faithful wasting their time on "silly unprofitable diversions." The future prime minister was never seen to play rugby at Dalhousie, it has been noted. But according to another historian, "Bennett with his back up could be a chalcenterous animal," which sounds like a hockey appraisal even before I get to the dictionary. It could be the perfect hockey adjective, from the Greek, meaning *tough, of brazen bowels.*

William Lyon Mackenzie King bought himself a pair of skates in January of 1901. He paid $5.50, or about twice the price of the ticket he bought that month for a sleeping-car berth from Ottawa to Toronto. He took the skating slowly, waiting until 1903 to learn the first principles of ice waltzing. "I think I will learn as I am sure I would enjoy it greatly," he told his diary. The winter after that he took to the ice at Government House, but only shyly. "Wd. rather have skated in a less conspicuous place." We don't know how he fared with the waltzing. We can say that as PM he attended Ottawa Senators games, including one in 1925 that sparked, in the pages of King's diary anyway, a second unsung King-Byng Affair, after the governor general and Lady Byng failed to invite him into the vice-regal box, rendering him mightily miffed.

In the 1960s, Lester Pearson railed at the malign influence of the NHL: "every good player in Canada under the age of 10 is on the negotiating list, at least, of some professional club," and wasn't it time we protected our young? This was around 1964, when U.S. President Lyndon B. Johnson toasted Pearson at the White House: "a loyal neighbour, a durable ally, hockey star, and a good and most understanding friend."

"Sometimes," Pearson waxed late in his life, "I would rather have played for the Toronto Maple Leafs than been prime minister of Canada."

He probably could have done it, too. In 1921, he joined the Oxford touring team as it departed for Christmas visits to Belgium and Switzerland. It was a distinguished lineup, with sons of Montreal and famous Manitoba legal families in the ranks, along with a future mayor of Winnipeg and (as a sub) governor-general-to-be Roland Michener. They beat the Belgian national team, and in Switzerland, Oxford tutored Cambridge 27–0 in just two periods, with the third called off for mercy. Pearson's stickhandling impressed the spectators: they called him "Herr Zigzag."

"Our matches with the European clubs were also easy victories," he said, "so we thought, naturally, that we were better than we actually were by Canadian standards." He played for Switzerland in the European Championships, and England wanted him to suit up for them at Chamonix in 1924. Hockey wasn't his only strong sporting suit. In England he was a lacrosse star. During the Second World War, he was applauded on the front page of the *Times* for having thrown a cricket ball farther than any man on record.

Stephen Harper may be the first PM to wield hockey as an instrument of foreign policy. At home, he's been an exemplary first fan, faithfully attending Flames games and World Junior practices, dropping in to chat with the broadcast boys on TSN. "I love my job as prime minister," he'll happily Pearson, "but if you could be a hockey player, what could be better than that?"

It has been suggested that it's as much political as true patriot love. I don't know if that's fair, but before he published his book last year, it seemed arguable. Even more so, perhaps, after Montreal's *Gazette* disclosed that Harper had been seeking the advice of a prominent U.S. strategist, the Republican spinmeister Frank Luntz. He was the guy who famously gave George W. Bush his winning communications strategy for global warming: do what you can to confuse people and you should be fine. Once he'd tailored his advice for a northern client, his scheme revealed a ruthless perception. "If there is some way to link hockey to what you all do," Luntz is supposed to have recommended to the PM, "I would try to do it."

I'm sure that didn't have anything to do with the 2007 trip the PM took to the war in Afghanistan to visit the troops. This was the week after I went to Ottawa for the SIHR congress. The Senators were on their way to the Stanley Cup finals that spring and the prime minister's itinerary would get him back just in time to see them play. In the meantime, he had important work to do at the front, showing the flag, pressing the flesh, visiting the in-country Tim Hortons. He also had an appointment to meet his Afghan counterpart, Hamid Karzai, to do what he could to bolster the Afghan backbone in the fight against the Taliban.

First, though, he had presents to offer, including what was described in the non-domestic press as "a pint-sized bodysuit of a top ice hockey side"—a miniature Ottawa Senators uniform for Mr. Karzai's newborn son, Mirwais. Harper said he wanted to help the boy start out life in the right way. "Well," Karzai replied, "I would like him to play hockey as soon as he can walk on his feet." No word on how that's been going.

AT SMITHS FALLS, some passengers disembarked and others climbed aboard. I was ready to move my books at the first sign that someone needed the seat next to me. I was on alert, in case of company, for that person to take notice of the hockey novels and require an explanation. There were lots of seats, though, and nobody wanted mine, or any explanations.

Why are the so-many hockey novels so decidedly not-all-that-great? It's a refrain that echoes across the land, always has, and it's of utmost importance, because if hockey is such a vital organ of the culture, an engine of who we are, why wouldn't we have a longer, fuller, prouder shelf of hockey books?

The echo is relatively young, thirty-something, if that. No one seems to have worried too much about hockey lacking a literature back, say, in 1953 when Bill Roche was putting together *The Hockey Book*, his ebullient anthology of party-piece anecdotes from hockey's early days. His major concern was that many of the best hockey stories could never be printed: they were too pungent for family reading. The dire state of hockey lit wasn't a pressing issue either for Bruce Kidd and John Macfarlane when they wrote about child exploitation and selling our national soul in *The Death of Hockey*.

I don't know who was first when it came to klaxoning the emergency. Doug Beardsley was saying in 1987 that aside from Dryden and Roy MacGregor ("Hockey's Faulkner," his publisher would soon after be advertising), the landscape was bare. Don Gillmor in *The Walrus* in 2006, in a piece headlined "Hockey: The Great Literary Shutout," wrote that he'd vote *The Game* and *The Hockey Sweater* to the canon, that's all, if there were such a thing. Beardsley would seem to point the finger at the writers as having failed the game, whereas Gillmor chooses a hockey construction in suggesting the opposite, as though he were talking about a wayward right winger: *it has not produced*. In a 2006 essay in the *New York Times Book Review*, Keith Gessen frames the game as a down-on-his-luck hitchhiker, just can't catch a ride, and all those speeding potential rides just keep on passing by. To Gessen, *The Game* is "the last great hockey book," which is to say he's hoping it's not the final one, I think, rather than declaring the door shut. Don DeLillo's *Amazons* is "the other monument of hockey literature thus far"—mostly because its subject is not so much hockey but (like all of DeLillo's novels) America, "the dark schizy heart of it." It's a book, Gessen writes, that's "not about hockey in just the right way."

Is it the game's violence that limits its literature? Rick Salutin, who wrote the game's unsurpassed play, *Les Canadiens* (1977), is someone whose hockey thoughts I'd just as soon hear as anyone's. He says it's us, Canadians. We haven't elevated the game to myth. It's too bad we're so satiric, too ironic, all of it having to do with our national shyness and sense of inferiority. But does that really account for, say, Mordecai Richler's only having touched on the game in his novels? What's wrong with our novelists? Are their feelings too sensitive for the job? Do they know something we don't?

George Plimpton has his small-ball theory, which in hockey terms amounts to this: blame the puck. He argues that it's the sports that propel the bigger objects—footballs, basketballs—that have the meatier literatures, and maybe what golf and hockey and marbles need to consider is upsizing their balls and pucks, see where that gets them.

Don DeLillo is like a skateguard that won't shake loose: very irksome. Not just because he's refused to allow *Amazons* to be reprinted, or even ever to acknowledge that he wrote it. (His heroine, Cleo Birdwell, has taken the credit from the start.) No: what rankles just as much is that here's a novelist who saved for his 1997 novel *Underworld* one of the sharpest, most evocative depictions of a sporting event ever written and it's . . . baseball.

I'D EVENTUALLY WORK up a whole page of questions for the PM, but that was much later, in the fall of 2013, after he'd published his book. Before that, he'd contributed a long essay to *How Hockey Explains Canada* (2011) by Jim Prime and Paul Henderson, which I can say I enjoyed even as I try to remember the pith of the explanation. "Hockey is one of our greatest exports," is something the PM says there. He also describes the "so-called hockey room upstairs" at 24 Sussex Drive where he keeps "a veritable library of history books, including some short-run first editions" that people have sent him, along with his autographed sweaters from Vladislav Tretiak and the 1967 Leafs.

I'd like to know—but he actually answers this one on the page—yes, if he were the boss of the NHL, rinks would be bigger. The whole Sidney Crosby concussion business made him "just furious." Did you *see* that hit? The PM couldn't believe it wasn't a penalty. Never would have happened to Gretzky. "I'm mystified by it, but I hope that the powers that be wake up." For half a sentence I thought this might be where Harper answered the call from *Maclean's* that *he* was the man to save hockey in the way that U.S. President Theodore Roosevelt brought football back from the brink in the early 1900s. Could it be? Would he dare? No. If Harper has a comprehensive vision for what the game needs, and the will to implement it from on high, we haven't heard about it yet.

The reviews of Harper's *A Great Game* (2013) mixed terms like *disappointing, eye-glazing, agonizing pages* with the more palatable(ish) *surprisingly readable* and *overly engaged nostalgist.* "It is as if," wrote Jeff Z. Klein in the *New York Times,* "President Obama published a densely researched study of early basketball in Chicago. Harper has written a finely detailed history of the struggle between professionalism and amateurism in early 20th-century Ontario hockey."

I was fascinated, but then, overly engaged and a nostalgist, of course I was. The struggle was serious. It was, in the PM's telling, touch-and-go for a while there. Was it okay for hockey players to skate for money, or was the spread of the professional scourge endangering the morals and very manhood of those who succumbed?

I didn't know if I'd get close enough for a question in Ottawa. Maybe he wasn't even taking questions. Why would he? Best to have one ready. So maybe, *is hockey a Canadian value as far as…?* No. *Does hockey, in your opinion, need…So football, back in the…* Come on. Concentrate.

So what's this so-called hockey room like, upstairs?

It was no good, and anyway, it didn't matter. Arriving late on Friday, I missed the conference cocktail party, which is when the PM showed up to chat and answer other people's smart questions. Saturday, when I arrived for the AGM proper, one of the name tags on the registration table was for

Stephen Harper
Member—Alberta

It remained there all day.

Mid-morning, in a room with a convenient view of Parliament Hill, we welcomed Leo Gravelle to talk about his life in hockey. Gravelle played four-and-a-half seasons in the NHL, 1946 through 1951, for Montreal and Detroit. When I looked him up later, the profiles said *fine* and *industrious* and *the blond Bomber.* "Leo Gravelle swished in Glen Harmon's shot" is a sentence you might have seen after Montreal beat Chicago in 1947. He was born in Aylmer, Quebec. His nickname was the Gazelle. When he stood to talk, it was like a spell he was speaking. "I've had a good life," he said.

A lot of people, they think it's easy the start in life. We didn't have electricity until I was seventeen years old. When it comes time to play, I'm gonna tell you the truth. In those days the skates are not like today. It's just a leather thing. When it gets wet it expands. I had to wear my cousin's skates. At four o'clock in the afternoon it was my turn. I put on six pairs of socks. I don't know if you still have your mother or not, but after you lose her you miss her a lot. I had a good father. Sometimes he had to walk from Hull to Aylmer after working his day's work. We didn't have radios. We had a hockey team. I will tell you what we used to do. Shin pads, it was a piece of felt. Hockey sticks, we were paying twenty-five cents. Excuse me, ladies, if I'm swearing sometimes. I was an altar boy for eight years. Have you heard of a hockey game after midnight mass? It was the choir versus the altar boys. In the morning when I got up there was an apple, an orange, and a piece of paper. Thank you, Lord. What do you get for Christmas today? I was working for the government, office boy, thirty-nine dollars a month. My first suit cost me thirty-nine dollars, so my mother had to pay my streetcar for the next month. I was play-ing Juvenile at seventeen years old. Port Colborne. At St. Mike's the coach was Joe Primeau. When you win the Memorial Cup, a fellow has to be proud. I went to the Montreal Royals. I had a line with Floyd Curry and Howard Riopelle. I could name you some names. When you play for a team like Montreal, they can decide to send you to Buffalo. They sent me to Houston. The next year they brought me up to Buffalo. Then I graduate to Montreal. Then this guy, Kenny Reardon. He used to call me Gravel. We did some damage. That was another thing that went by. I got traded for Bert Olmstead. I think I can brag about this. I'm the only one who played with Howe and Richard. Sid Abel was injured. I played with Gordie Howe and Ted Lindsay. Then Sid Abel came back. I sat on the bench for thirteen games. Then they sent me down to Indianapolis. Jack Adams said, Leo Gravelle will never play another game in the NHL. I never did. I learned one thing in my life, when you go in to get a job, when they tap you on the back, that means they don't want you. But I've had a good life. What I've told you today, it's from the bottom of my heart. The Rocket could score on his knees. Gordie Howe was sort of a brute. They were two good guys for me. I don't know how I've still got my nose, my face. Black Jack Stewart, he picked me up and drove me into the end. I didn't know where I was.

WHEN THE DAWSON CITY Klondikes challenged for the Stanley Cup in 1905, they took the train from Seattle to Ottawa and did their calisthenics in the smoking car as they rattled east. Did they at least discuss trying to flood a boxcar, leaving January to freeze it in time for a scrimmage as they crossed North Dakota?

The first thing we have to acknowledge is that, a hundred years ago, hockey players were not only themselves rolling stock, but the railroad was what delivered them. Without it, where would hockey be? Stuck by the side of the road is where. P.A. Macdonald never would have made it to Winnipeg carrying his stick. Okay, maybe he would eventually have made it, picked up as a hitchhiker.

From its earliest advent, hockey took the train. When the CPR spread its lines into southern Saskatchewan in the 1880s, teams spread with them, from Moosomin to Swift Current. Is it just coincidence that so many hockey fathers worked on the railway? Nels Stewart's dad did his time, and so did Duke Keats's and Bill Gadsby's (a CPR baggage man for fifty years) and Paul Henderson's. Jack Adams's was an engineer in Fort William, Ontario; in fact, he helped to lay the tracks west out of town.

And as trains approached, and the lonesome plaint of the whistle haunted the town, the people would stream out to the station. During the silver boom in Cobalt, Ontario, the hockey teams riding the old T&NO line would change at North Bay, and all the boys from the town would be out on the platform to watch for Newsy Lalonde and Cyclone Taylor, and this alone, just the sight of a hockey player on the platform, the hockey books say, might change a young boy's life forever.

A train Normie Smith never saw pretty much spelled the end of his NHL career in 1938. Adams was Detroit manager by then, and Smith, the goalie, missed the team's departure from New York (he was staying with friends). Adams fined him $150 and sent him to the Minors, to which Smith said he wouldn't go, and quit. Linesman George Hayes was someone else who got into railway trouble when NHL president Clarence Campbell suspended him in 1961 for riding to Chicago in a day-coach rather than a sleeper berth. To be an official in the NHL, Campbell solemnly declared, you had to ride first class to make sure you got a good night's sleep before the game you were working.

Quarrington's King Leary says, "Train travel was the worst thing about my professional hockey career." I can't see it, though. Life on the trains sounds great to me. In the 1930s, the Leafs used to have their own private car—ML1, it was designated—that they'd hook up to the regular New York train. The journey took thirteen hours and ten minutes, Union Station to Grand Central, with a quick stop at Sunnyside to pick up the west-end players, like Hap Day. Conn Smythe insisted the players dress properly and behave themselves. Arriving at 4:10 in the afternoon, they'd play the Rangers from 8:00 until 10:45. They'd be back on the train at 11:25 PM.

Stories of the hockey teams on trains are built on phrases like *Murph Chamberlain would hang a good snootful of liquor on himself before dinner* and *King Clancy, who had just boomed the boys at rummy.* Clancy recalled a tour of Western Canada that the Ottawa Senators took after the 1922–23 season: "I got on the train to find our Pullman car like a brewery on rails. There were cases of beer everywhere, even in the ladies' room, but that was okay because we had the car all to ourselves." (Clancy didn't drink.) In Toronto, someone "smuggled" a piano aboard. Eddie Gerard, the only other teetotaller on the team, played all the way to Sudbury.

Frank Boucher recalled a trip that the Canadiens took to Victoria in 1925. At the station in Montreal, well-wishers loaded up their car with cases of gin and brandy plus seventy-eight quarts of beer, a supply that only lasted as far as the Manitoba border, according to Sprague Cleghorn. On the way back, in Banff, Alberta, the team uncoupled its car from the homebound train and stayed for a week, parked at a siding purely for the party of it.

In 1943, the Leafs embarked on a six-day trip, with games in New York, Boston, and Detroit. Veterans got the lower berths, rookies had to climb. As much as possible, a player's berth number corresponded with the number on his sweater, with Turk Broda, number 1 on the ice, in Lower 1, number 4 Bob Davidson, in Lower 4, etc. Ted Kennedy (Upper 12) had the privilege of sleeping above Leafs trainer Tim Daly, famous as, quote, the world's champion snorer. The fine if you were caught smoking outside the smoker was twenty-five dollars. Other than rummy, the games they played were hearts, euchre, bridge, and cribbage. Wagers were limited to a top stake of twenty-five cents per game, or a cent a point. Poker was strictly taboo.

Among the Black Hawks, Max Bentley was the self-appointed commander of the team's on-board reading material, comic books and detective stories, mostly.

If the Leafs played a Saturday night game at the Gardens, sometimes the schedule dictated a Sunday engagement in Montreal. Trainer Daly would pack up the team's equipment as soon as they were off the ice, and down to Union Station it went in Finkle's truck. Players followed by car or subway. On board, they'd change into their pajamas and gather in the smoker to talk about the game. Hugh Bolton always brought a jar of fruit salad. If they left at 11:00 they'd be in at Windsor Station by 7:40 AM. Everyone contributed a quarter towards the porter's tip. The Leafs' regular porter was Pinky Lewis, whom Conn Smythe called "a fine Canadian," a faithful worker with a spirit so infectious, the team couldn't help but contract his will to win.

In New York they'd stay at the Commodore Hotel. In Chicago, it was the La Salle. After the game, they'd buy train-station sandwiches and a six-pack of Budweiser. Tim Horton always bought wine, Mogen David, two or three bottles, to take home to his wife, Lori. A win meant a party. Billy Harris figured that during the 1950s, Leaf players spent as many as four hundred hours together each season on the trains.

John Ferguson says the train was the reason there was no discord between the French- and English-speaking players on the Canadiens. "When you were all huddled together in a lounge or smoking car, it was hard not to be sociable, especially when the train ride extended overnight, which it usually did." The main card game, in those days, featured Big Jean, the Pocket Rocket, Jean-Guy Talbot, and Claude Provost, while Ferguson played gin rummy with Ralph Backstrom, Bugsy, and Gump. "One night the train, stuck in a blizzard, couldn't move an inch for hours. Gump and I should have gotten into *The Guinness Book of World Records*. We played gin for twenty-four hours straight."

Howie Morenz was a big gambler at railway cards. And, quote, when the deck went cold, he would haul out his ukulele and sing. Rocket Richard, meanwhile, was not so sociable, teammate Ken Reardon recalled: "He used to ride all the way to Chicago, sitting in a corner. He didn't even read a book." Other times, the Rocket was known to sit in the men's room of the Montreal-Detroit sleeper reading until the porter filled the room with hockey players' shoes for shining.

For Gump Worsley, fun was a titanic pillow fight that almost got several Canadiens kicked off the train. As a player, Toe Blake would buy live eels and hide them in Bunny Dame's upper berth. A hot-foot was always good for a laugh, of course: crawling up on a teammate and sticking a lit match in his shoe.

In the 1960s, Montreal was one of the last teams to make the switch from train to air travel. It was the efficient thing to do, of course, though it also seriously upset Worsley. He may have hated flying even more than Wayne Gretzky did. Once, on a stopover in Chicago as

Montreal flew west, Gump left the flight to complete the trip to Los Angeles by train. The psychologists he saw couldn't help him.

For a while after the Canadiens took to the air, they were still catching trains to Toronto, with Jean Béliveau's approval. "It gives you a chance to catch your breath, talk for a while," he said. "I always enjoyed the train hops . . . There was plenty of kidding around. That's not so easy on a plane, and the stewardesses don't like it too much."

IT WAS SCOTT YOUNG who hatched the prototypical hockey hero, starting him off in *Scrubs on Skates* in 1951, following up with *Boy on Defence* (1962) and *A Boy at the Leafs' Camp* (1963). The first three books are fairly straightforward Boys' Own books in the Frank Merriwell mould, brisk in their plots, with no sudden movements to frighten anybody. Other than the violence on the ice, *Scrubs on Skates* is, true to its times and audience, scrubbed fairly clean: even when things get tense, Pete Gordon can muster nothing saltier than a forceful "Gol darn it!"

Pete is the star player for Northwest High, a Winnipeg high school team. At first he seems to be the central character. He's switched schools, and his problem is that he's not sure he can come up with the enthusiasm to play for a new and mediocre team. He does, though, and he plays well, and watching him we meet the team. What a motley bunch they are. How can they ever hope to come together as one? Which, of course, is the fuel that fires the whole engine.

Here's where you have to be paying attention. Like many hockey novels, *Scrubs on Skates* employs a helpful newspaperman as a character, Lee Vincent of the *Telegram* in this case, and he sits in the stands and watches Northwest practice. Here's a man who understands the value of a good read. He laps up the list of the team's players as "a man who loved line-ups, because to him the line-ups always told the true story of sport." The names he sees there are as Canadian as can be, a mix as rich and thick as ever you'll see in a melting pot—or whatever it is you get when you put a melting pot on ice. There's Horatio Big Canoe ("the tall lanky Indian boy") and Benny Wong, Rosario Duplessis, Winston Kryschuk. The captain is Grouchy DeGruchy, a son of Dutch parents. "He would remember"—this is the narrative voice speaking up for Lee Vincent—"all the names on this team and know that people of all races could get along when they had something in common, a puck or a ball."

Bill Spunska doesn't make the melting pot at first; he keeps to the background. He's got a square face, he's big in the body, he speaks with an English accent. He's new at the school, it's only his second year on skates, and when you hear what he's been through—how does he do it? He's a striver, that's how. Lumbering around the ice, he doesn't impress anyone until during a scrimmage on page 26 he steps up into this sentence: "But everybody had reckoned without Spunska." Boom! He lays out DeGruchy with a thunderful bodycheck—for which he promptly apologizes. "I'm sorry if I hurt you."

He's Polish, we learn. Just like Stan Mikita, he's a DP, a Displaced Person. His parents fled to England when he was five, and then his dad moved on to Canada, with Bill and his mother eventually following. The upshot of this is that he didn't see his dad for eight whole years. He doesn't play in Northwest's first game, but the coach sees fit to tell the boys, last thing before they head out to the ice, that Bill is so committed to improving that he borrows the key to the rink and he's out there every morning skating hard. Inspiring example, but not quite enough to win the game for Northwest. One of the problems is the disappointing play of Pete Gordon. What's wrong with this kid? He's got all the tools but there's something seriously the matter with his toolbox. Or maybe he realizes he's no longer the main character he thought he was. But Pete takes it well, and he's allowed one brave act before he evaporates entirely, saving a goal even as he's getting his leg sliced by an errant skate.

Pete isn't a bad kid, but he becomes the bad example to Spunska's good. Spunska has no toolbox whatever. He has to build his from scratch, finding all the hammers and awls and spirit-levels to put in it. Spunska is pure effort, a tool-making marvel, plus his mother lies gravely ill, which can't be easy for him. She's the one who, in a lucid moment, spells out for us all what the novel is actually about, and more than that, what hockey means. She's never paid too much attention to the games boys play. "But it seems to me this sport is different," she tells Bill from her sickbed. "It is what you are, not what you have been or what your parents have been."

And that's why Bill prospers. And just in case we need the point underlined, there's the true villain of the piece, a rival centreman, Forsyth. He's good—"a real hot hockey player"—but he's got a motor on his mouth. He calls Rosy *a big Frog* and Benny Wong *a yellow Chink*, and after that, well, can you blame the big mild-mannered defenceman who loses his temper and lines up Forsyth and clocks him? This is how hockey judges the wicked. Though hockey justice is a little more complicated: a two-step process whereby first Forsyth is laid out for his transgressions and then there's an inquiry into whether or not the hit was legal. But that's just bureaucracy. The point is, Bill Spunska is a good guy and hockey is both the proving ground for this and the gateway to being a Canadian. Of course, there remains the question of whether Forsyth, for his sins, ought to be cast out of hockey and country. It's a troubling one, so it's lucky that he's not a central character and we can forget him as easily as we forget a loss in the pre-season.

Scrubs on Skates ends on a high, to the point that you find it hard imagine there's anywhere else that Bill can go. Until you actually start on the imagining, that is, at which point the answer turns out to be fairly obvious.

IS HOCKEY LIKE life? The soldiers who took the time to play the game in nineteenth-century Kingston were seeking to escape the dull routines of their garrison lives: pucks and sticks measured the distance they could create to leave those lives behind. On harbour ice in front of the town they strayed as far as they were going to; any farther and they'd be nearing open water.

So, I guess that's a no. Hockey has a lifelike look, except for all the padding and the sticks. Also, for most of the world, levelled ice is strange. In "The African Hockey Poems," Richard Harrison writes of walking the streets of Côte d'Ivoire with a hockey stick in hand and the people look at him in awe and bewilderment just as—this is lovely—

the inland farmers who had never seen the
sea stared at Ulysses with his oar.

Roch Carrier's other hockey book, the one that's not *The Hockey Sweater*, is *Our Life with The Rocket* (2002). To Carrier, the real world is contained in neither books nor hockey. Growing up in turbulent Quebec, hockey and books were escapes from real life, with its cold and its hunger and striking miners fighting Maurice Duplessis's police in Louiseville.

Once it's on the ice, hockey has no mining and only occasional police. Sometimes there's weather, wildlife only rarely. It does without commerce and cooking and real conversation. Affection is limited to the ritualized embraces after a goal is scored, and maybe some of that comes close to love, briefly. There's obviously no sex, except as it pertains to conditioning. Like Jack Adams in Detroit, Eddie Shore had his views on sex and hockey when he was running the show in Springfield: during a losing streak he'd call in players and wives to the dressing room to demand cutbacks until the team starting winning again.

Easier insisted upon than actually legislated, if hockey's fiction is any guide. Most of the love there is, prudently, practised with skates off. Not that the hockey ever drifts too far from mind. In *The Last Season*, Batterinski grunts and shunts with a girl called Lucille: "This was harder than starts and stops in practice." There's a case to be made that Don DeLillo's *Amazons* features more sex than hockey, though his narrator, Cleo, does seem to be able to maintain a high level of play even with all the fucking. Known, she narrates, for "her plucky work in the corners" as well as "her taut ass and firm breasts," she first hooks up with a tennis player (who falls asleep) before moving on to coaches, general managers, and defencemen ("I realized I had him effectively pinned. Like a player in a hockey fight."). Sounds licentious, but it's more playful than pornographic. Hockey makes men sexy, Cleo muses: "Years of physical stress have made the players look noble and battered and ancient Greeklike, except for goaltenders, who look like mounds of vanilla horsemeat, by and large." The sight of the defenceman's nicks and scars makes her think that "this would be like wartime sex with a fellow who was due to hit the beaches at dawn." But she reminds herself, "They were entertainment wounds, and nothing to get emotional about."

Life laps up to the edge of the rink, where it stops. Mike Keenan coached Wayne Gretzky at the 1987 Canada Cup, and he'd watch him make his way to practice through the thickets of retainers and reporters, poachers of autographs, and he saw Gretzky's eyes when he finally reached the ice—the peace that filled them when he could glide away from the grasping world. "It was the one domain where he was just free to play hockey, away from everything else."

The frontier between life and hockey is the opening faceoff. Or actually, no, before that, because where else do we stand and remove our hats to hear national anthems, ours and other people's? After that, real life takes its seat on one side of the glass while hockey goes about its business on the other. It's no great distance between the two, other than in the essential things: footing (frozen), time (hockey has its own big clock), what you can get away with (assault).

As coaches tell their players, history doesn't matter once the game has started. For all the money that surrounds the professional game, the politics, the branding, the selling, once the game starts, that's all part of what hockey shuts out. That's why the hockey we watch in the stands and on television and listen to on the radio doesn't deal in current events. Why should it? The whole point is that we've agreed here to a break from life. It's the pact that we make and that broadcasters uphold. It's why you get no mentions of Arctic sovereignty or appointments to the Supreme Court on *Hockey Night in Canada*. "How about that Keystone XL?" That's what I'd love to hear from the broadcast booth as we're waiting to watch the start of a playoff overtime, the score 4–4, Jonathan Quick just about to lead his Kings back on the ice to face the Rangers. Or: "Okay, Simmer, let me just hold you there on your Edward Snowden thoughts until we get a whistle here."

I don't know how much I want real life intervening on the rink, after all. Historically, when that happens it's mostly a case of a Richard Riot or a medical emergency.

And it's true that I'm still perplexed by the exception hockey makes for military operations in its ignore-the-world policy. For all the respect I have for the character and contributions of the armed services (a lot), I still need someone to explain to me the NHL's ever more prevalent eagerness to honour wars and warriors on the pre-game ice with light armoured vehicles and infantry rappelling from the rafters. After all the trouble hockey has taken to distance itself from real life, the connection isn't as explicit as we're supposed to believe.

A pair of books that appeared in the fall of 2013 detailed pivotal struggles that gripped the sport in the dawning years of the twentieth century. While Stephen Harper investigated the Athletic War, so-called, historian Craig Bowlsby bore down on the rule changes that transformed the game in *1913: The Year They Invented the Future of Hockey*. Both books also provided important backgrounds on an era when real life and hockey were almost one. Spectators kept close to the ice in those years. If you didn't like what you saw at Dey's Arena in 1912, you said so by throwing stuff, reaching for whatever was at hand, coins, shoes, fish. If the situation demanded it, you reached out and grabbed the cover-point as he skated by. Or ran out to chase the referee until the policemen came after you. That's just how it worked back in the good old golden days.

MAJOR FREDERIC McLAUGHLIN, who owned the Chicago Black Hawks from 1926 to 1944, had some strange ideas about hockey players. Max Bentley talked about this, the way McLaughlin measured their worth in terms other than how they played the game. He'd hold on to a middling defenceman for years because he was polite. "The Major," Bentley recalled, "had a tendency to rate his hockey players on personality, appearance, and their ability to talk." After home games, the Hawks were obliged to report to McLaughlin's office. "They sat in rows while the Major told them what was wrong with them, individually and collectively."

In 1940, Syl Apps had to decide between hockey and politics. "Right now," he said, "I don't know how I'll play hockey and conduct an election campaign at the same time." He ended up running for the federal National Government Party in the Ontario riding of Brant.

And lost. Which pleased Conn Smythe. (After hockey, Apps was elected to the Ontario Legislature.) The conflict implied could have been one of time and focus, but it leaves an opening for another explanation. Maybe the two just aren't compatible: politics is another realm altogether and hockey has no place there. Or maybe hockey had warped Apps so much already that it would have been impossible to straighten him out for serious work in Ottawa. Hockey is clearly the lesser calling, politics the more meaningful job, real adult work.

Other Leafs politicked and played at the same time, among them Howie Meeker and Red Kelly, who served as MPs in Ottawa. Referees used to tease Meeker: "Your Honour," they'd call him at faceoffs. Kelly believed that hockey prepares you for life. It's "a wonderful introduction," recommended to all, leaving you "better able to cope with various situations and personalities." There are two lessons you should take from hockey, he thought, "the ability to work with others and to get along with them," and anyone who learns those "is one up on life when he enters the business world." Also, keep your head. In hockey, you will be *dumped*. "There is no need to feel humiliation at attacking a check and being knocked down, and it will never help your cause one bit to lose your head over it."

"Life," wrote Vladislav Tretiak, "checks us for strength at every step."

In September of 2001, with Canadian players gathered in Calgary for a quick national team camp to help prepare for the following February's Olympics, word came from Montreal that Habs captain Saku Koivu had been diagnosed with abdominal cancer. "It's really demoralizing," said Keith Primeau. "Ultimately what we do is just play a game." Montreal team president Pierre Boivin said everybody was praying. "Everything else can wait for later," he said.

Mario Lemieux had survived cancer. Of Koivu he said, "He's always battling and hopefully that will translate into his private life." Koivu asked teammate Craig Rivet to bring him a copy of Lance

Armstrong's *It's Not About the Bike.* "I just think Saku wants to read something, a good story, that says there are other sports figures that do have these types of illnesses." Columnist Damien Cox said that stories of hockey-player disease and death add humanity to "a game that's often brutal and inhumane."

NHL training camps were getting going that week. In a couple of days the exhibition schedule would start. Then came Tuesday, September 11.

In New York, Rangers team members on their way to Madison Square Garden watched one of the World Trade Center towers drop. Some of their colleagues were in Penn Station scribbling autographs. Nobody knew what was happening. Eric Lindros called his parents to say he was okay. At 2:00 PM, the NHL's Manhattan head offices were evacuated.

In Toronto, Tie Domi wondered: What was the point of training camp? "What we do doesn't matter." But the Leafs were supposed to be heading out to Newfoundland. They'd already sent their equipment, so there was some planning to do. League officials wondered about the games coming up, cancel them or no?

The Ontario Hockey League postponed the start of its season. In Germany, the Nuremberg Ice Tigers voted not to play a scheduled game. Along with everyone else, hockey tried to find its feet. The papers asked psychologists about the value of sports in times like these. We need trivia, some columnists said, and a refuge from reality. People need to escape their fear and sadness.

IN *A BOY AT THE LEAFS' CAMP*, Bill Spunska takes a tentative first step into the big world beyond home and high school when he's invited to try out for the Leafs. He's eighteen now, and here he is, skating the Canadian dream, headed for his first big-league training camp in—it's true—Peterborough, Ontario. The fall there smells of burning leaves.

At the Leafs' hotel—I'm pretty certain it's the old Empress on Charlotte Street—the opportunity that has opened up to him is represented at the breakfast buffet. Here Bill sees more fruit than he could have imagined. It's a potent scene showing what it means to have arrived at the doorstep of your dreams: if there are this many apples and apricots at training camp, imagine the bounty waiting once you get to Toronto.

You begin to realize that hockey imposes certain restrictions of movement on novels. Basically, you've got the hockey on one side and life on the other. Yet the problems in life are in fact spilled-over problems from hockey. Bill gets into a hoo-ha with Benny Moore, a brutish winger. Is he also falling in love? Maybe, but this is kind of a hockey problem, too, insofar as Pam is a sister to the brute. So everything is routed through the rink. If he can overcome the difficulties there, well, life off the ice will be easy.

As in *Scrubs on Skates*, Bill lets go with a thunderous hit. Sends Benny Moore into next week, two postal codes over. It's nothing if not an attention-grabber and all good. But Bill, predictably, suffers an attack of conscience. The hockey men advise him not to worry, to lie low, say nothing. An old Leaf hand warns about the sportswriters who'll be spreading word of the feud across the country, those damnable writers, playing into the hands of the people who'd use the hit to raise the cry of *blood sport!* against good old hockey.

Here beginneth the lesson. Spunska is getting advice from all sides. Through it all, he keeps his head, which is useful, because he's about to make the most important commitment of his life, the one in which he vows never to hurt anyone. And that's it. Hockey doesn't matter as much as how you live your life: that's what Billy discovers in Peterborough.

A Boy at the Leafs' Camp ends in what I can only call a Canadian key. Bill doesn't make the team. His dream evaporates. But in Scott Young's telling, the opposite of success isn't necessarily failure. What if the dream is only postponed? And what if the alternative, the next step, is even better than what Peterborough offered? In the last few pages of the novel he finds out that the University of British Columbia wants him. Education shines its light all the way across the country. Not only that, but he can play in the Olympics. The Olympics! Bill goes out with a smile on his face and the promise of a sequel to fill with new exploits. To me (and I guess to Young), this is a much more satisfactory end than the obvious one, where Bill joins the Leafs and we follow him through a succession of novels, *A Youth Who Didn't Finish His Education on the Leafs' Blueline* and *Thirty-Two-Year-Old Journeyman Who Blew Out His Knee Traded to California Golden Seals for Future Considerations*. I don't know if it's everyone's idea of a happy hockey ending, though, or just the readers among us.

CURRENT EVENTS, AND LIFE, threatened to overwhelm hockey in 1936: they wouldn't leave hockey alone. Because it's impossible to measure the contamination of hockey by life in, say, parts-per-million, you're left to draw more of an impressionistic conclusion. Certainly in 1936 the Nazis were a big part of this; what they were doing then and were yet to do makes hockey seem like a fast-moving irrelevance. The Nazis themselves thought otherwise: they were only too pleased to use the Olympics (they had both winter and summer that year) to show off their uncanny Aryan superiority in all things involving sliding on ice and speeding through snow.

There's altogether too much Hitler in 1936, a foul glut of Herman Goering and Joseph Goebbels. Nazis menace the story of the

Sportbegeisterten: Goebbels and Hitler sign Olympic autographs during the Canada-U.S. game on February 16, 1936.

Olympic hockey tournament that took place that year in Garmisch-Partenkirchen, filling its photos with their madman smiles as they look down from the stands of the Kunsteisstadion, hanging a ghastly pall over the whole enterprise.

Can you winnow out the sophisticated evil of the Nazis looking on from the simple game they were watching? Is it possible to shift over as soon as this very sentence to a discussion of the Port Arthur Bearcats? "Canada's aroused puckmen" was what one paper called them, which sounds naughtier now than it would have done at the time. Elsewhere they're described as *determined* and *unperturbed*. Ahead of the Olympics, there was a great fuss involving who was going to play for Canada in Germany; it was supposed to be a Halifax team originally. Strong words were spoken, and at an exhibition game in the Nova Scotia capital the night before they sailed, fans tossed bottles at the interloper Olympians.

The three important non-Nazi-related lessons of the 1936 Olympics are (1) Canada lost; (2) the world didn't end; and (3) we didn't brood too much in defeat. Furthermore, in at least one of our games, against Hungary, the quality of the hockey was so soaringly high that spectators were fainting from pure bedazzlement. And not only spectators: the Hungarian goalie was overcome too, and had to be replaced. Can there be anything better than that in hockey? For all the praise lavished on Canada's golden team at the 2014 Sochi Olympics, theirs was never so wonderful a display that those of us watching couldn't stay conscious.

Going to Garmisch, Canadian teams had won all four previous Olympic hockey titles with ease, outscoring the opposition 209–8 as they did it. They'd sailed to those early Olympics on ships called *Melita* and *Montcalm* and *Arabic*. In 1936, the team boarded the *Duchess of Atholl*, steaming out past Chebucto Head with, quote, a quiet feeling of confidence and good fellowship. Experienced passengers had another name for the ship, the *Rocking Duchess*, so maybe the players expected the crossing to Liverpool to be as rough as it was. Herman Murray, the team captain, was sickest of the bunch.

News of King George v's death reached the ship mid-Atlantic, and the players went ashore wearing black armbands. In London, they joined the queue at Westminster Hall to pay their respects at the King's lying-in-state. I've seen a tantalizing reference to the team having attended the royal funeral, which can't be true, much as I like the notion of Bearcats clumping past the catafalque in St. George's Chapel, heads bowed, sticks raised. I do know that back home in the Dominion, Conn Smythe called up Frank Calder and the two men agreed to postpone the Leafs game against the Canadiens. In Shelburne, Ontario, the sad news arrived as a Junior game was about to start, and the players and spectators stood silent for two minutes, while outside a gale howled, and then everybody sang "God Save the King." In St. Catharines, a game between the Colonels and Merritton was halted and not resumed.

By the time the Canadians made it to Germany, the International Olympic Committee had convinced the Nazis to remove the roadsigns banning wild dogs and Jews from Garmisch.

The German coach—the *Reichstrainer*—was Saskatoon's own Val Hoffinger, who'd played a handful of games for the Chicago Black Hawks. Their manager was Bobby Bell, who probably wasn't the German spy the Belgian police thought he was in 1941 when they shot him. For six weeks leading up to the 1936 Olympics, the Germans had a *Lermanshaft*, a training team that eventually included eight Canadians. Hoffinger did his best to teach his boys the Canadian game. A reporter watching them before the Games noted that they had a tendency on the attack to swerve towards the corners, and they liked to grab their opponents' sticks, but nonetheless deemed them a "smooth-skating, thoroughly disciplined corps."

Another of the regime's thoughtful concessions was the presence on their squad of a right winger, helpfully identified by the *Toronto Daily Star* as the "non-Aryan" Rudi Ball. Any proof you needed that all was well in Germany, according to Avery Brundage, president of the U.S. Olympic committee, was there in the flesh thanks to Ball. The fans loved him, cheered him loudest of all. "The Nazis were fine," Brundage breezed when he got home. "You saw a lot of young fellows in uniform around Garmisch-Partenkirchen, but that's a sort of national whim these days. Just a whim."

Hitler presided over the opening ceremonies before a crowd of fifty thousand. In "glistening uniforms of red and white," the Canadians looked the smartest of the contingents, in the opinion of some Canadian journalists. *Der Reichskanzler* was a man, said *Time*, who'd never sat on a bobsled, but he looked proud as the bells rang and the cannons boomed and the army bands "tootled merrily."

As the athletes passed the reviewing stand, they gave the Olympic salute which, conveniently or not, involved raising up a straight right arm. Hitler liked it so much he straight-armed them back. The Americans were the only team not to salute. "Naturally we didn't get any cheers," said Brundage, who thought his team's uniforms made them look like streetcar conductors.

Then, hockey. The fifteen-team tournament started that same day, with the Americans suiting up against the hosts at the main stadium. Canada met the Poles in the afternoon over on the smaller of Garmisch's two rinks, out on the open ice of Lake Riessersee in front of a crowd of three hundred. The weather couldn't deter the Canadians, but it tried. "So heavy was the snowstorm," the *Star* reported, "the spectators saw more snow shovelling than hockey." They lost the puck at one point and it took a while to find—under the shoe of a rink attendant.

The Poles we taught an 8–1 lesson, with special emphasis on how to be shoved back "almost into their own net." Next day, the Latvians got an 11–0 schooling. There was another blizzard blowing as the teams took to the ice, but the sun came through when the game began. It was scarcely more than a workout for the Dominion puck-men. Our defencemen had so little to do that they joined the attack. Ah, but the innocence was almost at an end. Another storm, this one political, was brewing.

You'd think that after all the years of our helping the foreigners find their hockey way they'd thank us, or if they had no thanks, then at least play fair. We didn't mind Canadians playing for other teams, notably the British; what we didn't like was that their papers weren't in order. The goalie, for one, Jimmy Foster, who'd worked in the CPR yards in Winnipeg and played for the Moncton Hawks, fine, good for him, best of luck. But Jimmy, and Alex Archer, too, a defenceman, had neglected to obtain proper permissions from Canadian hockey authorities before signing up to play for Great Britain. For this, they'd been suspended in Canada. Letters had gone out from said authorities the previous fall, noting that the suspensions travelled with the players, but the British had failed to uphold those sanctions. We weren't happy either about being made to look like the villains of the piece when we objected.

There was a vote. Foster and Archer were ruled ineligible for Olympic play. Out! In response, the entire British team threatened to withdraw from the tournament. It was all a big shame, said Lou Marsh in Toronto's *Daily Star*; the players just wanted to play hockey, but there you go, sorry, boys, safe trip home, see you later. Except that almost as quickly as Canada had made its point, we let the whole matter drop. Never mind! Magnanimous once again, the Canadian delegation said Foster and Archer could skate after all. *No problemo! Our pleasure!*

On Saturday, February 8, the Canadians played a morning game at 10:30, which was off-putting, the coach had to admit, and that's probably why we could muster only a modest rout. Instead of hammering the Austrians, the best we could manage was a bleary malleting, 5–2. That night, the Americans lost to the Italians. The hockey cognoscenti agreed: Uncle Sam hadn't sent a strong team. The *Star* relayed the news home: "Canada should experience little difficulty retaining the championship."

Also in the news that week at home: according to Harold Varney, the minister of a small independent congregation in Toronto, Armageddon was coming, and fast. The part-time prophet had been studying his Bible and making calculations. Canada would have time to play three last games, but by the end of the week, before any medals were awarded, God was going to put an end to the world.

One of the last-ever editions of the *Globe* carried even worse news next morning. "We are feeling pretty sick here today," Matthew Halton wrote from Germany. It's not that Canada didn't deserve to win; in fact, we did everything right. "Hockey managers dream of players who back-check like fiends, are on the puck like lightning and who keep play in the opponents' territory all through the game," Halton wrote. "Such a team was Canada last night. Beyond doubt they played rings around England for 80 per cent of the game—but they lost."

The score was 2–1. It was a story of goalies, two goalie stories side by side, ours first, then theirs. Dinty Moore wore the maple leaf, from Port Colborne, Ontario. What nobody writing for a Canadian news-paper could understand was how he could have let that first puck pass him, a mere thirty seconds into the game. A *sneaker* they called it, there had to be an explanation. Maybe (wrote one columnist) "Dinty had just lamped a new blonde in the grandstand . . . or the snow got in his eyes?" A British forward named Gerry Davey had grabbed the puck, shrugged off the flu (he'd been sick in bed before the game), shot, scored. He was out beyond the blueline.

Canada's Ralph St. Germain then tied it up. After that it was all Jimmy Foster. *Impregnable*, he was called. And *thousand-eyed. The wonder goalkeeper, remarkable for the size of his hands.* He was nick-named the Parson. A *withering puck bombardment* ensued, but despite the *avalanche of pucks* under which the Canadians all but buried him, he would not, *in his super-brilliance,* be pregnated. Rush upon rush, the Candians *steamed* into British ice, their *cunning tactics* and *great speed bewildered* the Britons time and again, only for Foster to turn them back *as if by black magic.*

This was the Canadian view, anyway. In days to come the history we wrote as losers expanded on the theme of just how Canadian the

British team really was—just as an interesting bit of trivia, of course, and not by way of griping or guffawing, much less crying foul.

Twelve minutes from the end, Gordon Dailley (Winnipeg-born) tore in on Dinty Moore, feinted him to the side, and flicked a pass to Chirp Brenchley for the winning goal.

The Canadian manager had no excuses to make for the Canadian defeat. No squawk would he raise regarding British players who were really Canadians and never should have been playing in the first place. Marsh wrote:

> The lesson is plain . . . Canada will have to do as the other nations are doing . . . select and train a real all-star team to carry the red Maple Leafs in future Olympic hockey tournaments. Canada has a good team over there . . . one that should, and probably will, win out . . . but we could have been represented by a stronger side.

Back at home, the *Star* went to the streets to see what the citizens of the nation thought about the big fluke. Chin up, no doubt the loss would put a spur to our boys. That's what Ace Bailey thought. "The defeat should sharpen them," he said. Still, who better to beat us than the Brits? That was another sentiment that came up, hurrah for Great olde Britain! When else would we be able to say that *Kid England* had whipped *Battling Canada* and welcome to it! We were disappointed, sure, but also we were elated. And maybe this strong joy was what powered the *Star* to send up north to a municipal office where British goal scorer Gerry Davey's birth certificate showed that he was born in Port Arthur and even if that didn't make him a turncoat and charlatan, he too had departed our ice without the proper transfers.

We still had a chance to win the Olympics. We played the Hungarians next, beat them 11–0, with everybody fainting. We played the

Germans and the Americans, too, and though we played well, and won those games, the gold medal went to the British.

If this had been 1972 in Moscow, the oceans would have risen while the earth quaked. In 1936 in Germany, we said, *Not a worry!* We were gracious and humble in defeat. As a people we said, *You know what? That was fun. Just to see you guys loving hockey so much is such a great gift to us. And all the Canadians who've gone over to your countries and you've made them feel at home and given them jobs, that's great of you to have done that, too. So that's about all, except to say, Can't wait to get together in four years' time to do it all again. See you in Sapporo in 1940!*

Everybody had a great time that week. Hitler was at a lot of the games, with Goering and Dr. Goebbels, who dressed up in Daniel Boone frontier garb for some of them. At the Canada game with the U.S., Herr Hitler signed autographs. Of all the unlikely photographs from 1936, there's one of this scene that I keep going back to with a strange fascination. It's a view of the good seats, sun shining down, everybody looks warm and relaxed. They're all smiling, except for the young ss officer with the death's head insignia on his cap sitting directly behind Hitler. Because down below, in front of the stand showing the Olympic rings, a crowd is gathered and they're handing up postcards and notebooks and Goebbels is signing a card for the man in the soft hat with the tartan scarf. Hitler is a little harder to read. The photographer has caught him in the middle of accepting a notebook from the hockey-gloved hand of an unidentifiable Canadian player. Unless it's Hitler handing down *his* autograph book. They're both smiling.

I don't know how many hockey games Hitler saw in Garmisch, but he kept coming back. Goering seems to have loved the game. Goebbels stood up to calm the crowd when they booed Canadian bodychecks. On the Sunday we beat the United States 1–0 on a goal from Dave Neville. There was good feeling between the two teams, notwithstanding the violent mix-up in front of the Canadian net, where Ray

Milton lost several teeth. Hitler's favourite player was American Phil Labatte, touted as French Canadian though he was actually born in Minneapolis, star of the Baltimore Orioles of the U.S. Eastern Amateur League. "Hitler applauded Labatte frequently during the joust," reporters noted.

Hockey-maddened, Hitler is said to have taken a keen interest in the field game at Berlin's Summer Olympics later that same year. The final had India beating Germany 8–1 in a squally wind, with Dhyan Chand scoring six goals and losing one tooth. Chand's adjectives include *clever*, *dazzling*, *barefoot*, and *greatest of all time*. Hitler's that day are supposed to have run to *frustrated* and *angry*; he's said to have left the game early in his disgust. Next day, though, he summoned Chand to his box at the Olympic Stadium, where he showed him the view and invited him to come and live in Germany. Supposedly. A lot of field hockey people don't think it ever happened. Others say that when Chand said that he was a soldier in the Indian Army, Hitler offered him a commission in the Wehrmacht—as a field marshal, says one source, confidently.

Back in Toronto, on that final Friday night, intrepid reporters had waited outside the prophet Harold Varney's door to see the heavens crash down. As the days passed, Varney had some tricky questions to answer. He'd made some mistakes, he admitted, his Bible-math was a little off. "The Almighty has seen fit to grant an extension of time so that those who are not right with God can get that way." Reporters who'd been at his house wondered why he had put his bottles out Friday night for the milkman, with the hellfire on its way.

"You know," he said, "it is just like the Lord to give us a little longer." Every day now was a day of grace. God wasn't angry. People could laugh. "I expect judgment day to start at any hour ... Might not the storms reported in all parts of the world be an indication of the beginning of the end?"

[Second]

I'm telling you boys / This game is so fuckin simple.
STEPHEN SCRIVER (1981)

THIS IS NOT the book I was planning to write. That book was going to be called *Ear to the Ice*, and it was meant to focus on what happened in 1972, complete with bold conclusions to the effect that rather than glorify our game and ennoble us as a nation, what the Canada-Soviet experience did was tarnish and taint and shame us, exposing us as blowhards and bullies and—I had a whole indictment scaffolded up. Sticking with the internal medicine/hockey model, I was prepared to conclude that, really, the only way to think about the Summit was (and is) as a virulent national stomach virus from which we've never fully recovered. I wanted to understand why, for as long as it's been our passion, hockey has never really reflected so well on our national reason and probity. For the title, I had in mind the cowboy trick of listening to railway tracks for distant reverberations. If you think about laying your actual ear down on the ice, though, that's where the title begins to fail, especially if there's any kind of actual hockey going on nearby. If you don't get a skate in the head, it'll be a puck. That scotched *Ear to the Ice*.

There was a Walter Gretzky book I never wrote, too. When Wayne's dad was planning an autobiography, I auditioned for the job of ghosting it. The hockey, obviously, was to be a big part of it, but mostly it was a survival story, Walter having suffered a stroke and recovered.

This was explained to me, first by the publisher, next by the man from the Heart & Stroke Foundation who met me in a murmurous under-lit restaurant in Brantford, near the salad bar, on a gleaming bright spring day. This was the first of my vettings. It was like descending into a cave, that restaurant, and we sat there looking at one another by the reflected light of carrots and whittled radishes. When I'd passed the restaurant test, I moved on to the house that Wayne built. The family home, anyway: a perfectly regular house on a perfectly pleasant small-town street with three black and lustrous Lincoln Continentals parked in the driveway.

Walter wasn't home, and neither was Phyllis. The next of my vettings was conducted by Wayne's brother Glen, whose career statistics you won't find anywhere online. We chatted. It made sense that he was expecting me to come with readymade notions of what kind of book Walter and I would be writing, a prepared vision. It made sense, yes, but no one had told me. I had ideas, but not as many as I would have had if I'd prepared, plus it was hard to concentrate. Glen had to move the Continentals from time to time, there was some kind of a parking situation that only Glen was authorized to resolve, and I'd chat for a minute to Glen's girlfriend, then back again to the book, until another Gretzky walked in. I met sister Kim as she passed through, and brother Keith, too. Gretzkys kept appearing from door-ways, down staircases, it was like a play we were in, a dress rehearsal of Beckett's lesser-known *Waiting for Brent*. (Spoiler alert: he never shows.) And after a while of not really having very good answers for Glen, more and more my mind roamed towards the basement stairs. I could see them from the couch: they were right there. Maybe could we pop down and look at the memorabilia? Walter Gretzky's base-ment is second in fame only to his backyard rink, which we did see, or at least the physical space the famous ice had once occupied. It's dedicated now to a swimming pool. Looking at the pool, not far from the top of the stairs, was as close as I got to seeing Wayne's trophies in Walter's basement.

Later, when the publisher called to say they were going with another writer, I think I may have regretted the burst I didn't make down those stairs more than the book I didn't get to write with the man I never met. They thought you were maybe too interested in the hockey, is what the publisher told me. Nothing wrong with that, she said, perhaps they just wanted someone who could balance it more with the heart and the stroke.

And the 1972 book? Well, 1972 wasn't the problem. Yes, it did kind of leave me cold and prone to wincing once I started catching up on what had happened, watching all the games in real time, reading all the books already published on the subject. The truth is, I missed 1972, the original one, so I have none of the foundational memories of those who were there, school cancelled for the afternoon, everybody in the gym watching the TV they wheeled in, *Henderson scores for Canada!* Nothing. Remember, says my friend Evan, the rumour about Tretiak? What rumour? "The reason he was so good was that the Russians had all his ligaments removed." I have to shake my head. Evan knows it's just the kind of the thing I'd love to be remembering. "The great part is," he says, "we had no idea what ligaments were."

Abroad was where I was, taken on sabbatical with my parents, both academics. I was six years old, so I had to go along, my brother and sister, too. We lived in an English village, across the bridge, turn right at the pub, down the long pebbly drive. The pub had a name, the Greyhound, and so did the house, as houses abroad sometimes do when you're six years old: Tanglewood. There was a brick well in the big garden and a wood and a roaming tortoise named Ferdinand. Back near the bridge was the riverbank from *The Wind in the Willows*, and beyond that, the house where Kenneth Grahame wrote about it, including winter scenes, though no hockey. We watched the river that year, same as Ratty and Mole, but it wouldn't freeze.

I had no idea what I was missing, being abroad, nobody having taken the trouble to tell me about the hockey history that was about to be made in Canada and the USSR. This may have been part of the plan. What I didn't know I didn't worry about. And it's not as though I didn't have new interests in England—for instance, tracking down roving tortoises and epic games of kick-the-can at the vicarage. I also took a furious interest in Lord Nelson and what he'd done at the Battle of Trafalgar with just one arm and a single eye and not very much of his life left to live.

In E.M. Forster's novels, anxious mothers whisk their young daughters out of the country at the slightest hint that they might be in danger of falling in love with the wrong young men. Later, briefly, I wondered if that sort of thing might have happened to me. Maybe my parents had somehow foreseen the way it was going to unfold, all the ugliness of 1972 that no parent could hope to explain, the jingoism and the slashing, chairs thrown onto the ice, throat-cutting gestures. They knew they couldn't fight with my blood, teeming as it was with hockey. Had they decided to leave the country to prevent their six-year-old from seeing the Soviets toy with our Canadian professionals and—worse still—how the professionals would respond?

I phoned my mother, gave her the conspiracy pitch. She laughed. "No," she said.

I asked my father, "Were we keeping up with the hockey while we were over there?" He thought about this. "Keeping up how?" I don't know. Radio Canada International. Taking the train to London to read day-old *Globe and Mail*s at Canada House. "No. Could be. Possibly."

It's not as if it would have been easy for him, with his hockey past, captain of the team, Smoothy Smith of yore. He would have had to have been fighting the hockey in his blood in 1972 to exile himself like that.

By the time we left for England, hockey was everything to me. In 1972, other than going to school, hockey was all I was doing. When I wasn't lining up on the ice for All Saints, I was playing road hockey in Dave Bodrug's driveway or knee hockey in Peter Wearing's basement. I studied *The Hockey Encyclopedia* with a young monk's devotion. Ian Lamont and I, serious stockpilers of hockey cards, would fill entire weekends with endless bonspiels of leansies, topsies, and farthies. We played pretty much continuously from 1971 through 1975, when I gave all my cards away—a huge mistake, I realized almost at once, triggered by the false impression that nine was the age at which you outgrow both hockey cards and the foresight to hang onto them long enough to sell them on eBay, whenever it might be invented. I hadn't yet learned any of the aphorisms about the place hockey colonizes in Canadian society, our hearth and our heartbeat, our national conversation, our theatre, our daily bread, the church where we worship, our very faith and creed—I didn't need to know any of that, because my blood knew.

The sheer broadside brutality of the Royal Navy's fighting fleet circa 1805 served me well during that year in England, fulfilling my need for obsession, and for that I'm grateful. When we got back home to Canada in the spring, though, it was all hockey again. I don't have much of a memory of the summer of 1973, but I'm assuming some of it was spent absorbing the free-floating atmospheric national joy left over from when we'd beaten the Soviets. Friends must have told me what happened, if only so I could play my part in the road-hockey reconstructions. Without knowing much about it, I was pleased and proud. We'd won, hadn't we?

That's the thing about hockey-blood, it updates automatically, like the operating system on my Mac.

THERE WERE FOUR games in four Canadian cities in September of 1972, you'll remember, four more in the enemy capital. At home, we lost two, won one, tied another. We lost again in Moscow, then won the final three games. No need to worry about the three European exhibition games. Final score: yay us!

I came to fret about how it had all played out: the shock of that opening loss, the nation's agitation, distraught Phil Esposito, bad Bobby Clarke, overwrought Paul Henderson. No sooner had I consoled myself by recalling the skill with which Pete Mahovlich scored short-handed in Game 2 than I'd happen on some ugly reminder of how messy the whole enterprise was: Canadian allegations, for instance, from Game 7 that Vladimir Vikulov kicked Yvan Cournoyer (once) and Gary Bergman (five times). I was irked at first when I read about a Polish reporter in Moscow who told his readers that because the Canadians, so much older than their Soviet opponents, were still somehow faster and stronger and more spirited, it probably meant they were on drugs. Later, though, I wondered whether this wasn't a kind of a compliment: to some, our healthy, free-range hockey looks hopped-up.

I loved the stories about how the devilish Soviets schemed to steal the three hundred steaks and eight thousand beers Team Canada brought to Moscow. (We also imported two hundred litres of Finnish milk.) And I continue to revere the sweaty rawness of Esposito's Vancouver speech — "To the people across Canada: we tried, we gave it our best" — after the home crowd booed the Canadian loss. The desperate wheedling heartfelt passion of his plea was like the voice of the country giving itself a talking-to.

Icy niceties: Alexander Ragulin (left) discusses the situation with Canada's voluble Phil Esposito during Moscow's Game 7, September 26, 1972.

I was thoroughly chuffed to read, without entirely believing, that on the day of the final game, not only did Canada's federal election freeze in its tracks, but crime and punishment, too, as courts were adjourned and the crime rate dropped to nothing. I lapped up new Summit Series books as fast as they appeared, from Dave Bidini's tiny radiant *A Wild Stab for It* (2012) to the no-stat-left-behind immensity of Richard Bendell's *1972: The Summit Series*, published that same year.

I finally watched the games, loading in the DVDs over the course of a weekend up north. My wife, Sarah, checked in on the score now and again, and so did the friends who were staying. Mostly it was just me and my friends' eight-year-old son glued to the thirty-six-year-old TV feed from Finland. It was all new to him, too, though he knew things I didn't. "Bobby Orr is playing for the Russians," he mentioned halfway through the first period of Game 5. Nothing I could say would convince him otherwise. Before I brought in the books to contradict him, he'd identified Orr on the ice and—*fine, have it your way, he looks good, doesn't he?* We were both disappointed when Paul Henderson scored, but I told him not to worry, there was still another game to go. "The Russians win," I said. I later felt terrible about that.

In truth, Orr hadn't been healthy enough to play. Dave Keon's absence concerned me too; he should have been on the team, shouldn't he? Not to mention Bobby Hull and, on the Soviet side, Anatoli Firsov. I wished Anatoli Tarasov was still coaching the Soviets instead of having been dismissed for murky reasons earlier that year.

These contributed to my disaffection, as did the mayhem of the two Swedish games we played in between Vancouver and Moscow. And also:

- The brazen blinkered Canadian arrogance beforehand where everybody confidently predicted that we'd win every game (Alan Eagleson expected an eight-game sweep).
- Clarke's slash on Kharlamov's ankle in the sixth game, cruel, calculated, witless, along with all the post-slash justifying and remorselessness and general lack of Canadian outrage.
- Harry Sinden, in his book *Hockey Showdown* (1972), dissing anybody who doubted, deplored, or second-guessed Team Canada: "I feel sorry for these people. I know many of them, and they all have one thing in common—they're losers. And they'll be losers all their lives."
- Paul Henderson, in his book, reporting how he ran into the Soviet goalie, Tretiak, in a hallway after the final game and told Tretiak to go to hell. That seemed unnecessary.

- The suggestion in *Canada Russia '72*, the dramatized mini-series that retold the Summit on CBC in 2006, that our team was 75 per cent boors and jerks. What if that were non-fiction?

And the Canadian team left the ice after the devastating opening game in Montreal without shaking hands. Everybody thought we were soreheads, admitted coach Harry Sinden later, but, hey, who knew you were supposed to shake? Other than Ken Dryden: *he* shook hands. You learn only when you lose, Dryden said. He couldn't believe it, but not a single NHL team sent scouts to the games in Toronto and Montreal. "Setbacks can be very useful in sport, since they help analyze correctly your flops and excite the striving for revenge," said Tarasov. "For some unknown reason, defeats do not worry the Canadian hockey leaders."

I was left queasy by the idea that in winning, Canada had planted a secret seed in Russian hockey, the noxious weed that grew inside their game and choked it. Bobby Clarke has suggested as much:

It used to be that when two national teams would get out on the ice, you could see the difference in styles immediately. Now everybody plays the same type of hockey. And it's the North American type. In our time Soviet players never dumped the puck into the zone. They would rather turn around at the blue line and pass backwards to start a play all over again. Now they do it our way more often. I think that after 1972 the Russians learned that it's more effective to get the puck into the opposite end and play physical hockey there.

After the Montreal game, Ken Dryden questioned whether he would *ever* be able to cope with Russians. Wandering the city, he ate terrible hamburgers in an awful restaurant. He wondered whether it was all a bad dream. He ran into the Montreal sportswriter Red

Fisher, who was as bereft as he was. They both felt as though something had been taken away from them.

They needn't have worried, of course, because twenty-six days later, Canada was crime-free and triumphant. Bobby Orr said that it proved we were the best hockey players in the world. For the games in Canada, he opined, the only real problem had been conditioning. Asked about Canada's many Moscow penalties, he said, "Players like Paul Henderson, Gary Bergman, and Bobby Clarke never look for trouble in the NHL. If they're losing their tempers here there must be some reason for it."

I CONFESS THAT I didn't read a single hockey book either on the nine-and-half-hour flight from Toronto to Moscow or during the week I spent in Russia in the summer of 1997, following the hockey players. There were three of them: Viacheslav Fetisov, Vyacheslav Kozlov, and Igor Larionov. They were Detroit Red Wings at this point, and having won the Stanley Cup that spring, they were exercising the champions' right to take the trophy home to meet the family. As big a deal as it was for the NHL and Moscow, it was a much bigger one for Larionov and Fetisov, legends of Soviet hockey who'd also railed against the strictures of its systems. After a long struggle they'd escaped—soon enough that their giant talents weren't exhausted when they came to play in North America. Both had written autobiographies, and I was looking forward to sitting down in Moscow to talk to them about the journeys they'd taken and the hockey they'd played.

And one day, maybe, that will happen. In Moscow, only once did I see the hockey players seated; the rest of the time they were on the move, enclosed by crowds of family, friends, NHL officials, owners of the Detroit Red Wings, journalists and photographers, fans, startled tourists who wondered what the fuss was about, and a few of the young army recruits you used to see loitering all over Moscow at that time (often by car windows asking for money when the traffic lights turned red). When I wasn't grumbling at the hangers-on who were blocking my view of the hockey players, I did my best to get out of the way of those people whose view I was obscuring. The night I did manage to shake Igor Larionov's hand, we were in a Canadian bar, the Hungry Duck, where the beer was Labatt's. "Congratulations," I said, just before he sat down at a table with no place at it for me.

WHATEVER ELSE RUSSIAN blood contains, hockey wasn't in the mix originally: it had to be introduced. There's a song they sing some-times at Russian hockey games—you can find it on YouTube—that includes the verse:

> The most fitting game for our Russian guys
> Was accidentally born in Canada

The story of how Russians came to hockey is altogether clearer than ours, but it does come with a bit of a tangled-up provenance, some mist, and a Chekhovian touch of men arguing offstage. Here's how I under-stand it. Before 1946, Russians mostly played soccer in the summer and bandy—*russki hokkei*—when winter came. They'd been doing it, in one form or another, since Peter the Great's time. *Canatsky hokkei* (ours) wasn't unknown, especially in the Baltics, but mostly they ban-died, chasing a ball, with eleven-man teams skating on a rink the size of a soccer field. Sticks were short and curled and wrapped in cord.

What happened in 1946? Possibly it was a case of Moscow Dynamo, the famous soccer club, touring Britain in 1945 and in their spare time attending a game in which visiting (probably military)

Canadians were playing hockey. Like so many others before and later, they were captivated. Clarence Campbell, still a soldier, was in England at this time, prosecuting Nazi war criminals, and that's what *he* thought happened.

Ah, the Soviets. They had such a hockey plan, a big one, which was more or less the same as their foreign policy: they wanted to rule the world as soon as possible. Hockey-wise (if not geopolitically), we thought they were adorable, trying so hard with their funny helmets and their aluminum shin pads. At first the notice we paid was none. The next stage was when they started to look pretty good and we thought, *Not bad*. They got better and better. They started beating the teams we sent over to Europe, which was kind of rude, especially since we're talking here about the East York Lyndhursts. It wasn't as if they were beating our best teams. Not that we'd even bother to play them with our best teams. What would be the point?

When the first league started up in December of 1946, some of the players had never seen a puck before. The plan was to run a season lasting two months. Boris Kulagin was one of the draftees. "We did not have big crowds," the coach of the 1972 Soviet team said, "and we were seen as some kind of fools for playing a completely alien game." Vsevolod Bobrov was one of the stars of the Moscow Dynamo soccer team when it travelled to London in 1945. When he took up hockey, he was bewildered, helpless. However, he floundered but briefly; soon "he made the puck obey him."

An American writer named Drew Middleton went to see an early Moscow game in January of 1947: Red Army versus Dynamo. He reported that they might give a New Jersey high school team a good match "on an off-day for the latter." A player shouted "please!" to a teammate when he wanted a pass. In the intermission, a song called "Let Mother Discover We Are in Love" gusted from the loudspeakers. In his opinion, neither Red Army nor Dynamo would be going anywhere fast until they dispensed with the long woollen underwear they wore in favour of proper hockey togs. "The drawers," Middleton wrote, "seemed to get in the way."

At the rink at the Moscow Physical Training Institute, the boards were just six inches high. Local journalists who watched couldn't get a grasp on the game. Players struggled to lift the puck off the ice. The new stick was a puzzle. The blade was absurd. Bandy goalies go stickless, so to have one thrust on them was irritating. They couldn't get used to it. They flung it away.

"We learned the game out of a void," Anatoli Tarasov wrote.

Kulagin tells of an early Canadian offer to send coaches, but the hockey authorities agreed that the best way to learn the game was by themselves, organically, free of foreign additives. Although another version of this is that when the Soviets proposed to Canadian officials an exchange of coaches after the 1954 World Championships, they were snubbed. No one would come to watch Russians play in Canada, they said they were told.

At home, there were those who said that Canadian hockey was folly. Boris Arkadyev, the national soccer coach, for one. Writing in the newspaper *Sovsport*, he reproved those who, he said, wished to "bury alive" the Russian form of the game, which he recommended as a more practical winter pastime for soccer players.

Tarasov was one of the Russian hockey pioneers, players "of the first call-up" is his phrase. Later, North Americans came to hear about his dominion over the Soviet game, to size him up as the Plato of Russian hockey, and maybe also its Dalai Lama. The first defencemen of Soviet hockey never hit. There was no ramming, Tarasov writes. "They played quite a soft game, almost gentle." Sometimes they felt awkward, embarrassed, playing rough teams. They stayed calm. There was no retaliation. They were considerate. Patience would win. "Victory, we thought, is good compensation for injustice."

This didn't necessarily last.

The first real test came in the third February of Russian (Canadian) hockey in 1948, when LTC Prague arrived in Moscow to play a series of exhibitions. Too soon, some said. Tarasov was one of the organizing coaches. His brother Yuri played, and so did Bobrov. Elbow pads and knee pads were "cotton wads," and players wore soccer shin pads. "Helmets and cups were non-existent in our country in those days," Tarasov notes. The only skates they had were long-bladed. But from bandy they brought speed and pinpoint passing. Tarasov says they won that first game—6–3—on desire alone. Collectivism and valour perplexed the Czechs.

The first indoor rink in the Soviet Union didn't open until 1956. No worries. "The players," said Tarasov, "felt much better on outdoor rinks with a slight wind and frost." If you read the Russian hockey books in translation, there's plenty of lusty ideology: *Ice hockey is the display of a man's best qualities: kindness and courage, fidelity to one's comrades and moral stamina.* There's no mention of violence. A lot of tough talk, yes, but it's mostly in a theoretical vein, so that when Alfred Kuchevsky says "ice hockey is a fight," he doesn't mean a punching-fight so much as "an opportunity to prove that you're stronger than your opponent. To prove you're a real man." When the other fighting does come up, it's a perplexity—"sometimes the spectators are puzzled: isn't there too much rudeness in the game?"—or a disgrace to the game. "Respect towards one's rival does not allow a player to behave dishonestly, to attack, for instance, a player who falls down."

"Personally, I seek happiness in ice hockey," confides Alexander Ragulin, Merited Master of Sports.

Eventually, reading the Russian hockey books you can without a translator's help, you get to the secret. It's a wonder they give it up so readily.

[E]ven when the boys leave hockey they will take into life with them the most valuable human qualities acquired in the game: a readiness to help your team-mate, friendship.

Hockey helps a young man enter adult life strong and courageous.

There is also a feed-back in this sport, however—most significant success comes to kind-hearted and good people, to those who honestly and faithfully serve the interest of their team, their teammates.

ON THE MORNING of the day I followed the hockey players to Voskresensk, I walked along the Moscow River down below the Kremlin and tried to take a photograph of the man with the small brown bear on a leash. The man nodded when I gestured with my camera and I was all ready to go until he spoke what may have been his only English words: *fifty bucks.* I probably would have paid if this were a hockey-playing bear; as it was, I kept going, on to the Metropole Hotel. With a reporter from the *Detroit Free Press,* I spent my money on hiring a driver instead. In his big mustard-coloured Mercedes with no seat-belts, the three of us headed out of the city, downriver, following Larionov and Kozlov as they carried the Cup to see their hometown, an hour or so to the southeast. (Fetisov is a Muscovite.) On the road, the North Americans in the car discussed everything from anxiety and fear to the possible cultural reasons why we had to drive so fast and pass every last slow-moving beet truck on the highway when oncoming traffic was equally fast-speeding and constant.

In addition to the beets, we outran the minivan carrying the Stanley Cup. We came into Voskresensk through the concrete district, slowing down briefly in the dusty-car quarter. On the far side of town the sky was filled with fuming clouds so thick that smoke-stacks had formed underneath, dangling like stalactites. A crowd was already gathered at the rink when we got there. As we pulled up, they gave us a cheer that died of disappointment as soon as they realized we had no hockey players with us and no silverware to show off.

Over and beyond Larionov and Kozlov, the list of local hockey talent is long, and lush with surnames like Ragulin, Kamensky, Markov, Zelepukin. You can't really help but echo the question that's at the front, if not the centre, of Larionov's autobiography: Why *is* Voskresensk the hockey capital of the world? It is remarkably Peterboronov when it comes to size and proximity to a larger city. Rivers help define both cities (Otonabee v. Moscow), as do industries (Quaker Oats and General Electric in Peterborough v. chemical works for Voskresensk—the hockey team is called Khimik, or Chemists). With several dozen other people, I climbed up to the roof of the Sports Palace for a better view. It wasn't much: trees and drifting dust, rooftops, cloves of church steeples. Larionov refers to the city as *out of the way* and *God forsaken* (*sic*). According to him, the reason he and others found and thrived at hockey here comes down to one man, a famous coach with a passion: Nikolai Epshtein. That's it; that's all. Nothing in the water here but heavy metals.

Cheering greeted the Cup in its minivan, along with swarming and reaching and rubbing. If it's true that you'll never win the Cup if you touch it without having played for it properly in the NHL, then I watched a whole generation of Russian children and their mothers curse themselves below me. Inside, the rink was modest, smaller than the Memorial Centre at home. I may have been hoping for a big Lenin portrait down at the far end; there was none. It was as dim and as close as the inside of a dryer, and it took a moment, coming in from the rooftop, to see that there was second crowd waiting in here in the stands. On the ice, Minor-leaguers in yellow Khimik uniforms stood beside stooped bemedalled veterans and, over by the penalty boxes, a battalion of drum majorettes.

I don't know that the speeches touched on the history of Russia going back to the first tsars, but they did go on for a long time. If they included any jokes, no one was laughing. I walked around the ice taking pictures of old soldiers and young goalies, at the risk of offending the majorettes.

Later I read that Larionov's grandfather spent fourteen years in a labour camp for something unflattering he said about Stalin. His family paid, too. They were banned from Moscow and exiled south to the chemical city.

BECAUSE IT WAS written in my notebook that Valeri Kharlamov was born "near the Sokol subway stop," I went there to take a look, once we got back to the capital. In 1948, his mother was in an ambulance on her way to Maternity Hospital Number 16 when he was born. For me, it was a fifty-minute round-trip from the hotel, and while there was nothing really to see when I surfaced from underground, just more low sandy-coloured blocks of apartments and many grim un-crossable lanes of traffic, I felt like it was worth the journey.

I've read as much as I can about Kharlamov, and if I end up learning Russian it will be to start on his autobiography, Хоккей—моя стихия (1977). A measure of his importance that's greater than any paltry pilgrimage of mine is the minor planet that's named after him. Proper Canadian procedure for honouring hockey players is insistently terrestrial: we raise monuments, sometimes we brand rinks or roads. As Wayne Gretzky, you get it all: statues in Los Angeles and Edmonton, a Drive in Edmonton and a Way in Toronto, and in hometown Brantford, a Parkway and a Sports Centre. Kharlamov's eponymous Ice Palace is in Klin, northwest of the capital. I didn't get there, and I can't say where in the cosmos his planet is, or what its atmosphere might be like, though I do know its number: 10675. If I wanted to guess, I'd say that it looks not unlike the geographer's planet in The Little Prince.

Late as I was in acquiring them, lots of my best 1972 memories are of Kharlamov, who introduced himself that first game in September by scoring a pair of sublime goals. Canadian coach Harry Sinden says that the only emotion the Russians showed that night came when Phil Esposito punched one of them in the face—and the guy grinned. Sinden doesn't say who it was, but I can't help casting Kharlamov in the role, smiling with sincere unruly happiness rather than mockery or sarcasm. Kharlamov's first goal stunned our team with its magnificence, though they didn't want to let on at the time. "He's a helluva hockey player," Sinden was finally able to concede.

Once we discovered him, Canadians liked how tough Kharlamov was. He had sand, he had sinew, he was as resilient as he was imaginative. *This Chagall of hockey*, wrote Lawrence Martin; *the deadly little scorer*, Frank Orr called him. "He had more moves than Nureyev," Ken Dryden said. Harold Ballard wanted to pay CSKA Moscow a million dollars to bring him to Toronto. Kharlamov's was the wrong generation, though: it was the next one that managed to leave the Soviet Union behind.

If he couldn't come to play for Western cash or Stanley Cups, we in Canada nonetheless showed our appreciation with our sticks and our hips and our elbows. I'm sure it didn't feel like it at the time, but in Game 6, when Bobby Clarke axed at Kharlamov's already injured ankle, he delivered on our behalf the highest hockey honour we could bestow: a Sher-Wood Order of Merit to go with his Soviet Medal of Labour Valour. In film and fable, Clarke was under orders, though he's denied it. Either way, it wasn't a random hobbling. Clarke's chop was specific and heartfelt, guaranteeing the honouree a lifetime's supply of admiring Canadian abuse, renewable any time his team came to North America.

Descriptions of Kharlamov's goals often have the word *dancing* in them, and sometimes the phrase *he loved to stickhandle*. Against the

Toronto Marlboros in 1975 he scored a goal that because you weren't there to see it, you just would not believe, unless you watch a lot of *Star Trek*. "It was as if he had disintegrated on his way over the blue line," Jim Proudfoot wrote, "only to reassemble his molecules on Palmateer's doorstep. Better plays are just not made."

Vladislav Tretiak said his effort, the way he strove to be the best, should be taught in every hockey school. In personality, said Tretiak, he was like the great cosmonaut Yuri Gagarin: "similarly unaffected, bright, and modest. Fame did not influence his character—he remained benevolent, open to all, cheerful, and always smiling." His favourite food was pancakes. In Montreal in 1972, Dryden noticed that he drank six or seven Cokes for breakfast, same again at lunch and supper. When he came to lunch, the mood of the team changed: everyone laughed.

Later Jim Proudfoot reported that the Canadian players were calling him "the Derek Sanderson of Moscow" for all the "punishment" he dealt out to everybody who approached him. In return, the Canadians accorded him "a thorough going over." This subtle narrative, that Kharlamov got what he deserved, is picked up in *Canada Russia '72*. Movie-Bobby Clarke hates him from the start. "Eat shit, you little prick," is Clarke's first—only?—line in the whole epic. Later, we watch assistant coach John Ferguson whispering in Clarke's ear. Movie-Paul Henderson looks horrified.

In 1974, when the WHA took a team to Moscow for the less-famous follow-up with the Soviets, Canadian defenceman Rick Ley felt he'd suffered insult and indignity from Kharlamov after the sixth game's final whistle. Canada had lost 5–2 and Kharlamov had "jostled" and grinned at Ley. So Ley didn't hesitate to punch him to the ice. Actually, the newspaper reports say he *flew* at him, punching with both hands, continuing the onslaught when Kharlamov was down. If Soviet coach Boris Kulagin didn't understand the nuances of our Kharlamovian rituals—"Under Soviet law, he should be jailed for fifteen days for attacking and injuring our player," he said—the man himself knew what was going on. The next day, Ley was waiting for him after practice. *Sorry*, he said, *for punching you in the face, nothing personal, just got frustrated.* Kharlamov said he understood. The two men shook hands.

Ed Van Impe was the last Canadian to remind him of our national respect, I think. This was in the game in Philadelphia in January of 1976, just after CSKA played its famous New Year's Eve game against the Canadiens in Montreal. Van Impe dropped Kharlamov to the ice with a nasty blindside check. When no penalty was called, the Russians refused to play on. They came back, under protest, to lose. Another Flyer defenceman, Moose Dupont, said he thought Kharlamov was playing Hamlet when he went down. "They're not so great," he said. "They looked like fools today." That February in Innsbruck, Kharlamov scored the goal that won the Soviets the Olympic gold medal.

He got married in the spring. Two weeks later, Kharlamov and his wife were in their car on the Leningradskoye, the road of his birth. The car swerved off the road and hit a pole. Kharlamov's legs were broken just above the ankles, his ribs were fractured, his brain concussed. All that summer he lay in a hospital bed. As soon as he could walk he was at practice. "I was good at first, not so good later," he said. In 1981, still active with CSKA, he and his wife were involved in another highway collision; this one killed them both. Kharlamov was thirty-three.

The back of a Russian DVD I watched bears this frail found poem of an English translation:

We should be proud,
that in our country of veins
such person

and hockey player
Valeri Kharlamov.
Twice Olympic champion,
the eightfold world champion and
the sevenfold champion of the Europe.
Its game amazed imagination.
In its life was a lot of fatal and mystical.
Valeri was born in the machine
and has died too in the machine,
in the age of 33th years.
It was the unique person. It all loved.

The Stanley Cup and I met up again a few more times before we had to head home to Toronto. There was a press conference at the Ministry of Sport and a big buffet lunch (with caviar and vodka) at the CSKA Hockey School. We attended a hockey game together, too, which is where I bought my white CCCP sweater that I still wear for shinny, number 8, with Larionov's name across the shoulders.

On the Monday, we took a walk on Red Square, just me and the Cup and dozens of its admirers. I'd been in to see Lenin a few days earlier on my own, and I had no real desire to gaze at his slumbering raw-potato face again or to be hurried along by the guards in the big hats who refused to answer questions asked in English about how often he changed his spotted tie. Still, I would have been glad to go back with Fetisov if he'd invited me to join his wife and kids when they took the Stanley Cup in for their private visit with the Chairman of the Council of People's Commissars of the Soviet Union. In life, the last thing Lenin would have known about it, assuming he was paying attention before he died in January of 1924, was that Frank Nighbor's Ottawa Senators were looking like a good bet to repeat as champions.

EIGHT YEARS IT took the Russians to catch up on the ice. Back in Canada we'd developed a cruel model for Europeans embracing hockey. First we welcomed the acolytes, arms open, big hug for loving our game. We gave them as much support as possible, sticks and pucks and skates, coaches, mentors, all on the condition that they never rose as a hockey-playing nation to anything above mediocrity. As with the pesky North Koreans and their nuclear program, we insisted on being allowed to send inspectors every once in a while to beat them 22–0 and thereby verify that they weren't producing weapons-grade hockey that would one day devastate our pride and dignity.

This worked well, year after year. Until the spring of 1954. *Hockey Pictorial* framed the health crisis that was developing thousands of miles way:

Hockey's Biggest Headache:
What *Will* Canada *Do*
About Moscow?

The East York Lyndhursts had travelled to Stockholm to represent Canada in the World Championships. The Lyndhursts were a Senior B team from Toronto and they did fine right up until the final, when they met Moscow Dynamo. *Hockey Pictorial*'s Bob Hesketh described the distress that resulted back home:

Startled Canadians choked on their breakfast cereal as they split their morning papers at the sport page and read that Russia had defeated Canada in a game of hockey. Smugness fell inert to the floor as though it had been struck by a poison dart.

The score was 7–2. When the second-place Lyndhursts straggled back home, the men from the morning papers were waiting. First to touch down in the terminal was centreman Eric Unger. Reporters discovered him in the bathroom at the Malton airport, where they squeezed a confession out of him. "I don't know whether I should say this or not, but they outplayed us by more than five goals in that one game." The Soviets weren't good stickhandlers, but they could skate and they sure knew how to pass. On their bench during the game, they had twelve guys in black coats and black fedoras. At the hotel, the players wore track shoes with no laces—Unger didn't know whether maybe that was part of their training.

The Swedish fans had been pro-Russian, as was the press. When Lyndhursts goalie Don Lockhart disembarked, he revealed that all the Soviet shots he'd faced had no fakery in them, they shot straight on. "If they played our rules, we could knock them flying." They were so weak, another player said, that even the Czechs could have beaten them, if they hadn't laid back. Right winger Bill Shill was covered in Russian bruises from Russian sticks. "They have plenty of speed but no actual hockey ability," he said. Their equipment was pretty poor, and too much—they even wore a belly pad. "I would have liked to have taken them on in a four-of-seven series," Eric Unger said before the reporters let him go home.

Conn Smythe had a better idea: the Toronto Maple Leafs would go to Moscow that very May to take on all comers as long as one of them was Moscow Dynamo. It wouldn't cost the Soviet Union a ruble, this generous offer of international hockey goodwill. The chairman of the board of Maple Leaf Gardens fired off a cable to the Soviet ambassador in Ottawa to seek permission. This was "a national blot," he said, and it needed to be cleansed. Smythe's assistant, Hap Day, wasn't so sure. He was going on holidays after the season ended, not to Russia. And the coach, King Clancy, had to work. He could only go, he said, if Russia was within seven miles of Ottawa, where his construction business needed him. Clarence Campbell worried that the team would end up trapped behind the Iron Curtain. In the meantime, a fan could dream, and so could a capitalist. Watch out, Red Square, for Ted Kennedy! Hey, Nevsky Prospekt! Ever met Tim Horton? All our vengeful behemoths, over there, unblotting the nation. Rudy Migay! Fern Flaman!

It just wasn't to be, though, and almost as soon as it was proposed, the plan had to be stowed. Not that the Leafs weren't welcome, the Russians politely said, it was just that by the time they got there in May, all the rinks in Moscow would be melted.

SWEDEN HAD THE words for hockey before it got the actual game: I picture them drifting like catkins over snow, waiting for their future to arrive, *smäll* (whack), *klampa* (clump), *sus* (swish), *slagsmål* (rough house), *slagsmål* (scuffle), and *slagsmål* (fisticuffs).

The Swedes didn't need hockey. They were doing fine, in 1920, with none. I don't know what it is about their national blood that resisted it, but for years of Swedish history, the people did extremely well with football and skiing, and also bandy. The bandy microbe was coursing strongly in the national bloodstream for a long time before the men with hockey in mind met at a Stockholm restaurant in 1919.

They were three: a sportswriter, the guy in charge of Swedish soccer, and an American former speedskater who worked for MGM. With the first Winter Olympics coming up in less than a year, you'd think maybe they'd elect to take it slowly, go to Belgium to observe, aim for the 1924 Olympics. No. They couldn't wait. Hockey—*ishockey*—was too good to resist. They wanted in. I just wonder, if they'd known the pain that lay ahead, the abuse Swedish hockey was in for, would that have squashed their enthusiasm?

There was lots of good stuff to come as well, though—and glory. There would be Sven Tumba and Ulf Sterner, not to mention Peter Forsberg, and what about Olympic gold medals and the Sedin twins and Henrik Zetterberg? Tumba's hockey books include the not-so-definitive *Tumba säger allt* (*Tumba Says It All*) from 1958 and 1995's *Mitt rika liv eller den nakna sanningen* (*My Rich Life or The Naked Truth*), for neither one of which have I, to date, collected enough Swedish to read. Tumba was the first European-trained player to be invited to an NHL training camp, in 1957, but when he didn't make the team, he decided not to sign a contract with the Minor-league Quebec Aces, which would mean losing his amateur status. He went home.

It was *going* to be great. Except for, somehow, the Swedes would have years of Canadian derision to navigate, invective, slurs, punching. We called them "Chicken Swedes" and our crowds chanted: "Kill the Swede!" We didn't like them. It's better now, but it's only fairly recently that we decided to forgive the Swedes for whatever it was we felt they did to us in the course of embracing hockey. Was it something they said in 1920? Did they look at the Winnipeg Falcons the wrong way as they succumbed 12–1 in Antwerp?

Is there solace in the fact that we looked down our noses for so long at the Americans, too, even as we played in their cities in front of their paying customers? Playing for Boston in 1926, Duke Keats said that 99 per cent of American fans had not the foggiest idea what was going on in front of them. Steering the Rangers in 1928, Lester Patrick pointed out that American players didn't start out skating early enough, which was why they couldn't develop a proper *full-leg stride*, so you could always tell what they were going to do on the ice.

If anything, the Swedes played as Canadianly as we did right from the start. The Russians might have refused our coaches, insisted on going it alone, but the Swedes were all too willing to follow in our tracks. Before they arrived in Belgium, they only ever practised with bandy sticks and a rubber ball. They wore no shin pads. What they lacked in finesse, they made up for in ardour. "They didn't spare one another in practice," reported a Canadian observer, "but smashed and crashed each other into the boards without the slightest hesitation."

The very first game they played in 1920—it was actually the first game ever in Olympic hockey history—they swamped the poor Belgians 8–0. The home crowd didn't like their tactics, which were described as *rough and ready*: they knocked down any Belgian as soon as he got the puck and the Canadian referee had to ask them not to carry their sticks so high. When the Falcons got home, they said the Swedes would be hard to beat in a year's time. They'd joined the Czechs in buying all the Americans' equipment and tried to buy the Canadians', too.

So that was encouraging. It had to make us proud. Why then, after that, is the rink of our dealings with the Swedes so littered with *kiv* (squabble) and *ruskighet* (nastiness)? I'm not talking here about the early rudeness of wallopings—22–0 in 1924; 11–0 in 1928—but of the increasingly hostile attitude we took to the Swedes.

They were always whining, said the president of the Ontario Hockey Association in 1961 when the Trail Smoke Eaters toured Sweden and defenceman Darryl Sly was charged by police for assaulting a Swede on the ice. You never heard a peep out of the Czechs or the Russians; maybe the answer was to avoid Sweden altogether. Sly, for his part, said the reason that Swedes got hurt was that they were soft.

"This is not hockey," Swedish papers said. Next time, maybe, they'd have to bring in Sweden's national boxing squad.

The Swedes buckled down, studied harder. While the Soviets and Czechs went to war at the 1969 World Championships, the under-card featured Sweden undoing Canada 5–1. Afterwards, the Swedes bemoaned Canada's rough play. Swedish coach Arne Stromberg complained about the refereeing and catalogued his wounded: "This was not one of our best games. Our team was trying to avoid being slaughtered by these boys."

Ulf Sterner was speared under the arm "and the blood flowed constantly." Lars-Erik Sjoberg had "a broken lip." Sterner returned to knee Canadian goalie Wayne Stephenson, who left the game with a bad charley horse.

It's hard to say when the counterattack had begun in earnest. As early as 1949, when the Sudbury Wolves travelled to Stockholm for the World Championships, the local press called them "dangerous men." When it was time to play the home team, thousands of fans tried to prevent the Canadians from entering the rink. (Maybe. The fans may simply have been trying to get in themselves.) The game, a 2–2 tie, was "bitter." On the second Swedish goal, a spectator reached over the boards and held Joe Tergesen's stick. Police had to escort the Canadians in and out of their dressing room.

"We in Europe are trying to make ice hockey a little more human," said a Swedish official. "We do not like the North American tendency to brutalize the game."

They were crafty, those Swedes. In 1965, they tried to outflank us psychologically, with the announcement from their national hockey federation that money was being set aside to provide financial assistance to Canadian amateur hockey, essential as it was to the well-being of world hockey, if sadly underfunded. *Fuck you very much,* Canada said.

In 1969, a Canadian ex-pat living in Stockholm explained the attitude of the Swedish press: "Canadian hockey ranks probably somewhere below the slaughter of baby seals." He kept a scrapbook that he'd filled with local newspaper clippings devoted to Canadian visits over the years. In 1968, the newspaper *Aftonbladet* sent a lawyer to the rink to watch the Canadian Nationals. He cited nine instances where players would be charged if they'd done what they did off the ice instead of on.

In 1973, the Toronto Maple Leafs signed two stars of Swedish hockey, Inge Hammarstrom and Borje Salming. For their first road game of the season, the Swedes got to visit Philadelphia. Dave Schultz punched Salming whenever he got the chance. "I don't think they like Swedish boys," Salming said. "They don't play hard, they play dirty. But it's no problem." Flyers defenceman Ed Van Impe, who took a five-minute penalty for spearing Salming, said it was accidental—he was falling at the time.

Here's what Anatoli Tarasov had to say about Ulf Sterner:

> Can anyone else in world hockey, including the professionals, pass the puck with such skilled faking, with such precisely judged force? His passes are not only mathematically precise, timed just right, but they are very easy to receive; it comes to the blade of a teammate's stick almost as if carried by hand.

The Rangers signed Sterner in 1964, then sent him down to the Minors, beckoning him back when he started to score. The *Washington Post* reported: "The rugged Canadians who dominate professional hockey consider it a matter of routine to give any rookie the test—a physical pounding, both legal and illegal."

It was said he couldn't get used to the hitting. The Rangers played harder against him in practice, he said, than they did against the opposition in games. Down with the farm team in Omaha, he put the puck in his own net on a delayed penalty, and oh, how the North Americans laughed.

"I like rough hockey," he would say, and then, waving his stick: "But this I don't like."

Eventually he gave up. "I suspect that Ulfie has never recovered from his NHL experience," said Ken Dryden. And that seems to have been the case. In 1963, he clobbered a Swedish fan with his stick, which he also later used to attack a Finnish opponent. In both cases the talk that he'd end up in jail came to nothing. He was suspended for two months in 1970 for punching a referee. In 1972, it was Sterner who cut Wayne Cashman's tongue in two with his stick.

THE REVEREND MR. Wood wasn't attacking the game itself. We should be clear about that. His complaint was precision itself, a finger pointing out a specific transgression, a matter of timing, rather than a general indictment. Just a strong opinion, judging from the report in the *Canadian Independent* in 1890.

It was a winter's Sunday in Ottawa, and at the Congregational Church at the corner of Elgin and Albert, Reverend Wood gave a Bible reading on the law of God in regard to the Sabbath and the example of the Saviour and His apostles to its observance. Word had come from the governor general's residence, Rideau Hall, that people were playing Sunday hockey on the vice-regal grounds. Wood didn't like to believe it, but how could he ignore the letter in the paper from someone who'd taken part and "gloried in his shame"? It was unbelievable. Set aside God for a moment: What would Queen Victoria think? "He was sure Her Majesty would not allow such a thing in the grounds of Windsor Castle." On he railed. Wealth, he reminded the congregation, was no excuse: the divine laws apply to rich as to poor.

It's good for hockey, healthy even, to sit in the pews and listen to the naysayers. Because there are, no doubt, plenty of people who have problems with the game, and not just in terms of Sabbath-breaking.

It helps to look the doubters in the eye, and to hear their concerns. Maybe we can help them. The thing, I think, is to distinguish the veins of complaint, to separate the merely indifferent from the mildly irked, the fatally bored from the outright haters.

Roger Angell says that "bad hockey is the worst of all spectator sports." The fact that Angell, venerable, veteran *New Yorker* writer and editor, has chosen to illuminate baseball more than hockey in his career is disappointing, but at least he's a fan. More worrying are those who've looked to the ice and felt nothing. Maybe they just haven't seen enough hockey or haven't seen the right kind. For all those, like Faulkner, who've seen the game and misconstrued, misunderstood, or malspoken it, how many innocents are there who just need a bit of tutoring, as opposed to those we should outright ignore?

Take Pierre de Coubertin, the French founder of the modern Olympics, for instance. This is more of a slight than an outright insult, and a slight slight at that. De Coubertin believed—there's an entire article he wrote about this in 1909—that hockey was no more than a means to an end. Hockey had no mental or moral qualities, or if it did, they didn't matter. The only reason to play hockey was to improve your skating. You know how fencing on horseback makes you a better rider? No, I hadn't heard that one, either. Same sort of thing, though. Hockey teaches the skater how to start, stop, pirouette, jump. Also boosts your mettle: "The hockey player fears no obstacle and willingly launches himself into the unknown."

There are those who only see hockey as a scourge to skating. An article in an 1863 edition of a British magazine waxed this way, starting with this ode: "I do believe that skating is the nearest approach to flying of which the human being is as yet capable." So why ruin it? The hockey here is the massed antique version, fifty or a hundred people chasing a ball over frozen glens and ponds—and wrong, wrong,

wrong. It's unworthy of the *true skater's attention*, an illegitimate use of the skate, and worse, the writer says cricket is *degraded* when it's played on ice. "I should be truly glad," he finishes, with a flourish, "to see the police interfere whenever hockey is commenced."

Put-downs by smart people we thought of as friends stab at the chests of those of us who love the game, if I may speak for the group. Maybe because he himself likes Canadians, the American novelist Richard Ford leaves it to his character Frank Bascombe to call hockey an uninteresting game played by Canadians that's only redeemed because a sportswriter friend of his can sometimes make it seem more than uninteresting. That stings, especially the fine-tuned implication that *Canadians* is a sufficient insult all on its own.

It's not as if we can't take a joke. We love jokes. We'd just like to be sure that a joke *is* a joke and not just the kind of slur American writer Roy Blount Jr. perpetrates when he says, "Personally, I love NASCAR about as much as I do hockey. The only thing that would get me to watch a car race on TV would be if they ran over a hockey player every couple of laps."

Bunny Ahearne always did hate us, so much so that he master-minded the robbery (by confusing rules) of Olympic gold in 1936, plus here was (another) foreigner who never played the game and (also) unless your last name is Larocque, Bunny just isn't going to fly as a first name. For all those reasons, we can ignore what the vitriolic president of the International Ice Hockey Federation said when we'd beaten the Soviets in 1972. "I don't think the Canadians will wake up. They're too small-minded. Now they'll start to think up alibis."

Alexander Solzhenitsyn isn't so easily shrugged off. In *The Gulag Archipelago*, he poses this question: If you are arrested by the KGB, interrogated in the Lubyanka, pressed to incriminate your friend, what do you talk about instead? Not the latest arrests. Not collective farms.

It is fine if you talked about hockey—that, friends, is in all cases the least troublesome! Or about women, or even about science. Then you can repeat what was said. (Science is not too far removed from hockey, but in our time everything to do with science is classified information and they may get you for a violation of the Decree on Revealing State Secrets.)

In all cases the least troublesome. To have it suggested that hockey doesn't matter, even if it's a help to someone under KGB interrogation? That hurts.

Once again comes the fear that there just isn't enough grist in hockey for writers to mill. We worry that the emperor has no clothes. Or is it what the game reveals about us—its votaries, its guardians, its apologists—that we fear? It's in our sensitive national nature that when someone criticizes the game that's ours, we suspect—we fear— that somehow our own tacit decree on revealing state secrets has been violated. It doesn't even have to be criticism. Sometimes just getting a glimpse of how others size us up can be demoralizing. One short paragraph in German can be enough, if it's like the one in Karl Adolf Scherer's history of the International Ice Hockey Federation. It's in the chapter called "Eishockey Mutterland Kanada," a seductive phrase in its own right, and one that I defy you not to bark at the next person who walks into the room. Towards the end of the chapter, Scherer confides,

Die Kanadier sind die Erfinder des Körpereinsatzes (Bodycheck), der Strafbank und der allgemeinen Zuchschauer-Auffassassung, daß körperlos spielende Athleten "Drückeberger" sind.

O, Kanadier. This is us?

The Canadians were the inventors of the bodycheck, the penalty bench (the "sin bin" or "cooler") and the widespread view of fans that athletes who shirk bodily contact are "pansies."

ULF STERNER ENDED up suing hockey. Not hockey, directly. Hockey would not be putting up a defence or paying any damages. In 2008, at the age of sixty-seven, he launched a lawsuit in Sweden against his insurance fund in order to win damages for injuries he'd suffered during his playing career. He said, "I will go all the way to the European Court of Justice, if necessary." What sounds better is to say that he sued hockey for hurting him so much, which it did; specifically, his spine, ankles, hips, and elbows. At one point he could barely get out of bed in the morning. These were occupational injuries, he told the court when the time came. And the court agreed, awarding him an annuity as compensation.

So hockey hurts. This is easy to say, and it's even easier to feel. In today's NHL, you don't talk about injuries, not out of delicacy but as a matter of operational security. Is it going to aid and abet the New York Rangers if you let on that Carey Price torqued his medial collateral ligament? Maybe not, but safer to call it a *Lower Body Injury* anyway.

In Finland, hockey used to hurt less. In a study comparing the incidence, type, and mechanisms of hockey injuries in that country from the 1970s through to the 1990s, it was discovered that due to a rise in the rate of "checking and unintentional collision," contusions and sprains were increasing significantly decade after decade.

Ted Green's wife noted an odd thing: players seem to be *tickled pink* when they get injured. "It's the nature of the beast, I suppose."

How do you know, in hockey, when you're hurt? This is a tricky problem. In regular life, the blood and the pain flag it for you, letting you know to stop what you're doing and summon a doctor. In hockey, not so much: you see blood, you keep going. Feeling fine? That's when you have to worry. Philadelphia Flyers coach Bill Barber at the start of the 2002 playoffs: "If you're healthy, if you're totally bruise-free, maybe you shouldn't be in the lineup."

The least of hockey aches would have to be a puck in the skate, *bees in the boot*. *Lace bite* sounds benign, but it's awful, an affliction of dorsal tendons that makes tying your skates extremely painful. Don't underestimate the *hip pointer* (*höften pekkare* in Swedish). *Back spasms*, I have no doubt, feel worse than they sound.

An unredacted register of injured NHLers from January of 2000 catalogues bruised Dave Reids, fractured Jere Lehtinens, and wonky-kneed Grant Fuhrs. *Hamstrung, sore, lacerated, sprained, partially torn, contused, herniated,* and *compressed,* Bob Essensa, Mark Janssens, Derian Hatcher, Antti Aalto, Brian Skrudland, Kirk Maltby, Sean Burke, and Frank Musil waited for their respective hamstrings, backs, calf muscles, ankles, left elbows, chests, thumb ligaments, abdomens, and vertebrae to heal up. Meanwhile, a groin epidemic was sweeping the continent, a contagion linking Dominik Hasek, Jamie Allison, Joe Hulbig, Steve Staios, Jean-Yves Leroux, Peter Popovic, Sean Hill, Grant Marshall, Craig Rivet, and Darren Langdon in a belt-range band of discomfort that they'd probably prefer not to have us dwell on in too much detail.

I DON'T THINK goalposts hated Howie Morenz—there's no good proof of that. From time to time they hurt him, but you could reasonably argue that in those cases he was as much to blame as they were. Did they go out of their way to *attack* him? I don't believe it. What could the goalposts possibly have had against poor old Howie?

Morenz was speedy and didn't back down and, well, he was Morenz, so other teams paid him a lot of what still gets called *attention*, the hockey version of which differs from the regular real-life stuff in that it can often be elbow-shaped and/or crafted out of second-growth ash, graphite, or titanium. But whether your name is Morenz or something plainer and hardly adjectived at all, doesn't matter, the story's the same: the game is out to get you.

In 1924, his first season as a professional, Morenz developed stiffness against Ottawa, before badly bruising a hip just before he won his first Stanley Cup. In February of 1926, he hurt an ankle in a goal-post crash. A month later, playing Pittsburgh, he had to be carted from the ice after bruising the same ankle in a collision with the Big Train himself, Lionel Conacher.

Morenz went into another post in late 1927. Opening night, Madison Square Garden: fans in fur and finery, the West Point Army Band, New York's mayor was there to drop the puck between Morenz and the Amerks' Billy Burch. Early on, Burch banged up a knee in what looked like a serious way while Morenz stayed around long enough to score a pair of goals. The *smash-up* in the second period does sound like a highway disaster: six players went down in the Canadiens' net. "Driven against the stout iron support," Morenz suffered "a severe bruise on his left side and possible kidney injury."

Hec Kilrea slashed him over the head in Ottawa in 1928, not really but maybe sort of on purpose. Three years later, Boston's Eddie Shore smote him on the *fore*head, though it was Shore's teammate, George Owen, who got the blame and the penalty. With Kilrea, he and Morenz were "exchanging compliments." Then (from the *Ottawa Citizen*):

Morenz turned Kilrea around completely with a jab in the mouth, and as the blonde left winger was whirling, his stick caught Morenz over the right temple, inflicting a gash of about two inches.

Four stitches bound the wound; Morenz returned in the third period. Kilrea said he was *very* sorry; Morenz told reporters Kilrea wasn't the type to injure a man deliberately. "Bright particular star of the Canadien sextet," the *New York Times* was saying a few days later, Morenz was still sporting plasters, "although his brain is said to be functioning fairly well."

How did he keep going?

- November, 1930: nursing severely strained back.
- January, 1931: hurt an ankle playing the Rangers and — cautious — checked into Sir Henry Gray's Hospital in Montreal. Suffering from a sore wrist at this time, too, as well as a charley horse.
- April, 1931: Chicago's Taffy Abel caught him heavily on the shoulder; "in fairly bad shape."

In 1934, he damaged his left ankle in a Maroons-related incident then, next game, there was a tangle in the Rangers' goalmouth and maybe the post dunnit, maybe not, Morenz's ankle was twisted, badly, again. Back at St. Henry Gray's again, doctors applied a cast he kept for a month. In February, he skated, carefully, and started on his way back to finding his old form.

Is it worth noting here that he gave as good as he got? Or, another way of looking at it: playing hockey, you're at risk not only of getting hurt but of hurting others. For Morenz, this meant:

- March, 1930: clashed with Chicago's Ty Arbour behind the net. Arbour went off with torn ligament, Morenz to the penalty bench.
- April, 1931: Chicago again. Skating with Tom Cook at centre ice. "Morenz flung the light Hawk player to the ice, hurting his face. Both were penalized and Chuck Gardiner skated up to protest."

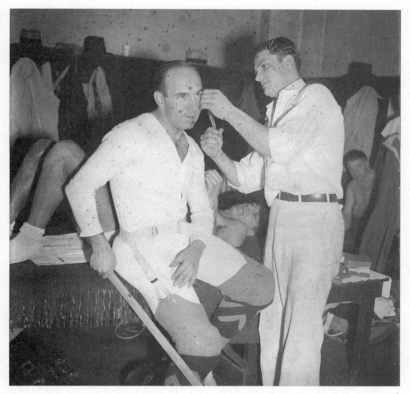

Sew there: Chicago's Howie Morenz takes stitches in a Boston dressing room in the mid-1930s.

- March, 1934: Morenz would surely have incurred another of his goalpost injuries if he hadn't crashed into Detroit goalie Normie Smith while scoring on him. Wounded "about the head," Smith left the game to spend four months in hospital to heal his fractures.

It was Morenz, too, who broke Clint Benedict's nose with a shot in 1930, forcing the Maroons goalie out of the game and, a little while later, out of his career. I'm not saying that was Morenz's fault: the evidence seems to show that Benedict's nerves were already well crushed. A month later, when he returned, he was wearing the nose-guard that may or may not have been the NHL's first goalie mask. It looked strange and vexed Benedict's vision so much that he's supposed to have discarded it before the game against Ottawa, that March, when someone fell on him. He decided to retire. Possibly another shot of Morenz's might have caught him in the throat at some point in here, too.

Can we agree, also, that Morenz didn't necessarily need hockey to hurt himself?

In 1932, he had his mother-in-law staying over at his house in Montreal, 4420 Coolbrook Avenue. Streetview it on Google and you can imagine him standing there on the porch surveying—actually, no, not really. Too many silver Hondas and Kias parked in front, now, all those twenty-first-century strewn garbage bins. It looks like a pleasant street, calm and leafy.

Morenz drove Mrs. Stewart home to her house on Jeanne-Mance, not far, a grey street on the day Google scoped by, with its trees looking spindly. Turn the view around and you can admire the big cross up on Mont-Royal.

Possibly Mrs. Stewart was giving Morenz hockey advice all the way home, stuff he wasn't hearing anywhere else, and he took it, too, and prospered, and no one ever knew but them. You don't know. Without a photograph at hand, you're free to assign her a prim, tweedy, bespectacled look, but is that fair? The door of her house was unlocked when they got there. In they walked. Mrs. Stewart turned on the light and that's when the tall man stepped out from behind the door with a revolver in hand. He said either "Give me money" or "Give me money before I shoot you." Accounts vary.

Morenz stayed cool. The season had been over for a month, but he still had his hockey wits about him. He told the guy, careful with that gun. He said, "If you shoot Mrs. S. you'll be in the hoosegow a long time." Not those exact words, but close. Did the guy know who it was, threatening him with hypothetical jail sentences? Was he a tall Habs fan? Impossible to say. We do know that Morenz jumped him. Think of that! Little Morenz! He pulled down the guy's over-coat—smart—partially *trussing him*. This all has to have been fast and frenzied; newspaper accounts slow it to sludge. The *thug*, they said. He got an arm free and *slashed* Morenz "several times over the head and temple." With a hockey stick no one previously noticed? No: the gun. He added another bash as he shed his coat, then he was gone, running south on Jeanne-Mance, disappearing down Fairmont.

Mrs. Stewart telephoned the police. Special constables Geraldeau and Laroche came immediately. From reading too many Tintin books, I see Morenz sitting on the floor, legs splayed, hand to head, stars and punctuation and musical notes orbiting. He gave the policemen a good description of the suspect: thirty-fiveish, dark suit, grey fedora. They couldn't figure out how the guy got in. In his abandoned coat they found a flashlight. The cut on Morenz's head looked bad, but he said he was okay with some first aid. He didn't go to the hospital.

Also, back in 1928, while Morenz was golfing at Montreal's Forest Hill course, lightning just missed him. There was a sharp crackle, a flash; the club he'd been about to swing was left twisted and split. Morenz and his caddy both said they felt a jolt.

A *SCRAP* IS what happens when, in 1973, Norm Dube of the Kansas City Scouts tries to clear Minnesota's Dennis O'Brien from the front of the net and they *tangle*, resulting in five-minute majors. Except that O'Brien doesn't want to let the matter drop, forcing the referee to send him to the dressing room, but instead of going there, O'Brien goes after Dube again. Hockey has lots of different words for fights: *fireworks* and *bouts*, *spats* and *imbroglios*. It used to have *shindigs* and *tong wars* and *schemozzles*, great words all.

Hockey likes to drape the spectacle of its millionaires wailing fists into one another's skulls with words that cloak the stupidity, smudge the inanity into harmlessness. *Chucking the knuckles* sounds kind of fun, like a game at a summer fair. *Dropping the mittens*. *Tilt* is a hockey-fight word, and so too are *bout* and *set-to*. An *argy-bargy* is a soccer hoo-ha, as much as it sounds like another name for the Falklands War. A Canadian version might be *argle-bargle*, which has a hockey air to it; in fact, it's defined as the sound made by seabirds. We've already decided that *donnybrook* is foreign and obsolete. A *scuffle, altercation, melee*; or how about *brouhaha*? The *extra-curricular*, Craig Simpson sometimes says on *Hockey Night in Canada*, suggesting chess club or mathletics. Clarence Campbell preferred the respectable Marquis-of-Queensberry formality of *fisticuffs*. As in: "I have been in hockey forty years," he said in 1971, "and I can think of only one incident in which a man has been seriously injured in a personal fisticuffs by a punch in the nose."

In Chicago in 1953, during a disagreement between Black Hawks and Bruins, the attendant manning the door to one of the benches took fright and abandoned his post. The players fell into the Chicago bench area and were rolling about, among them my old History teacher, Mr. Armstrong. That was a *rumpus*.

A *fracas* is what happens in Paris, France, on a Sunday in 1933, when a visiting Toronto team loses the game, then gets into a *kerfuffle* at a restaurant with some locals that sends a defenceman to hospital and the coach, Harold Ballard, to police court.

Dropping the buckets is hockey terminology associated, usually, with an intention to *chuck the knuckles*.

They're throwing them from Port Arthur is an admiring phrase you might have heard Don Cherry use to approve a particularly vivid fight. The five reasons to throw, according to one who threw: (1) an opponent ill-treats one of your stars or (2) they abuse your goalie; (3) you want to change the momentum of the game or (4) you're trying goad the other team into a penalty; or (5) you don't like someone.

Jokey terms for fighters: *head-boppers*, *pot-stirrers*, *Bob Gainey's new windup toy*. Players not known for fighting who drop their gloves sometimes come in for gentle ribbing, as in: hey, did you catch the *powder puff* between Spezza and Markov?

Goon is another funny word, though not necessarily one that the goons themselves like to be called. It does carry big baggage, it's true, a whole Samsonite's worth of unflattering definitions: "stupid or oafish person," for one, derived from *gony* ("simpleton," 1850). Or the term applied by sailors to the albatross and similar large, clumsy birds (1839). Or in the sense of "hired thug," first noted in 1938, probably with a nod to Alice the Goon, a muscle-bound dull-wit in E.C. Segar's original Popeye comic strip.

You don't call a goon a *goon*, because if you do, Bob Probert's wife might tell you that you don't know him and you don't know hockey. *Rent-a-goon* is no better. *Heavyweight? Tough guy? Badman* used to be a popular term, in reference to Bad Joe Hall or Sprague Cleghorn, or (in 1956) Lou Fontinato, who was a *blockbuster*, giving a *larruping* Ted Lindsay a run for his money in riot-producing badman honours. The list of badmen carries on: Billy Coutu, Eddie Shore, Red Horner. The last of the breed may have been Detroit's Howie Young. In the early 1960s, the *Saturday Evening Post* took the measure of the average badman as being "long on muscle and short on Freud."

Enforcer seems to have entered hockey's lexicon in or about 1939 without anyone really asking the question, what does the enforcer enforce? Not the rules, given that fighting lies beyond their limits. *Policeman* is an odd designation, too, though it's one that Marty McSorley liked "in a romantic sense." *Vigilante* is more appropriate given that any policing that's done on the ice is the work of referees, linesmen, and actual uniformed police officers. *Tough guy* does have a bit of a musty, Damon Runyon ring to it. *Pugilist* is mock-archaic. *Gladiator?* The players who fill these roles are often provided with names that seem strangely appropriate to the job they perform. Does Domi not sound like a curt warning muttered at the boards behind the net? Grimson, Boogaard, Kordic, Kurtenbach, Kocur: they all have the ring of violent threats, of bad outcomes. (Although John Ferguson sounds harmless enough. And Fergie makes him sound as plush as a toy palomino pony.)

Because fighting is such a, quote, shitty job, fighters actually love the game more than anyone else. "They have to," Kris King has said, "because they're setting aside part of their dream to do it."

Hockey-fighting is harder than boxing, said Rod Gilbert. Scoring a goal is easier, according to Rob Ray. You need a strong character to punch and be punched. Big hands are recommended. Ferguson was super-motivated, plus he despised the opposition, plus he studied other fighters to figure out who went for the legs, who backed off, who (looking at you, Carl Brewer) didn't drop their stick. You can start a fight with a flick of a finger, rub a guy's elbow, or say a word or two.

The main technical difficulty involves, according to Gilbert and Brad Park, keeping your balance. Nick Metz advised getting up on your toes. Gordie Howe said you hold on to your stick until the other guy drops his. Tie Domi didn't have a fighting style. Just grab hold, said Tony Twist, throw your fists, see what happens. You have to get the first punch, Lou Fontinato, among others, felt. Although for

Dave Schultz, the priority was to get a good grip on the guy's collar, even if that meant allowing him a couple of first punches. Orland Kurtenbach stood back until you came at him, which is when he got you with his reach, which was tremendous. He stood back, cocked his arm, *boomba*.

It's almost like shooting the puck, said Bobby Orr, you want to be getting as much power into your punch as you can. Being a lefty helps, too. Guys have real trouble with lefties.

Wait a minute. *Bobby Orr?*

Yes, true: he has a helpful section in his how-to book, from 1974, where he shares his secrets. "Some people think fighting is terrible," he explained to *Life* in 1970, "but I think the odd scrap—without sticks—is part of the game."

Don Cherry used to file his fingernails to prepare. He said he was never mad when he fought, ever. Mick Vukota was firmly in the face-plant camp: "You pick the guy up, get the elbow across the head, and slam him into the ice." Kevin Lowe says that when Dave Semenko fought, he destroyed guys, traumatizing both teams. "Not only was the opposition devastated, *we* were devastated."

Keith Magnuson never minded losing a fight. "I really mean this," he said. Not that he didn't work at his craft. After his rookie season, he took boxing lessons from former world bantamweight champion Johnny Coulon. That was the year he had a fight a game, serving 291 penalty minutes, or almost five hours in the box.

Bang your hands on the floor while you're watching TV: Tony Twist learned from a kickboxer that's how you condition your knuckles. The swelling makes your tendons stronger.

If you're going to fight, *fight*. Stand there and give it, and take it— after you get rid of your gloves and stick and take off your helmet, of course. Then, punch. That's what veteran sportswriter Stan Fischler's

2008 formula for fixing hockey amounted to: more haymakers! Back to the days of pure and simple punching. If you wrestle or pull the guy's shirt over his head, waltz around without punching, then sorry, pal, that's extra penalties for you, because it's boring.

Some say that the greatest fight ever in the NHL may have been the mutual wailing that Chicago's Johnny Mariucci and Black Jack Stewart from Detroit laid on one another in the late 1940s. Twenty minutes it's supposed to have lasted, on the ice and into the penalty box, the most brutal battle Gordie Howe ever saw.

Frightful hockey sounds:

- *whop-whop-whop:* sound of Gordie Howe's punches in 1959 when he battered Lou Fontinato. A witness said they sounded "just like someone chopping wood." Fischler described Howe's fists as moving "like locomotive pistons," though the sound was decidedly equestrian: "Clop! Clop! Clop!" Howe: "He was coming like a madman. It took me a while to get the gloves off and then things were busy."
- *like a .22 shot:* goon's head fictionally hitting the ice after Roy MacGregor's Batterinski fells him in a fight.
- *like a hollow wild cucumber we used to fire against trucks on Highway 60 so drivers would think they'd struck something big:* sound of a fan's head on the ice after one of Batterinski's teammates hipchecks the guy for trespassing.
- *crackling:* sound reported in 1933 after Eddie Shore hit Ace Bailey and Bailey's head struck the ice, sending shivers through "experienced spectators in the press section."
- *whack:* Shore's head meeting ice not too much later, not far away.

If you saw Todd Bertuzzi skate down Steve Moore in 2004 and punch him in the back of the head—with the result that Moore will never play another NHL game in his life—maybe you heard Ken Dryden say it was like watching a National Geographic special with the lion taking down the antelope.

Pierre Pilote's dad was an amateur boxer nicknamed Kayo. "The first English words I ever learned were, 'Do you want to fight?'" Pilote said. "I averaged a fight a week and won my share. I had that animal instinct, you might say."

John Ferguson's knuckles always bled. Sometimes, the day after a fight with Stu Grimson, hockey players who suited up again for the next game found that they couldn't turn left or simply fell down. Defencemen have told doctors that once in every four or five fights, they'd get stung, the sky would change colours, and they'd find themselves in a daze.

The NHL got a new rule in 1977 whereby the "third man" into a fight would be ejected from the game and fined one hundred dollars. That would make the violence more sensible, some said. "You'll always have fights as long as you have hockey," Chicago coach Billy Reay reminded the pacifists. Clarence Campbell: "Hockey takes the position that if a man considers himself badly used he may want to punch the offender in the nose. This is certainly preferable to having him strike him with stick or skate." After three decades at the NHL helm, Campbell gave way that year to John Ziegler. "We're going to put some attention on fighting at our annual meeting," the new president said at the beginning of his reign. "But with the cost of players, there just aren't that many goons around any more."

In 1999, when Scott Parker's helmet fell off, Bob Probert threw the hardest punch Scotty Bowman ever saw in hockey, and when Parker went down, Probert told him, "Well, I guess I broke ya."

That was six years into Gary Bettman's tenure as NHL commissioner. Fourteen years after that, he was interviewed by the CBC's Peter Mansbridge, and cautioned, "Before you make a fundamental change and say, okay, we're changing the rule on fighting—you know, you fight, you're gone for two weeks—you have to be very careful. It needs to evolve. Because for every action there's probably an unintended consequence that you weren't aware of."

WE KNOW THEIR names now, the doctors of hockey, they're in the news as much as their patients. Dr. Micky Collins was the concussion specialist who spoke first at Sidney Crosby's famous state-of-the-skull address in September of 2011. He talked about *fog* and *Ferraris*, *herding cows back into the barn*. He cited *deficits* and *impacts*, and introduced us to the word *vestibular*. Dr. Ted Carrick was there, too, explaining *small perturbations* and *great perturbations*. He stayed in the news, having loaded Crosby into a *whole-body gyroscope* and turned him all around as part of his treatment.

Dr. Joseph Maroon also tended Crosby, and both he and Dr. Collins were advising Philadelphia's Chris Pronger that same week to park his shaken brain for the rest of the season. It was Toronto neurosurgeon Dr. Michael Cusimano who said (the same week) that the NHL wasn't doing enough to protect its players. Earlier that fall, he and Dr. Paul Echlin from London, Ontario, had unveiled a study of two Junior teams that found that 25 per cent of the players had suffered concussions.

It was Dr. Ann McKee from Boston's University Center for the Study of Traumatic Encephalopathy who studied Derek Boogaard's brain after his death in 2011. Dr. Charles Tator was the Toronto neurosurgeon who said, "We in science can dot the line between blows to the head, brain degeneration and all of these other issues. So in my view, it's time for the leagues to acknowledge this serious issue and take steps to reduce blows to the brain."

And then there's Dr. Ruben Echemendia, director of the concussion working group that answers to the NHL and the NHLPA. He was the one who, like league commissioner Gary Bettman, wasn't sure about the whole supposed connection between brain damage and hits to hockey heads. "I think it's an opinion based on limited data," he told the *New York Times* in 2011. "My perspective is, we should not make wholesale changes until we have more than opinion and speculation."

Hockey has always had doctors, of course, it's just that their names tend to fade once their patients are discharged, and if anyone's thinking about installing a commemorative gurney in their honour at Toronto's Hockey Hall of Fame, it hasn't yet been announced.

Dr. Henry O. Clauss treated New York Americans left winger Shorty Green in 1927. Green was known as one of the lightest men in professional hockey, at just 136 pounds, or approximately one-half of Zdeno Chara. Also, it was said that Green was one of the game's *most aggressive* players and also one of its *gamest*. He'd served with the Canadian Army at Vimy Ridge and was gassed at some point, but he survived the war. Then on this night in 1927, he got into a *mix-up* during a game against the cross-town Rangers and had his left kidney dislocated. Dr. B.A. Sinclair at New York's Polyclinic Hospital removed it, after a priest had prepared the patient for the procedure by giving him the last rites. Green couldn't play any more hockey after that, but he did go on to coach the Americans. Clauss remained the house doctor at Madison Square Garden for many years, and once remarked that the toughest sport he ever saw was six-day bicycle racing.

In 1930, Dr. Clauss told Rangers defenceman Ching Johnson that his broken jaw would keep him out of the playoffs. Johnson is supposed to have said, "My ankles and shoulders are all right, and they're the important things in hockey. Your jaw doesn't count. What if I can't open my teeth? You're not allowed to bite in this game."

Dr. Clauss said, "I guess his brain is gone. He won't be able to chew his meat until next August." Johnson: "We'll see."

A long-time Leafs doctor named Dr. Jim Murray was the one who went with Team Canada in 1972. After the two exhibition games in Sweden, he asked coach Harry Sinden, "What the hell way are we playing hockey out there?" Sinden wasn't happy: he had to, he said, straighten Dr. Murray out.

I don't have an exact number on how many of Bobby Orr's nineteen knee operations Dr. Carter Rowe performed but we'll just assume, for now, a plurality.

Hard to say whether Gordie Howe holds the mark for most career attending doctors, but it's a good bet, given his longevity. Several of them:

- Dr. Frederic Schreiber, the neurosurgeon who bored an emergency hole in Howe's head in 1950, two inches in front of his right ear, to drain fluid after the twenty-two-year-old star fell into the boards with or without the aid of Toronto's Ted Kennedy.
- Dr. Charles Karibo, the Red Wings team doctor who examined Howe in 1961 at Osteopathic Hospital after he'd collided with Toronto's Eddie Shack.
- Dr. John Finley, a long-serving Detroit team doctor who in 2012 published hockey's first medical memoir, *Hockeytown Doc*.
- Dr. Vincent J. Turco, the man whom a fifty-two-year-old Howe consulted when he suffered dizzy spells during the New England Whalers training camp: "Like a drunk without the beer," Howe said. "I'm no doctor, but I figure it's related to blood sugars." Dr. Turco said he wouldn't be held responsible if Howe continued to play.

Dr. G. Lynde Gately was on duty one night in 1933 at what was then still the Boston Madison Square Garden, when the Maple Leafs were

Post-rumpus: On December 13, 1933, after Boston's Eddie Shore (prostrate, right) felled Toronto's Ace Bailey (his feet are visible, far left), Red Horner dropped Shore.

in town to play the Bruins. The *New York Times*: "Both teams were guilty of almost every crime in the hockey code during the slam-bang first session." In the second, Eddie Shore skated in behind Ace Bailey, and "jamming his knee in behind Ace's leg, and at the same time putting his elbow across his forehead, turned him upside down."

Afterwards, Frank Selke said, Shore stood there "grinning like a big farmer." The rural glee ended, presumably, when the Leafs' Red Horner punched him in the jaw, a heavy right that knocked Shore flat, cracking his head on the ice. Horner broke his fist.

The *rumpus*, the *Globe* called it. Other contemporary accounts preferred *the smashup*. Dr. Gately was treating a Garden ticket agent who'd been punched in the chin by a scalper. "I had just finished with him when a police officer was brought in with a finger someone had tried to chew off. I sewed him up and just then the Leafs appeared carrying Bailey and the Bruins were carrying Shore, both out cold."

Dr. Martin Crotty, the Bruins' team doctor, was working on Shore, so Dr. Gately looked after Bailey. Gately's diagnosis was *lacerated brain*. (Later, what he told the papers was *cerebral concussion with convulsions*.)

When Bailey woke up, Dr. Gately asked him what team he played for. "The Cubs," he said.

Later he tried again.

"The Maple Leafs."

Who's your captain?

"Day," Bailey said. He wanted to go back to the ice.

When a revived Shore came in, he said, "I'm awfully sorry. I didn't mean it." Bailey looked up, according to Dr. Gately's recollection, and replied, "It's all in the game, Eddie."

Drs. Gately and Crotty both rode in the ambulance that took Bailey to Audubon Hospital. Dr. Donald Munro was the one who trepanned Bailey's brain there, twice. His 1938 book, *Cranio-Cerebral Injuries: Their Diagnosis and Treatment*, is one I reviewed so that you'll never have to: not a word about hockey.

Once a trepan was a military siege engine for holing stubborn walls. In the hands of non-medieval surgeons it's a crown saw. A trephine is an improved version, with a transverse handle as well as a sharp steel centre-pin which is fixed on the bone to steady the movement in operating. Some accounts of the Bailey case say *trepan*, some *trephine*. Either way, Dr. Munro tapped Bailey's spine first, on December 14, to drain the fluid. Then he went into the skull, removing damaged tissue and tying up bleeding vessels.

On December 17, Dr. Munro operated again. Afterwards, he said that Bailey's brain had been more seriously damaged on the left side than the right, even though the skull fracture was on the right. Also, the intra-ventricular hemorrhage that Bailey had suffered usually proved fatal.

On December 21, Bailey recognized his wife. Next day, Dr. Munro declared that he was out of danger and that his four-year-old daughter, Joan, could visit. On Christmas Day, *Time* wondered whether hockey was getting too violent. By the New Year, Bailey had been released from all dietary restrictions; his doctors said he could even have a steak if he wanted.

Toronto manager Conn Smythe complained that the Leafs had spent $2,500 on medical bills, which included a silver plate inserted into Bailey's skull. He called for Shore to be suspended for as long as Bailey was out. Toronto would never play the Bruins again if Shore was on the ice. At the NHL, Frank Calder was still thinking. Shore, for his part, had no interest in playing any hockey. "I'm still very nervous," he said. He sailed to Bermuda with his wife, Katie, for three weeks.

January 2 was when Bailey sat up for the first time. A week later Smythe got a letter from Mrs. Bailey reporting that Dr. Munro had told her husband he wouldn't be playing any more hockey. On the bright side, Bailey was shaving for himself again.

On January 4, Calder absolved Shore of any deliberate attempt to injure. "Preponderance of testimony," said NHL managing director Frank Patrick, "is that the contact was accidental." Shore would be allowed to play again on January 28. On January 12, the *Monarch of Bermuda* docked at New York and the Shores stepped ashore looking tanned and refreshed.

Bailey went on to coach university hockey, and he was a time-keeper at Maple Leaf Gardens for years, until Harold Ballard fired him. Later he recalled, "During the first year and a half I suffered some bad after-effects of the injury. Since then, I've felt fine. For probably a year after I was hurt, I got the jitters just watching hockey. I could see an injury shaping up every time there was a solid check. But that wore off, too. No, I never bore any ill-will toward Shore. He and I are good friends."

A HISTORY OF hockey booing could start with Gordie Drillon. Not that he was the first to suffer, but his suffering has a landmark quality. For those of us who never saw him play, someone who did called him *another Frank Mahovlich*, which is helpful, so long as you're old enough to remember Mahovlich before he went to the Senate. Drillon was *big* and he was *good-looking*, a *champion goal-getter*, a *scoring magician*, an *ace*. Also: *happy-go-lucky*, *youth personified*, *a heck of a player*, *a wonderful friend of hockey*. Journalist John Robertson likened him to "a big blue submarine rigged for silent running." His six years in Toronto were packed with successes: a couple of first-team all-star selections, an NHL scoring title, a Lady Byng Trophy in 1938. Four years later, he helped the Leafs win a Stanley Cup. Well, he was on the team. Playing Detroit in the finals that year, the Leafs lost the first two games and coach Hap Day took measures, as coaches do. One of them was benching Drillon—on general manager Conn Smythe's orders, it should be said. Training with his army unit at Petawawa, Ontario, Smythe phoned Day with instructions to sideline Drillon for his lack of toughness.

Nobody likes an enigma, I guess. That's what the *Toronto Star* called him in 1941. "Good one night, bad until the fit comes on him again. He's the inexplicable unit."

"I used to be afraid to put on my skates," Drillon said, years later, after it was over. "They booed me even when I was warming up." For a while he couldn't walk a street in Toronto without being jeered. Scott

Young: "Kids threw snowballs and worse at his house and car." It's the mysterious *and worse* that's both disturbing and tantalizing here.

Star sports editor Andy Lytle took the time to examine his own part in the piece. He'd been hard on Drillon all winter, goalie Turk Broda, too. Then everybody started. "Comes a night when the morons in the crowd boo Drillon and Broda." The players resented it, but they carried on. Drillon was the leading scorer in the playoffs. Still with the booing. Nothing Drillon could do would stop it. "So he plays carelessly purposely so he will be sold next fall. Toronto will lose a wonderful player."

And so it happened. Come the fall, the Leafs put Drillon out of his misery, or theirs, selling him for $30,000 to Montreal, where the children were better supervised and the packing snow not so prevalent. Of course, they'd booed their own in Montreal before and they'd boo them again—Howie Morenz, Bill Durnan, greats of the game, they both suffered. Drillon appeared to have escaped it, but he played just a year for the Canadiens before he went off to the war.

Morenz had a slow start in the fall of 1933. He had a sore ankle, missed a month, put on weight, shed stamina. When he returned to the ice the fans wanted full flight from him, that's what they were used to. When they didn't get it, they not only jeered, they hissed. Morenz went home in tears. Booing is big and clumsy, and sometimes it's just clowning. Hissing is something different, sharper, directed, mean—maybe it's just the edge of it that's vicious, but an edge is enough—and it's as scary as a snake. Canadiens manager Leo Dandurand couldn't stand to see it, didn't have the heart to let it continue. Thinking the unthinkable and then actually doing it, he traded Morenz to Chicago.

Bill Durnan didn't go home to cry, he did it right in the rink. Rocket Richard remembered this: Durnan coming back bawling to the dressing room after a game. Like Drillon in Toronto, he had a sterling record, one of the best ever in the NHL to that point, five Vezina Trophies to his name, also the all-time shutout record of 309 consecutive minutes. And the fans hounded him. In 1947, in the Forum, they constantly chanted for Durnan's predecessor in the Canadiens' net: "We want Bibeault, we want Bibeault." They were still at it in February of 1950, when Montreal was hosting Chicago: "The enraged fans screamed their invective at Durnan as the Hawks went wild and hammered in nine goals on the demoralized Canadiens."

Oh, Montreal. In 1955, it was Boom-Boom Geoffrion's turn to suffer. The fans didn't even need a bad game from him: if anything, Geoffrion was too good. This was the year of the Richard Riot, and in March, with the Rocket suspended for the remainder of the season, Geoffrion overtook him for the NHL's scoring lead. The fans hated him for that and made his life miserable. Geoffrion, just twenty-four, didn't know what to do. He thought maybe he'd retire. "I couldn't deliberately not score," he said. "So I was sick of the whole thing. Even thinking about hockey made me throw up."

In New York, at a time when they were booing Rangers defenceman Rod Seiling, a writer asked how it made him feel. Oh, he didn't mind too much. "The fans pay their money," he allowed. "They have a right to say what they want." The writer waited a moment: the truth can take time, coming out. "Screw them. What the hell do they know?"

But of course, they don't have to know anything, the booers, that's not in their job description. They boo because they can. In September 1972, when Canada lost that first game to the perplexing Soviets, it may have been that the fans in Montreal were too shocked to boo. This can happen. Three games later, in Vancouver, they found their scorn, and by then it may have been that they were booing on behalf of the whole country. Also maybe pre-emptively, in case Canada lost all four games in Moscow.

Frank Mahovlich got it going. The Soviet goalie was out of his net and Mahovlich did what any self-respecting forechecker would do in a similar situation, which is to say he lay on him. Phil Esposito thought it was a great play. The fans did not. The Soviets won, 5–3. The crowd not only booed their own, they also cheered the Soviets.

Esposito couldn't believe it; he'll never forget it. He says this in the second of his autobiographies. In the first, published in 1973, he doesn't really mention it much, a terse paragraph is all Game 4 gets. The fans were yelling obscenities, he reports thirty years later, though he doesn't, strangely, cite the specifics. It may be the only page in the entire book that's curse-free.

Esposito was Canada's player of the game, and when CTV's Johnny Esaw interviewed him, that's when he let go. He was so angry. The whole team was—or at least, all those who wrote memoirs later, other than goalie Ken Dryden, who understood. Bill Goldsworthy was ashamed to be a Canadian. Paul Henderson considered retribution: "Honest to goodness, I almost felt like wading into the crowd with my stick, to use it as a skewer on some of them."

You might have expected Esposito to follow Henderson into the stands, handing him new sticks as needed, maybe kebabbing a few fans for himself. And yet when Esaw put a microphone in front of him after the game it was a promise he made rather than a threat. Later on, he'd write about how unfair it was, look at what the poor pros had to sacrifice to play this series—"money, our vacations"—but at the time, in Vancouver, he told the viewers that if the Russians booed their players in Moscow then Esposito would be back to apologize—but he didn't think he'd be back.

Everybody had something to say about the booing. Letters filled newspaper pages, more voices of the people, except this time many of them were lambasting the "booing herd," telling the country not to worry, have faith, let's just go over there to Moscow and beat the

Commies. Actually, said the head of the Canadian Ski Federation, "they're booing themselves, booing the Canadian way of life."

Meanwhile, Paul Henderson explained some of the rules of the business. For example, if a guy is playing for the Leafs, where he's being paid for it, and things aren't going well, then okay, a few cat-calls might be expected. But "it's a whole different thing when you're playing against a different country and you're doing it for your country."

IT MAY BE that the Petun who used to live near my rink played *lacrosse* or Huron *hubbub* or a version of *tabegasi*, which is what the Omahas used to play in Nebraska. There are, of course, any number of not-hockey games they could have taken up. If you read the books, they're full of what are referred to as Indian games, many of them hockey-like. They had it all figured out, other than the skates.

The Walapai and the Mohave played *tas-a-va* in Arizona, arguing over whose ball to use. The Mohave (says historian Andrew McFarland Davis) usually gave in, knowing that they could win anyway, no matter whose ball was in play. The Makah in the Pacific Northwest used a ball of whalefin cartilage. For a while they only played to celebrate the capture of a whale, but later they played whenever they felt like it. In what's now Michigan, the Passamaquoddy had *e-bes-qua-mo̓gan*, which they suspected the spirits played also. That's what the aurora borealis was, a big game under the lights.

A lot of these games were lacrosse or like lacrosse, and they allow you to make the connection between the game they used to call the Little Brother of War and its twenty-first-century incarnation. White observers of the time used to say that if you happened upon a game in open country, you might take it for serious combat. In 1667, the trader and government agent Nicolas Perrot watched Miamis near Sault Ste. Marie play a game of lacrosse with two thousand players: "a constant movement of all these crosses which made a noise like that of arms which one hears during a battle."

The purpose of the games, in many cases, was to prepare young warriors for war. The Dakotas, before they played their ball game, invoked the aid of supernatural influences. In the Choctaw Nation, injuries inflicted upon a man during sport were often avenged by the player's relatives. Women had key supportive roles here, too, giving the men hot coffee as they played and also, quirt in hand, lashing out at anyone who wasn't competing hard enough.

An observer of the Mississauga at play near Rice Lake, Ontario:

> No one is heard to complain, though he be bruised severely or his nose come in close communion with a club. If the last-mentioned catastrophe befell him, he is up in a trice, and sets his laugh forth as loud as the rest, though it be floated at first on a tide of blood.

Here's a French Jesuit, Pierre de Charlevoix, watching a Huron game of *platter* in 1721:

> They sometimes lose their rest and in some degree their very senses at it. They stake all they are worth, and several of them have been known to continue at it till they have stript themselves stark naked and lost all their movables in their cabin. Some have been known to stake their liberty for a certain time. This circumstance proves beyond all doubt how passionately fond they are of it, there being no people in the world more jealous of their liberty than our Indians.

Games lasted for five or six days. Spectators watching were many times "in such an agitation as to be transported out of themselves to such a degree that they quarrel and fight, which never happens to the Hurons, except on these occasions or when they are drunk."

Here's author A.W. Chase reporting on Oregons in the 1880s playing a game, he said, that appeared *identical* to hockey:

> Sides being chosen, each endeavours to drive a hard ball of pine wood around a stake and in different directions; stripped to the buff they display great activity and strength, whacking away at each other's shins, if they are in the way, with a refreshing disregard of bruises.

Abbé Ferland, a later observer, talked about a particular ball-carrier's defensive measure: holding the ball between the feet while opponents tried to clout it loose.

> Should he happen to be wounded at this juncture, he alone is responsible for it. It has happened that some have had their legs broken, others their arms and some have been killed. It is not uncommon to see among them those who are crippled for life and who could only be at such a game by an act of sheer obstinacy. When accidents of this kind happen, the unfortunate withdraws quietly from the game if he can do so. If his injury will not permit him, his relations carry him to the cabin and the game continues until it is finished as if nothing bad happened.

The Cherokee of North Carolina played a ball-game called *anetsa*. Matches took place every other week, and when the Cherokee weren't playing they were training. The serious player observed a strict diet. He wouldn't eat the flesh of a rabbit because the rabbit was too timid, easily put to flight, liable to drop its wits when chased by the hunter. Also off-limits were frogs (too brittle-boned) and the fish known as the hog-sucker (sluggish). And salt and hot food and women. Plus, if a woman so much as touched his stick on the eve of the game? "It is thereby rendered unfit for use," reported an interested observer.

And what about the Jesuit *Relations* from 1636? We have to acknowledge Jean de Brébeuf and his accounts of watching Huron sports in southern Ontario, even though it's hard to separate Brébeuf from his death, which came gruesomely in 1649 when he and his fellow Jesuit Gabriel Lalement were captured by Iroquois raiders, tortured to death, and eaten. Accounts of Brébeuf's ordeal talk about the fleshy parts of his arms and thighs, and they use the word *succulent*. He died after three hours. Lalement survived for fifteen hours in a suit of burning bark. Brébeuf had the skin of his head torn off and his heart extracted while he was still alive, and some Iroquois ate that too, believing that "nothing so much contributes to courage in war as to eat the heart of brave men, unless it's drinking their blood." All of which, for me, more or less obliterates the rest of his life, including his sports commentaries.

Still, in happier days Brébeuf had watched the Hurons play at their field games. He's the one who's said to have given lacrosse its name, although there are those who claim Rabelais described it in books he wrote a hundred years earlier. These games, Brébeuf noted, were thought to be supremely good for the health. Sometimes an ailing man was commanded to play to save his own life. Some other times— a hockey reverie if ever there was one—the invalid himself dreamt that he would die unless the country engaged in a game of lacrosse, a.k.a. *cross*, in aid of his health. "Sometimes also one of their medicine men will say that the whole country is ill and that a game of cross is needed for its cure," Brébeuf further noted. "The chiefs in each village give orders that all the youths shall do their duty in this respect otherwise some great calamity will overtake the country."

BILL GADSBY CLAIMS a career total of 640, which seems like a big number the first time you see it. Bigger, for example, than the number of points he scored as an NHL defenceman (568). Averaged out over his 1,248 career games, it works out to about 0.51 per game. To put that in perspective, Wayne Gretzky, over his career, averaged 1.92. Though, of course, with Gretzky what we're talking about is points per game, while Gadsby's tally is for stitches to the skin.

There are several levels of meaning to sutures in hockey, starting with the useful medical purpose of closing a deep cut. Beyond that they serve as a gauge of many hockey attributes, including durability, tenacity, willingness to suffer, poor timing, and bad luck of a kind measured out in monofilament.

It may take a period of adjustment for newcomers to the game to figure out how to read their hieroglyphics. Unlike thread-count in bedsheets, the numbers don't automatically indicate quality. Before he coached Pittsburgh's Penguins, while he was still playing for the Anaheim Mighty Ducks, Dan Bylsma said he stopped counting when he'd accumulated 550. "Stitches are a routine thing," Bill Goldsworthy's biographers shrug. "Once he had his tongue split open. This required ten stitches to close."

Derek Sanderson was eight years old when a puck hit him in the face at practice one day. Blood everywhere, Sanderson remembers. His dad, Harold, told him to keep going. "So I bled for the entire practice, and when it was over he took me to the hospital where I had three stitches." They started a ritual after that: when the stitches were plucked, the remnants went into a little plastic box. "Harold saved every one of my first hundred stitches," Sanderson says, "and, pretty soon, I started to become proud of them."

"The reason I know how many stitches I had," Gadsby writes in his cheery autobiography, "is that my dear wife, Edna, kept a log of how many times I was hurt, just like some spouses keep a list of birthdays and anniversary dates." And it was worthwhile: Gadsby was one of the NHLers who bought stitch insurance in the 1950s. A hundred-dollar-a-year policy paid out five dollars for each stitch it took to close a hockey cut. Sounds like a story, but no. One year, Gadsby bled so much he ended up making a fifty dollar profit.

It's not a competition, of course, but if it were, how many stitches would it take to win the all-time NHL sweepstakes?

Borje Salming took three hundred in his face on just one night in 1987 after Gerard Gallant's skate puzzled it. Same count for Buffalo goalie Clint Malarchuk, who barely survived a skate in the neck two years later. Jacques Plante says he had two hundred stitches by the time he started wearing his mask in 1959. Gump Worsley tallied 250; Johnny Bower, 280.

There's a photo of Terry Sawchuk you shouldn't show to a child. It's painful to look at, even if it was doctored to illustrate a career's accumulation. Before he put on a mask in 1962, goalie Sawchuk was up to 350. A subsequent count tallied more than four hundred stitches to his face and head alone, including three inside his right eye.

Theo Fleury estimates five hundred for his career. "Most people who don't know I play hockey," he once said, "think I was thrown through a plate-glass window or something." Keith Magnuson estimated that in a typical NHL month, seven hundred stitches were "dealt out" across the league.

I've taken the liberty of organizing Lionel Conacher's list of career wounds in case anyone—Leonard Cohen?—feels the urge to put it to song:

Nose broken eight times,
leg and arm broken,
several broken bones in hands,

ten cracked ribs,

a skate-gash across the throat near my jugular which almost dropped
the curtain on me and required sixteen stitches to pull together,

another skate-gash near my mastoid which again had me a matter of
inches away from eternity,

a four-square-inch slash of a razor-edged skate on my thigh,

which resulted in gangrene and a red-hot bout
with the Grim Reaper,

two smashed knee cartilages which resulted in
surgical operations,

a total of more than 500 stitches in my face and head,

another 150 or so in the rest of my gnarled anatomy.

Then, those innumerable routine injuries, classed as 'minor,' which
include sundry sprains, pulled ligaments, twisted muscles, black eyes,
bumps, aches, bruises,

Hallelujah, Hallelujah . . .

Saga magazine's November 1968 issue ran an article titled "Gordie
Howe: Hockey's Man Of 1000 Stitches," but somehow that just seems
like a speculative number conjured up by editors. Mr. Hockey does
make a good case for his claim on most career stitches at gordiehowe.
com. Enduring a career of "crippling injuries," he amassed five hundred stitches in his face alone. The skin over the bridge of Howe's
nose was so often sewn that it took a particularly firm hand in later
years just to get a needle in. Howe, incidentally, blamed himself for
many of his sutures:

I was taught to put a lot of weight on my stick, so I'd lean on it. In
order for a player to hook my stick off the puck, they would use a lot
of strength. When they'd get ready to pull up my stick, I'd pull it out
of the way, and their blade would hit me in the face. It would've been

prevented if I left my stick where it was. About three hundred of my stitches were mistakes.

Between 1925 and 1940, Eddie Shore "received" six hundred stitches, which makes them sound like birthday wishes. I've also seen estimates of 900 and 978; Trent Frayne says 964. A 1947 report prefers "taken" for a stitching verb, and adds that Shore acquired them all "without ether." He also had his nose shattered fourteen times and accepted five broken jaws.

It's with stitch stories that hockey's trainers come into the historical limelight. In the early days, the trainers were the ones with the needles and surgical thread. Bill Head did the job for years for the Canadiens. Like Bill Gadsby, Montreal defenceman Dollard St. Laurent was stitch-insured, and he recalls sometimes asking for more than actually needed, seven or eight when four would have done the job. Ed Froelich, the trainer for the Chicago Black Hawks and the Brooklyn Dodgers, had fond memories of goalie Charlie Gardiner in the final game of the 1932 finals. He went into that game with six stitches closing a wound over one eye, a further four eyebrowing the other, and ten more closing a wound on his scalp. "He had the wounds covered and wore a football helmet for additional protection and went out and held the Bruins scoreless to give the Black Hawks the championship."

Leafs doctor Jim Murray was so trusted by the players that when they got cut during games on the road, they left their wounds unstitched until he could tend to them at home. Bobby Baun said, "He'd come at you with those fingers and they were just so big, you'd wonder how he was ever able to stitch as neat as he did." (Another careful counter, Baun estimated that Dr. Murray applied half of his 143 career stitches.)

Whether or not Gadsby holds the record, his experience is memorable. One year (could be the year he was making all his stitch money) he took on sixty. In one lip he had thirty-one, inside and out, thanks to an unseen Tim Horton shot. His gums turned black. For two weeks he couldn't eat. "The sorest stitches I ever had," he said, "were inside my nose." Marcel Bonin had followed through on a shot. Doc Nardiello told him it was going to hurt. Doc was right.

A CRUCIAL QUESTION about the game in its earliest incarnations has to be: How did the rules hold up? More to the point, were there fights? I have a theory about this, just a small one, easy to fold, fits in your pocket. Here it is: If at the original organized game in Montreal in 1875 there was a fight—or not even a fight, but a terrible slash—what if right then and there, at the very first opportunity, someone had objected? The prime minister or the governor general, say. There's no evidence that they were there on the night, but if they had been, they could have stepped up and said, "Look, hold on, I think the way we're going to do this is with no fights or grievous slashes, you're simply going to have to restrain yourself." I believe an announcement like that would have stuck.

Anger is an unavoidable hockey emotion, a fuel and a byproduct, undeniably a part of the game. But does it help you as a player or hinder you? In April of 2007, *Hockey Night in Canada* commentator Harry Neale watched Dallas centre Mike Modano take a petulant slashing penalty. "Anger," he thought, "is just one letter short of danger." In Ralph Henry Barbour's *Guarding His Goal*, it's a risk you run, though help is as close as the blanket on your bed, as our narrator explains: "Violent emotions such as anger generate a poison, the scientists tell us, and sleep is one of the antidotes." What to do, though, if you can't catch a nap on the ice?

An old hockey word for angry is *ornery*, one that's often associated with Ted Lindsay. A *crackling* competitor, *Look* magazine called him in 1952. Descriptions of volatile players often emphasize the contrast between their demeanour on the ice and off, and *Look*'s is no exception. In the drawing room, Lindsay exuded gentility and charm. He wore quiet clothes. He was not unhandsome. His name suggested a minor diplomat or maybe the local harpsichord teacher. Even his lungs were peaceful: a cigarette made him sick when he was seven, so he never lit another. Hockey transformed him. It was the *devil's brew* that turned Jekyll to Hyde. *Brattish, snippy, a picture of unmitigated villainy*. Gus Mortson from the Leafs was his good friend, but never mind, he'd brawl him anytime. Doug Bentley said you'd be a fool to take your eye off him. He called him *the little so-and-so*.

This is all played for chuckles, which is to say in the standard way for hockey profiles, now as then. *Al Shields was rough when he had to be, but easygoing without his skates.* The idea here, I suspect, is to establish clean character; otherwise, why would they be let loose on the ice where the law can't reach? Especially since hockey anger is a stronger proof than the regular civilian stuff.

Roy MacGregor's Felix Batterinski is a reliable guide on this, noting that when he starts to feel "anger akin to hockey anger" he's talking about the high-test, blinding, swing-your-stick variety. At the rink it's important to distinguish further, Batterinski explains. Playing in Finland, he suffers that dread Canadian affliction, a penalty called by an idiot foreign referee for a perfectly clean bodycheck. When he's thrown out of the game for abusing the dumb Finn-of-a-moron, it's not the bad call that incenses him, but the fact that his feelings have been misconstrued. He wasn't *angry* at the ref, only frustrated. "There is fury against an opponent, which is something I enjoy, and there is frustration, which I despise. Yet they call it anger." If they'd just understood his right to be frustrated and let it run its course, things would have been fine. Instead, the ref's failure to properly identify his mood flares in the empty dressing room, where—anger? you want anger?—he destroys Kohos, stomps a mask, smashes a toilet seat, murders a sink. "Frustration," says Batterinski, "has no cure."

Maurice Richard would stab his stick at fans. His, of course, was some of the most notorious anger to have fuelled a hockey career. Ed Fitkin: "When he blows his top the result is atomic. No one can pacify him, it seems, until the rage within him runs its course." Hugh MacLennan explained that Richard was affable once upon a time, "but ten years of being close-checked and nagged by lesser men have given him a trigger temper."

INTIMIDATION IS A common hockey tactic, attempting to cow an opponent by threats or taunts or just by being someone named Georges Laraque or Bob Probert or John Ferguson. Making the other guy mad is another way to go, as in the case of Howie Morenz's winger Aurèle Joliat, who used to wear a black baseball cap when he played to cover a growing bald spot. The word on Joliat was that if you kept knocking the hat to the ice he'd get so mad he couldn't take a pass. He finally abandoned the cap.

Newsy Lalonde used his anger, in fiction, at least. In *Hockey Night in the Dominion of Canada*, Eric Zweig gives him an uncle who tells him never to smile when he's carrying the puck. "You should snarl," he advises. "A hockey player should have no friends on the ice." In Quarrington's *King Leary*, Lalonde glares with eyes "black as a nun's habit." When he's angry (always) they take on a "lunatic" glimmer. "Many a player was beaten just by a look at those eyes."

As a coach, you want to keep all your players firing on all their cylinders. One of the big worries that dogged men like Jack Adams and Conn Smythe was that marriage sapped players of their vital antipathy. *Sports Illustrated* suspected in 1960 that the Rangers' Lou Fontinato had been, quote, tamed by the happiness of his marriage. (They were glad to report his eventual recovery.) When Ted Lindsay got himself engaged in 1951, Adams wasn't sure what to expect. The happy couple appeared in a Detroit newspaper that year in an ad for electric stoves. "I think he's so much in love, he may be softening up," Adams said. Not to worry, though. While Adams was speculating, Lindsay had raised his stick as though—this is how it was reported—to decapitate New York defenceman Hy Buller. The game after that, he punched his good buddy Bill Ezinicki, who punched back.

In Rob Ritchie's 2006 novel *Orphans of Winter*, a bodycheck is "a release of hatred." The main character, Stephen, remembers his father telling him what Gordie Howe once said: "Hockey is an angry sport." That's how you have to play, he's told, again and again: "For best results play angry, like there's a storm inside you." But if you draw on anger to win, you should be prepared also for the anger of losing, one of the symptoms of which is throwing equipment, such as skates, down stairs (a ten-year-old character in Pete McCormack's *Understanding Ken*) and sticks out of hotel windows in Krefeld, Germany (real-life Soviet forwards after losing to Canada in 1955).

THE FIGHT AGAINST fighting presupposes that hockey and fighting can be separated, and that like Peter Pan and his shadow, the two come easily apart. But maybe the fighting is what makes the hockey possible? When Bobby Orr first got to Boston, manager Wren Blair was quick to identify a problem: "Bobby's polite, friendly nature." The league's tough players were pushing him around. "You must stand up to them," Blair counselled. "Show them that you're willing to fight and before long they'll stop bothering you. Then your hockey ability can take over."

Let's accept for the moment that there's no divide: be it resolved that fights are a part of the game (which, by the way, is a *man's game*). Also, they're inevitable. Plus, they're a safety valve, releasing naturally occurring anger and frustration, all of hockey's volatile gases that would otherwise build up and explode. And there's the argument, too, that a punch to the head is good for you once in a while, a shot of wake-up tonic.

That last one is borrowed, in fact, from boxing, and while I've never seen it offered as a defence of hockey fighting, it's probably only a matter of time before someone reaches that way. It comes from a study that was published in the *Journal of the American Medical Association* in 1954 asserting that a blow to the head (by a gloved fist) rarely produces cerebral changes. Moreover, Drs. Kaplan and Browder found that while some punches "may stun," others can cause the brain to be—ready?—"altered to alertness."

Certainly fights do alter the fans, or some fans. The ones who look happy when the fight starts, they stand up, hammer on the glass. The TV cameras catch their smiles. This is what Conn Smythe was talking about when he said, "We've got to stamp out this sort of thing, or people are going to keep on buying tickets."

You don't have to want it, but you have to expect it. This is the argument of older men in big collars on TV. Tiger Williams said you consent to assault every time you lace on your skates. "It's what hockey is all about." Fighting, you see, is a byproduct of the swiftness and excitement of the game, "inevitable," said Billy Reay, "with spirited men."

Purist fans may dislike the brawls, as do a large number of the players. But coaches and players both know that there is no way to avoid them and remain competitive.

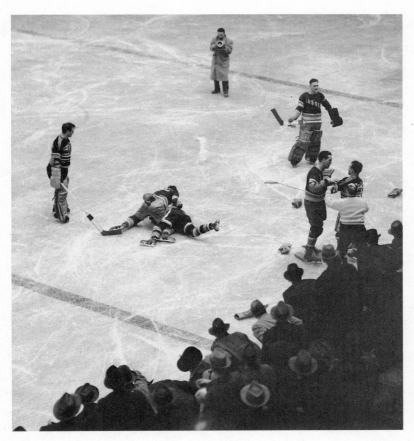

Madison Square brouhaha: Rangers and Black Hawks square off in a 1941 game in New York. Note the eager photographer up by the blueline.

There must have been a first fight. The history books didn't get it down—who was involved, where, why—not even the histories of violence, like Ira Gitler's *Blood on the Ice*. He says it's a delusion to think that the game was genteel until it moved north into the mining towns where the miners corrupted it. For evidence, he points to Toronto's Granite Club in the 1890s, where players and spectators alike forgot themselves (as the *Globe* reported) and ended up in the newspaper followed by the words *fisticuffs*, *regretted*, and *deplored*.

There was more open-ice bodychecking in the early days. The game, all those old players agree, was rougher or, to use Sprague Cleghorn's word, *tougher*. It was just a more robust world back then. Frank Boucher said that it's hard to pinpoint when the toughness stopped and the violence started. Straightforward fist-to-fist combat was never a threat, according to Scott Young in 1955. He'd been watching the game since the 1920s: "If fighting had been going to kill the game, it would have died in infancy."

At some point the sticks came into play, which is to say that when players got irked, annoyed, angry, or blinded by vengeance, they might just as well choose to use them for weapons. This was frowned upon at the time, though maybe not as much as now.

If it happened in the late 1930s that Baldy Northcott of the Montreal Maroons commenced swinging sticks with Babe Siebert of the Canadiens, nobody condoned that. Were they shocked when a fist-fight followed, combined with a wrestling match down on the ice? No: hockey is a game of frictions and reactions. Then, in the penalty box, they went at it again, and Northcott went down and Herbie Cain jumped Siebert, bringing Stew Evans hurtling over the boards, after which nobody saw what happened down in the rumpus until Northcott emerged with blood in a gush down his face and said Siebert had kicked him, though Siebert said it was his fist and the referees said they would report Siebert for *bicycling*, and later Maroons coach King Clancy challenged Siebert to a fight and later still Siebert said, "Sure, I bicycled when I was down on my back on the ice, but I didn't kick with my skates on the bench," and Tommy Gorman said, "That guy Siebert has been kicking with his skates for ten years in this league." Canadiens goalie Wilf Cude, who didn't like to lose, stood by with tears in his eyes.

As early as 1918 it was serious enough in the newborn NHL that president Frank Calder had a warning for players who assaulted other players on the ice: Don't even think about it. Or—go ahead.

Try it. Be his guest. In which case, he'd launch them right out of the league. "He says that he will not allow $60-a-week rowdies to wreck enterprises in which several thousand dollars have been sunk," the *Globe* reported. The *Toronto Star* applauded the toughness of the talk. "Rough-house rowdism will kill any sport, and it will kill pro hockey if it is allowed to flourish."

Rowdism? Rowdyism was the more common term, and from contemporary reports, it was rife in the early days of hockey, just a scourge on the game. It seems to have covered a wide swath of unpleasantry, from a Brooklyn player clubbing another from the New York Athletic Club over the head with his stick, the latter collapsing on the ice bleeding, while the former was pursued off the ice by spectators, all the way to a punch-up between timekeepers at an early OHA game. After a 1918 stick brawl in Toronto, Alf Skinner and Joe Hall were convicted of disorderly conduct and given suspended sentences. The First World War was still on, which explains the notice Toronto manager Charlie Querrie pinned up in the dressing room: "It does not require bravery to hit another man over the head with a stick. If you want to fight, go to France."

Lately, the fighters themselves have started to fret. In 2006, Georges Laraque, then with Phoenix, sounded sick with worry when asked by Canadian Press about "his craft."

"I know that within two years there won't be any fighters in the league anymore," he said. "Within two years, I'm serious, because this is how it's going. More and more teams don't have fighters." CP did the math: eleven teams were regularly dressing tough guys, seven others occasionally, twelve more not really at all.

Laraque:

I'm depressed about it because I sympathize with the guys who do my job. Those are my brothers. I was lucky that it wasn't this way when I started nine years ago. If I lost my job tomorrow I could say I played a decade in the NHL. I've been fortunate. But the younger guys like McGrattan, I feel bad for them. They may not have a job soon.

Remember the old days when Probert and Domi fought? People would line up three hours before the game. They were so excited and would talk about it for days. It was crazy. Now we talk about revenue sharing and things like that. We're turning hockey into a ballet league.

MICHAEL CUSACK HAD an idea. He also had a preamble. This is going back to the late days of 1884, about a decade after hockey had organized itself in Montreal in 1875, and to Ireland, where Cusack was born in 1847. He was a schoolteacher and a civil servant, also an athlete, strident in all his dealings, and he believed that traditional Irish games were fading. This, to Cusack, constituted several sorts of shame, including one that was cultural and even metaphysical—the notion being that a nation that loses its games loses into the bargain bits of its soul and nerve, many of its better angels, not to mention its mojo. So he thought he'd do something about it.

Ireland's famine wasn't too far in the past at the time, and English rule was very much in the present. Along with everything else the English were imposing on Ireland were English games like rugby. Worn down by their historical hunger, the Irish weren't up to resisting. "The tyranny of imported and enforced customs and manners," Cusack decried in "A Word About Irish Athletics," an article he published (unsigned) in October of 1884. The games of the people must be preserved, he said. "Voluntary neglect of such pastimes is a sure sign of national decay."

In November, in the billiard room of Miss Hayes' Commercial Hotel in Thurles, County Tipperary, Cusack and a company of like-minded men founded the Gaelic Athletic Association for the Preservation and Cultivation of National Pastimes (GAA). There was handball and there was rounders, but the main GAA sports were (and continue to be) hurling and Gaelic football. The early rules that were laid down the year following are like commandments anywhere: they have a tendency to bark at you in a way that makes you want to break them, just because. Lots of *There shall be*s and *must*s. They measure the field and outline the fouls. What they don't tell you is how to comport yourself, what to think of your opponent. And though the Archbishop of Cashel, T.W. Croke, did suggest amendments banning the sale of porter and ale and alcoholic drinks on match days, for the most part the GAA rules steer clear of moral instruction and behavioural prompts.

Then there's the preamble. It sounds like a little stroll you take before a bigger hike, but in fact it's important. You wonder if hockey, with a similar vision enshrined from the start—a graceful few paragraphs to guide its principles, some declaration of spirit and intent—might look different today. Cusack published his preamble on February 21, 1885:

> [W]hether it is granted or not that with the decline of the Irish language came a decline of religion, of morals, and of intellect, I am sure no sensible person will deny that, as a nation, we have very considerably declined physically since we gave up our national game of Hurling.

The game is called *baire*, in Irish, and the hurley is called *caman*. The goalkeeper is *cul-baire*. The game is probably the oldest game extant. There is not a shadow of doubt that it was played in Ireland two thousand years ago. It was the training of the hurling field that made the men and boys of the Irish Brigade.

> Guard the game well. But in doing so it will be necessary to play without anger or passion. Irishmen have endured many agonies for the sake of their country without going mad. Why, then, should we gratify our enemies by getting up an unseemly row because one of us get an accidental crack of a stick from a fellow-workman?

Other sports? Baseball's rules come with a Foreword, but other than a quick wag of the finger—the popularity of the game will grow only if everybody respects "the discipline of its code of rules"—it's straight to business. Given the geography of baseball's diamond, all that fair territory and foul, you'd think there'd be room in the rules for some light moral guidance, but the best baseball can do is a few pointers on good grooming. Otherwise, zilch.

Basketball has a no-nonsense addendum, the "Comments on the Rules," that manages to maintain a friendly, just-giving-everybody-a-heads-up kind of a tone. Section K covers "Punching, Fighting, and Elbow Fouls." No room for confusion here: "Violent acts of any nature on the court will not be tolerated." Towards the end, there's this plain warning:

> There is absolutely no justification for fighting in an NBA game. The fact that you may feel provoked by another player is not an acceptable excuse. If a player takes it upon himself to retaliate, he can expect to be subject to appropriate penalties. .

As if this didn't wave its arms and point at hockey's silence, there's always the NBA's Section N: "Guidelines for Infection Control." This is the one that stipulates procedures in case a player sustains "a laceration or a wound where bleeding occurs or if blood is visible." Of course, what happens is that the ref "shall suspend the game" and get the guy some help, also he'll want to be on the watch for "any lesion, wound or dermatitis," making sure it's patched up, because of course no sense risking "contamination to and/or from other sources." The NBA's rules take a stand on taunting, too. I'm just saying.

Over at the NFL, if you look at football's rules, there's no mission stated there, no rousing reminders on conduct other than a brief review of "Unfair Acts." As for the other football, the Beautiful Game, you'd think maybe that might be the sport to trump all the others in eloquent outline of values and verities. It's not so: soccer's laws are as prosaic as any.

The early rules of hockey have a Shaker simplicity. It might have been an elegant argument for deregulation they were making, a willingness by the game's founders and their heirs to keep things simple, stay out of the way, let the market decide. Turns out, hockey's rulebook is the wrong place to look for philosophy or oratory; there's no preamble to be found. It's probably too late anyway. The whole problem with preambles is the pre-ness involved. If you don't get in there right at the start, you find that the pre has already ambled. You can't unring the bell, as the poet says.

Unless you, um, simply decide the time has come for a change. Take cricket, for example, which enshrined its preamble in 2000, introducing a preface to its rules called Spirit of Cricket. The Laws, as cricket calls its rules, are strong and Biblical, riding along on words like *obey* and *responsibility*. The bit I like right at the beginning is this: "Any action which is seen to abuse this spirit causes injury to the game itself." There's the reminder to RESPECT, all caps, your opponents, your own captain, the work of the umpires, and the game's, quote, traditional values. There's the decree against "cheating or any sharp practice." And there's point number 6, just the summary conviction: "There is no place for any act of violence on the field of play." Cricket is four centuries old; its preamble, a decade and a half. It gives you hope.

WILLIAM BEERS WAS our Michael Cusack, a tireless organizer and promoter of sport, a fervent nationalist, a great Canadian, and a dentist. More, too: Beers is the man who's usually credited with having started dental journalism in this country, establishing several journals, and when he died, he left behind the most extensive dental library in the country. But, sport: Beers really had room in his heart for only one, and it wasn't hockey.

He was called, quote, a flaming lacrosse evangelist. In 1869, he published a book, *Lacrosse: Canada's National Game*, claiming his subtitle had been officially ratified by an act of Parliament, which isn't true, no matter what you may have heard. Lacrosse, Beers wrote, "dislikes all hypocrisy, unnaturalness, and assumption, and it is the very thing to knock all such out of a man." Which is impressive, you have to admit, and possibly enough to keep the game on the ascendant. Undeniably, by the mid-1880s, it was breaking out all across the country, and Beers was leading teams overseas, including a famous tour of Great Britain that used lacrosse as a vivid advertisement for emigration to Canada. Sprague and Odie's father, William Cleghorn, was on that tour, along with Caughnawaga Iroquois players named Deer Whispering, Strong Arm, and June Stand Up. They travelled ten thousand miles, handed out half-a-million brochures, and played 452 games. If any sport seemed to have momentum on its side, a bright, expansive future both amateur and professional, it would have to look like lacrosse.

So what happened? Lacrosse didn't die out entirely, of course, but nor did it grow in the way that hockey did in the early years of the twentieth century. One wag blamed big business: "Its destruction began when business enterprises—railways, ferry companies, wealthy individuals—started spending large sums on the purchase and salaries of players." The best players were thereby lured away to the big cities, which discouraged local pride, and that's why the patient died.

Perhaps it was the roughness. Or the terrible refereeing. Newsy Lalonde starred at lacrosse and hockey; he thought it was the war. Four hundred good lacrosse players went overseas to fight in 1914–18, he said, and the game was never the same again after that. In 1958, Clarence Campbell told a panel in Ottawa that Henry Ford was to blame. "The man who ruined lacrosse," he said, apparently in earnest, "was the man who provided the people with a means of going for a drive on a Saturday afternoon."

This is just one more hunch, I admit, but was the demise dental? When Beers died in 1900, widowing his library, he left the nation's dentists without a strong voice to rally them to the game he so loved. Sure enough, the evidence of more and more hockey-minded dentists starts to accumulate in the first decade of the new century. Could there have been a recognition—how to put this? Did they see in hockey's hard ice, her free-flying pucks and elbows, the creative high-sticking—was there simply more professional potential for dentists? It's impossible to say. All I can do is plead the facts, one of which is that by 1916, one of the stronger teams on the OHA senior circuit was the Toronto Dentals, also known as the Toothpullers.

YOUR TEETH TAKE their chances. Harry Howell kept all of his through a career of 1,411 NHL games. Goalie Ed Giacomin's survived 609. Another New York Ranger, Rod Gilbert, lost four to a puck when he was fifteen, but no more after that. But don't count on preservation. You never should. No-teeth is a defining feature for hockey players, better than a driver's licence, as detailed by Don DeLillo in *Amazons*: "Bent noses, glazed eyes, those gaps in their teeth." When Dave Bidini calls a chapter in *Tropic of Hockey* (2000) "Bobby Clarke's Teeth" to evoke an old rink attendant in the Chinese city of Harbin, nobody who watched the Flyers in the 1970s (or beer commercials thirty years later) has any trouble picturing the man's ruined grin.

In 1971, according to a survey of NHL gums, 68 per cent of players had sacrificed at least one tooth to the cause. I've heard it said, off-handedly, that Eddie Shore had every living tooth in his head knocked out during his career, though that may just be antique newspaper shorthand from a time when American newspapers were still trying to understand why these Canadians took the game so seriously.

Teeth out, dentures laid aside, hockey players show mouths that look like they're *old apples* (Mike Cassidy in Quinn McIlhone's *Trade Rumours*, 1985). Andy Bathgate was a boy who whacked his head one time, lost one tooth, cracked another. The attending dentist told him to suck it up. "Andy," he said, "just remember you can never be a hockey player if you've got your teeth." He could and he didn't. Flash forward twenty-few years to a 1959 *Sports Illustrated* sighting: "The hollow-cheeked look he has on the ice is due to the fact that he has no upper teeth and leaves his plate in the locker room."

Not everyone sacrifices teeth so cheaply. Colleen Howe, Gordie's wife, explains what's at stake in her book *My Three Hockey Players*: "To a hockey wife and/or mother, teeth are more precious than dia-monds. No stranger can fully appreciate the joy we feel at seeing a child smile with teeth that are his own." As coach of CSKA Moscow, Konstantin Loktev felt the same way about his players, which is why he pulled them off the ice one night in Philadelphia. Later, Loktev said he didn't want his players losing teeth. To which Milt Dunnell, in the *Toronto Star*, growled, "Anybody who wants teeth doesn't belong in the NHL."

In Roy MacGregor's *The Last Season*, all your teeth intact is a letter you wear, big and scarlet enough to condemn an entire continent. Felix Batterinski looks around his Finnish dressing room at his new teammates:

> They all have their teeth. All of them, all of their teeth. And that says all anyone ever needs to know about European hockey, as far as this boy's concerned.

In North America, the pre-game routine in the dressing room includes everybody stashing their crowns and bridges away in a paper cup or plastic case. A funny hockey joke used to be for someone to sneak in and switch around all the false teeth. Vic Hadfield couldn't resist, neither could goalie Eddie Giacomin. In Giacomin's case, he reports that in practice, vengeful teammates would swear at him and shoot at his face, try to break *his* teeth. One of Sweden's all-time greats, Sven Tumba, tried the same prank at the Boston training camp in 1957, which may be one reason why he was mailed back to Sweden without having played a single NHL game.

Doug Burns is the hero of Fred Stenson's funny novel titled *Teeth*. Burns is pretty good, a goal scorer who's never lost one. This unEddie Shore is a first-round draft choice, just into his fourth season with the NHL Bisons; his secret is steady brushing, determined flossing, and the painstaking avoidance of all fights, elbows, highsticks, or errant pucks. He loses his first to a Montreal madman, who drives his helmeted head into Burns's mouth. Knocks his left front tooth clean out. His first reaction is to retire. That's it, enough, game over. "A missing tooth is a hole in your head for life."

But that's patent absurdity, of course, a hockey player quitting because he lost a single tooth, a fine Canadian joke. Funnier still is what he wants to do next: write a book. "So many hockey nobodies had done this that I thought, why not me too?" But publishers aren't interested. His is a regional reputation. What about a book for hockey parents on the care of their children's teeth? (Sample chapter: "Teeth as a Determiner of Personal Identity.")

In *The Last Season*, Batterinski goes down to block a shot. He does it well, too, if he does say so himself: "Bill Gadsby-style—knees flat out, hands to the side the way Al Jolson finished 'Mammy.'" When the slapshot crashes into his mouth, he describes "a painless, almost soft, certainly silent push against my mouth." It leaves him spitting into the faceoff circle, blood and the last of his premolars. "There was no pain whatsoever." Plenty of rage, though: he believes that the shot was aimed with malice aforethought.

Fiction tries its best, but reality trumps it every time. Circa 1968, in a game against the Oakland Seals, Philadelphia's Ed Van Impe took Wayne Muloin's slapshot full in the mouth. "Three or four teeth on the lower jaw and seven on the upper jaw had been smashed," recalled broadcaster Gene Hart, "and after being sutured up to stop the bleeding, Eddie had gone back out and finished the game." The stitch-count came in at thirty-five for Van Impe's mouth and gums and a further seventeen for his tongue. After the game, his wife shuttled him over to Philadelphia's Lankenau Hospital for surgery to uproot the shattered battlements of his smile. U.S. Senator Hubert Humphrey wrote him a letter conveying his congratulations.

HOCKEY IS *RIOT* and *schemozzle*, but it isn't war. Lacrosse used to be war, we're told. Soccer causes wars if it's not careful: for example, the one between Honduras and El Salvador in the summer of 1969. Not hockey, though. "I'm amazed everyone takes Canada Cup nationalism so seriously," Brett Hull mused in a memoir he published under the bellicose title *Shootin' and Smilin'* (1991). "I never viewed it as Canada vs. USA. I hate the whole anthem aspect of the tournament. We're not going to war; we're playing hockey." Igor Larionov agreed. "I always preferred the word 'rival' to 'opponent,' which somehow seemed to grate upon the ears. It sounded too much like 'enemy,' and we were playing a game, not going to war."

Almost, though. The closest hockey has come to spilling into international conflict may have been in the spring of the year of the Soccer War. Nothing to do with us: this was in Czechoslovakia, a year after the Soviet Union had invaded. Continuing unrest in the former had the latter revving up its armoured units. Careful, the Kremlin warned, any more of your agitating and we'll send in the tanks to run over demonstrators. In March, the 36th World Hockey Championships got underway in Stockholm. On March 21, the Czechs beat the Soviets 1–0. They did it again, 4–3, on March 28. In Prague, the people poured into the streets to celebrate, bait any Soviets they could find, and trash their national airline offices. Happy hockey fans smashed windows and built a bonfire of chairs and desks. They burned all the models of Aeroflot airplanes and the pictures of Lenin. In this, perhaps, they mistook hockey for life: the results in Stockholm didn't, in the end, change anything in Prague. In fact, they didn't even win the Czechs the championship, which the Soviets took home a few days later. Czechoslovakia ended up third. For one night it didn't matter, though. The people wore paper hats and the hats said 4–3 and the chants in the streets of the capital were "Russians go home!" and "Today Tarasov, tomorrow Brezhnev."

Wartime can present a major existential test for hockey. The First World War was a serious war, hockey was firmly established, and people had had time to connect the two: hockey as a preparation for war, an incubator for soldiers. Not in quite the doctrinaire way that the Soviets later would apply it, but it was a start.

Reading about the hockey of this era, you detect just the tiniest hint of rivalry, a sense that war was a bit of a nuisance to hockey, in an upstart WHA sort of a way. The NHL was still a few years away, but its forerunner, the National Hockey Association, had already suspended a player named Art Ross, who'd been bruiting the idea of a rival league in 1914.

In August of that year it was still possible to imagine business as usual, to ignore the silliness that was starting up in Belgium and France. There was a British letter, reported in the *Times* that summer. B.M. Patton, captain of London's Princes Club, wrote to his counterpart at the hockey department of the Berlin Skating Club. "It is our warmest wish that the good relations between our two clubs remain unclouded in the interest of sport, independently of anything that may happen." He looked forward to next winter's championship. He sent his greetings to all ice hockey players in Germany.

In Canada, when war broke out and the clouds lowered over Europe, more and more players were joining the ranks. Who better to fight? In 1916, the MP and soldier Colonel J.A. Currie published a book called *The Red Watch* in which he praised the vigour with which lacrosse and hockey players had taken to the ranks of Canadian imperial battalions for overseas service. "It was afterwards to be shown," he enthused,

> that the manly and strenuous native Canadian sports, lacrosse and hockey, practiced by almost every boy in the country from the time he is able to walk, are of a character admirably suited to produce bold and courageous soldiers. Boys who have been accustomed to handle lacrosse and hockey sticks, develop arm and shoulder muscles that make the carrying and use of the rifle easy. Firing for hours during a hot and sustained engagement does not fatigue nor exhaust them as it otherwise would. In the rough work of the bayonet charge they

Shadowy men in a shadowy Garden: Bruins host Maroons on spectral Boston ice in the early 1930s.

keep their heads, and have confidence in their ability at close quarters to overcome their antagonist. They do not dread a blow or a bayonet, for they have been accustomed to roughing it all their lives. When it comes to "cold steel" it is the man who has the courage and confidence in himself that wins, for nineteen times out of twenty the other man is dominated before blades are crossed, and at once either throws up his hands or runs.

Fine words, and a good reason to keep on taking all those cross-checks. And yet: Was it possible to play hockey without insulting the serious work at the front? Was it right for young men to be out on ice in Canada while their peers were overseas facing the fight?

The president of the Amateur Athletic Union of Canada addressed this at the start of 1917. Praising those who'd joined up, he also wanted to reassure their stay-at-home friends. "To those who for various reasons cannot go," he said, "I would ask of you to keep the game going, and the sacrifice of your time and experience for the training up of the younger generation in clean, manly sport, so that we may always be prepared for any emergency."

War maimed and killed hockey players just like it did to everyone else. Having carried your stick to boost your bicep only took you so far. Red Dutton played for the Maroons and the Americans, but in 1917 he was nineteen-year-old Private Mervyn Dutton, a member of Princess Patricia's Canadian Light Infantry, when a German barrage filled his legs with shrapnel. Bullet Joe Simpson, one of the first players to be called "the Babe Ruth of hockey," served with the Cameron Highlanders and won a Military Medal for bravery. Twice he was wounded, "once by machine gun bullets in his legs," though "good surgery kept him from lameness." His forte, said the *New Yorker*, was "solo goal-shooting from mid-ice." There's no way of calculating how much post-traumatic stress hockey absorbed when the war was over and the hockey players returned, just as the NHL was making its debut in 1918.

Lest we forget: Frank McGee lost the sight in one eye to a puck in 1900, retired as a player, refereed, but couldn't stay away, and so came back. In 1905, he helped the Ottawa Silver Seven beat Dawson City to win the 1905 Stanley Cup, scoring fourteen goals in one game. Don Reddick wrote a novel, *Killing Frank McGee* (2000), in which a character observes, "He doesn't look like a hockeyist, he looks like an altar boy." He was thirty-two when he somehow passed his medical to enlist in 1914; he died a lieutenant at the Somme in 1916. His body was never recovered.

Nobody talks much about Scotty Davidson, but some people who saw him play rated him the best ever. He's in the Hall of Fame, like McGee; Stephen Harper also has a (passing) place for him in his book: the PM calls him a *power forward*. In 1914, six months after captaining the Toronto Blueshirts to Stanley Cup victory, Davidson signed up to serve with the Canadian Expeditionary Force. He was twenty-three. Nine months later he was in France, a lance-corporal with E Company, 2nd Battalion, Eastern Ontario Regiment. Volunteering for a bombing party, he handed over his bayonet and watch to his friend George Richardson, another hockey player, saying, "I may never come back, but those Germans are going to catch blazes before morning." He was within a few feet of an enemy trench when his companions withdrew. He stayed to get rid of his grenades. By Richardson's account, German soldiers surrounded him, called on him to surrender, and heard him refuse. He *crashed* his last grenade against the body of a German officer. When friends retrieved Davidson's body next morning, it was torn with bullets and bayonet wounds. He deserved a Victoria Cross, they said.

NO MORE, SAID Clarence Campbell in December of 1948; he'd had enough, and he wrote a letter to the NHL's general managers to tell them so. Was he demanding an end to fighting? Nixing all ear-chewing? The ambushing of referees, the selling of their whistles for scrap?

No. The president had decided that indiscriminate profanity by players, coaches, and trainers had to stop. It was getting worse and the fans—certain fans—needed protection. "In our game," he wrote, "the best and most high-priced seats are located in the vicinity of the players benches and closest to the ice. It is very offensive indeed, particularly to women, and contributes absolutely nothing to our spectacle and will inevitably drive some people out of the rinks."

It was that old tension between the realities of the game and the demands (and perceived sensitivities) of the paying public. Campbell increasingly found himself standing up in defence of the sensitivities. On the practical side, as Dave Bidini says, "There's no room for polite in hockey."

Insults are a part of the game, always have been. Tempers fray and flare, but the burn is fast. "Sure there's cussing out there," referee Wally Harris once shrugged. "It's just like it is anywhere men get together."

Percy LeSueur's 1909 primer *How to Play Hockey* included advice: "Do not listen to remarks from the spectators. It is a habit, particularly at the general admission end of the rinks, to call all kinds of things at the goalkeeper and he cannot listen to them and keep his mind on the game."

There are some hold-outs. Eddie Bush, an early mentor to Paul Henderson, was known as a coach who stood on the bench and screamed when he helmed the Hamilton Red Wings in the 1960s. But in his dressing rooms (which he insisted on keeping spotless), Bush kept a cuss book, logging fines of five to twenty-five cents against players caught bluing the atmosphere. In the NHL, there have are documented abstainers: Milt Schmidt of the Bruins was a gentleman, says Rocket Richard, and so was the second Harry Watson, who played for the Leafs and didn't antagonize any Americans in 1924. Syl Apps, too: "Never, absolutely never, would he say anything on the ice." Igor Larionov has good things to say about the Swede Kent Nilsson (he was *open, free*; Larionov saw in him "somewhat of a Russian soul") and the Czech goalie Dushan Pasek ("kind-hearted, approachable, a well-wishing person").

On the other side of the ledger: nobody could cuss like the Gump, according to Vic Hadfield. And what about the spitters? Georges Vézina, Paddy Moran, and Nels Stewart are all supposed to have chewed tobacco when they played in order to have a cheekful at the ready to unleash into opponents' faces.

In southern Ontario in 1914, Frank Selke was coaching his home-town team, the Berlin Union Jacks, when war broke out. It was two years before the city changed its name—Industria, Newborn, and Confidence were in the running before Kitchener was finally chosen—but in the meantime:

> We were called "Baby-killers," "Pro-Germans," "Flatheads"; and many other grossly insulting names. Often we had to fight our way bitterly out of the arenas when we were playing away from home.

"The language could get real thick," says Red Storey, who refereed through the 1950s. Herbert Warren Wind observed that Phil Watson, when he played for the Rangers in the 1940s, believed that the worst slur was to suggest that a rival was fading. "You damn been-has!" Watson might cry. "*Pollution!* I run you up two trees, you no-brains, *mal de tête*, mother of pig, *fils de chien!*"

Dennis Hull says that Gordie Howe *never* talked to rivals. Maurice Richard, he says, was selective: he only insulted stars, players in his own orbit. From the Rocket's brother, Henri, Hull always heard the same thing, which, in his autobiography, he thoughtfully renders in his best Henri accent: "My brudder is bedder dan your brudder."

Henri figures in a lot of trash-talking tales of old. Toronto's sly Bobby Baun: "I never dared look at Henri and call him a 'frog'; instead, I used to call him 'gorf.'" Hull says that his Chicago teammate

Stan Mikita hated Henri, and vice versa. Mikita talks about this: "Henri would call me a 'DP' and I'd snap back with 'Frog' or 'Pea Soup'... Words led to fists and penalties." It was nothing Mikita hadn't heard before. As he writes in his autobiography, "Among the first words I heard from Canadian boys were 'foreigner' and 'DP' and even before I knew what the words meant their tone stung me like a sharp knife." In 1962, he wrote about what he'd learned about NHL needling. "In the heat of the game... when the pressure is on... if you talk to an opposing player, find his weak spot... bug him, the chances are that he's going to come after you." He goes on:

> Needling is an art. There are some players you just can't get excited, no matter what you say or do to them. These include Andy Bathgate, Gordie Howe, Johnny Bucyk, Red Kelly, Dave Keon, and Alex Delvecchio. You can usually accomplish a lot by needling Brewer... Carl is also a pretty good needler himself. It's very easy to irritate Eddie Shack. All you have to do is use psychology.

Ted Lindsay used as much as he could when he played against Maurice Richard. "I used to go to the Rocket and I'd say, 'You dumb fuckin' Frenchman, I'm going to take your head off your shoulders with this stick.' And before you know it, he's forgetting the puck." On his side, Richard acknowledged that Lindsay was the "worst" he faced. "It wasn't so much that he was a dirty player, but as far as I am concerned he had a dirty mouth. He swore at everybody on the ice."

Ken Dryden says, "the most damnable thing an NHL player can be called is a 'snow thrower.'" Which sounds like Dryden wasn't paying close attention.

In 2004, Ontario's Junior Hockey League announced that it was suspending for five games a Plymouth Whalers defenceman who'd called an opponent a "Euro." A year later it happened again, same word, new suspension. "This comes under our non-tolerance in the area of diversity," said OHL director of operations Ted Baker. "We don't feel there was any intentional malice, but we've taken a strong stance on any type of reference to a player's country of origin." In this case it was a Slovakian player, Stefan Ruzicka, who'd been targeted— by young Jonas Fiedler, from the Czech Republic.

If only Clarence Campbell had succeeded in stamping out foul language in 1948. In 1955, Campbell started the year at a Canadiens-Red Wings game. Another three months and he'd be in the middle of the Richard Riot. (He was already investigating Richard for having slapped linesman George Hayes across the face.) For now, he was concerned that Detroit was sullying the game with bad words. Hockey is a business in which obscenity has no place, he said, "can't benefit anyone and can have no defender." Sure, once in a while, hockey's strenuous pace and the resulting "harassed feelings" might generate the odd mild curse, "such as when you hit your thumb with a hammer."

> But it is revolting to make obscenity part of standard speech and it is on this basis I am approaching the situation. It is not a matter of disciplinary action against individuals; it is something that has to do with [the] standard of conduct of our organization.

During the game in question, Campbell was sitting too close to the Detroit bench to ignore coach Jimmy Skinner's squalls of profanity. He felt he had no choice but to intercede and quell them.

"It was the most absurd thing I had ever heard of," Red Wings manager Jack Adams said afterwards; he wanted the NHL governors to censure the president. Skinner, for his part, had told Campbell to sit back down: "You're only a spectator at this hockey game." Campbell agreed with this version of events. For some reason, though, he wouldn't go into specifics. "In effect he told me to mind my own business," was the most he'd say to reporters.

IN EARLY SEPTEMBER of 1939, as Canada's Parliament met to decide whether the country should go to war or not, the NHL's rules committee was mulling over some important questions of its own. Should the league continue to compel referees to delay a game every time one of the coaches wanted to debate a decision made on the ice? What about the penalty-shot rule? Leave it as is? There was time still, of course, to deliberate before the new season opened in early November, and if weightier decisions needed to be made, well, the league's full board of governors was meeting in Detroit in a few weeks' time.

League president Frank Calder addressed the larger pending storm. If the government felt that they shouldn't play, they wouldn't. "Professional hockey," he said, "is just as patriotic as any other endeavour." Players who wanted to volunteer for the fight would be aided in every way. Still, though, "we feel that well-conducted sport will be of great benefit to the national morale in these days of worry and mental stress."

Meanwhile, the NHL soldiered on. The Rangers won the first wartime Stanley Cup in 1940, beating the Leafs. Given the times, there wasn't room for news of the win on the front page of the *Globe and Mail*, which is fair enough with serious matters afoot, the British having taken control of Narvik in Norway, for instance. Maybe if the Leafs had won, they'd have it made it to page one. Overall, there was a new sobriety to the coverage, a self-subduing instinct.

By the start of the next hockey season, Red Dutton's New York Americans had lost fourteen of sixteen players, mostly to the Canadian Army. (Eventually, Boston's Art Ross would call for all wartime records to be expunged from the books on account of the weakness of the teams.) Again there was debate about the role of sports in wartime, none of it too fierce: by this time there was no real doubt about their value. After the United States joined the war, Paul V. McNutt, the federal commissioner of Manpower, made the point that baseball was the number one recreational diversion and morale-builder for both soldiers and the home-front working man (movies were number two). He had the stats handy: fully 70 per cent of the news cabled overseas by the Office of War Information was sporting news.

The war would see some sports curtailed—so long, golf and bowling—but baseball would go on. He said, "No concessions will be made to baseball, but no cease-and-desist order will be given either." Seventy-five per cent of the Major League's players were serving in the armed forces. That didn't mean there wouldn't be changes: game times were shifted to 10:30 AM to help war workers and the teams cut back on travelling. Colleges shut down football for the duration, and campus rinks that used oil to drive the refrigeration were closed. To keep students active, one paper reported, "simple games, such as softball and touch football, and games that have a carry-over value in after-life, like tennis and squash, will be taught and played."

Ahead of the 1942 season, the NHL showed its warlike resolve by doing away with overtime. There were discussions about shaving club rosters from fifteen to twelve. Editorial pages murmured impatiently now and then. Said the *Globe* in 1942: "Hockey battles strengthen the conviction that the game has produced a fine crop of prospective Commando troops, and that the sooner they are in uniform the sooner the war will end."

As NHLers flocked to the war effort, the war effort gave back what it could. For example, in 1942 a young machinist helping with the manufacture of Ram tanks at the Montreal Locomotive Works was invited to try out for the Montreal Canadiens. (An ankle hockey broke kept him out of the Army.) He himself had a hard time believing the Habs wanted him, for though he'd been playing for their affiliate team in the Quebec Senior League, he'd got himself a reputation as fragile, plus Maurice Richard had scored eight meagre goals the previous year.

There were those who argued that wartime presented a perfect opportunity to reshape the rickety edifice not just of hockey but of the whole tenement neighbourhood of sport—tear it down and rebuild, they cried. John R. Tunis wrote a long article in *Harper's* suggesting that here was a chance "to institute a program of sport for everyone, the only system worthy of a nation calling itself a democracy." Canada was a good example: "Hockey is Canada's national game and every Canadian can skate because every small town in the Dominion has a municipal rink." That was the way, he said, to build "a race of outdoor-loving and outdoor-living people."

ANTHROPOLOGISTS AND social psychologists have wondered whether sports might be a means by which societies manage aggressive behaviour. Using words like *recrudescence* (a great potential hockey word) in close proximity to terms like *ergic tension* and *substitute discharge* (sounds uncomfortable as well as messy), social scientists have had a lot to say about combative sports and the societies who practise them. A Toronto lawyer made news in 1973 when he said that there was a good reason Canada didn't send troops to Vietnam: we already had all the fight we needed in hockey. Do peaceful peoples use them as an alternative to war? That is, they don't need to fight, having burned off all their aggression on the field, or the rink, of play?

Most of us would probably lean the other way, towards the idea that, actually, it's the warlike people who are more likely to play at combative sports, that their violent pastimes embody who they are as a people rather than separate them from their identity. Richard Sipes's research bears this out. In 1973, Sipes published a holocultural correlation study looking at a sample of twenty societies from world history, and while I was hoping he'd chosen Peterborough or Flin Flon as one of them, the closest he came was the Copper Inuit of what is today Nunavut.

His definition of combative sport:

> There is actual or potential body contact between opponents, either direct or through real or simulated weapons. One of the objectives of the sport appears to be inflicting real or symbolic bodily harm on the opponent or gaining playing field territory from the opponent.

He looked at Hutterites and Dorobos, Tikopians and Abipons. Guess what? Those societies that tended to be always attacking other peoples played aggressive games, except for the anomalous Tikopians, who rarely bothered anyone, despite their enthusiasm for a zestful game in which the object was to advance on the opposing team and smack them on the head or the ribs with a sago-leaf stick.

WOULD THERE BE enough sticks and pucks to keep going? Wartime put a stop to the manufacture of bowling pins, to save on maple, and in 1941, the war in the Pacific cut off the supply of crude rubber. Stockpiles would last for a while, but reserves of corsets, golf balls, and sink stoppers would be gone by the end of 1942. Still, it was

February of 1943 before the U.S. government put shoes under rationing, including boots attached to ice and roller skates. (Boudoir and ballet slippers were exempted.)

The Chicago Black Hawks appealed to their fans:

> It would be a shame to see a great sport and morale-building game like hockey go into the discards because of a shortage of pucks. That's why we call upon our fans to throw back our pucks in the interest of sport and conservation of valuable defense material.

Lots of players served both hockey and military, keeping their skates when they donned the uniform, like Max Bentley, if not Hec Kilrea. After a long NHL career with Ottawa, Toronto, and Detroit, Kilrea fought with the U.S. Army at Anzio in Italy and then participated in the push across Alsace into Germany in the war's last winter. He won a Purple Heart and the Combat Infantryman Badge, and twice saved his company from what the citation for his Distinguished Service Cross called *peril* by personally stopping two German tanks with a bazooka. He ended up wounded, taking sixty-six pieces of shrapnel. Said Hec: "War is almost as dangerous as hockey."

In 1944, Canada's Defence minister announced that army teams and personnel were hereafter banned from participating in the Allan and Memorial Cup playdowns. "The Canadian Army," he said, "has always regarded hockey as a great sport, but now we must carry the puck to Berlin."

Red Dutton, meanwhile, advised that players returning from battlefield to rink would need some specialized conditioning. He was thinking back to his own experience following the First World War. "We could stickhandle just as well as before going to war," he said. The problem was that all the military marching and physical training developed the wrong muscles for a puckster. It would take hockey's soldiers a while to regain their skating legs.

HIS NICKNAME WAS Terrible, as in Ivan the. His given names were Blake and Theodore, but people used to say better options might have been Vicious or Venal. He was *no choirboy* and played like *a Tasmanian devil*. Accounts of his career tend to include words like *bloodshed* and *waged war*. Even teammates hated Ted Lindsay sometimes, because of what he did to them in practice. *A mean sucker*, they said, *don't get too close to him or you'll bleed.*

In March of 1956, someone telephoned a threat to shoot him dead on the ice, his teammate Gordie Howe, too, if they attempted to play against the Leafs that night in Toronto. The police said they'd be on their guard. Two peculiar things happened: first, *Toronto Star* sportswriter Jim Hunt dressed up in a long coat and hat and went into Maple Leaf Gardens shaded behind sunglasses and carrying a fake wooden rifle in a real shotgun case. He sat with it between his knees for the first period and then laid it down under his seat. No one noticed. Second, in overtime, Lindsay scored the winning goal for Detroit and afterwards, to show his sense of humour, he skated to centre ice and raised up his stick, blade to his shoulder. Then he pretended to machine-gun the Toronto fans. At Lindsay's website, where he raises money for autism research, you can buy an autographed commemorative photo from that night, US$125 for the shot of Lindsay taking aim at the stands.

"Fully three-quarters of the men in this Hall of Fame are sons of bitches!" says Quarrington's King Leary. Because it helps?

Some, maybe, can't avoid it: Eddie Shore, says Michael Farber, was "preternaturally mean." Sprague Cleghorn, too, maybe, although he pleaded self-defence: "I never did anything to anybody who never did anything to me." You can understand anger having a hockey use, as a motivator, as fuel. Mean could have a tactical application, helping you to crush the spirit out of a rival by, say, breaking his ankle with a lumberjackly swipe of a slash. To some it might seem a viable option. Mostly, though, mean seems like a nasty indulgence, a personal style, a question of what you can get away with. Ed Van Impe, one of Kharlamov's many attackers, wasn't mean, according to a long-time Philadelphia broadcaster; that was just his approach to the game.

Mean is the protagonist's brother, Kirby, in Steven Galloway's charming first novel, *Finnie Walsh* (2000). Playing road hockey and executing what in the playoffs of 2014 became known as a *Lucic*, "his favourite trick was to come at you from behind, put his stick between your legs and then pull back, sending the blade into your crotch. He called this 'harpooning the whale.'"

When Howie Morenz first came to Montreal from Stratford, Cleghorn was one of the veterans who wouldn't talk to him. Billy Coutu and Bert Corbeau wouldn't talk to him, either, but Cleghorn is suggested to have been more extra-insidiously silent. Later, Cleghorn and Morenz were good friends, and liked to kick up their heels by stocking up on, quote, cannon firecrackers, which they'd toss under police cars in Montreal traffic jams. "They'd howl in glee," the story goes, "when the cops came tumbling out of each side of the patrol car drawing revolvers."

In Chicago, Stan Mikita was mean but Bobby Hull wasn't. Billy Reay, their coach, testified to this. "Bobby is just a big, easygoing kind of guy," he said. Hull was handsomer, too. Mikita's scars, his battered nose, "Slavic features," cold brown eyes: "Put it all together, it doesn't exactly spell mother." Bob Gassoff—he played for St. Louis in the 1970s—was the meanest of the mean, says Tiger Williams. "He would do anything to get an advantage: gouge your eyes, kick, spear, even push his finger into your nose and twist it to increase the pain." Also: "He was mentally tough in a way that Dave Schultz will never know about."

The word *mean* has many meanings, including an older sense signifying communion and fellowship and intercourse. As an adjective, it's a benign enough word for intermediary, and also signifies inferiority and smallness of character, pettiness. *He swings a mean stick* can be both a censure and approbation. *Disobliging, unkind, vicious,* and *cruel*—that's the hockey usage.

Is the ice to blame? What is it about stepping out to skate that turns a man? It's a strand that runs through the hockey books. In *Net Worth* (1991), David Cruise and Alison Griffiths write of former Toronto defenceman Carl Brewer: "Though often a mass of nerves before games, once on the ice Brewer played with such coolness that observers wondered whether it was the same man."

Often it's framed as a kind of an apology or disclaimer. Here's a former Toronto Maple Leaf, Kris King:

> Many fans who come to the games are under the impression that those of us who play tough hockey have tough personalities away from the rink, but that isn't the case. People who know me on the ice are surprised to see me off the ice. I'm a laid-back kind of guy. After the season, my family and I head right back to our cottage in Ontario where I love to fish. I try to do a bit of charity work . . .

Away from hockey, Montreal's fearsome John Ferguson was cited as "the type of fellow who washes the floors for his wife." You have to admit: a willingness to do housework makes for a convincing plea of innocence. Elmer Lach might have been one of the most-penalized players of his day but, said the *Saturday Evening Post* in 1950, "he wears sports clothes in good taste." Mostly, though, it's hobbies that are entered into evidence. Deadly Dave Schultz? "He tends his lawn and shrubs as if he were a landscape gardener," the *Miami News* reported in 1975. Boston's nefarious John Wensink was a dollhouse enthusiast. Montreal's *Gazette* profiled the Canadiens' Babe Siebert in 1939 and found, guess what? On the ice he was "a roaring, driving charging demon." Off ice, in the dressing room:

> Siebert sat in a corner by himself, smoking. He never bothered anyone; talked only when spoken to. Even on trips . . . you'd find the Babe curled up in his lower berth examining fondly a new rod or reel, some new line or a set of flies he had just bought. For he was a confirmed fisherman and hunter.

In *Hockey: For Spectator, Coach and Player* (1939), Richard Vaughan and Holcomb York called it "The Dual Personality:"

> The most puzzling of all personal problems is this: How is it possible for a grand fellow off the ice—courteous, thoughtful of your interests, and devoted to the idea of fair play—to discard all this the moment he gets on the ice and become mean, to go out of his way to relieve a personal grudge, and to take all the fun out of the game through his constant crabbing and lack of good sportsmanship?

If players let off steam, well, would they be human if they didn't? The best players smile after the explosion, and isn't it a wonderful thing. The problem? "The fellow with a dual personality is the victim of an inferiority complex, and he puts the game on a personal basis as a part of his defense mechanism." He's not beyond help:

> To put a stop to this dualism it is necessary to reveal to the individual concerned a contrasting picture of what he thinks he is doing on the ice and what he is actually doing. I have had some fellows react to this

by saying that they just can't help it, that [it] is a part of a nature. To this the reply is, 'Bosh!' What is will power for, if it is not for the kind of self-control that will enable us to do our best?

And you can thrive as a player without being mean. You can be Jean Ratelle, for instance, who played for Canada in 1972, a two-time Lady Byng winner. His teammate Dennis Hull called him "one of the nicest people I met in my career in the NHL." Bill Quackenbush, who played with my History teacher, was one of the game's cleanest players. Rocket Richard? He was rated, in his time, *aloof, sullen, moody, peculiar*. But, says Frank Selke: "There is no meanness in Maurice Richard. He's 100 per cent solid gold; someone you'd be proud to have as the husband of one of your daughters."

When Jaromir Jagr came from Czechoslovakia to his first NHL training camp as a bright young phenom, he navigated a new language, a new culture, and the wariness of new teammates. "The best players were the friendliest to me, which is understandable because they had nothing to be afraid of. The others treated me more or less normally, although some of them glared at me a little. Those were the ones who felt threatened." Once the season began, he quickly found out about Montreal's Claude Lemieux:

He was unbearable. He constantly fought, provoked people and poked and stabbed with his stick behind the back of the referee. He wasn't even very well liked by his teammates. He was always complaining. The food was bad; his gear wet; the bus was too cold or too hot.

Ebbie Goodfellow had a theory that truly mean players didn't last, that word got around. "Somebody would say, 'That dirty sonofabitch gave me the stick' and the other guys would then lay for him and straighten him out."

I don't know how this squares with Ted Lindsay, who just seems to be a case study for mean. Or what about his fellow bullseye, Gordie Howe? Howe also had a strong reputation for meanness. It's on the record. John Ferguson said, "Somebody like Howe, he never said much at all. He didn't have to. He was a mean bastard, and that look of disgust he'd give you made you want to crawl into the ice." Phil Esposito recalls Howe spearing a guy "in the balls" during an old-timers' game. Gary Ronberg is one who cautions a wider perspective: "Despite all the stories about Howe's meanness, he probably never hurt another player unless he felt that the guy deserved it, or that it was necessary for self-preservation."

Lindsay retired from the Chicago Black Hawks at the end of the 1959–60 season and went to work in the automotive industry, but he returned to the Red Wings for one more season in 1964. Clarence Campbell tried to persuade him not to, but he couldn't resist and back he came, aged thirty-nine. It was tough. "In business, you get so you love everybody," he said halfway through the year, "but in this game you have to be mean or you're going to get pushed around. I keep telling myself, *Be mean! Be mean!*"

The first time King Clancy played against Montreal's Bert Corbeau, Corbeau cross-checked him headfirst into the chicken wire and then dropped down on his back with both his knees. (They got to be pretty good friends, later, Clancy chirrups.) Red Storey said that Corbeau taught him how to break a man's ankle and not get caught by the officials. Corbeau said, too, that no one ever got by him twice. "A guy passed me once and the next time I broke every muscle in his stomach." Which does sound exceptionally spiteful.

THERE'S NO MORE famous lack of teeth than Bobby Clarke's, a front-upper gap, four-wide, with the gums glistening Flyers-red, a smile so famous maybe it's the Canadian Mona Lisa, and as with Mona Lisa, we can't be certain just what Clarke is smiling at. The 1970s were good to the Philadelphia team he led, bestowing two Stanley Cups. Is it the happy warrior he's advertising, livid as his welts, in photos from those years? There's a seven-year-old's gleam in Clarke's eyes, proud and defiant, a wildness that you have to assume he was relying on to terrify future opponents who might be looking on, especially Russians.

He was twenty-three when he was named captain, the youngest ever in the NHL until Steve Yzerman showed up. In 1976, he was elected to the presidency of the players' union, and so it was on his watch that the NHLPA declared that the players wanted all fighting gone, whether by stick or fist, time to rid the game. The previous fall, under the direction of Ontario Attorney General Roy McMurtry, police in Toronto had started charging hockey players for alleged criminal acts committed on the ice. Five were headed to court. The players were concerned. They didn't have specific suggestions, so far. They wanted to parley with the league's owners.

Bernie Parent said that Clarke reminded him of Jean Béliveau. "Both are very quiet, but they are great leaders. Clarkie's judgment is amazing." Really? Béliveau? Denis Potvin said Clarke only appeared to be working hard. "The fact is, he takes two strides and assumes that desperate look of his because he's such a poor skater...Bobby skates with so much desire that it inevitably rubs off on his teammates." Dennis Hextall called Clarke's style "cute dirty," and a good part of it was his ability to keep from getting caught. "I've already told him he's the dirtiest SOB in hockey today, but I don't hold that against him." Dave Schultz, former Philadelphia enforcer, echoed that assessment:

"The funny thing is that when people talk about Clarke, the cute little word 'chippy' keeps popping up. Chippy! How about 'dirty'?"

I watched the broadcast of that Moscow Game 6 again. Second period, Canada leading 3–1. There's 10:22 left in the period. Gary Bergman runs into Kharlamov near the Canadian blueline. Foster Hewitt: "Bergman was particular, how he handled him." Yes, true: he shoves gloves in his face, pushes him down. Clarke gets the puck, backhands it high into the Soviet end. Icing. They're four-on-four. Also on the ice for Canada: Paul Henderson and Guy Lapointe. Faceoff to Ken Dryden's right, Clarke and Kharlamov. Kharlamov snaffles the puck back to the point. The whistle goes but the Canadians keep skating and, man, are they peeved when they have to stop. Hewitt: "It's awfully hard to hear it." Canadian players throw up their arms, the universal *would-you-believe-these-fucking-foreign-joker-referees?* gesture. The camera swings over to the visitors' bench where Peter Mahovlich, looking seriously pissed, throws his stick on the ice just to illustrate how seriously pissed he is.

Faceoff, Clarke and Vladimir Vikulov. Clarke wins. Puck goes down, Soviets bring it back. Kharlamov carries through centre, primes to shoot—it's just him and the withdrawing defenceman, with Clarke cruising just behind to his left. As Kharlamov crosses the line, Clarke slides his hands up his stick. Starts his swing. Never seen a photograph of this. Slo-mo it and you see Kharlamov has no clue. It's a full Clarkovian backswing that's delivered just as Kharlamov backhands a pass to his trailing winger. *Attawapiskat!* He doesn't go down. "Here's a roller in front," Hewitt says, eye on the puck. Whistle. Clarke is on his knees. Kharlamov stands over him. Dryden is looking on. The referee is chopping on his arm. Clarke is facing the camera, talking to Kharlamov, who push-punches him, skates away. Bergman chases. "That nearly started something," Foster Hewitt says just before the TV feed cuts out. "Because they don't understand English," Hewitt reports, "it doesn't really mean whatever they're saying." *Clarke's mix-up*, he calls it, like a bowl of nuts. Kharlamov, he notes, "seems to be exhausted from whatever check he took."

Clarke's penalty is two minutes for slashing, ten for misconduct.

"I gave him a good rap on the ankle," Clarke says after the game. Henderson protests that *he* was the one who was slashed: "I get axed and we get the penalty."

The *nasty and premeditated slash* it's sometimes been called since. The Hockey Hall of Fame prefers *aggressive chop*.

John Ferguson did later confess that he'd given Clarke the word, though Clarke says that was just Fergie being gentlemanly.

"What the hell," the assistant coach also said, "I would have done it myself if I had to."

Clarke in 1981: "I'm surprised he can walk after the shot I gave him."

The *ultimate compliment*, Canadian Press wrote on one of the anniversaries.

Henderson in 2005: "Obviously, I look at it a little differently today. Hindsight is 20–20 for all of us. But I really don't think any part of that should ever be in the game. But in '72, I thought it was fine."

Clarke: "We didn't win because of the slash."

He explained it to his daughter, Jakki, for her book, *Flyer Lives*, in 2012. "If I hadn't learned to lay a two-hander once in a while, I never would've left Flin Flon." While we still weren't quite yet beating Latvia during the 2014 Olympics, her sister Jody took to Twitter to suggest that a Bobbyesque slash might help the cause, quote, #sorrynotsorry #dontjudge #proudofdad.

Kharlamov spoke up, too, before his death. "I looked into his angry eyes, saw his stick which he wielded like a sword, and didn't understand what he was doing. It had nothing to do with hockey."

IF MEAN IS a satellite of angry, where does hate fit in? Because hate is another thing entirely; it can be a crime, not a word to use lightly and one that all upstanding people would say there's no place for in hockey. Where you do hear it is in the phrase *get a hate on*, or players you hear about who *hate to lose*, but it's understood that the sense is mostly figurative, or as the dictionary designates *a strong aversion*, "Now chiefly *poet.*"

John Ferguson advised Peter Mahovlich when the latter first came to Montreal: "You've got the size and ability. Get mad and start leaning on people. You gotta hate those other guys." Or Denis Potvin, who wrote in his book *Power on Ice* (1977), "I hated the entire Toronto club—but especially their captain, George Armstrong, who was half Indian."

Anatoli Tarasov admired Canadians, loved Americans, but the Czechs—he hated the Czechs because the Czechs hated him. They used to shoot pucks his way, aiming to hit him behind the bench. Was that Canada's problem in 1972: the team only discovered its hate halfway through the series, waiting for them in Sweden? Frank Mahovlich seems to have hated the Soviets going in, but it took a while for the feeling to spread, and there's a strong case to be made that it was largely Swede-hate that drove the team in Moscow. *Canada Russia '72* follows the flow of the team's anger: losing in Montreal is embarrassing, and the team plays better. By the time they get to Vancouver, they're furious at the nation for booing how hard they're trying. So they take this anger over to Sweden, where they generate some more. In Moscow, Canadian ire nearly razes the rink.

It wasn't that simple, of course, but that's the narrative that we're left with, along with the iconic images of J.P. Parise swinging his stick at a referee. If you read the biographies, the hate is unavoidable. Channelling Paul Henderson a year after it was all over, author John

Gault wrote that he'd come to despise Russians, Communism, the Soviet hockey system: *everything*.

Hate is a regular feature of playoff hockey. Its absence was the reason (pundits said) that Philadelphia couldn't beat New Jersey in the second round of the 2012 playoffs. This allowed the Devils to spare their reserves of acrimony for the semifinal against the New York Rangers, a team they hated so much that when they'd met previously during the regular season, three fights broke out in the first three seconds of the game. Where else in civil society do you see the word *hate* used so casually, without question or qualification? Maybe you thought that speed or excitement is the prime NHL product. Not according to Colin Campbell, the league's director of hockey operations who in 2007 told Randy Starkman from the *Toronto Star* that he didn't believe that bad hits in hockey happened because players lacked or had misplaced their respect for another.

A *crock*, he called that. "I just think that that's overblown and the players who say it don't understand. Players are competitive. We sell hate. Our game sells hate. You guys, the media, sell hate." It was worse when he played in the 1970s, he added, either wistfully or as a proud measure of progress.

Back in 1975, when she was a columnist at the *Globe and Mail*, Christie Blatchford wrote in defence of hate as an essential commodity in the hockey world. Like it or not, she argued, there's a vein of madness that runs through sport, a current of illogic that is not only normal but necessary. That's hate, and it's what non-hockey people don't understand, "just as they find little beauty in the sound of a body hitting the boards." To be great you have to embrace the hate. "That's our game, guys," says Blatchford. Here's the recipe:

bravado + bravery + (some) phony machismo + (a dash of) meanness

Maybe it's not a draft that's going to cure anybody's cold or even refresh you much: it doesn't taste like raspberries, but it is what it is and who are you to fool with the formula? In fact, you should be vigilant that no one spikes the brew, or worse, dilutes it. "If we're not careful," Blatchford rails, "somebody's going to take what's hard out of hockey." You know who'll be happy when that happens? The Swedes.

> Our country has a surplus of nice athletes who play by the rules and play clean and never stoop to try anything for an edge. They don't hate. And they hardly ever win.

THE HOCKEY HALL of Fame used to keep its archives in downtown Toronto, upstairs from the vaults where the cups and hallowed members are honoured, Gretzky's sticks and the two thousand pucks, all the hanging sweaters, and the portraits of players. You came in the doors by the sculpture of the boys on the boards and took an elevator to the second floor.

The fame wasn't so well organized up there in the archives. It looked like the building had bred memorabilia overnight and piled it by the wall. Beneath the massive Jean Béliveau portrait, a table teemed with hockey cards and heaped photographs. Thickets of sticks crowded up against trophies whose tarnish had rubbed off on someone's famous golf bags, next to meaningful old slatted seats from an old arena somewhere.

One morning, looking for traces of Sprague Cleghorn, I pulled out a file: Hockey Related Deaths. It was an altogether unhappy index, but contained no surprises. Hockey can, and often does, kill, though you'd think it might kill more. All those skates and sticks, the slippery ice, the collisions and confrontations, all that male anger moving at high speed. Looking on the bright side, as per the *Saturday Evening Post* circa 1938: "Though battles waged during the thirty years of professional hockey have stained the ice of a thousand rinks, only one player died as a result. And he was a minor leaguer."

The *Toronto Star*, from the evidence here, may have at one time been the official crier of subsequent hockey deaths.

Head hit ice in fall
Thorold player dies

Town in mourning
over young referee
Killed by a puck

Begged For A Chance
But Hockey Player Dies

Hit in neck by puck
goalkeeper, 13, dies

Death Stuns Team
Game goes on

The bad news covered the table with its headlines. "Player dies during game," was one more. Steven Dale Hedtrath, from Coon Rapids, Minnesota, was seventeen. He was considered one of the hottest prospects in the state, and he had died at the Cook Arena on Wednesday night when he swallowed his mouthpiece.

One more, from 1978, "Untimely Death" the headline. A family friend reported what the boy's father said when they told him his boy was gone: "I dreamed too much for my son."

[Third]

"We didn't have much heart for hockey after he died."

**TOE BLAKE, IN 1956, ON THE MOOD IN THE MONTREAL CANADIENS
LOCKER ROOM AFTER HOWIE MORENZ DIED**

EVELYN MORETON WAS eight in 1878, when she came from England with her family to live at Rideau Hall in Ottawa. As comptroller, her father looked after the governor general's books while her mother coddled resentments. As Evelyn told it later, her mother was unhappy in Canada even before the weather turned, on account of the *pitiful amenities* of our *lacklustre* and *graceless* society. But it was the monstrous cold that really repelled her, and before the year was out the Moretons were on their way back home.

There's plenty to say about Evelyn, but what's pertinent here is that in due course she grew up, met Old Bungo, and married him. Sir Julian Byng, her husband, had commanded Canadian troops in France during the First World War, most famously at Vimy Ridge, and he was never happier than when Winston Churchill sent him to Canada to be governor general in 1921. Evelyn returned to Rideau Hall with a new name, Lady Byng of Vimy, and that's the one under which she did her best to save hockey from itself.

Winters in Ottawa were a *harsh bondage*, and the viscountess never really got used to them. Beautiful? Yes, but the birds didn't sing and middle-aged people could only watch as the young enjoyed themselves. The Byngs tried to learn to skate, pushing chairs around

Lady Byng and Old Bungo: Lady Byng, the woman who tried to save hockey from itself, and Governor General Viscount Byng of Vimy in 1922.

vice-regal rinks, but they kept falling down. Finally, with relief, they gave away their skates.

There were no plays to see in the capital, because Canadians weren't theatre-minded. That's how the Byngs ended up, more or less, loving hockey. They watched the Toronto St. Patricks beat the home-town defending champion Senators 5–4: that was their first game, in 1921. Ottawa captain Eddie Gerard presented Lady Byng with a bouquet of American Beauty roses; Lord Byng dropped the puck. Later, both teams joined in giving their Excellencies three hearty cheers. The hockey, said the *Globe*, was some of the most thrilling ever to have been played on Ottawa ice. There wasn't a single penalty.

After five happy hockey-filled years, with many Saturday nights spent rooting for the Senators, Lady Byng could count many favourite players—Gerard, Frank Nighbor, and King Clancy were among them—and just two grievances. Needless rough play, she felt, was a threat to the future of the game. As for those childish spectators who insisted on showering the ice with rubbish at the slightest annoyance, didn't they realize the danger they were putting the players in?

She was right, of course. It was childish and dangerous, and over the years the list of players felled by debris grew long. It took many decades for hockey to arrive at today's state, where bombarding the ice is a scourge prohibited by the NHL. Lady Byng would be proud of the Senators and their reminder to fans, in 2013, that:

Anyone caught throwing an object onto the ice is subject to ejection from Scotiabank Place and/or criminal prosecution.

"If you're skating along the smooth surface and suddenly your skate goes over a coin or a paper clip, there's no way to defend yourself," says Andy Bathgate. "It can be a terrifying moment." Everybody on the ice is in equal danger, all the players, the referees, and the linesmen. "An unseen object flying through the air can put an eye out. An unseen object lying on the ice is the worst hazard in hockey."

Coins "of every denomination" were on the ice when Montreal's Gilles Tremblay broke his leg in 1964. Just before his NHL debut, playing in Guelph, Ontario, Rod Gilbert skated over a cardboard lid from an ice-cream cup. He ended up with a broken back and a spinal fusion. He describes the mechanics of the crash in his autobiography: "I immediately fell forward and, because of the great speed I had developed, crashed into the hard wood boards at the side of the rink."

He must have known the story of Jack McMaster, a standout Junior with the Toronto Marlboros who'd gone on to sign for the Senior A Kitchener-Waterloo Dutchmen. He'd been the leading playoff scorer for the 1957–58 season. The following season, taking a shot on the Sudbury goal in the second period, he crashed hard into the endboards. "Hockey fans were at a loss to explain McMaster's fall," the *Star* reported. "No one was near him." He was carried off with broken vertebrae and other injuries to the spinal cord. He never played another game of hockey and he never walked again. He'd skated over a paperclip.

Hats, programs, newspapers, packets of cigarettes, coins: these are the everyday ammunition of hockey barrages, and have been for years. Belts and watches speak of a more committed abuser, someone willing to divest themselves of useful property as an investment in insult. A whole tray of ice-cream cups coming over the glass in Bloomington, Minnesota, shows a creative flair. In Toronto in 1918, a fan—"a plutocrat in the gallery," the *Star* called him—either dropped a large gin bottle or whizzed it past Alf Skinner's head. I don't know whether it was a spontaneous review of the book or the reffing or both, but in a raucous 1944 playoff game in Chicago, a plummeting library copy of the Dorsha Hayes novel *Mrs. Heaton's Daughter* struck a woman over the eye. The *New York Times* had felt more or less the same when it first appeared: "No distinction of style or great depth of character."

A 1927 Boston crowd watching Bruins and St. Pats scattered:

- one bottle
- the yolks and whites of four eggs
- 65 cigar and cigarette butts
- 76 American pennies
- one Canadian penny

A rubber ball thrown after Montreal's Terry Harper scores a goal circa 1964 says *hooray*, just the opposite of its billiard cousin hurtling past goalie Terry Sawchuk in Boston in 1957. Nails say *If I had a ham-*

mer, while a crutch hoisted over the glass in Toronto in the early 1990s at Los Angeles enforcer Marty McSorley, that's more of an *I wish you needed this*. On Christmas Day of 1925, fans in Saskatoon pelted a referee with mud, coal, and peanuts. In Toronto's old Maple Leaf Gardens, on a Sunday night, a fan sometimes threw a bottle of ink or plastic mustard containers. At least once they threw a persimmon. But the Leafs probably had that coming.

It's only very occasionally that players return the fire of fans. Brad Park remembers teammate Vic Hadfield, in Toronto, tossing Leafs goalie Bernie Parent's mask into the crowd. As a Junior in 1962, goalie Wayne Rutledge roared around "in a riotous mood" after a goal was scored against him. He harangued the goal judge and threw a selection of rubbers (including the puck) back at the crowd. Also, spat. No penalty.

Eggs have a special place in hockey, which is to say, *splat*, on the ice. That's the transitive verb we'll assign to them as they hit; as Scott Young says, the rightful noun for the puddle they make is *plat* ("a flat ornament of gold," one of its dictionary definings). In *The Leafs I Knew*, Young charts the source of Toronto eggs (usually the second balcony) and the reaction (nobody comments), and introduces us to the guy charged with cleaning up. He wears a brown fedora and a sweater of yellow and black; his trousers are baggy. His operation has two parts: first he appears with a long-handled ice knife and broom. When he's transformed plat to pile, he goes back for his shovel. Always he's applauded, and every time, he raises his hat in response.

An egg is inherently humorous, but even with an egg, as with anything, funny has its limits. Gump Worsley took one in the head at New York's Madison Square Garden one night, no joke at all: "Gump was badly shaken and had to be hospitalized," his Canadiens teammate John Ferguson recorded. "He had suffered a concussion." (New York policemen caught the thrower, a high school student, and brought him down to the dressing room in case Worsley wanted to punch him out, which he didn't.) The dinner knife someone fired at Worsley in 1969? He kept it for a souvenir.

In 1936, Montreal's Maroons battled the Detroit Red Wings into six overtimes before Mud Bruneteau finally won it for the Wings. It's still the longest game in the league's history, and lucrative, too, for the Wings. Jubilant fans stuffed dollar bills into Bruneteau's equipment as he left the ice, and he moved slowly enough that when he came to divvy up the cash, he paid out twenty-two dollars to each member of the team, including the trainer and the kid tending the sticks.

Before the Richard Riot, toe-rubbers were generally tossed as a currency of approval: score a goal in the Forum and the men would reach down and remove a precious winter overshoe, hurl it happily to the ice. One rubber emboldens another: Was there ever a fan who just threw one? Red Storey tells of five hundred collected in one night, but that's galoshes, too, and he doesn't specifically indicate what the mood was at the Forum that evening. Dennis Hull's dad went to Montreal to watch him play for Chicago. "When you're out there tonight," he told his son, "and Béliveau scores, get me a size ten-and-a-half."

On one occasion in Chicago, a fan threw a fish that landed in the lap of Bill Gadsby's wife. Bobby Hull recalls a live rabbit and dead squirrels. Also, firecrackers and a life-sized dummy of Frank Mahovlich wearing a noose around its neck—though attendants confiscated mannequin-Frank before he got to the ice. In Minnesota, someone once tossed a bag, and inside the bag, just like a joke waiting for a punchline, were a duck and a pheasant, both alive. Red Berenson—"an outdoorsman," Bill Goldsworthy explains—escorted the birds from the ice.

"An octopus cannot be accurately thrown," Dick Beddoes wrote, regarding the fabled Detroit tradition that carries on to this day.

A NOTE FROM
THE BLACKHAWKS

FANS, we BLACKHAWKS, when we're playing a hockey game, are engaged in a very serious and hazardous occupation. Despite the exactions of the game, we try with every ounce of strength we possess to win.

In a great measure your support and cooperation are tremendous factors in our success. Without your help, we would find it extremely difficult to win. May we go a little further and ask for a bit more of your cooperation to

AID US IN DISCOURAGING THE GROWING
PRACTICE OF THROWING OBJECTS ON THE
ICE DURING THE PROGRESS OF A GAME

We, like yourselves, are often subject to over enthusiasm. Who in the of a hard fought battle isn't ? It is only when that enthusiasm reache danger point that we feel we must call on you for help.

The smallest article on the ice, even a piece of paper, may cause a trip that will send us crashing on the ice or into the side boards, perhaps ending a hockey career. The danger involved and the upsetting delay to the game are harmful to us an we ask all sportsmen to help us stop it.

THE CHICAGO BLACKHAWKS

MARTY BURKE	JOHNNY GOTTSELIG	DOC ROMNES
LORNE CHABOT	BILLY KENDALL	PAUL THOMPSON
TOMMY COOK	NORMAN LOCKING	LOUIS TRUDELL
	MUSH MARCH	
ART COULTER	HOWIE MORENZ	ART WIEBE
LOLO COUTURE	DONNIE McFADYEN	CLEM LOUGHLIN

Game of throwns: A January 1935 handbill distributed at Chicago's Stadium asked fans to keep their enthusiasm from reaching "the danger point." It's said to have worked, at least for a night: debris on the ice was limited to "one lemon and one half-folded newspaper."

George Plimpton notes that the fan who started the whole business only ever tried to hit one player in all his years, Toronto's Ted Kennedy. He missed, and hit Detroit's own Vic Lynn.

As a Ranger playing in Boston, Brad Park nearly took a "45-rpm phonograph record" to the head. When a whiskey bottle clonked a Chicago fan named Joe Fusco on his brow, the Black Hawks offered a $250 reward to anyone who could identify the bottler. During the

1943–44 season, Detroit at Chicago, the Black Hawks were leading 2–0 with two minutes to play when the Red Wings came roaring back to tie the game. Charles Coleman describes what happened next: "A roll of adding machine paper was thrown from an upper balcony that struck linesman Steve Meuri on the head and knocked him down."

When it comes to throwing stuff, there's really no bigger night in hockey than that of Thursday, March 17, 1955. The next morning, *Toronto Star* correspondent Frank Teskey reported from the front: "A grapefruit from the grays hit my camera and knocked it spinning." (There are a few more expressive sentences in hockey's literature, but only a few.) Montreal's beloved Maurice Richard had been ruled out of his team's final three games and all the playoffs. Four days earlier, playing in Boston, Richard had gotten into it with Hal Laycoe. The *gory affair*, newspapers called it, and the *brannigan*, and they threw in *wild scene* and *most vicious* and said *Montreal's fiery Rocket exploded*. The *irate French battler* ended up punching a linesman in the eye; the linesman tried to punch him back. Asked later what had happened, Richard said, "Ask Laycoe." Boston police wanted to arrest Richard, but they were persuaded that this was a matter of hockey lawlessness that hockey's peace officers would address.

They didn't like the suspension in Montreal, and they didn't like the suspender, so when Clarence Campbell showed up at the Forum to see the Habs host Detroit, Montrealers had a brannigan of their own waiting for him. The *Toronto Star* reported: "Campbell, after being punched in the face, was buried under an avalanche of rubbers, peanuts, programs, eggs, tomatoes, and pennies." Someone threw what was later described as "a U.S. Army–type teargas bomb." That's when the smoke began to billow, "as if from a miniature atom bomb." The organist played "My Heart Cries for You." Later, of course, the riot spilled out into the streets of Montreal. Cars burned, looters sacked stores.

Conn Smythe said it could never happen in Toronto. "Well, just let anyone try to make it happen," he threatened. Jack Adams said the same on Detroit's behalf. Montreal pampered the Rocket, that was the real trouble, according to him. When the Rangers played the Forum the following Saturday, two hundred policeman stood guard, backed up by a fire hose. People were selling looted watches and rings "at ridiculous prices." A few nights later, back in Montreal for a game against Boston, five hundred policemen joined Campbell in the crowd. On the night of the riot he'd been accompanied at the game by "three girl secretaries from his office," one of whom, Phyllis King, the papers commended for coolness under fire. "Although she was struck several times by flying boots, rubbers and fruit," a correspondent wrote, "Miss King never once suggested they leave." Campbell was down to a single secretary for the Boston game—again, the "attractive" Miss King, his future wife.

AN EARLIER MONTREAL game, in March of 1923, sounds almost as wild, and so appalled General Sir Arthur Currie that he felt moved to comment publicly. The Canadiens were hosting Ottawa's Senators in the first game of the NHL championship that night, the victor of the two-game series winning the right to head out west to play for the Stanley Cup. "Riotous Scene," the Ottawa paper reported next morning, and "Disgraceful Attacks." Montreal's Sprague Cleghorn was in there, certainly, but it was his teammate Billy Coutu who did most of the damage, and most of it to Ottawa's Cy Denneny. A word-cloud depicting the worst of it would look like this:

deliberately slugged **head** cowardly blow from behind
blood heap rolled around
match foul **several stitches**

The crowd, enraged, threw papers and bottles at the referees and Ottawa players, also fruit. Twice the game had to be stopped to clear the ice. One of the referees, Cooper Smeaton—he'd served in the First World War and been wounded—got himself a megaphone to appeal for a calm that he couldn't, in the end, command. General Currie was president of McGill University at this time, having led the Canadian Corps through some of the bloodiest days of the war. After the game he issued a blazing statement:

> I would rather see every grandstand in the country burned down than a repetition of the disgraceful scenes which took place in the Mount Royal Arena.

Which would have been one way to go. Lady Byng thought of another. If she couldn't stamp out hockey's littering problem, what about the behaviour so shocking to General Currie? She tried. In 1925, she wrote a letter to NHL supremo Frank Calder.

> Feeling a great desire to help your effort to clean up hockey and elimi-nate the needless rough play that at present is a threat to the national game... I am convinced that the public desires good sport, not the injuring of players, and if, by donating this challenge cup, I can in any way help towards this end, it will give me a great deal of pleasure.

The Lady Byng of Vimy Cup was intended to reward the fairest, most effective, and most sportsmanlike player in the NHL. Her Excellency invited hook-checking Frank Nighbor over to Rideau Hall to ask him what he thought about it and—surprise!—tell him he was the first winner. A committee of sports editors took over the administration after that, rewarding Nighbor again in 1926, before Frank Boucher began his run in 1927. After he won the trophy seven times in eight years, Lady Byng gave him the cup outright in 1935. There was a third edition cast in 1949, after its benefactor's death, and that's when it became the Lady Byng Memorial Trophy. That original cup perished in a fire at Boucher's son's house in 1965, after mice chewed the wiring.

Did Lady Byng's honest effort to reform the game help? Hard to say. Billy Burch slipped in to win it pre-Boucher, post-Nighbor, and he's supposed to have been an awful hothead early in his career before (as a newspaper said in 1925) "taking himself in hand." But that would seem to have come before there was any trophy up for grabs. Browsing the list of winners, all the Max Bentleys and Jean Ratelles, Wayne Gretzkys through Pavel Datsyuks, I think the conclusion you'd have to draw is that it's done exactly what it was intended to do, celebrating the silver good citizenship of exemplary hockey citizens. It doesn't appear to have had any effect whatever on the bad.

OTHERS HAVE TRIED other fixes. Quitting hockey altogether was Bobby Hull's dramatic gambit in October of 1975. The violence just got to be too much. Hockey had fallen so far that it wasn't his game any longer, and so, seven games into the Winnipeg Jets' season, at the age of thirty-six, the Golden Jet walked away in protest.

Or did he? It was front-page news across Canada, but the front pages hadn't heard from Hull himself and there was some doubt about where he'd gone and why. His general manager, Rudy Pilous, said, "It's been buggin' him for a long time, last year as well as this." The Jets released a statement announcing that Hull had been excused from practice and the following game in order to protest hockey's brutality "and the type of goon hockey that has been played recently." Events in a game earlier that week seemed to have propelled him out the door. The Jets' talented Finnish centreman, Veli-Pekka Ketola, had scored, and three members of the Cincinnati Stingers had, as the *Toronto Star* said, jumped him "out of frustration."

Hull's Goon Hockey Boycott, some of the papers called it. Pilous hoped Hull would be back soon; he wasn't sure what good the walkout would do. He himself thought the Cincinnati game wasn't so terribly rough, though another of his players, Perry Miller, had suffered an eye injury fighting three opponents at once. That was pretty bad. But what are you going to do?

"That's not hockey," Hull said.

Everybody had an opinion. Christie Blatchford knew an un-hater when she saw one, and believed Hull had grown old and weary, and that was fine. His gesture was probably a pretty good indicator that he was done, because you're never going to win with that attitude. The Cincinnati coach concurred: it was an easy way for Hull to retire. Toronto defenceman Jim Dorey believed that a lot of the roughness wasn't necessary, though, you know, the word on stopping the Jets was, go after Hull's Swedish linemates, Ulf Nilsson and Anders Hedberg. On the whole, the Jets rarely retaliated when the going got nasty, which only seemed to confirm that they could be intimidated. Complicating the issue, their lineup, which included seven Swedes and two Finns, superior skaters all, was seen as a provocation, causing "frustrated opponents [to] resort to all kinds of foul play."

World Hockey Association president Ben Hatskin tended to blame the Europeans, too. They were so fast on their skates that it was almost a natural reaction of North American players to take a swing at them—imagine, again, the frustration—when they skated by. It wasn't pretty, maybe, but if things really got out of hand, there were fines and suspensions. "That's all you can do," was his answer.

Frank Mahovlich said the game was more brutal than when he and Hull had arrived in the NHL in 1957. "It seems to be keeping pace with everything else: more murders, more crime," he said, a sentence I admit to having tried out aloud in my best imitation Eeyore drone.

It was an ugly time for hockey: 1975 had started with the Boston Bruins' Dave Forbes attacking Minnesota's Henry Boucha. A *scuffle* the papers called it, though the Hennepin County Attorney's Office wasn't sure that was the appropriate term. The reigning Stanley Cup champions were Broad Street's Bullies, the Philadelphia Flyers. In Ottawa, an MP was worried about violence on TV, and not just gratuitous gunfights or massacres with machetes. "I think," said James McGrath, "the most violent aspect of Canadian television is *Hockey Night in Canada.*"

A few months after Bobby Hull returned to the ice—yes, after missing a single game, he was back, scoring a goal—well, nothing had really changed. The NHL didn't have anything to say because it didn't have to. Hockey wouldn't be making any promises to reform. There would be no going down on bended shin pad and apologizing to Bobby Hull. Or anyone else. The editorial writers and columnists weighed in. He should suck it up, they all said, other than the ones who thought hockey was the one that needed to get help.

If you were trapped in a library that year, with no view of rinks or televised games, you could have read your way to the same conclusion that Hull had reached: hockey was in trouble, had lost its way, what was it thinking? The shelves were full of it: Gary Ronberg's *The Violent Game* was just out in 1975, or what about Ira Gitler's *Blood on the Ice*, with chapters titled "Woodchopping Galore" and "Death and Helmets" and "Techniques of Mayhem."

Over in fiction, you'd find long gone the era of making-the-team stories featuring Bill Spunska and his ilk (Frank Orr's Spunskavian Buck Martin, for one). Hockey's novels had entered a whole new phase, one that went beyond reflecting the ugliness of hockey, achieving a sort of novelistic equivalent of method acting in which the story itself was so noxious that, as with John Craig's *Power Play*, if you chanced to put it down, it was almost impossible to pick it up again.

NO ONE DREAMS as a boy of growing up to be a referee, say the referees. "It's a hell of a job," said Clarence Campbell. "A man has to have iron in his soul, the will to command. And he can't be a drinker—he'll have thousands of hours with nothing to do."

In the early days their names were Lou Marsh, Cooper Smeaton, Mike Rodden, and, yes, Clarence Campbell, too. They were born in tiny towns like Fleming, Saskatchewan, where their fathers sold lumber, or maybe in Allandale, Ontario, and the doctor who delivered them was the one to nickname them Buster, which stuck. Some of them were lacrosse or football stars as well as referees. King Clancy and Sylvio Mantha both played in the NHL before they took up a whistle; there have been many others.

Campbell said it was a "personality job," which means, I guess, you have to have a good one. When King Clancy started as a linesman, the veteran Mickey Ion was by his side for his debut at Madison Square Garden. Said Ion, "There are only two sane people in the house—you and I. All the rest are crazy. Just remember that and you won't be nervous."

A new rule in the NHL in 1933 forbade any club employee from "entering into an acrimonious argument with a referee on or off the ice." First to be fined was Detroit's manager, Jack Adams, who paid one hundred dollars to yell at Bill Stewart.

Thankless is a word you often see in referee books, of which there are a few, with titles like *Black and White and Never Right*, *Final Call*, and *Lone Wolf*. Sometimes in the literature referees are called:

Reftop: Whistle-tooting Lou Marsh practises his penalty calls above Toronto in the 1920s.

- *inefficient whistle-tooters* (said of Eusebe Daigneault and Odie Cleghorn, 1933, by the *Boston Post*)
- *a name* (Stephane Auger, 2003, by Joe Thornton)
- *a liar* (Jack Mehlenbacher, 1955, by Phil Watson)
- *a fat pig* (Don Koharski, 1988, by Jim Schoenfeld)

Lou Marsh is supposed to have weaponized his whistle, attaching "a small handle" with which, the papers said, to defend himself.

In 1928, a Quebec judge must have lifted the spirits of the whole profession when he ruled that an assault committed against a hockey referee is more serious than any perpetrated on an ordinary person.

HOCKEY'S NOVELS HAD a go at fixing the game, too, by showing how much worse life can be than hockey. This was in the late 1960s, early 1970s. Reading the books from this period, I developed the following test for hockey novels: using your imagination, extract all the hockey from the story and see what's left. Any residual character and plot at all, and there's a chance you've got a book you're not going to be tempted to hoist onto the ice the next time you're at the Air Canada Centre.

Scott Young's Bill Spunska novels bend and flop with the hockey taken out. The characters don't have much to talk about, have nowhere to go. There's a lot of staring into corners. Most important, without hockey Bill has nothing to grasp for, no agency by which to make himself into a full-blown Canadian.

With all the hockey wrung out of Craig's *Power Play*, you're left with a dark love story. When I say dark, I mean turbid, and by turbid, I mean it's probably best if we leave the hockey in. Les Burton is captain of the Falcons; Lori Adams, an "entertainer" of what I'd better call ravishing beauty. They fall in love and they're great together, except they can't make it work. The world won't let them. "Oh, Les," says Lori. "Oh, Lori," Les says. And I quote.

I may have missed the scene where they explain what divides them. Hockey, I think, is part of the wedge. TV might also be to blame, if I don't miss my mark. If I do, it could be hockey on TV. The message here may be that hockey and TV can't be together. *Power Play* is a bit of screed when it comes to TV: it makes the hockey less real, more of an act. It changes the light at rinks.

It's also a timely novel about players' rights, their emancipation from indenture, for this was the age in which the first players' association arose. (Alan Eagleson is a character.) The Falcons go on strike before the sixth game of the Stanley Cup finals. The players in *Power Play* haven't read their contracts. But the book's prevailing pitch is one of nostalgia: it's about what used to be, before hockey was seized from the hockey men. "It's not fair," says a coach, but it's true.

To say that *Power Play* ushers in a new age in hockey fiction is to load a lot on a flimsy structure. Let's just say that there's a dark, murky time in hockey literature of which *Power Play* is a good—which is to say, bad—example. In fact, there's a sullen sameness to the novels that followed *Power Play* and the world they depict, and the hockey that's played there would terrify Bill Spunska.

In the 1970s, hockey itself became a bit of an enemy. Early hockey heroes just wanted to make the team; now they struggled to subdue the game itself, to serve their dream. Scott Young published a new novel, *Face-Off*, in 1971 that must have been much anticipated by Spunska enthusiasts. They might have had a moment's pause when they saw on the title page the name of a second author, George Robertson, and this ominous credit: *A novel based on an idea created by John Bassett.*

No room in that brainstorm for Spunska. In the book and a subsequent movie (it's *fine*), he cedes the ice to Billy Duke, an altogether different kind of a hero. Chapter one, first paragraph, he's parading naked, which pretty much sets the tone for the rest of the novel. The hockey and the sex are wrestling around together right from the start, at which point we make the acquaintance, page two, of Billy's penis. Whom he calls, endearingly, Mister. What a crazy pair! They go everywhere together and get into all kinds of trouble.

Billy is big news as a player, third in the exalted line of Canadian hockey prodigies after Bobbys Hull and Orr. Billy skates like Orr, shoots like Hull. And he's also smart: the papers (he narrates) always mention how articulate he is, his many scholarships. On page four, it's back over to Mister and how, aged fifteen, *he* meets a dark beauty named Adelaide whose clothes have a distracting habit of rustling against her legs and breasts.

Billy and Mister both hail from Sunset, Ontario, a small town north of—where else?—Peterborough. "Did you know," he confides, "that according to official tests conducted by Lloyd Percival at the Fitness Institute, I have the best blood-oxygen supply in hockey?" He's savvy and his talk is straight, he calls a spade a *spade* and referees *assholes* and he's as wise as Derek Sanderson in the ways of selling himself. He knows that if you're squirting champagne after winning the Memorial Cup, you make sure you sign a contract with the champagne company first. ("You are advertising it, and for that you should get paid.")

There's lots here to amuse a hockey fan, including a villainous rival named Sprague Lowther ("a real rack-em-up kind of defence-man"). Like Spunska before him, Billy's drafted by the Leafs. He signs a big fat contract, buys himself a Firebird convertible, becomes an instant Canadian idol. "You're every kid who ever laced on a pair of skates," he muses. "I mean they'd give anything to be you." He's living Spunska's dream, as long as that dream includes, lingering beyond the dressing room door, "luscious, juicy dolls just waiting to be plucked."

But here's where Billy and Mister go their separate ways, if that's possible. Because whatever Mister's preference, Billy has no time for doll-plucking. He spies a singer in a rock group, Sherri Lee Nelson, and with her he finds joy and fulfillment and "all the tenderness and soft yielding warmth of woman."

So, three years and a few dozen pages on, we're more or less at the same cross in the roads Les faced in *Power Play*. Was this really the only fictional possibility for the time? At least in *Face-Off*, the split, when it comes, is a little clearer. For Billy, it's when the hockey starts to sour. Away from the game he's doing fine, on TV they're showing features about him titled "The Hottest Rookie." But the hockey is letting him down. All of a sudden he's lost his touch, can't score, can't fight, and here's the terrible dilemma: is it the life that's ruining the hockey or the hockey that's such a poison to the life?

None of it is too appetizing. Billy fights, he loses all his front teeth. The crisis comes when Billy battles Brad Park and bleeds; Sherri Lee flees Maple Leaf Gardens and vomits. When Billy's friend and team- mate Sangster scores and gets slashed down and slams into a goalpost, Billy does the only sensible thing: he punches out the referee, Art Skov. "Even in the NHL," he dryly allows, "that is a rarity."

"Cool it," advises novel-Bobby Orr. "Do you want to get life?"

It doesn't end well for Billy and Sherri. Not to give too much away, but Billy's in a taxi looking for Sherri when he spies a wrecked sports car and the driver says, "Looks like an accident." Later there's a morgue scene. Hockey wins, Sherri dies.

Billy sleeps. When he dreams, it's about a defenceman who won't let him get to Sherri. There's a bit in here about how hockey has to change, but it's not too convincing, and anyway what does hockey matter at a time like this? He's a zombie as he wanders around Yorkville. He goes back to his bed, cries and moans, then wakes and drives up Church Street. Because, though life can be cruel and empty of all meaning, the Buffalo Sabres are in town, and if there's a sin that's unpardonable, it's showing up late for the game.

So far, two novels, two wins for hockey, two defeats for life and its beautiful women.

Billy Duke is one of the last rookies to stand at centre stage in a hockey novel. As the 1970s give way to the 1980s, the heroes (and heroines) move along in years and careers. Once the novels were about being young and breaking into the big time. Now they're about hanging on down at the end of the bench. Our heroes are a collection of wounded veterans for the most part, a wry, cynical bunch trying not to think about what lies beyond.

YOU COULD ALWAYS ban hockey outright. There are, after all, precedents for this.

An English king, Edward III, nixed *hoquet* and football and cricket in 1363 because they "interfered" with archery. The law stayed on the books until 1784. American football was famously under siege in the early years of the twentieth century because it was deemed too dangerous, with many American colleges putting a stop to it. Harvard was one: in 1907, the president declared it "an undesirable game for gentlemen to play, or for multitudes of spectators to watch." Hockey and basketball weren't much better, in his opinion: all three sports were wastes of money, and the "furious spasms" of competitive sport did nothing to protect players from immorality and vice. Their extreme recklessness exhausted the players and made them incapable of intellectual work. A year earlier, Maine's colleges attempted to eradicate the scourge of basketball, "one of the greatest evils" with which they had to contend. "Records show," said a member of the faculty at Bates, "that it causes an enlargement of the heart and a consequent weakening of the health. It is played indoors where the air is foul and dust thick." To replace it? "Ice hockey is none the less strenuous, but it has the advantage of being played outdoors in the cool fresh air."

More recently, the regional parliament in Spanish Cataluña voted to ban bullfighting. And in Venezuela, the late president Hugo Chávez pondered doing away with golf as an altogether bourgeois pursuit.

Maybe down deep in our blood we've got snowshoe racing lying latent? Canadians couldn't get enough of it at one point. Same with tobogganing. Those aren't team sports, though, I'll grant you that. Curling? Field hockey?

Bandy should be easy to love. It's a sort-of hockey anyway. Teemu Selanne used to play it in Finland as a boy and loved it, so it has that going for it. It almost made it into the Olympics, in 1952. We already have a national bandy team, in fact, and at the Bandy World Championships just before the Sochi Olympics, we . . . Oh. So, bandying, we lost 22–1 to the Russians.

Montreal people who saw a display of lacrosse on ice in 1877 reported back that the rapidity of the skaters was almost *inconceivable*. The dodging was *magnificent* and the stopping—*almost instantaneous*. In 1917, it was touted as a game that was twice as strenuous as its grassy cousin. Next year there would be a league with half a dozen teams. Not sure what happened to that.

It's not easy to think of anything better than ice lacrosse except for, maybe—slippery tennis? The father of the lawn game, Major Walter Wingfield, first lobbed the idea as early as 1874, but it was in New York in 1916 that the game caught on. With black lines painted on the ice, using "old" tennis balls (they tried squash balls first), Watson Washburn and Dean Mathey took on F.B. Alexander and Theodore Roosevelt Pell at the Ice Skating Palace, 181st Street and Broadway. They wore full hockey gear, apparently, and once the match got going, sharp volleying was the order of the day. Mathey and Washburn were intent on playing a forecourt game, which was a mistake, since they kept having to scurry back to the baseline and lost, three sets to zip. The game required "more prompt and decisive action even than hockey." Altogether it was, observers concurred, "far from being an experiment," not only "feasible" but "exciting" and "worthy of being classed a real game."

By 1920 in Cleveland, hockey was forced into a back seat by a double whammy of ice baseball (a six-team league, games every Sunday, twenty thousand spectators) and ("the real thriller") ice boxing. At Rockefeller Park, the fighters were "heavily dressed" in sweaters. "Aside from having to dodge the blows," an eyewitness reported, "contestants experienced much trouble in keeping their feet when they missed their blows." The ring was expanded, to give the fighters more room to work with, and regular boxing regulations were amended to allow for wrestling.

Hockey was probably too young to understand fully the existential threat it faced down in the 1890s. Two words: bicycle skates. A young mechanic in New York by the name of Mike Murphy was the inventor. With a long-bladed skate clamped to the front wheel of his safety bicycle, which was fixed straight, he got his power from the rear wheel. In trials, Murphy attained "astonishing speeds." Smart people who'd seen him go predicted he'd be knocking down speed records just as soon as he could find a straightaway stretch of ice where he didn't have to take any corners, which the bicycle skate couldn't really manage due to rear-wheel slippage. Also, there was trouble with keeping your feet on the pedals, which spun superfast. Can't imagine how it never caught on.

HOCKEY HAD ITS own reforming crusader in John Farina. And if the cure killed the patient? Actually, that was the whole idea. If Farina could have raised up his hand and cleared our winters of pucks and players with a single sweep, he wouldn't have hesitated.

Briefly, in November of 1957 he was the talk of the nation, and on an early Saturday of that month he shared the front page of the *Toronto Star* with Maurice Richard. The Rocket, who'd just scored the five hundredth goal of his career, had been summoned to meet the governor general aboard the vice-regal train, parked in a siding in Montreal. He was the first athlete ever to have been sought out for an audience by a Canadian GG, and he and his wife had visited the Rt. Hon. Vincent Massey's private car, where they talked hockey for thirty-five minutes, after which His Excellency gave Mrs. Richard a white rabbit for her daughter, Suzanne.

Professor Farina was handing out no rabbits. Hockey deserved none. If Richard never scored another goal again, fine. The headline

Condemns All Sports/
They Breed Cheaters/
Doubts Their Value

barely understated the assault he'd made on hockey at a speech the day before, addressing the leadership of the Boys Clubs of Canada, a national organization with some sixty thousand members. He told them that all sports encourage "cheating, larceny, fighting and downright sadism" but he pinned hockey with the prize-ribbon of "most degenerate sport in the world."

You can see how Farina might have caught hockey's attention. He was a sociologist and professor at the University of Toronto's school of social work at the time. In the only photograph I've seen of him, he looks like Jerry Lewis playing the part in bow tie and big glasses with a sprung forelock and a goofy smile. Sports, he'd gone on to say, held scarcely any practical value.

Let's face it, aside from the possible development of skill of questionable use, and perhaps physical development, there is very little use in sport and recreation activities themselves.

It's ridiculous to say running will contribute to character. Running where? Along a back alley or on a cinder track? Running with what motivation—to win a prize, for the joy of running, or from a cop?

The true value of such activities, is their popularity as a medium in which community leaders can effectively transmit our social and cultural values from one generation to the next. The product of such a process is to be a socially adjusted, participating and democratic citizen.

To those who argued that youth clubs got boys off the street, Professor Farina answered that the clubs were of no benefit whatever. "The boys are just as well off left on the street," he said. One of his beefs with boys' clubs was the leadership. "Too many coaches teach boys that the only important thing is winning and not how you play the game," said Professor Farina. Sports should be about the fun, never mind who was watching, and also, the referee needed stronger support: "the only person who represents integrity in the game." About hockey specifically, he thought it bred bad habits.

How many times have you seen one player trip another going in to score? The defenceman figures he'll get a two-minute penalty and it's worth it if he can prevent a goal. He plays the percentages that the other team won't score when he's off. And what do you find boys talking about after the game? The good sportsmanship that has been displayed? No. The fights they saw. They'll look up to these players as heroes. Look what happened to Clarence Campbell after he suspended Rocket Richard.

He was rolling now. He cited American studies that denied any relationship between recreation and low delinquency rates. "If there is evidence that sports and recreation do not necessarily prevent juvenile delinquency and do not alleviate modern stresses leading to mental breakdown, what is their value?"

As word got out, Farina had questions coming back at him. Who was he, anyway? Why should anyone listen to him, yammering away from his ivoried tower? Had he ever played the game, any game at all? When his sporting credentials were examined, well, okay, he'd played baseball and lacrosse, and it was true, too, that he was a big football guy, a former professional referee, and he'd quarterbacked and coached for the University of British Columbia.

Good for him. But his grapes were sour. The president of Toronto's Minor hockey league stepped up to say there were ninety thousand hockey-playing boys under the age of eighteen across the country, "and if that many kids love the game, the whole nation must be degenerate." The president wondered about Farina's intestines. Where other men keep their fortitude? Farina's had to be empty.

Jim Vipond, in the *Globe*, called the professor extravagant. It had to be admitted that there had been incidents in hockey to create such thinking in the minds of social workers. But the chief of referees had a program in place to steer back to wide-open hockey, away from "modern mayhem." The proof of this was that Rocket Richard had been given but a single penalty in thirteen games. More broadly speaking, closer attention should be paid to the nation's fitness. Said Vipond, "We cannot forget the high rate of military rejections for the Korean campaign as compared to the health records of the Russian population." Serious days lay ahead. Who knew what might happen in the next few months? That's why our military men had to be ready, which was to say, our sportsmen: "Canada's armed forces have a history in which the inspirational leadership of men who played sports, and played them hard, meant the difference between winning and losing. The whole history of the British Empire has a sports background."

The *Globe* sent a reporter to the professor's home, and in his own living room Farina said his comments had been twisted around in the uproar. All he was trying to say was that sports should try to "develop the muscles between the head as well as the others."

"The inherent value lies in the leadership and the standards set by the leaders in sports." Here was the problem: sports were too much in the hands of the promoters when it should be the participants in charge. "If sports are maintained to build and develop 'social beings,' they can be of value," he said.

The *Globe*'s editorial page felt the need to wag its finger. The evidence seemed to lie on the side of the sociologist. Hadn't a Junior A player just been suspended for kicking an opponent in the stomach? Farina should be heard. "If he is proved wrong, the error will impose its own penalty on his professional status; if he is right, the motivations of our sports should be examined and corrected."

Scott Young said it was old hat.

A professor comes out of the wings and proclaims professional sport as a degenerating influence. Bystanders nod their heads. Sportswriters try to shout down the professor. Sports promoters, players, and others connected with the game keep largely quiet, except perhaps for one or two soft renditions of that realistic old refrain: We're going to have to cut out this kind of stuff. Or we're going to have to print more tickets.

Young didn't like fights in sports, either, "but since degeneracy, like anything else, is a matter of degree, I don't feel that these fights are signs of degeneracy. If they are signs of anything at all, it is that human beings are present." There were worse things than hockey's violence. What about drunkenness? How about sexual promiscuity, theft, prostitution, neglect of children, crowded housing, and war? "Does any reasonable person believe that that a fight between a couple of well-padded athletes belongs in the above listing of social evils? I don't." The windmill Farina had chosen to charge, said Young, was tiny enough to fit atop a beanie. Clarence Campbell said the man should be thrown out of his job.

Somebody who might have been listening to Farina—maybe he even agreed with him—was Vincent Massey. Maybe the governor general was never going to invite him aboard his private car or give him a white rabbit, but Massey had thought about where hockey was headed, to the point that his idea of the Canadian Pattern had shifted significantly since he'd seen our soldiers strolling the streets of London. In 1949, three years before he moved into Government House, Massey had given the Centennial Address at the Royal Canadian Institute, a speech illustrated with "lantern slides."

Unable to trace the original text, I rely on contemporary news-paper reports for a glimpse of its grain: Canada was in danger of destroying hockey like it had ruined lacrosse, by playing it in the wrong spirit. That's right! Wake up, everybody! And what was wrong, precisely, with this spirit? Details are sketchy, but it was nasty and ultimately destructive. There was no reason why our games shouldn't embody the standards of decent sportsmanship and fair play which, Massey said, we quite rightly label *British*.

I SHOULD HAVE been a goalie, I think, although of course it's too late now. I hurt easily and, also, it may be that I'm too tall. Plus, fear. Pucks scare me. Failure, too, which goalies have to face up to in a more direct way than their teammates, along with the ridicule and targeted booing. Isolation. Scrutiny. Both Tiny Thompson and Charlie Gardiner gave up reading, for God's sake, which they loved but which saps the vision. "After all," said Thompson, "the only thing a goaltender has is his eyes." But more than all that, I'm disturbed by

No reading in the net: Bruins goalie Tiny Thompson shows his 1930s goal-guarding style.

the tortured testimony of the men who've done the job. Glenn Hall, for instance: "I hate every minute I play."

You hear a lot about the eccentricities of goalies, Jacques Plante knitting his own toques ("I use four-ply wool," he said), Patrick Roy talking to his goalposts. Eccentric? To me, goalies just seem more interesting than other players. And maybe, is it possible that they could be the key to hockey's salvation?

They used to not wear masks in order that everybody could see their misery and know. They used to say—Gump Worsley said—it helps to be crazy. They'd promise you that the goaltender is the loneliest man in the world. Sorry, on the ice. That was Emile Francis. They used to fine a goalie two dollars if he fell down to stop a shot. It was another three dollars for a second offence—and a five-minute penalty.

None of the reasons famous goalies give for going into the nets ever came up for me. Worsley's grocer in Montreal told him he was too small to be anything but a goalie; in Peterborough, at the A&P, nobody said a word to me. Bernie Parent's brothers noticed how well balanced he was and that, combined with Bernie's poor skating, convinced them he ought to try net. I'll give my brother the benefit of the doubt: it may be that my balance was nothing special.

In Floral, Saskatchewan, young Gordie Howe was having such trouble on his skates that his teacher decided he'd be better off standing still in the goal. Vladislav Tretiak is supposed to have volunteered himself for the net because he couldn't bear to be cold and thought that the goalie's equipment would be warmer. Before he departed for right wing, Yvan Cournoyer kept to the net so that he'd never have to leave the ice. "It's a chance for a shy person to be onstage," Chico Resch said. Gilles Gratton, for whom shyness doesn't seem to have been an issue, told teammates that he was fated to tend goal by what he'd done in a former life, in Biblical times, when he'd stoned someone to death.

Asthma sent Plante to the net, where he wouldn't tax his lungs so much. For Ed Belfour it was the lure of the equipment, especially the masks, which were "awesome looking," back when he was a boy. Parent says that at the age of three he used to play policeman and "sit" in the middle of the street to flag down trucks. "If you read deeply into behaviour like that," writes Parent, "maybe I was showing then I could handle danger and eventually be a goaltender."

The truth is, as to the cloth, you have to be called to the net. Steven Galloway touches on this in *Finnie Walsh*.

There is a difference between someone who plays goal and a goalie: Finnie Walsh was a goalie. He believed it was his mission, his *duty*, to keep pucks out of nets and, in the larger scheme of things, to keep tennis balls from hitting sleeping mill workers' garage doors.

To Worsley, embarrassment was the key: you stopped the puck to keep the shame at bay. The most difficult position in all of sport, Gary Ronberg says. An almost wholly negative duty, the stopping of pucks, the preventing of goals, the disappointing of would-be scorers.

I drew goalies. For a long time they were all I drew: many Parents, Gilles Gilberts, the odd Ken Dryden, some Grattons and Doug Favells, and a single tactical Dave Dryden. Before the goalies, I was drawing a lot of retreats from Moscow and slews of pirates. In 1972, I sketched a famous still life depicting a detachment from the French Foreign Legion overseeing rehearsal by an orchestra. There's a lot going on in this drawing, but mostly it comes down to the sabres and bassoons, timpani and rifles. In other words, the hardware is what mattered, as in the goalie drawings, with their blockers and masks and goalie sticks.

In my Dave Dryden drawing, when I look at it now, I can see no Dave Dryden. Studying the eyes—well, there aren't any, just a vacant mask. The rest of his equipment is stacked up artfully, with the help of coat hangers or pipe cleaners. Dave himself didn't even notice this, or else he was too polite to say anything. I'd sent the drawing to my grandfather in Edmonton, and he'd passed it on to the Oilers. What was I thinking, sending him a drawing of his empty equipment? He autographed it anyway, and returned it with his regards.

I never would have said so to my grandfather, but Dave was always my second-favourite Dryden. Dave probably got a lot of this, likely still does. Is it fair that Ken won all the Stanley Cups, beat the Russians, wrote all the books, had all the novels and poems written about him? No, probably not.

"A strange and lonely occupation," says Grant Fuhr. The burden is fourfold, or so it was said to be in a 1959 article, because the goalie

1. has to stand still. Other players get to roam, but the goalie is so heavily padded that he had only his own marinade in which to stew while waiting for the return of the puck.
2. gets lonely.
3. bears 65 per cent responsibility for the success of his team.
4. is terribly scared.

There's some dispute about 3: Jacques Plante calculated that it might be as low as 50 per cent; Scotty Bowman put it at 75.

Dryden, Ken, didn't like to think of himself as a mere target, another piece of the net, preferring to believe that the goalie creates action rather than denies it.

Oh, but the tortures. Goaltending of old truly does sound like testimony from the trenches of Flanders, complete with rubber shock ("a first cousin to shell shock," according to Ed Chadwick, who played for the Leafs) and walking wounded (Tiny Thompson had to be helped across a street after a bad game).

Gerry Desjardins once caught a slapshot of Bobby Hull's on his leg. It was still sore two months later. Another Hull, brother Dennis, used to say to himself before every game, "I hope I don't hurt a goalie tonight." Not that he had a lot of choice in the matter; much depends on how the puck decides to hit you, in Gump Worsley's experience. If it comes in flat, a puck can stun, slice, or knock you silly. "But for some reason the puck is more dangerous when it hits you straight on. Then, it's like a sabre. It has a cutting edge. Maybe it's something like the difference between slapping someone in the face and hitting them with your fist."

Most goaltenders drink beer, Worsley said. They dream of scoring seventy-five goals as a left winger. There's no goalie alive who doesn't dream that, according, again, to Ken Dryden. Your mistakes will stand out like sore thumbs, Gordie Howe warned. You must have intestinal fortitude or, to put it bluntly, the guts of a burglar, Emile Francis thought you might like to know. When you get a shutout, you feel nine feet tall! (Howe again.) Stay on your feet! (And again.)

Good goalies have different physiologies than the rest of us. Jack Adams said that Turk Broda had not a nerve in his body. "He could tend goal in a tornado and never blink an eye." Do the pucks drive you to eccentricity, or is it the eccentricity that keeps you from the maniacal laughter? Either way, quirky behaviour is expected, forgiven, enshrined in anecdote. Bob Froese used to bark like a dog.

It's the waiting that gets to you, goalies agree, all the spare time. Murder, said Worsley. Butterflies plagued Plante before a game, and shivers buzzled between his shoulder blades. Mark Jarman has a goalie who lines up three coffees in paper cups, lets them cool, and gulps them just before the game.

Glenn Hall would puke if you talked to him. Or if you didn't. Hall's stomach and his habit of throwing up before each game is a standby of hockey lore. It's dutifully mentioned in his biography at the Hockey Hall of Fame. "We'd hear him in the bathroom," teammate Bob Plager said, that's how they knew he was ready to go. *His penchant*, it's sometimes called. Every game he puked? If that's so, then the NHL (and maybe even gastrological) record would have to sit in the vomit of 906 regular season games and a further 115 in the playoffs.

Hall himself thought the media went a little overboard reporting on all this.

A taste of Gump Worsley's seven-point recipe for goalie survival might include (1) forget your mistakes, (3) don't expect too much of life, (6) chew gum ("best tension-breaker I know for someone who has to stay in one spot"), and (7) read mystery stories. *After* the game, once you're home. No better way to (1).

What does it take to be counted as one of the greats of the goal? When Dryden came into the NHL late in the 1971–72 season, leading the Canadiens to the Cup and winning the Conn Smythe Trophy as playoff MVP, Plante cautioned wariness. It takes four, five seasons to determine how good a goalie is, he said. The shooters don't know him to start with, let them learn and then decide. "When they get to know him and he *still* stops them, then you've got a great goaler."

Though, of course, nobody liked Plante, according to Maurice Richard, not in Montreal and not in New York. He got on people's nerves and he never took any blame for anything—a requirement of the job that, strangely, Plante fails to mention in his book.

Thirty-six years after they skated on Luzhniki ice in Moscow, Phil Esposito turned his lip as he said that Tretiak was one of the worst goalies he ever faced. A little surprising, that. Tretiak learned at the blocker of Viktor Konovalenko, the great CSKA Moscow goalie. He looked ungainly. He never complained. After a puck got by him, he'd mutter to himself, "Outwitted, outwitted . . ."

Sometimes what happens with goalies is that they grow old and forget to duck. This was Bernie Parent's fate, at the age of thirty-four, when a stick from a passing Ranger poked into his eye through the hole in his mask. *Subluxed* is the medical term for *pushed back*, and that's what the doctor saw when he looked, a *permanent sublux of the lens of the eye*. What Parent saw was no more hockey. Of retirement he said:

It's an awful feeling. I loved being a goalie. I loved the responsibility it demanded, the spotlight it brought with it. My job was to give the team what it needed, when it needed it. Not when I was uninjured, untired, unsick, unworried enough to give it, not when I felt like giving it, when *the team* needed it.

Frank McCool, in a snub to his own surname, quit when he was twenty-eight and severely ulcerated. Bill Durnan said, "It had gotten so bad that I couldn't sleep the night before the game. I couldn't keep my meals down. The job—it was with me all the time, wherever I went. Nothing is worth that kind of agony." Durnan quit Montreal in the middle of the Stanley Cup playoffs. His successor, Gerry McNeil, gave up the game to preserve, he said, his health and his sanity.

The famous story about Detroit's Wilf Cude is that he was at home eating supper one night when his wife asked him about a goal he'd allowed. He picked up the steak he was eating and hurled it at the wall. That's how he knew his goalie years were over.

YOU CAN TAKE your pick of Ken Drydens, or not. It's true that not everyone is as sympathetic to Dryden as I am, and while his gifts are granted, these people would prefer not to hear from any of hims. There are those, too, who say that while they wish him no actual harm, the idea of Dryden is one that tempts them with dreams of firing a puck at his mask. I'm not entirely sure why one of the most incisive thinkers on the game—a man who happens also to have been one of the best goalies it ever saw—inspires such negative feelings. I sometimes wish the derision surprised me more, and that it didn't typify so much of hockey's self-protective armour.

Is it because he turned his back on the game when he was still at his best? Did it have to do with his opinion that there were other things more important than stopping pucks? For a while, the Dryden I liked the least was poem-Ken Dryden, who's enshrined in Milton Acorn's "Dryden in the Net." "Stone face of a pharaoh" is memorable, but I didn't understand the part about Dryden's "arrogance." I guess that's what a lot of people saw, and see, in him, though.

Where you stand on Dryden can depend on your view of the game. To some, his curiosity, the incessant need to study and analyze, made him suspect. In the old NHL, the law degree he was determined to pursue in the 1970s looked like an insult to hockey. It showed a lack of appreciation. Guy's got hockey, a Stanley Cup, a Conn Smythe, what more can he want? Why couldn't he be satisfied being what he did?

Dryden may be the multiest-media hockey player, which is to say the most widely represented across the culture. Richard and Gretzky have their statues, Bobby Orr, too, outside the Bruins' rink in Boston. Howe, Orr, Gretzky, Crosby: all the greats show up in children's picture books, though Orr may be one of the few (along with Derek Sanderson) to have been immortalized in full-frontal naked glory by the American painter Kurt Kauper. But not since Rocket Richard has a hockey player been so widely represented across so many different canvasses—novels, memoirs, articles, and *Hansard* as well as moviescreens, plinths, and actual painterly canvasses.

And yet, for all those, it's hard to tell whether we really know him.

Goalie-Ken Dryden I admire almost unconditionally. In Peterborough in the 1970s, on CHEX-TV, we used to get the Canadiens' broadcast on *Hockey Night in Canada*. I suppose you could have driven down to Port Hope to catch the Leafs, though I never heard of anyone doing that: it was Dryden's Habs, after all, who were winning Stanley Cups in those years. I can't recall much of Dryden's actual goaling, no particular saves leap to memory, but then Dryden says that's true too for him: fifteen saves he can recall from his career, max. He had a great defence, as everybody knows. Phil Esposito called him a "thieving giraffe," which is pretty good. What was important about goalie-Dryden was his mask—and his calm.

When he first came into the NHL, and also against the Soviets, Dryden wore one of the ugliest masks known to men, the one that made him look like an Orc chieftan weeping blood in *The Lord of the*

Rings. His more famous second mask had loops of blue and red, modern, friendly, as cool as a Danish dinnerplate. It complemented the famous Dryden stance, enhanced its portrait of his calm, and maybe even his virtue, as the game skittered on at the far end of the rink.

In Pete McCormack's *Understanding Ken*, the ten-year-old hero thinks he looks like God. The *New Yorker's* Herbert Warren Wind described it this way: "He stands up straight in front of the goal and, with his hands and arms resting on his stick in a way that suggests Cincinnatus at his plow, surveys the distant proceedings." Cincinnatus, if you look him up, was a benign Roman dictator, which doesn't really fit Dryden.

Nowhere, I submit, is he better summed up than in kids'-book-Dryden. The book in question is *Hockey Showdown* (1979), a picture book by Bruce Kidd. It's the story of Domingos, six years old, who watches Dryden tend the goal for Team Canada that September, and of course, he wants to get out there in the driveway to practise making the save for himself. But: the big fat mean neighbour, Mr. Sheppard, hates kids. Keeps your tennis ball, if he can grab it. Calls the police on you. So Domingos has to skulk, and what kind of hockey is skulking ball hockey? No kind. Fortunately, Ken Dryden's aunt lives on the street, and along comes Ken for a visit. He sees Domingos and wants to play.

Wouldn't he have a clause in his contract forbidding him from playing street hockey? If so, he doesn't care. Just then, Bill the Cop shows up. Mr. Sheppard has sounded the alarm on kids disturbing the peace. But Bill the Cop wants to play, too. This is Ken Dryden, after all. He's wowed. Next thing you know, Mr. Sheppard has joined in. You see what's happening here and you can guess the message: something to do with simple pleasures and being a good neighbour, or that there are things more important than hockey. That would be a typical Ken Dryden message. In some ways, that's the message of his whole career on the ice.

Shockingly grammatical: Goalie Dryden faces the shooter in his rookie season, 1972.

Once, when he was starting out, people worried about Dryden, but later a lot of them grew to be annoyed. First of all, though, he surprised them. This surprise has been traditionally expressed in two forms. One is to wonder: What's a smart kid like him doing playing hockey? The second is closely related: this kid's not like any hockey player we've seen before. Sometimes in the early profiles the surprise is mock surprise, but mostly it's authentic enough. When the novelist Jack Ludwig profiled him in 1976, he heralded his intelligent listening, "small cussage" (he hardly swore), and articulate answers. He was "shockingly grammatical." Phil Esposito had his carnal pre-game rite ahead of Game 1 in Montreal; in Moscow, the night before Game 8, Dryden went to the Bolshoi

Theatre to see *Anna Karenina*. "Unlike a true NHL player, Dryden didn't have himself a pile of paperbacks girlied up or severely bloodied."

There are those who've resented over the years all his book-learning, note-taking, glasses-wearing, thought-thinking, meaning-wondering. The mini-series *Canada Russia '72* pays tribute to their derision with Gabriel Hogan's performance. Whatever his puckstopping skills, movie-Dryden is a bumbler, telling his tape recorder what hockey means when he should be getting geared up, forlorn, bewildered by his own braininess maybe, visibly taken aback by his brash, guffawing teammates. Either way, Jack Ludwig's right: it's impossible to ignore the hockey meaning of Dryden.

Boston drafted him in 1964, but when he wouldn't sign, a trade sent him to Montreal. Three things that worried the Canadiens were one and two, his eyes, and three, the path he was looking to follow. The eyes were tested, and Dryden was fitted for contact lenses. As for his attitude, Scotty Bowman called it a "lack of ambition." The trouble? "He kept talking about going to school instead of playing Junior A."

He refused to go to Peterborough, a bitter repudiation, hard to comprehend. How are you going to get to the NHL if not via Highway 28 on your way to the Lansdowne Street exit? But to Dryden and his family, school was more important. Instead of Peterborough, he headed for Ithaca, New York, to study and skate at Cornell University. The team there was good in those years: *Newsweek* called the 1967–68 version the "Royal Canadians," and in fine Canadian fashion, they clobbered most comers, including Yale (19–1). At Harvard, students hung a sign proclaiming *Stand Up For America*; at Brown it was *Welcome Home, Future Farmers of Canada*. In three years, Dryden's record was 76–4–1.

In 1969, the Canadiens again tried to harness him to their plan. Dryden wanted to go to law school. Joining Canada's national team seemed like the perfect compromise: he could play and study at the University of Manitoba, in Winnipeg, where the team was based. Perfect. What could go wrong?

There wasn't much respect, though, for the Nationals. They were seen to be stealing away perfectly good hockey talent and even (a commonly held opinion) souring the skills of some of those players. Then the Nats got whacked for not winning, and why would anybody want to be associated with losers? In the end, the National Team ceased to operate in 1969. Stories that the Canadiens were behind its demise, doing whatever was necessary to get Dryden to Montreal, were not true. But Sam Pollock did set him up finally so that he could study at McGill and play for the Canadiens.

Even so, the NHL couldn't bend Dryden's will. He sat out a year when he felt that Montreal wasn't paying him his worth, articled for a Toronto law firm, played defence in a beer league. There was talk he'd leap to the WHA, play for the hometown Toros. And he wrote, including an article in *Sports Canada* where he noted our "smug proprietary attitude towards ice hockey," among other things.

Other countries can take a game and make refinements to fit their emotional make-up—the rejection of violence in the game, for example. When they do this they quite properly believe they have made an improvement.

He went back to the Canadiens, of course. Andy O'Brien called him the "most unusual personality" in the NHL. The *New York Times* tracked him down in Washington the summer before his first full NHL season, immediately detecting "a Naderesque earnestness," maybe what you'd call an "impassioned common sense."

Out on the ice it didn't matter what people said, because the Canadiens were winning. Oh, but everybody *had* to have their say.

Don Cherry: "He had a law degree and a great pair of legs." That kind of thing. Dennis Hull thought he was *more* normal than most goalies. "The only strange thing about Dryden was you needed a thesaurus to figure out what he was talking about." He offended Boston's Derek Sanderson, even his own teammate John Ferguson. "I don't like his attitude," Sanderson grumbled, "the way he approaches my game. He comes in for a couple of years, then he'll be gone. Hockey doesn't have to be his life—I resent that. He's like a psychiatrist always analyzing things." Ferguson thought he was cheap (topping Red Berenson, another college boy, in "the Department of Ridiculous Frugality") and uppity and you know what? Mediocre.

> He definitely had an attitude problem. He was a rookie who had expected to be treated like a veteran, and he was the most selfish kid who ever came up. As for his goaltending, just look at the record overall—we had to score six goals in some of the games to win it for him. He wasn't that great.

Dryden played eight seasons. He said he knew it was over when the best part of hockey was the showers, which is to say 1979, when the Canadiens had won their fourth consecutive Stanley Cup. When he gave up the games, he wrote *The Game*. He said none of the books he'd read reflected what he'd known on the ice.

Is *The Game* the best hockey book ever written, now and forever, amen? I'd say first that it depends on what you like to read; there's no way to gauge *best* and no real point in it, for me. I'd add: the revolution doesn't start here. If we're talking about non-fiction, the short shelf of books I keep returning to includes Lawrence Martin's *The Red Machine* (1990), Carrier's *Our Life with the Rocket*, Lawrence Scanlan's *Grace Under Fire* (2003), and Jack Batten's *The Leafs in Autumn* (1975). I'm fond of oral histories like Stan Fischler's *Those*

Were The Days and also *The Habs* (1991) by Dick Irvin. In a sport that can be so earnest about itself, there's no funnier book than Plimpton's *Open Net*. Bidini's *Tropic of Hockey* is great, and Roy MacGregor's collected columns, and all of Trent Frayne. Oh, and my copy of Gzowski's *The Game of Our Lives* is going to pieces from too much admiration.

It's no secret why *The Game* has lasted. It's because Dryden played— and at such a high level. No other hockey writer has that, blended with the focus, curiosity, and self-awareness that he brings to the page. Because he can tell a story, which isn't easy to do. Because of his love for the game; because that love makes him more truthful, not less. I'd go on, but every time I get going on *The Game* I just end up re-reading it again. I recommend that.

For all the acclaim he enjoys, Dryden is noteworthy, too, for the degree and consistency with which he has annoyed the hockey establishment with his commentary, discussion, analysis. Will the man never stop thinking? His forty-dollar words! What a bag of gas! "If you ask him the time, he'll build you a watch," snarled Bobby Clarke. "You didn't dare ask him a question because you had to stand and listen to him spout off for half an hour."

For a while, hockey-Dryden was subsumed by House-of-Commons-Dryden. He rose to begin debate on motions urging the Government of Canada to withdraw from Iran, and said things like "Mr. Speaker, is the minister saying that the childcare providers of Napanee and Halifax-Dartmouth are not telling the truth?" Once in a while he looked back to his hockey-playing days. In 2006, in the running to lead the Liberal Party of Canada, his stump speech bracketed references to his dad's backyard rink. How could he avoid it? That October he told party members at the final leadership debate that in the 1970s, Montreal had had no choice but to defeat the Philadelphia Flyers because they were bad for hockey. Same with the Conservatives. "Only twice in my life have I felt as if I was on a mission against an opponent," he thundered. "The first time was against the Flyers, the second is in terms of beating Stephen Harper and the Conservatives."

Stirring stuff, though Dryden lost the leadership race. His indictment did rouse Clarke's slumbering wrath in Philadelphia. "Not relevant to anything," he muttered in response to a reporter's (possibly leading) inquiry. "He thinks he looks good? He looks like an idiot saying something like that." Clarke's father and grandfather had always been Liberals to the core, back in Manitoba, but now because of Dryden, he'd have to dump that family tradition. In theory, at least. If he was a voter in Canada, Clarke said, his ballot would go Conservative.

HOCKEY DOES HAVE a history of adapting, which has to be encouraging. Think of smoking. Hockey used to have a lot more smoking, back in William Faulkner's day and before that, too. Now you almost never see it. Or what about helmets?

To me, the first mention of the word *stickfight* would have been the sign that the time was right to put on a helmet. But hockey never liked a helmet much. You can't hear in a helmet, it's too hot, it raises a question regarding your manlihood, it compromises your hair. And it's not as if anyone *died* from not wearing a helmet.

Even when someone did, it wasn't hockey's fault so much as a problem of personal responsibility. Take Edgar W. Hawthorne, for instance, a goalie playing for the Royal Bank in Toronto in 1921. The puck that hit him in the head did cause his death, yes, technically, but there was more to it than that, as the *Toronto Daily Star* pointed out: improvements in sticks and shooting methods had made hockey so exceedingly lethal that players could now, quote, knock down an infant elephant with their shots. "The first goalie who has the moral courage to come out and wear a real protection for his head," the *Star* intoned, "will earn the thanks of right-thinking hockey fans."

This is the history of the helmet debate: clusters of outcry around terrible injuries and awful deaths (Ace Bailey's trauma in 1933 prompted the first NHL-wide discussion), followed by a few more converts to the cause, mixed with some general naysaying leading up to a long silence, until the next time.

In 1937, the *New York Times* reported that the Rangers, to a man, refused to protect their heads. Visiting teams were a different story. If fancy headgear could be considered a means of mockery, well, maybe that's what they were up to, their "heads upholstered in color combinations and designs that suit their own fancy." Detroit's Ebbie Goodfellow wore a helmet of "slashed type that gave him a dashing appearance and plenty of ventilation." His teammate Doug Young's was black and streamlined and "cut so well over his dark hair that it was almost invisible from the gallery." Wilfred McDonald's was deep as a dish, tan-coloured, with criss-crossed bars of leather that fairly "shrieked for attention." Ralph Bowman had a saucy midget model that perched (a trifle) on the side of his head. Why no Rangers helmets? It was a minor mystery, the *Times* declared. So far as the paper's reporter could tell, they weren't a hindrance, causing "no drag on the head," which is to say that players needn't worry that their heads would slow them as they tried to build up breakaway speed.

The helmet that Boston defenceman Johnny Crawford donned in the 1950s was said to be a cover for his baldness as much as protection for his skull. It had a coiled white intestinal look to it and may have been on NHL president Clarence Campbell's mind when he dismissed helmets as "too undignified." Fans had a hard time telling helmeted players apart. This was another opinion of Campbell's: helmets stole players' individuality.

Clarence Campbell repelling boarders isn't a surprise. That was his job, smacking down anyone who dared to opine on how the NHL ought to run its operation. It was predictable, then, that when yet another serious incident occurred, this one in March of 1950, Campbell was quick to shush at those who said that a helmet would have made a difference.

Toronto captain Teeder Kennedy had come at Gordie Howe and Howe had fallen and been grievously hurt. Detroit coach Tommy Ivan said Kennedy had butt-ended Howe, but players who'd been on the ice didn't entirely agree on whether there had been any contact between the two. Maybe Howe had only stumbled. Campbell was at the game, and his investigation cleared Kennedy of responsibility. It also served to dismiss the notion that a helmet would have helped. Campbell ruled that Howe had broken his nose on the dasher of the boards *by the force of his own speed*. Had he hit his head subsequently when he fell? Maybe, but the serious damage was already done.

Campbell had a surprising ally in his anti-helmet crusade: Ace Bailey. "Helmets are not necessary," he insisted, unless you wanted players to stand still. "Hockey players carry so much armour already, they can't bear any more." An injury like his, he said, was just a fluke, wouldn't happen twice in fifty years, he thought. This was a common enough sentiment. "Helmets would be beneficial to a lot of players," he said in 1970, "but that's not what's really necessary, not if the rules are enforced."

Some coaches concurred: one player lost in fifty years, what's the big fuss? As for players, Rod Gilbert pleaded the old-dog defence: he'd gone too long without one to make the switch. Plus, in a helmet, he sweated too much. This was Maurice Richard's peeve, too: when he tried one, his head overheated. Brad Park had worn one in Junior and it was awful: unhelmeted opponents would tap him on the head with their sticks. And what a nuisance: his sweat would freeze and his head would ache.

My old History teacher, Mr. Armstrong, said, "I tried it once but every time I touched somebody I felt like I was hiding behind the helmet." Plus the perspiration and the leather—"they used to stain us yellow."

Dave Balon argued that in most games you never took a hit to the head. Balon was on the ice in Minnesota one January night in 1968 when his teammate Bill Masterton was carrying the puck in the North Stars' zone. Two Oakland players came at him. He passed the puck to Balon, then fell, slamming his head on the ice. The blood was profuse when they carried him off. Five doctors worked to save him. He was dead at 1:55 AM.

"Quite a few of us on the club put on the helmet after Masterton died," said Balon. His coach, Wren Blair, tried to talk him out of it.

The Boston Bruins led the protection lobby. In 1969, the team filed a formal motion with the NHL rules committee asking that the wearing of helmets be mandatory. This was in 1969, right after Wayne Maki had chopped the Bruins' Ted Green over the head in Ottawa. The proposal was rejected when it came up for voting at the committee. Toronto's general manager, commenting on his team's decision to abstain from the vote, explained that there was no way he could tell a player like Tim Horton to wear a helmet.

He might have been alluding to what Brad Park so elegantly calls the *sissy connotation*. Somehow, if you wore a helmet you weren't as manful as the guy with his hair flapping free. By the sight of your forehead will we measure your mettle. When Felix Batterinski took his career to Finland he had no choice but to wear a helmet, that's the law of the land, but it didn't mean he couldn't complain about having to don "the ultimate suck symbol." Same with Phil Esposito at the

World Championships, 1977. Helmets were the rule, and when it was all over, Esposito threw his at the president of the governing IIHF to register his disgust.

Now that everybody goes helmeted, the stigma has transferred to visors. Many of the arguments are the same; today you display your true sinew by whether or not you wear the Plexiglas.

I don't know whether Guy Lafleur could have taken his place among Canadiens greats wearing the bobbleheaded helmet he sported when he first played in the NHL. In 1974, at training camp, the story goes that he left it in his hotel room. He'd been a bit of a dud up to then, and the sportswriters were ready to write him off. Without his helmet, blond hair free, he played with joy and with verve. The writers cheered. Right there, right then, he decided he'd never again cover his head. Biographer Georges-Hébert Germain: "As though by magic he had rediscovered the pleasure of playing." It wasn't what was on his head, of course, so much as in it. "But the helmet would be banished as a negative fetish for him, a bearer of unhappiness." Versus the Flyers that year, the Canadiens thought he should put the helmet back on. "He would hear none of it—it was a burden, slowed him down."

Guy's dad wasn't pleased, as noted in his autobiography. "I've always been afraid to see Guy play without a helmet." He and his wife worried when they saw him bareheaded, "especially when he falls or he's checked against the boards." When he asked Guy why, he said he'd damaged his helmet and the team hadn't got him a new one yet. "I never much believed in the story," his dad solemnly wrote.

Rocket Richard had a change of heart at the end of his career. This was around the same time he started to think before games about getting hit. "Everyone should wear helmets," he said. "It's just up in the mind. It would be a good thing. It's a dangerous spot, the head. We've tried; they bothered us, were too warm. But if everybody wore them it would be the same." It took another nineteen years, but by 1979 the NHL was mandating that all rookies joining the league would from now on be helmeted. Players were allowed to grandfather their bare heads, and a few, like Al Secord and Craig MacTavish, did so.

Right to the end of his tenure, Clarence Campbell battled the headgear. Players couldn't hear, helmets got knocked askew, and the constant need to adjust them detracted from the grace of the game. And: "A protective helmet also minimizes the sense of responsibility for those who should not be causing the injuries. If everybody wears helmets . . . What is the risk? Bang them on the coco if you have to, he isn't going to get hurt."

LLOYD PERCIVAL'S ADJECTIVES would have to include *embattled* and maybe *abrasive*. He himself might have added *misunderstood* and *underappreciated*. When he died in Montreal in 1974, the papers conferred *controversial*. His opus, *The Hockey Handbook*, won adjectival fanfare when it came out in 1951: *mumbo-jumbo*, the hockey writer Baz O'Meara called it, and *theoretical twaddle*, though it might have some useful diet suggestions. Dick Irvin the Elder said it was worthy of a three-year-old. Or rather, he said Percival *was* a three-year-old.

But that wasn't strictly true. He was by then a strapping thirty-eight-year-old champion tennis player, runner, and cricketer. In 1941, Percival founded the Sports College, a correspondence school for coaches and athletes conceived as a national radio show that ran, eventually, for twenty-one years on the CBC, with as many as eight hundred thousand subscribers at its peak. Queen Elizabeth II gave him a medal in 1953 for his contribution to Canadian sport.

Here's what I like about Percival: for all his emphasis on physical fitness, what he was campaigning for was readers. The road to improving yourself as a hockey player was paved, for Percival, with newspaper columns and the closely printed little booklets you could send away for, study, and absorb. He believed that you could read your way to hockey betterment.

The Hockey Handbook is a Canadian classic, as far as I'm concerned—up there with *Fifth Business* and *The Stone Angel*. What it's not is a scintillating story, but then that's not what he was peddling. With Percival, metaphors aren't important, only facts. Nor is there any kind of violence, which is a little strange, until you see that for all his practicality, Percival worked exclusively in ideals.

As far back as 1951, Percival's constant contradicting of what hockey people thought they knew kept getting him in trouble. He said, for instance, that Gordie Howe was, scientifically, a better right winger than Maurice Richard: that's the kind of thing that drove Dick Irvin batty. Sentences in *The Hockey Handbook* say things like *Speed is about twenty-five per cent mental* and *There's no such thing as a born skater*.

Scoot is an occasional hockey word, nowadays, but does anyone know the technical specifications? Percival has the goods. In 1951, *scooting* was one of the most overlooked of agility skating tricks. (Much as Percival would hate to hear it, that's still the case today.) Milt Schmidt was probably the best of the scooters. *Use it to shift around a checker! Break away suddenly from a melee of players for the purpose of receiving a pass! Go ahead! Don't be shy!* There are drills you can use to practise, for example, Scooting the Goal, Angle Scooting, and Scooting the Line. He tells us about Edgar Laprade's shooting percentage (one in four); most players are lucky to score a goal once in every ten shots.

Or take Red Horner. When he first tried to breach the NHL, his skating was *like something out of a comedy act*. People laughed at him. With a siege of hard work, he became a good skater. Skating complacency is hard to shake. Players think they can skate. They believe they have the

three key areas covered: *free skating, agility skating, backward skating.*
Wrong. They can do one of those, but not all of them. Do they fix the
problem? Rarely. It's not hard to do: all you have to do is attend to your
body lean and *foot action*. Free-skating faults include Skating Tension,
Bang the Foot, and Tight Roping. Simple.

His mantra is there on his PlayBetter pamphlets, scripted to fit a red
shield that would look good on the chest of a hometown superhero:

KEEP FIT

WORK HARD

PLAY FAIR

LIVE CLEAN

Harry Sinden was too busy to listen to him in 1972. Who knows
what would have happened if the coach had acknowledged just one
of Percival's letters (he sent three), offering counsel, films, all access
to the records at the Fitness Institute. "We had advice from so many
people, it was swamping us," Sinden said when it was all over. As it
was, the Soviets were the ones who used *The Hockey Handbook*: it
was their manual for undoing the Canadian professionals. High-
tempo skating, pattern-passing, tea-drinking between periods: that
was all from Percival. When he was still coach, Anatoli Tarasov sent
Percival a letter of his own: "I have read it like a schoolboy," he wrote
of the *Handbook*. "Thank you for a hockey science which is significant to world hockey."

Before he sought out Sinden for a pen pal, Percival had actually
given up trying to improve Canadians, so it's surprising that he
wrote at all. In 1968, he'd announced that no more would he be pur-
suing his lifelong dream of trying to transform Canada into a world
sporting power. "I can't fight the establishment any longer," he said.
"I guess I was too far ahead of my time, and it's been one of the great

disappointments of my life." Still, business did get a bump after the Summit Series. Detroit signed him to a two-year contract to help transform the Red Wings, and the WHA hoped he might be able to transform the upstart league.

The Hockey Handbook makes a cameo in *Canada Russia '72*. When the Canadian coaches see the Soviets' copy, they're confused and disgusted. "This Percival guy," movie-John Ferguson sneers, "he play hockey? He play?"

THERE'S NEVER BEEN a time in hockey's history when there hasn't been a parallel play-by-play on how to improve the game, patch up the punctures, renovate the front rooms, fix what's broken.

- No more forward passing in the defensive zone! said Newsy Lalonde in 1928.
- End summer hockey, said Wayne Gretzky, in 1996. Don't send the kids to hockey schools! "They should take their skates off and put them back on in September."
- Drop a player! Time to cut numbers on the ice, said the *Globe and Mail* in 1997: make the game five-a-side.
- Bigger nets! proposed Rick Dudley in 1999.

In February of 1973, four short months after Team Canada returned from Moscow, a national magazine ran an article titled "How We Can Jazz Up Hockey," in which Joe Crozier recommended more penalty shots and Norm Ullman wanted two referees and a better attitude from the press. Gordie Howe thought maybe it was time to bring back the old Beehive photos for the fans, and then Bobby Hull weighed in to say that players needed to show greater dedication to the game:

We should exhibit more pride in what we're doing, and we should be more conscious of public relations. I've seen guys just rip up fans' letters asking for pictures. That's no way to act. We've got to get back to where athletes are athletes and not long-haired goons. If they look like men, they'll act like men.

Unless that's the whole problem with hockey in the first place: too many man-looking men acting like men. It's not right that I've left it so late to talk about women's hockey, and even worse that I'm not really going to say very much, but still, here goes: What if the men's game were more like the women's? Better yet, forget the men. What if we just turned our attention to the women's game more often, flocked to its rinks, rejoiced in its stars and values? Governor General David Johnston was an accomplished defenceman at Harvard, knows hockey well, cares deeply about its future (it should be fight-free, he thinks). He suggested that the women's game "may just be the pinnacle of hockey." That was in 2013—a year before Canada's women won Olympic gold in Sochi, captivating the country with a performance against the United States that was every bit what Dave Bidini said it was: "one of the greatest games played in the history of sport."

Everybody has a formula for correcting the game's violence, and they always have. In 1950, Tommy Gorman wanted a penalty shot awarded for every major, with repeat offenders banned from the game for life. Blame the managers, cried a fan in 1953, for baiting referees, you know what we should do, fine all the teams $5,000 and close down the rinks for a month. "Then we might get a little sense drilled into the thick heads and get back to the hockey we all enjoyed." Or why not make it $10,000 charged to any player who drops his gloves? That's what two Minnesota legislators suggested in 1989 in a state bill that would surely have ended fighting. "I want hockey to remain an outstanding sport and not degenerate into a circus of blood," said State Representative Todd Otis. The bill vanished almost as soon as it was proposed.

Money has long been seen as a fix for hockey violence. The cost to Billy Coutu for knocking George Redding unconscious with his stick in 1928 was twenty-five dollars. In 1936, Art Ross paid a five-dollar fighting fine during a friendly benefit game. In 1961, when Montreal coach Toe Blake struck referee Dalton McArthur, the NHL hit him up for $2,000. Compare those to what New York Rangers coach John Tortorella paid in 2012 for saying not-nice things about referees: $30,000. (The price for linesmen who worked a game in 1963 without having shaved properly was fifty dollars. This was George Hayes again, the official whom Clarence Campbell penalized for taking the wrong kind of train between games.)

For a long time, referees had the power to fine players, and when I read the reports from the papers, it always sounds like they were collecting the cash on the ice as the game went along. There's no way to measure how well fines worked as a deterrent. To me, it seems like another case where real life stops rinkside: money only matters once the game ends and you've returned to terra firma. Fines were never going to change much. Near the end of his tenure, Clarence Campbell seemed to think it might be a good idea to enrich players rather than tax them. "The more affluent the players are," he observed in 1975, "the less inclined they are to violence."

The hockey books with an eye on rescuing hockey are called *The Good of the Game* and *Saving the Game* and *What in Hell's Wrong With You, Game?* Sometimes it's just a single chapter in a book that takes on the challenge, titled "Bringing the Game Back to Life" or "Sorting Things Out" or "The Game Plan." They all have good and carefully considered ideas that will probably be adopted soon and kick in, oh, at some point in the not-too-long-from-now so that nobody has to write the final installment in the celebrated *Death of Hockey* trilogy.

When it comes to fighting, the *Hockey News* is all for taking it slowly—implement a ban over three years, get everybody acclimatized. Sorry, *was*: that was in 1997, which meant that by the year 2000, when the NHL would finally be ejecting players who fought, everybody would be used to it.

The Toronto Board of Education had an idea for the TV networks in 1975: black out hockey broadcasts as soon as a fight starts. That's a long way from the fall of 2013 when Steve Yzerman, Hall of Famer and general manager of the Tampa Bay Lightning, said it was time for fights to be gone for good. "I believe," he said, "a player should get a game misconduct for fighting. We penalize and suspend players for making contact with the head while checking in an effort to reduce head injuries, yet we still allow fighting."

"It is the players," Clarence Campbell opined in 1950, "who decide what type of game it should be." By 1974 he was saying, "Fighting is not undesirable, because it's the best safety valve I know of in hockey." In Europe, they threw you out of the game if you fought—ridiculous. "It produces a more violent game."

DOES GOD HAVE time for hockey? It's a big question, not necessarily blasphemous, but probably insoluble. A smaller, and possibly more urgent, one is this: Did God lend a hand when Paul Henderson put that puck behind Vladislav Tretiak in 1972? Probably not. If he did, the troubling follow-ups include: Why couldn't we handle the Russians on our own? And does that mean, implicitly, that He was okay with the whole breaking-Kharlamov's-ankle situation?

Tretiak has said that he thinks the Lord himself gave the goal to Henderson. None of the Canadian players mention any such gift in their books, of which they've written many. Team Canada 1972 would have to be the most prolific team we've ever sent out to face the world in terms of hardcovers, a team with a lot to say, and not just because Ken Dryden was their goalie. It's not a straightforward calculation, but by my count there are as many as twenty-five books written or authorized or assisted by players and coaches from that team, three by Paul Henderson alone. For all that, Alan Eagleson is the only one to mention divine intervention, and that's in somebody else's book: the disgraced former player agent and man-behind-the-1972-curtain says (joking, I think) that if Henderson hadn't scored the goal, he wouldn't have had to take his turn to religion to show his gratitude.

There is a strange novel about 1972, Frank Cosentino's *Hockey Gods at the Summit* (2010), wherein an all-star team of dead Canadian hockey players manipulates the whole series from on high. God has delegated the job to Bad Joe Hall, Howie Morenz, Hod Stuart, and many bi-locating others. When things go bad for our flesh-and-bone boys, posthumous heroes drop into their bodies and take over. Georges Vézina occupies Dryden; Jack Darragh does the winning work that poor, mortal Henderson couldn't manage on his own. It's all very confusing, although we do learn that if there's one thing God can't stand, it's bad refereeing.

Is hockey polytheistic? It may just be a rhetorical plurality when coaches and commentators talk about the hockey gods, but if not, those gods are incredibly busy. They

- have long enjoyed tormenting New York;
- were thought to be more friendly to the Atlanta Thrashers on the road;
- can be cruel;
- anointed Tim Horton when he was seventeen;
- smiled on Ron Ellis by allowing him to be picked for Team Canada in 1972;

- never intended for the Cup to end up in Texas;
- are alone in knowing the potential of the Phoenix Coyotes; and
- sprinkled some kind of magic dust over the NHL schedule-makers so that Wayne Gretzky would arrive in Edmonton one point shy of becoming the NHL's all-time leading scorer.

Religion provides a rich fund of faith-and-devotion imagery, of course, especially in Quebec. It's also handy when Fred Shero wants to talk to his players about Bobby Orr ("We've got to stop treating him like God") or Montreal's Serge Savard has something to say after that famous New Year's Eve tie with CSKA Moscow ("God was Russian tonight. They had three chances to score and they scored on all three of them.").

One year, when the Leafs' Don Metz ran into Elmer Lach and broke Lach's jaw, Canadiens coach Dick Irvin felt that God would rule that it was a dirty play by allowing Montreal to win the Stanley Cup that year. In fact, the Leafs won.

Gretzky's dad, Walter, says that 99's talents were given to him by the Good Lord; Wayne himself is on the record as saying he learned them all for himself.

There's the *sin bin*, of course, which always seemed a half-hearted rhyme to me. I much prefer Zamboni interpretations: the "liquid absolution" that poet Matt Robinson writes about in *Tracery & Interplay* (2004), his collection of hockey poems.

In *Amazons*, Don DeLillo has an announcer giving a talk to delinquents on the subject "How goaltending prepares you to let Christ into your life." In *The Last Season*, Batterinski's buddy Torchy finds religion, though a teammate says it's just another form of superstition, like a rabbit's foot. In Fred Stenson's *Teeth*, the coach wants his boys to pray between periods, but there's a Russian who won't do it: "I no believe God. He dead."

For a more serious-minded approach, I recommend Bernard Palmer's 1957 novel *Danny Orlis Plays Hockey*. Orlis was new to me, but I'm determined, having found him, to venture deeper into the Palmer oeuvre, starting with *Danny Orlis and the Strange Forest Fire*, or maybe *Danny Orlis and the Rocks that Talk*. Eventually. I'm still digesting Danny's hockey adventure, in which characters say things like, "I've been a different woman since I took the Lord Jesus as my own."

How good is Danny? At one point he gets caught in a hunter's trap and has to take to the ice with just the one unmangled hand. "He called for a puck and darted at top speed from one goal to the other, dribbling it expertly." It wasn't as natural using one hand on the stick, but he could manage. Later, Rick—did I mention Rick?—Rick says, "I can't go on any longer, Danny. I've got to become a Christian." Someone else stops smoking and starts praying. Someone else: "With God's help, I'm going to live as He would have me to live from now on."

Actually, I've changed my mind: Danny is a big drag. Talking about a movie, he wonders was there anything in it that glorified Christ? Would it make you want to live a better life? Not so much, but there's lots to want to make you sin. "That's the reason I don't go to movies," he says.

Rob Ritchie's *Orphans of Winter* braids hockey and faith tightly enough that I wasn't able to discern the finer strands, or many of the broader ones for that matter. I believe it's about the Messiah making his return to the world of men, via Thunder Bay, as an undersized centre with not much of a shot but plenty of wile, including a tricky faceoff move that gets him a goal six seconds into his big-league debut. Again the question arises: "Why the hell would some Messiah waste his time playing hockey?" Casey Bruford is his name. I missed the answer to the question. Wolves also feature.

The most straightforward, unironic consideration of just how God fits with hockey has to be in Keith Magnuson's 1973 autobiography

None Against!, which is disarmingly guileless from the title on in. Magnuson tells us his dad put religion before hockey.

> With me, it's the other way around. Naturally I want God on my side because He has the power to deliver talent or take it away. And being a good Christian is the best way to help my own performance in hockey. Quite possibly this is sinful reasoning. But before games today, I still find myself telling God that if we win I'll become a better Christian. Then later, when we have won and I go out for a beer with the team, I'll say, "If you're up there, please don't strike me down." Whether I'm a hypocrite or just human, I'm convinced that if God has been listening to me all this time, He's thinking, "Well, to Hell with this guy." And so, whenever we lose a game, I'm sure it's some form of punishment.

In 1978, when Tom Edur couldn't reconcile his religious beliefs with hockey's brutality, he retired. Stu Grimson, on the other hand, saw no contradiction in his role as a hockey fighter. "Jesus was no wimp," he told an interviewer. "If there has to be a player in this team environment that sticks up for the smaller man, or the less physical athlete, why can't it be a Christian?"

An Irish kid from South Porcupine, Ontario, Les Costello won a Stanley Cup with Toronto in 1948. Words that adhere still to his playing career are *brash* and *feisty* and *shit disturber*. In the summer of 1950, he heard a voice saying, "I think you should try." The priesthood, that is. He steered past the Leafs' training camp and headed straight for the seminary. It shook his family and his teammates, but he never looked back. He'd had his eyes opened, he later said, playing Junior at St. Michael's in Toronto. "If you're not careful, you can get seduced by the pleasures of hockey," he said. "In some ways it could be a useless life."

Charlie Angus tells his story in *Les Costello: Canada's Flying Father* (2005), detailing his piety and good works (also largely shit disturbing) and how he ended up as the driving force behind the team of hockey-playing priests who entertained thousands throughout their years on the ice while raising millions of charitable dollars. In the 1980s, Disney came calling. There was a script involving skating movie-priests prevailing against wicked Soviets, but that's as far as it went. The priests didn't like some of the unholier subplots apparently, and then there was the problem with the young actor who flunked the screen test for the starring role: Wayne Gretzky.

I wish Father David Bauer had written a hockey book. I've even got a title for him: *Let the Spirit Prevail.* Bauer was a classmate of Les Costello's at St. Mike's, though as hockey players they won separate Memorial Cups in the 1940s. He wasn't the best hockey talent in the Bauer family; that would have to be his elder brother, Bobby, who joined Milt Schmidt and Porky Dumart to form the Boston Bruins' Kraut Line in late the 1930s and into the 1940s, when the adjectives he earned were *hard-working* and *seldom penalized;* he was known too as the *brains* of the outfit and the *balance-wheel.*

David went to war after he won his Memorial Cup, then the following year, he entered the novitiate of the Basilian Fathers to study for the priesthood. He didn't see any contradiction between the game and his faith. The Basilian motto could serve equally as a hockey slogan to make Anatoli Tarasov proud: Teach Me Goodness, Discipline, and Knowledge.

Father Bauer's greatest hockey legacy is his advocacy for an amateur national team built on a model in which sport and education were equal partners. He did this while coaching just such a team— the one that law-school-Ken Dryden joined—and in the years leading up to 1972, he was tireless and even heroic in trying to keep the program alive, despite steady opposition to such a hare-brained idea. Why would you bother? The Russians and the Czechs kept winning at the Olympics, and it was embarrassing to send our amateurs to play those wily Communists who were really pros anyway. The NHL didn't like Father Bauer's operation because it lured away their star youngsters when they should be concentrating on avoiding injury and readying themselves for the real big time. The country was disappointed because Father Bauer's teams weren't bringing home gold medals.

The plan that he hatched in 1962 and took to the Canadian Amateur Hockey Association echoes the plot of Foster Hewitt's 1950 novel, *Hello Canada! and Hockey Fans in the United States*, in which plucky, non-swearing, hard-studying Canadian lads called Crasher Kelly and Butch Batting and Buff Jones ("the colored boy") band together to play their way to the Olympics in Switzerland. While resisting the lures of pro scouts, they skate, skate, skate for four years until the time comes to head overseas with a mandate that includes not only winning, but being *nice* (important to make the people in other countries like us). They beat Poland and Britain, Switzerland, the U.S., the Netherlands, Belgium, Austria, and France, all despite the soft ice and inferior referees, and Czechoslovakia, too, in a tight gold medal game that redeems Canadian honour and pride and deserves cheers from us all. (This happens to be pretty much the plot of Scott Young's 1982 novel, *That Old Gang of Mine*, too—Spunska returns!—except that the Olympics are in Moscow. One more time: yay us!)

Father Bauer's real-life Olympic efforts were more or less like that, except for all the winning and widespread cheering. Still, he laboured on. His personal maxim was "Make use of technique, but let the spirit prevail." Why should it have been so difficult to understand? Some people appreciated what he was doing. Headlines from newspaper articles about Father Bauer's teams include "The Clean Canadians" and "Everybody Wants Them to Win."

But if Father Bauer's devotion to the national team still shines, it's not the main reason I admire him. For that, you have to go to the

Innsbruck Olympics in the winter of 1964. We're playing our old rivals, the pesty Swedes. A Swedish left winger by the name of Carl-Goran Oberg, having broken his stick while cross-checking a Canadian, skates past the Canadian bench on his way to the penalty box and throws a piece of broken stick that hits Father Bauer on the forehead and cuts him. Father Bauer bleeds, and is still bleeding half an hour after the game. When his players jump up to retaliate, Father Bauer tells them to sit down, which they do. There's no penalty. Father Bauer says he's convinced it's an accident, though there are witnesses who disagree: Öberg threw his stick in the coach's face. Instead of a brawl, the game goes on. Canada wins, 3–1.

There was aftermath: Öberg was suspended for a game and so was the Italian referee, who was deemed to have been negligent. Öberg apologized. Father Bauer invited him to join him to watch a game the next night. "He's a fine, clean-cut boy," Father Bauer said, "a little excitable, but I like him a lot." Another thing he said was, "Things like that happen in sport. I just happened to be in the way of the stick."

When it was all over, Canada finished up out of the medals that year, in fourth. But one member of the team received gold. So uncommon and meritorious was Father Bauer's behaviour—so shockingly unhockeylike—that the IIHF gave him a special medal. Father Bauer's players weren't there to see it. They felt they'd been cheated out of the bronze medal by tournament organizers, so they boycotted the ceremony.

THE *NEW YORKER* has kept an eye on hockey right from the start of the magazine in the 1920s, back in Harold Ross's day, when Niven Busch Jr. had the watch. Herbert Warren Wind, Roger Angell, and Charles McGrath have all taken monitoring duty over the years.

Today it's Charles's son Ben on the job, with Adam Gopnik, Alec Wilkinson, and Nick Paumgarten pacing the beat now and again. It was Wind who called hockey "inherently the most dangerous of team sports." Roger Angell said it was the most emotional and—it's almost enough to make our nation blush—dubbed it "this wingéd game."

Raised as a Montrealer, proudly a Habs fan, Gopnik has a hockey pedigree that boosts his authority above those others. He may be the most trenchant and sensible writer on the game since Rick Salutin's attention wandered away. In 2011, he was the (Vincent) Massey Lecturer, and once he'd crossed the country delivering the lecture in person, Gopnik published it as a sort-of-hockey book, *Winter: Five Windows on the Season.* Learned and lively, warm with wit, it covers a lot of frosty ground. Of all the games we play, Gopnik argues there, hockey is the mostest: most interesting, most rewarding, most consistently entertaining, most difficult, most beautiful. Also: brainy. You thought it was all chase and whack, a celebration of collision and bad temper, its actions naught but reactions, no time to think?

Wrong. Look at the patterns of the game, Gopnik says, all the angles, the vectors, the chess of the thing. He talks about different kinds of intelligence, spatial and emotional, and situational awareness. Those are the smarts that hockey players have and need, and that hockey reveals and rewards, and with everything happening at such a speed. Look at Wayne Gretzky. As a player, he wasn't big or fast or particularly powerful, but he had his skating and his brain. In no other sport is the brain so decisive a factor—and that's to be celebrated. As a friend of Gopnik's says, hockey is the only game in which a good mind can turn everything upside down.

The other part of Gopnik's appreciation of hockey has to do with fans and their brains. Maybe because I was always better at reading the game than playing it, this is the bit that I can more readily endorse. As much as we may love a show, we also crave a story.

Hockey provides both. "It looks like a reflex, rapture sport but is really a rational, reasoned one," Gopnik writes. He takes a quick dash through game theory, but what it comes down to is this: for all its apparent headlong chaos, a good hockey game is as complex and lastingly interesting as a good novel. Gopnik: "Hockey offers drama at first viewing, meaning on the second, and learning on the third and fourth, even forty years on."

It doesn't excuse all the bad games, of course, the boring, the banal. And it doesn't justify those parts of the game to which words like *brutality*, *thuggery*, *greed*, *degrade*, and *stupidity* apply.

Oh. Right. That.

"I have," Gopnik writes, "been inclined to abandon it."

I think it's just a warning—that's how I read it, anyway. *Winter* doesn't have any remedies to prescribe, just one more stern, loving, reasonable voice calling for hockey to use its brain. "With our selves invested in our games," he writes, "we have to save the game to save ourselves. It can be done."

NEWSPAPER NARRATIVES OF early games make it sound so cheerful, hale, and healthy, there's such an innocent enthusiasm for the spectacle at hand, just the tone alone has the feel of an elixir you could drink to tone up your skin and clean out your sinuses, restore your vitality. "It was a fierce hard contest," a *Toronto Daily Star* correspondent reported of a Toronto-Ottawa game in early 1915. "Players went down all over the ice, and it simply became a question of which team could stand the gruelling." Answer: Ottawa. But both teams suffered. Frank Foyston was so badly battered at the finish that he could scarcely walk, and Cully Wilson collapsed after it was over and had to be carried to bed. Art Ross ended up with two black eyes and a cut face.

A month later, the teams met again. Four men fought two fights on the night of February 17 at the Mutual Street Arena. Wilson, who played for Toronto, was up and about again, spry enough in the third period to skate into Ottawa goalie Clint Benedict, which started an argle-bargle that the referees tried their best to stop, and did. Benedict and Wilson were banished without further incident, other than Wilson whapped Benedict in the jaw with his stick and also, later, a spectator wrestled with one of the referees. The law looked the other way. Exhausted, maybe? Fresh out of handcuffs?

Police did lay charges against Art Ross and Toronto's Minnie McGiffen for their fight near the Ottawa goal, though just what it was that made their encounter more actionable than any of the others is hard to discern from the newspaper. "The men first tried to get at each other with their sticks, but finally dropped them and went to it with their fists." Businessman Lol Solman, a director of the arena, eventually bailed the players out of jail.

All this the *Star* duly reports on page 14 the next day. Three pages later, the story continues. The scene has moved two blocks south and seven to the west, from rink to police court. Inspector Geddes takes the stand to conjure the fight for the court. McGiffen and Ross had dropped their sticks, he says. The blows they exchanged were a dozen.

T.C. Robinette rises for the defence. "But you can't play hockey and be orderly," he says. "I am told the people won't attend the games unless there is some excitement, a little of the hot stuff. A tame game means an empty house."

Minnie McGiffen—sorry, your honour, *Roy* McGiffen—is sworn. He admits to fighting but, says he, not to worry, both players wore padded gloves. It's not as if they were going to hurt one another. The magistrate is His Worship Squire Ellis. He's bespectacled and white-haired, like Caesar (it's said) in the winter of life, a plain, practical man. "But when a great many people go to see a clean game," he suggests, reasonably enough, "they don't want to see rowdyism."

Inspector Geddes points out the danger "with feeling running high" and a big crowd on hand: "There is likely to be a riot on the ice, starting with a fight such as this one." Staff Sergeant McKinney pipes up on the larger issue: "Toronto's good name as a home of clean sport shouldn't be ruined by this sort of conduct."

Squire Ellis: What about the referee? Inspector Geddes: He was standing thirty feet away, and he didn't interfere until McGiffen fell down.

"I'd like to fine *him*," sniffs the magistrate, "but I can't." Instead he does what he can, fining McGiffen and Ross one dollar each plus costs for disorderly conduct, a price they presumably accept in place of the alternative: fifteen days in jail.

So hockey goes free, until the next time.

Cooper Smeaton was one of the referees that night. He'd started his career in 1913, patrolling a Canadiens and Wanderers game in which Newsy Lalonde is said to have taken issue with the very first offside he called. Smeaton fined him five dollars. It took nerve to referee in those years. That and a solid right hook. In 1917, Smeaton gave Howard McNamara of the 228th Battalion team two majors and tried the five-dollar treatment. McNamara rushed him, and the two men punched each other until other players intervened. You can see why Smeaton might have felt the need for a short sabbatical from hockey, which he took with the Canadian Expeditionary Force's McGill University Overseas Siege Battery (motto: By hard work, all things increase and grow).

After the war, Sergeant Smeaton returned to his insurance job in Montreal with a Military Medal on his tunic for bravery in the field. On the ice, he didn't delay in making his return to being battered and besieged domestically. In February of 1932, he was on duty at another game in Toronto, this one featuring Montreal's Maroons. You never saw such a sight, or at least the *Daily Star* never had. Imbroglios, free-for-alls. There was backbiting, haranguing, and gouging. It was one of the most disgraceful scenes in the history of Canadian hockey. The Sino-Japanese War—remember that joust?—was *pink tea* compared to Maroons and Maple Leafs. *Riotous* was a word you could use, but a weak one. Smeaton and his fellow referee, Mike Rodden, were said to be *powerless* and *under attack.*

Inspector Marshall from No. 2 Division, Toronto Police, had sixteen men in the building. Why hadn't any of them intervened? "It seems the only time the police step into hockey arguments is when a player strikes a spectator," he said, not sounding too sure. "The Crown attorney would only act on a complaint from the police." Anyway, the referees hadn't asked for help.

This continued. When sticks swung, suspensions were served and hockey authorities cleared their throats for more special pleading about hockey policing itself. Nothing to see here, no one to charge as you might be tempted to do in real life, move along, move along. Something about NHL rinks—maybe the rinky oxygen, an imbalance of ions—impairs the logic of policemen and prosecutors; whatever the case, it confuses the legal experts every time. Not just the legal establishment, of course; it confuses us all: What are we seeing here, a spectacle removed from the regular rules of society, a sanctuary, a spurline, self-regulating, with a unique auto-correct function? Anyway, it's not to be taken as seriously as real, regular life because— but this is where I always lose my grip and have to let go. Why, again, isn't it to be taken as seriously as real life?

Frank Udvari was the referee on duty when Rocket Richard and Hal Laycoe flailed sticks at one another's heads in 1955. Six years later, in Toronto, he invigilated a game between Chicago and Toronto, a 2–2 tie. In those years, referees were still levying fines as the game went on, taxes on abuse and dissent. In the second period, Udvari hit the Leafs' Billy Harris, for instance, with a twenty-five-dollar fine for questioning a penalty call. The worst of it came when Toronto's Eddie Shack angered Pierre Pilote with a hook and Pilote (as the *Globe*'s Red Burnett described it) "bounced a vicious two-handed stick slash off the shoulder, stick and head of the Leaf right winger." That was just the start. Bert Olmstead hit Pilote with a *snakey left jab*. Reg Fleming pounded Larry Hillman. A photo of Shack has him screaming at Stan Mikita as he brandishes a high fist to punch his head. From the Chicago bench, Tod Sloan and Bill Hay javelined their sticks at Shack and missed. "We didn't lose the game and we won the fight," Punch Imlach said when it was all over. Pilote said Shack had speared him in the stomach. "But it was a lot of fun, reminded me of my Junior days."

Red Burnett rated the night a *wild pier-sixer*, a *battle royal*, the least tame since the Toronto-Montreal *tong war* of December of 1953. (That one Burnett had described using the words *schemozzle, donnybrook, tangle, mix-up, hassle*, a 3–0 Leafs win with *a sock-sock ending*. The penalty box: the *sneezer*.) Before it was over, Udvari had called a total of forty penalties, an NHL record, including seven majors and eight misconducts. He'd also imposed $800 in fines. At least temporarily, he'd been reinforced by a Toronto police sergeant and three constables who'd ventured out onto the ice to try to help out with the ruckus near the Chicago bench. They didn't last long. Having tried without success to summon some of their colleagues, they retreated. To Burnett, the attempt was futile in the first place, and the task of peacemaking was left "in the rightful hands of the game officials."

Clarence Campbell wasn't happy. He couldn't believe it. "Police are never requested or desired to invade the ice during an NHL game," he bugled from Montreal. "It is a league matter that can be handled by our officials."

Word got to Conn Smythe in Florida, where the sunshine may have made the whole affair seem more amusing. "Only way I'd let a policeman on the ice," Smythe said, "would be if he qualified for the team."

Sparked by this "brutal brawl," the *Globe* didn't hesitate to brew up a long lead editorial, "Law on the Ice," which took the time to quote, for everybody's edification, section 230 of the *Criminal Code*:

A person commits an assault when, without the consent of the other person, or with consent when it is obtained by fraud, he applies force intentionally to the person of the other, directly or indirectly.

To which the *Globe* added:

Contact between the players had far exceeded anything permitted in the rules. Fine the managers and coaches, and may the fines be heavy... NHL players are regarded by thousands of people in this country, particularly by youngsters, as heroes. When they disregard the law, when they employ violence, they set an example which their admirers may be tempted to follow. Teen-agers cannot be expected to differentiate between violence on the ice and violence elsewhere. Let there be an end now to the notion that hockey teams and games have some form of immunity from the law.

The NHL investigated, and so did Toronto's deputy police chief, Robert Kerr. The sergeant and three constables at the Gardens, he said, were off-duty, and they were being paid to maintain order off the ice. Going *onto* the ice, he said, was a mistake. "The sergeant apparently interpreted a gesture by referee Udvari as a plea for assistance." But Udvari, in his report to NHL headquarters, insisted that he hadn't asked for any help.

It turned out, just to confuse things, that Stafford Smythe, chairman of the Leafs hockey committee, had asked other policemen, on the west side of the rink, to intervene. They had respectfully declined, saying they'd only go out there if they had to arrest somebody.

Campbell reiterated, "The referees don't require any outside assistance. They are capable of dealing with any situation. Police on the ice would only complicate matters." The police were there "to present an atmosphere of authority . . . They are to take care of the non-combatants, at least those who aren't players."

Chicago coach Rudy Pilous was reported to have said that such an outbreak couldn't occur in the Chicago Stadium because the police wouldn't tolerate it. Campbell ridiculed the suggestion.

"What a pop-off," said Campbell. "He should be squashed. They don't have police in attendance at games in Chicago. They have ushers."

A few days passed. The police had a new statement. They said they could do what they wanted, thank you very kindly, and the NHL should be grateful there were no assault charges. "It is a fallacy that no charge would succeed because an assaulted player in the same league wouldn't prefer charges," a police official said. Police officers witnessing the *donnybrook*—the *kapuskasing*, better yet?—would be enough. Had the brawl taken place on Carlton Street among civilians, they would likely have found themselves in the station cells for causing a disturbance, the police said. They were happy to quote the *Criminal Code*, too, specifically the part that says:

> Everyone who not being in a dwelling house causes a disturbance in
> or near a public place by fighting, shouting, swearing, screaming,
> singing, or using obscene or insulting language is guilty of an offence.

Under the *Criminal Code*, furthermore, prize fights are the only sports events in which assault charges can't be laid.

On March 28, Conn Smythe received a letter from his lawyer, Ian S. Johnston, Q.C. "You have asked my opinion as to whether the Editor of the *Globe and Mail* was correct in implying that the hockey players who became involved in the incident at the game on 11th March were guilty of assault."

Unlikely, he thought.

I am of the opinion that when a person volunteers to engage in a game of bodily contact he volunteers to accept the foreseeable results of his action and the possibility that he may become involved in a dispute with an opposing player which will result in the use of force. This same principle applies in civil matters: spectators are often held by Courts to have voluntarily accepted the risk of injury. In cases under the *Criminal Code* it has been held that where the issue of consent is material, the onus is on the Crown to prove lack of consent, and it would be extremely difficult for the Crown to satisfy the onus that the players involved had not consented.

There was a qualifier, though. If a player attacked another out of the blue, with no provocation, with the intent of harming him, thereby exceeding "the degree of roughness which a player normally expects to meet in a hockey game," then that would be something different, and possibly actionable.

But this didn't happen on March 11, Johnston didn't think.

SOMETIMES DURING THE reading-all-the-hockey-books years, I arranged to meet the hockey authors; occasionally we had lunch. By no means did I meet all the hockey authors, nor did I want to. I wanted to meet Dave Bidini, and we ate (vegan bacon cheeseburgers), and also Randall Maggs (quattro stagioni pizza), poet of Terry Sawchuk, author of *Night Work* (2008). Maggs said that some day he was going to write poetry women might like. We talked about goalies, and he described meeting Butch Bouchard and a trip to Ireland to read where people there who loved hurling found that they could love hockey poems, too:

> Reading to the Irish has deepened my knowledge of what this god-damn game is all about. I used to think these sports were civilizing things, this is how we got away from war, we play these sports. It's not, it's almost the opposite. It doesn't inspire you to go to war, but it preserves the qualities that you need so that you can protect yourself when you have to . . . It is a survival thing.

With Bidini it wasn't all Dave Keon but almost. What were the Leafs waiting for, not retiring his number 14? Titles he'd weighed before he got to *Keon and Me* (2013): *Eat, Pray, Leafs* and *Diary of a Loser*. He said: "One of the things I liked that Keon said, when I asked him about fighting—were you ever tempted—he was like, *All the time*. But he just didn't. He just didn't."

It was too early for lunch when I went to see Roy McMurtry at his law firm office high above downtown Toronto, but I took a coffee and for a few minutes studied the former Ontario chief justice's oil paintings, lakes and trees and skies, some of which he has hanging above his desk. You don't need to know that he was a friend of A.J. Casson's who joined him on sketching trips to hear that they're fine paintings, but he was and did, and they are. After a while, we sat down to talk about arresting hockey players.

Memories and Reflections (2013) isn't strictly a hockey book. Now aged eighty-two, McMurtry has a long and illustrious legal, political, and diplomatic career to chronicle. But he does take a chapter to recall what happened when he was appointed Ontario's attorney-general in 1975, just as the NHL's new season was getting underway.

"My brother really helped focus my attention on what was becoming a more serious issue," McMurtry says. Also a Toronto lawyer, Bill McMurtry had been commissioned in early 1974 to investigate the circumstances surrounding a violent Junior B game, which he duly did while also broadening his scope to take a frank look at the state of the sport in general. Bill, who died in 2007, was big news across the continent that year. His "Investigation and Inquiry into Violence in Amateur Hockey" (1974) was a tidy, eloquent little booklet with white covers that he delivered to the province's minister of Community and Social Services. It could have been a bestseller, too, except that they were giving it away for free at the government bookstore in Toronto.

If his substantive recommendations weren't exactly embraced by the hockey establishment, they did set the stage for the non-literary sequel that began to unfold soon after older brother Roy started his new job. One of the first letters he wrote as attorney-general went out to Clarence Campbell and Ben Hatskin, respective presidents of the NHL and WHA. McMurtry was instructing Toronto police, he informed them, to keep a close eye on professional hockey games played in Toronto. "I stressed that any clear infraction of the Canadian *Criminal Code* could attract a criminal charge."

And so it happened. In November, police charged Detroit's Dan Maloney with assault causing bodily harm after (McMurtry writes) "repeatedly banging the head of an unconscious Leaf defenceman, Brian Glennie, against the ice." Maloney was subsequently acquitted in court, but hockey was on notice, again. Clarence Campbell was sufficiently concerned that he sent a memo around the NHL. McMurtry smiles at the thought. "He told the league to be careful in Toronto because we've got this crazy attorney-general there."

Conn Smythe was writing, too. He was eighty by then, and very upset with McMurtry. The letter he fired off to the *Globe and Mail* on hockey's behalf captures a larger exasperation at the overbearing expectations of a civil society. Hockey dangerous? A threat to the population? Why, the *Globe* itself was reporting that 22 Canadians had been killed and 537 injured in snowmobile accidents just that year, a terrible toll, and McMurtry wanted to chase after hockey?

On April 26, 1976, Smythe addressed McMurtry himself:

> For as long as one can remember, it has brought fame and prestige to Canada. Professional hockey has produced as many or more decent Canadian citizens in every hamlet, town or city as any other Canadian profession. Like all other professions, there are problems. Those in charge of professional hockey have shown that over the years they have the ability to recognize these problems and are capable of getting the right solution.

As for the attorney-general, didn't he have enough on his plate? Toronto was in the grip of a "body-rub disgrace." Drugs were stalking our teenagers, drunken drivers killing our citizens. What about all the unsolved murders? "Why," Smythe wrote, "don't you mind your own business?"

On McMurtry's watch, Toronto police went on to charge four more hockey players the following spring, Philadelphia Flyers all. After they ended up pleading guilty to lesser assault charges that was pretty much the end of it, other than the shouting. McMurtry felt that he'd made his point and left hockey to its own devices. It's true that in 1977 the NHL did introduce new rules that sought to reduce fighting, though there's no way to gauge the McMurtry factor in those.

McMurtry says he still loves hockey. He played on into his 50s. Now, as a father to six and grandfather of twelve, he remains a true believer in the value of sport for social development. "I have a lower profile," he says, "but I've been working with Dr. Charles Tator, the neurosurgeon, and Ken Dryden. My concern relates simply to young people. I'm very distressed by the fact that tens of thousands of them have dropped out of hockey in the last thirty years." It's not just, he says, the "hooliganism and the chance of injury, the concussions and the fighting." The game is so expensive to play. What do we need to do to ensure that it's not only safe, going forward, but all-accessible?

"The NHL is well aware of the dropping enrolments in amateur hockey," he says. "My view is that they don't care because they know there will always be an inventory of elite young players who can feed their needs and that's all that matters to them."

As for fighting, he's as frustrated as ever:

> I really do believe they're an irresponsible bunch. And that includes the Players' Association. I'm pro-union, I don't have anything against unions, but they've got this crazy idea—in my view—that they have thirty or thirty-five members who are the so-called enforcers and they owe them representation. And part of their representation is to fight to maintain fighting as part of the hockey culture. I just don't know when people are going to wake up.

Thirty-seven years after he first wrote to Clarence Campbell, McMurtry still finds himself mulling strategy. What about sending in inspectors to the Air Canada Centre from Ontario's Ministry of Labour? "I've thought," he says, "it would surely shock the hell out of the NHL if *they* laid a charge. I mean, this all has to do with workplace safety."

ESCAPE VALVE IS something Clarence Campbell liked to talk about when he talked hockey fights in 1974. *Safety valve* was another favoured Campbell rhetorical fitting, and, I think, better suited to his line of arguing. *Safety* sounds more reassuring, for one thing—exactly what any responsible boss should provide to his workers when they are working in such dangerous, high-pressure conditions. *Escape* might cause a bit of a panic among the employees—why would they want to be escaping? And what exactly is an *escape valve* anyway? Wouldn't you want some sort of escape *pod* if you were planning to flee, roomy enough inside to allow for fisticuffs?

Hockey season was over when Bill McMurtry's inquiry got going in June of 1974, the game itself gone into hibernation, players and coaches flown to the south, or wherever it is hockey players settle in the summertime. But for five days that summer, hockey stood at a crossroads in the Ontario Room of the Macdonald Block, at Queen's Park in Toronto, trying to decide which way to go.

You can borrow McMurtry's forty-page report from the library, or you could buy your own copy online for about twenty-eight dollars. If you want the full story, the deluxe edition, you can visit the Ontario Archives in Toronto, where all 1,256 pages of transcript are collected in five volumes. I spent two summer afternoons there, trying to keep quiet amid the hush of deep research, reading my way through McMurtry's questions and the answers he got, or didn't get. It's a fascinating tale, though the plot wanders all over the place. The dialogue is the best part—well, it's *all* dialogue, really, the whole thing. If it were me, I'd have tightened up the characters, except for Commissioner McMurtry, who's pretty strong. Others are just not that convincing. With some it's hard to tell whether they're joking or not.

As Canadians we've grown used to committee rooms full of commissioners trying to find out what happened and why, and who's to blame, and if it seems like we live in a society in which public inquiries hum constantly in the background, well, don't they? What was going on over there in Somalia between those paratroopers and some of the local people? Did those policemen really need to Taser that man five times in that airport? What about that other man and his packets of cash to that former prime minister in the hotel room? It's easy to picture the tables and the witness chairs. It's a scene we know.

Bill McMurtry questioned some of the players who'd been involved in the original Junior B incident. Cal Herd was one of the first witnesses to be called, number 15 for the Hamilton Red Wings. He took questions from Mr. B. Templeton, representing the Red Wings.

Q. What do you understand as physical intimidation in a hockey game?
A. Taking your man out, taking your man hard when he has the puck and skating with your man.
Q. Anything else?
A. Bothering the man when he is on the ice.
Q. What is the best way to bother him?
A. To talk him [*sic*].
Q. Anything else?
A. Well, you can give him a few jabs with your elbow as he is going down the ice.
Q. Where did you learn this style of hockey?
A. I have always been brought up by that [*sic*].
Q. From what age?
A. I think ever since bantam, age 14.

At some point McMurtry decided that as much as his inquiry needed to hear from the likes of Cal Herd, it would also tilt its ear to experts from the wider world. Social scientists and psychologists were invited to contribute their views, and so were coaches, players, and administrators from the professional ranks. Players stayed away, most of them. Some, like Bobby Hull, were willing to talk but asked that their views not be publicized.

Clarence Campbell came willingly. I don't know if McMurtry was surprised to snare him. The president might have easily have avoided the Ontario Room, observed from afar, ignored the whole thing. But he came. The performance he gave was high in its dudgeon, couched in a vocabulary (if not a worldview) rooted firmly in 1931. He talked *fisticuffs* again, and mentioned a *roughy*, by which he meant a fight rather than a fish. He was a wonderful character, I have to say, right up there with Mordecai Richler's nefarious Hooded Fang in the way he came bursting in through the doors of the committee room, to wreak his havoc on the assembled body with fireballs and adamant denials. He twisted and turned, blamed helmets and referees, obfuscated, condescended. He seemed to say that fights in which no one is injured don't really count for anything and that demands for such a widened definition of violence—"anything that would possibly produce a serious injury"—meant that you might as well try to eliminate sticks and skates from the game as fighting.

It was June 3, after lunch, when Campbell was sworn. McMurtry asked what was the purpose of the National Hockey League? Business? Entertainment? Both?

A. Yes, it is a business of conducting the sport of hockey in a manner that will induce or be conducive to the support of it at the box office. I think that is reasonable.

Q. So in determining the rules, is one of the most important criteria what sells tickets?

A. Yes. We have two factors to keep in mind constantly. Show business, we are in the entertainment business and that can never be ignored. We must put on a spectacle that will attract people basically not in

Campbell court: NHL president Clarence Campbell passes sentence on Detroit's Ted Lindsay (left) and Boston's Bill Ezinicki (wounded) after their epic 1951 fight of fists and sticks. Both were suspended for three games and fined $300.

the short run but in the long run. We have to keep in mind a number of factors associated with it; that the game is one which entails the engagement or employment of human beings, players, to perform acts of skill and to try to develop the game in a way that will ensure your skills are constantly on display and to ensure that the minimum risk—they will be exposed to the minimum risk inherent in participation (I am talking about personal physical risks) not only because of the fact that it will be good for the spectacle but because of the fact that the value, the asset value of the player is of very great concern to the club contracting for his services. And of course it is completely destroyed by any serious loss of his competence by reason of physical injury.

McMurtry wondered whether the NHL felt it has any moral duty to society. "Well," said the president, "I would start out on the assumption we would not sanction or tolerate anything we consider to be basically anti-social at any time. I think that everyone's concern is to conduct our business in a manner acceptable to society and the environment in which we operate."

I said the story strays all over the place. There's a good bit where McMurtry cited a referee who quit the league because in his mind, the NHL was only interested in selling tickets to American fans and therefore wanted to encourage violence on the ice. "Well, let me put it this way," Campbell guffawed, "if you had not mentioned his name I would have forgotten him."

It went on like this, swipe and parry. McMurtry proposed that if you're a player who wants to remain in the NHL, you have no choice but to fight. "I think that is an absurd hypothesis," Campbell said. Okay, what about if Dave Schultz punches you in the face? "I don't think I want to indulge in hypothetical situations." McMurtry wasn't giving up. What if Schultz punches John Van Boxmeer in the face, which had happened recently, and knocks him out? *Well*, said Campbell, *we deal with it. We have our rules and we apply them.* The proper response to a Schultzing such as McMurtry was suggesting: a major penalty. "I think that is appropriate in the circumstances."

Q. In actual fact, sir, he was awarded a roughing penalty of two minutes.
A. Whatever it was.

Campbell paddled fast. He *should* have been assessed a major. McMurtry moved on.

Q. Do you not think that like every other contact sport in the world, with the exception of lacrosse, which is having its problems surviving and as I understand it is one of the reasons it almost passed as a professional sport; is there any other professional sport in the world which would tolerate such behaviour?

A. I don't know whether there is or not. I have never addressed myself to it for the reason that I think we have a problem to solve of our own. And I don't—while it is relevant to consider what other people are doing I don't think that necessarily sets a standard which we should accept.

This flummoxed McMurtry: "I do not follow you." Campbell splashed about: "If I express myself badly I apologize. I don't think we are under any obligation to accept somebody else's solutions for our problems."

I have to say, reading this, I barked out loud. In the archives, reading Campbell, he got a bark out of me and a bang of my knee on the table leg. Meanwhile, McMurtry was trying to widen the focus.

Q. Now, I suppose you are familiar—I think it was some 200 years ago and I think it was Edmund Burke who said example is a school of mankind. They will learn by no other. Do you think that is a fair statement?

Nice try. Campbell's lawyer interjected: this game didn't take place two hundred years ago. A quick tussle and McMurtry abandoned Burke.

Q. Do you not feel some moral responsibility to conduct yourself in a way which is conducive to the best interests of the children playing hockey?

A. Of course I do and I believe we do.

Q. Do you feel that the conduct which is sanctioned or condoned and in fact encouraged under your rules of physical intimidation by appearing—

A. Don't talk like that. I don't have to take your definition of what we do. If you wish to ask me do I support the play as it is conducted by the National Hockey League I will answer you.

Q. All right. I will take it one step at a time. Would you agree that to a greater extent in recent years there has become almost a science of intimidation in the way some teams approach hockey in the NHL. There has always been violence but now I would say it has become more deliberate and more of a science?

A. I do not concur in that.

McMurtry pressed on. What about Philadelphia, the Flyers? "Would you not believe that part of their game is physical intimidation of the other team?" There are no stage directions in the transcript, but I like to think of Campbell taking a moment to study the ceiling, maybe touching a finger to his lip. "That is a possibility. If you want to say they are being an intimidating team I would have to say they are not being very successful in that respect. I think it is their skill."

A wounded bear, they say, is the most dangerous bear.

McMurtry started to close in. Is it proper, McMurtry asked, to have players whose only job is to punch other players?

A. No, I don't think there are any such, regardless of what they may say.

Q. Regardless of what the player himself might say you disagree that is the case?

A. I don't think he has ever been appropriately quoted if he said he was employed to fight. I just don't believe he is ever correctly quoted, in addition to which I think he would be very quickly thwarted in his efforts.

On they go. You can almost feel Campbell relaxing. He was enjoying this now, the refreshing pirouettes, the bracing gainsaying.

McMurtry hammered on: "You are selling violence." "No, I am not selling violence." Teams are drafting fighters now, preferring them to skilled players. "You are so wrong."

Q. That is what the experts say. I am just quoting the general managers and the people who follow hockey much more closely than I do. The impression they had is that in the draft there is far greater emphasis on personal brawn than ability.

A. ... I don't care what they said. I am interested in the facts.

Here the roadrunner seemed, again, to have the wily coyote cornered.

Q. Is fighting undesirable as far as you are concerned?

A. Not necessarily. To excess it can be a terrible thing, but at the same time I have got to say that in my mind it is the best safety valve in the hockey game. It is the best safety valve I know.

Q. Notwithstanding the fact that every study that has been done by many social scientists would disagree with you.

A. I am not prepared to accept that conclusion either.

Q. Have you read any of the studies done by psychologists on the field?

A. Yes, I have.

Q. Are you aware of the fact that as far I know all of them have disagreed with your position that certainly the catharsis theory has no validity? It would appear there are theories now and some research indicates not only allowing violence in the context of hockey promotes further violence in hockey, but also promotes violence outside the context of hockey. Are you aware of this?

A. Yes. And all I say to you is this: within the framework of our operation—I say that it is much more likely to stimulate a different kind of violence which we think is more serious than the fisticuffs from which I have said time and time again is the least dangerous of all the fouls that are committed. The least dangerous.

Q. Is there any reason why if you discourage fighting necessarily you are going to encourage other fouls if in fact you call those fouls as well?

A. In point of fact it will just intensify it then, because the experience in international hockey and college hockey proved it is true.

Q. I am sorry, sir, but the experts I have talked to on both of those disagree with you completely and utterly.

Later, McMurtry floated a theory he had: it's as if, he said, we Canadians have a certain kind of conceit or arrogance about hockey, as if we are the only people who know it.

"That is right," says Campbell.

And here, at the end of a long afternoon's back-and-forth, just for a minute, we get a glimpse of Campbell's conception of the wider world, and maybe we need to put it to use to help us understand the rest of what he's been saying in the Ontario Room. To Campbell, hockey was a refuge from the wilderness we inhabit; far from being a venue for the worst of our angels, it was actually a safe haven, a sanctuary over which reasonable men preside. Under questioning from an OHA lawyer, he regretted the general erosion of discipline in the world we live in. "The degree of permissiveness has grown into our society in the past ten or twelve years certainly since the Vietnamese War and the race riots in the United States have changed things a great deal." Time was, nobody would dream of slapping a policeman's hat off his head or calling him a pig, but now? Society has to pick that policeman's hat up off the pavement and be ready to back him up.

Eventually they got back to hockey, and when they did, Campbell did his best to go out on the upbeat. Credit the NHL, he said, with the intelligence to understand that it has a vested interest in improving itself. "We got rid of the stick swinging," Campbell offered brightly.

But McMurtry was in no mood. "It is like saying shoplifting isn't as bad as bank robbers," he said, "and if you don't allow shoplifting you are going to get more bankrobbing."

THE TIME TO examine fighting's place in hockey was March of 2007, according to then-NHL director of hockey operations Colin Campbell. That was a month before a national Decima poll declared that 76 per cent of us who describe ourselves as *avid fans* opposed a ban on fighting. It was more than a year before Mitch Fritz, in his second NHL game, fought his first fight, challenging Georges Laraque, fully two years *after* Laraque's prediction that fighters would be extinct in two years. Across the NHL that year, the number of fights was actually up by 48 per cent. Fritz was six foot eight, 258 pounds, and had a left hand that was knuckled with scabs.

In February of 2009, I drove down to London, Ontario, for the Violence in Hockey Symposium. The highway country west of Toronto was bright and white and brittle as I went. I was almost sorry to have finished with the McMurtry/Campbell files: none of the other reports on hockey violence had quite the same piquant readability. Not the 1977 Citizen's Committee on Children report that advised Ottawa: "the fact of violence . . . in hockey cannot be denied and we should not attempt to shelter our children from all knowledge of its existence." Nor Gilles Néron's 1977 report of the Study Committee on Violence in Amateur Hockey in Quebec (referenced within another report, the Interim Report on Minor Amateur Hockey, 1979), noting that children tend to find heroes in NHL ranks and citing a case of Rocket Richardian frustration at the Montreal Forum during which he broke a dressing-room door. The following night there were "about 15" doors broken in Montreal arenas.

Organized by the Middlesex London Health Unit, this one-day gathering of doctors and coaches and parents and journalists convened to consider the game of hockey as they might swine flu or West Nile virus—as a public health issue. Brébeuf took note of the Huron playing lacrosse to cure the country in a time of illness: we were a long way from that. This was the country in a big meeting hall trying to cure the game that ails it.

Early on, someone said, "This is our game—this is *our* game—so maybe it's time we did something about it."

There were tales of referees locking themselves in dressing rooms after games. "How sad is that?" said someone else.

People agreed that unnecessary aggression was—is—the problem. "When hockey's played the way it's intended to be played, there's nothing better."

Journalist and author Bruce Dowbiggin was there. He called for rugged but not dirty hockey. He wondered: Why do we blame Americans? He also made the case that our national game doesn't reflect us. "We're *not* a nation of hooligans."

Ken Campbell from the *Hockey News* wondered about fighting: "If it's part of the game, why do they stop the clock?" Regarding the media: "Guess what? We're part of the problem."

Dave Simpson talked about the pressure in Junior hockey to drop the gloves. A son of London, brother of Craig, Simpson was a Junior star during many of the years that I never was. His adjectives from that time include *remarkable* (young man) and *league-leading* (thirty-nine goals). He said that he always tried to play the game as though his mother was in the stands. Which she was most nights, since he played for much of his career right there in his hometown.

A concussion doctor put the number of NHL concussions per season at seventy.

When Bryan Lewis, a former director of NHL refereeing, stood up to say that he believes fights *are* on their way out, most of us there in the room wanted to believe it, too. I feel obligated to report that some of us, however, couldn't keep from laughing aloud at his optimism.

At the end of the afternoon, for about twenty seconds, we watched monkey brains. It was an old film they used to show in medical schools, Dr. Ken Bocking told us, right before he said, "Maybe you don't want to watch this." For an experiment in the 1960s, researchers had sawed off the top of a rhesus monkey's skull, replaced it with Plexiglas, then filmed from overhead to record the effects of concussion on the brain. Say, for instance, the monkey took a high elbow to the ear as he was rushing the puck through the neutral zone, or maybe a left in the jaw during a *Pokemouche* behind the net. Imagine his head snapping back. In the old film, in black and white, we watched (if we watched) what would happen next, as his unstoppable brain went battering brutally back and forth inside his skull.

IN MAY OF 2014, as the playoffs roiled on, I made the mistake of picking up a newspaper that didn't have one nice thing to say about hockey, and the *déjà vu* blurred my eyes for a moment. American pediatricians were calling for a ban on bodychecking for players under fifteen. The NHL was looking into reports that some of its players were lying about head injuries during games in order to keep playing. Meanwhile, no one knew whether concussions were occurring less frequently or not, because the league was refusing to release statistics. Two pages away from the column about how playoff hockey encourages thoughts among players of how to hospitalize their opponents was another one explaining why the NHL's culture of late hits was flourishing. And two NHL players had been fined a total of $7,820.52 for maliciously squirting water at rivals.

I eventually found *one* nice thing: the *Globe and Mail* called Montreal's young winger Alex Galchenyuk *a shimmering bundle of puck skills and derring-do.*

THE END COMES quickly. One day, a quake in the chest, a flash of white light, and it's over, time to retire. Be careful, though. You don't want to go too soon. In the summer of 2008 and on through that fall, thirty-seven-year-old free agent Mats Sundin stayed off his skates trying to decide whether he'd had enough. Montreal wanted him and so did the New York Rangers, and of course, he was also welcome back, probably, maybe, we'll see, in Toronto. Everybody had advice about what he should do.

"People always told me: 'Play as long as you can,'" said Joe Nieuwendyk. Steve Yzerman: "If there's any doubt and guys aren't sure, I think they should be playing. You can be retired for the rest of your life. You'll know when you're done." Bob Gainey, who happened to be the Montreal general manager trying to sign Sundin, said: "I told him to make a decision. I said, if you feel like you want to retire, then retire. But if you're not sure, you should play and the emotion will come."

Towards the end of his career, Montreal's Bert Olmstead stayed on his farm in Saskatchewan to finish up the harvest before turning his mind to whether he'd play another season. Doug Harvey was one who kept going. In 1969, still playing the St. Louis blueline at the age of forty-four, he was asked why.

Because I'm a hockey player. I like the life of a player. I like the fun that goes with it. And I'm some use in here. I can quiet down the kids I play with on defence. I can show them what they're doing wrong while it's

End days: The Big Train, Lionel Conacher, as a Montreal Maroon in 1937, his last season in the NHL. Skates stowed, he was elected that year as an Ontario MPP. The Maroons weren't long for the ice, either: they suspended operations in 1938 and never played again.

still fresh in their mind. I can teach them how to avoid cheap penalties, maybe a bit of science. Defence, you know, seems to come a little later.

To leave hockey is to be diminished to the role of spectator. They stop accumulating your statistics; no longer is the Stanley Cup within your reach. It's a shock. Real players talk about how suddenly it comes, so it should be no surprise that the fictional ones do, too. Drinkwater, for example, in Mark Jarman's raucous *Salvage King, Ya!*:

One day you're a New York Ranger screwing *Vogue* models, doing coke off her famous belly; one day you're sleek as a whippet and smiling in sunglasses, you're media property, you're a midtown parade. The next day you're pumping gas at a Petro-Can in Moose Jaw or flinging yourself from a bridge in Flin-Flon.

So he weighs his options with care. On one hand:

Tired, TIRED! Jesus. Something is wrong. Am I too old? I am held together with velcro and tape, a king of shreds and patches, I no longer speak standard English. I think I need some time away from hockey, from humans, from the locomotion.

But the other side of it: "I can't imagine *not* playing. My body feels funny if I don't skate."

SOMETIMES YOU HAVE a job to do, other than hockey. Teeder Kennedy was twenty-nine in October of 1955 when he told *Hockey Pictorial* why he was finished with the NHL. "I've got a wonderful wife," he said, "a wonderful three-year-old-son, Mark, a horse, a Doberman Pinscher, my home, and a job that I really like." He'd been with Canada Building Materials for five years by then, and the company had been *very* understanding about his captaining the Leafs.

Sometimes it's the game that forces you out. "Don't like the scramble game the NHL plays," Sweeney Schriner announced as he departed Toronto for good at the end of the 1941–42 season, to the team's surprise. Other times, you just know it's time. For elite players, it can come down to painful acknowledgement that they can no longer do what they once did. Mike Bossy couldn't handle being a fifty-goal scorer in a five-goal scorer's body. "I hate," he said, "being ordinary."

Hanging them up: Sweaters, skates, and sticks belonging to the brothers Richard, Henri (#16) and Maurice (#9), in 1960.

Rocket Richard went to training camp in the fall of 1960, tanned, a little heavy. At the age of thirty-four, he was starting to slow, and the injuries were taking longer to heal. Earlier that year he'd been asked the dreaded question about retirement. "I'd like to leave the game before people criticize me, boo me," Richard said. "When I'm ready, I'll go tell Mr. Selke." A reporter took this to manager Frank Selke, who said, "I've been in hockey fifty-three years and I've never had an aging athlete admit he was through." In camp, Richard looked good. Jacques Plante said his release had never been quicker. One scrimmage, he scored four goals. But then came the practice where

Richard went from the ice straight into coach Toe Blake's office to tell him he was retiring. He was worried about his weight, about getting hurt. He said, "The dizziness, the pushing, and the fact that it was so hard to lose weight convinced me that I'd be better off retiring."

In 2011, Mike Modano announced his retirement on Facebook at the end of a summer of pondering.

Dit Clapper was thirty-nine, coaching while still playing for the Bruins, when he hurt a rib in a game in the spring of 1946. Between periods, Art Ross told him to take off his uniform, and then he told him again, and that was all for him. Clapper didn't know then he'd be back the following year; nor did his teammate, Bill Cowley, who asked if he could have his sock garters—"real rubber garters." Clapper handed them over.

Punch Imlach took the time, once, to explain the decay that occurs in hockey players. "As a guy gets older, he becomes less dedicated. Not only does he get a step slower, he also loses his desire to mix it up. He becomes more lover than fighter. This happens to everybody. It's human nature." Maybe his spirit is also being undermined inside his own house. "His wife may tell him not to get hurt. Maybe she doesn't like fighting, and subconsciously he's worried about that."

"A growing concern about injuries," said Andy Bathgate, "is a sure sign of a hockey player going over the hill. When a player starts thinking that the next bump may sideline him for good, his days as a topflighter are numbered." The pain saps the pleasure. Gordie Howe had an ailing wrist in 1971, he was forty-three, and he just wasn't having fun. In Detroit, too, his wife said, the crowds were smaller and meaner. Syl Apps was the same. "Hockey is work now," he said when he returned to the Leafs after the Second World War. "It's not fun anymore." He was gone at thirty-three.

The career-ending concussions we know about—Brett Lindros and Pat LaFontaine, for example—are nothing to those no one ever diagnosed, we have to bet.

Chicago's Kenny Wharram had a heart attack on the first day of training camp in 1969 and ended up with a heart infection. Bobby Orr said, "I'll play hockey until I can't skate anymore," which is pretty much what happened. By 1978, after all those surgeries, his knees weren't up to it. He was twenty-eight. The left one was a particular monstrosity. "I don't like looking at it, to be honest," said his Chicago teammate Bill White. Horrible, Stan Mikita said, like seeing some ghastly thing come down from outer space. "It is not very pleasant in there," Orr's doctor confirmed.

Don't bother trying to prepare yourself. "You can't," Batterinski says in MacGregor's *The Last Season*. "And anybody who says he does is lying. It's like a car accident. If you could prepare for that you'd avoid it, wouldn't you?"

Herbert Warren Wind from the *New Yorker* ran into a famous retiree and his wife at the Forum one night in the 1960s. "The Rocket's red glare was gradually replaced by a calm, relaxed expression—the heavy burden of not letting down himself, the team, his friends, the whole province had been lifted from his shoulders. He had become a man with a nice sense of humour and a basic ease of manner." He talked about fishing, catching a 920-pound tuna off Caraquet, New Brunswick. Retirement? "No, it wasn't hard at all. Not after those three injuries I had in those last three years." Mme. Richard spoke up, then. "He quit too soon," she said, with a wink. "Much too soon," said Richard, without one.

I CAN'T RECOMMEND that you read all the hockey novels, especially not in chronological order. If my own experience is any guide, even if you do make it all the way through, you run the risk of wooziness, light sensitivity, inability to focus—what's known in today's NHL as *concussion-like symptoms.*

It's not for me to dismiss the first fifty years of hockey fiction in a sentence, but if it were, I'd use the phrase *penny-dreadful* and mention weak plotting, dumb outcomes, and a truly shocking lack of Canadians. Like Scott Young's early hockey novels, they're all about plucky young lads who make the team just in time to score the winning goal that nobody thought they had it in them to score while a jealous teammate/scapegrace does his best to ruin everything. To say that the fiction improved vastly when Young came along isn't saying much: even with the *Scrubs on Skates* trilogy casting its genial glow, hockey fiction remained a bleak, bleak landscape for a long time before it found itself heading into the 1960s. Things got busy then, even if the prose and the plotting didn't necessarily get better. Where once our heroes hoped for glory, now, in novels like *Power Play* and *Face-Off*, they have it all: sublime hockey skills, massive contracts, the adulation of throngs of fans. They can't hang on to it, of course, it's just too much, the unyielding pressure and the constant sex and the endless drugs, they get lost, stumble, fall: just like that, it's over. Not even hockey can save them.

Hockey fiction's late period begins with Roy MacGregor's Batterinski in the mid-1980s. I think that's right. That's where I'd start if I were looking to read some of the more interesting hockey novels: I'd head straight for Quarrington, Stenson, McCormack, Johnston, Gaston, Jarman. They all have their own individual merits, of course. If they share anything, it's a tendency their battered heroes have to look to a horizon beyond the game. It's not necessarily that they want to: they don't have a choice. The hockey players in the late novels are wounded and wise: they ache and they know. Jarman's Drinkwater has a scar on his face where novel-Bobby Clarke slashed him for twenty-seven stitches; Gaston's Bonaduce wakes up to the jarring truth that he's "a man who had dedicated his life to working violently hard at preventing people with different-coloured uniforms from putting a puck in his net."

What now? But if I told you here, you wouldn't have to go to the trouble of reading all the latter-day hockey novels I've just finished recommending. Anyway, they don't really make as monolithic a corpus as I've suggested. Forgive me if I'm only just now mentioning *The Antagonist*, Lynn Coady's piercing 2011 novel, and Richard Wagamese's powerful *Indian Horse* (2012), even as I sweep them up into my neat little theory that what fuels the novels now, finally, is the need to remind hockey that it never escapes real life, and never should, regardless of the game's haughty notions. Of course, Al Purdy says it better than I ever could, in the poem "Hockey Players," when he takes us

thru the smoky end boards out of
sight and climbing up the Appalachian highlands
and racing breast to breast across laurentian barrens
over hudson's diamond bay and down the treeless tundra where
auroras are tubercular and awesome and
stopping isn't feasible or possible or lawful [...]

AS WITH ALL endings, talk of retirement can sound like talk of death. But unless you're Gordie Howe, one of the strange effects of retiring from hockey is to add life, strip away the years. "It's not every day you get to go from being an old hockey player to being a young man," said Trevor Linden when he got out in 2008, aged thirty-seven.

Joe Primeau retired at the end of the 1936 season. He was thirty. "I felt that I had devoted enough of my life to pro hockey," he said. "I had been married nine years and I wanted to spend more time with my wife and youngsters. Then, too, I had worked up a pretty good business in cement blocks and I figured it was time I stepped out and put my energy into my own concern." It turned out well enough: before he went back to the Leafs as coach in 1950, Joe Primeau Block was producing four thousand blocks a day, with stock on hand of two hundred thousand.

John Ferguson took his leave in the fall of 1970, at the age thirty-two, and went straight into the presidency of Butternut Enterprises, a knitwear company. ("I matched my colours and was never outlandish with my colour schemes," he writes in his autobiography.) He returned to the ice after a short stay away: Jean Béliveau asked him back, Sam Pollock gave him a raise. Lots of players have returned. Gordie Howe went down to Houston to play with his two sons.

In 1988, a couple of days after Guy Lafleur was inducted into the Hockey Hall of Fame, he decided he wanted back in. He felt he had some top-level hockey left in him. Plus his son, three-and-a-half, had never seen him play. His agent tried Los Angeles and Detroit, but they weren't interested. The New York Rangers were, but he had to make the team at training camp. He stopped smoking—for a month or so, at least, he put away the cigarettes. The coach said he was the best New York player in the pre-season. He scored forty-five points that year, and went on to play two more seasons after that with the Quebec Nordiques.

Mark Jarman's Drinkwater wasn't so lucky. He couldn't get past the wondering and wavering.

If I could just do another year or two, I could make a lot of money, the way salaries are going. I could get back what the agent has pilfered or gambled . . . The right team—I could help, show some young D-Men some tricks. I'm a role model.

Well, I'm not but I could be.

Forget it. It's over. I accept my demise.

HOCKEY NIGHT IN CANADA long ago lost its song, and within a few years it may be gone altogether from our Saturdays. Doesn't matter. A Saturday in wintertime is still the day of the week we'll always associate with hockey. That it also happens to be the day, statistically, most Canadians die is a fact as unlikely as it is true. It's probably just a coincidence, but can we accept it as proof that deep and mysterious forces flow below the ice?

You can't prepare yourself, not really. The best you can do is close your eyes, like Pete McCormack's wise young hero in *Understanding Ken*:

> And imagine dying! All that electricity sucked out of your ears and mouth and nose and then it's just like before you were here: no hockey, no anything.

In 1989, Doug Harvey was admitted to Montreal General Hospital suffering from cirrhosis of the liver. Before that he'd been living at an Ottawa racetrack in a marooned private railway car that had once accommodated John Diefenbaker when he was going places as prime minister. Confined to care, as preordained by Howie Morenz, Harvey had a long line of visitors: Orr and Béliveau; Lafleur; Geoffrion; friends who brought him contraband gifts, in Harvey's case mainly luncheon treats, smoked meat sandwiches, a lobster. He died on Boxing Day, though his life, a columnist wrote, had already ended forty-four years earlier, when he had to stop playing hockey.

Spanish flu kills hockey players. Near Gravenhurst, they collide head-on with a light panel truck, whose driver suffers only bruises while they, the hockey players, are pronounced dead at the scene from broken ribs that puncture their hearts. Drunkenly they take the wheel of a red Porsche 930 Turbo and hit a wall in front of a red brick schoolhouse on Somerdale Road. On vacation they die, suddenly, at Wasaga Beach, Ontario, and also diving in the Bay of Quinte where it's too shallow to be diving. They succumb to congestive heart failure and after heart surgery that gets complicated. Liver cancer and leukemia claim them. They fall asleep and don't wake up. Milt Dunnell said that Cyclone Taylor lived so long—ninety-four years—that countless Canadians thought he was a legend their grandfathers made up.

Johnny Bucyk once said he couldn't imagine the brothers Richard not playing hockey. He thought they'd die with their skates on. In May of 2000, more than 115,000 people filed past the Rocket's casket, and the next day some 2,700 mourners attended the funeral at the city's Notre Dame Basilica. Lucien Bouchard, premier of Quebec, said, "When we see him go today, we recall our youth, our childhood. He was the man of our childhood, for people of my generation. It's a bit of our childhood that disappears."

Terry Sawchuk got into a quarrel over money with his teammate Ron Stewart in their backyard on Long Island. There are different versions of what might have happened, some featuring a barbecue that Sawchuk fell on, but all ending with blood pooling in Sawchuk's liver and, at 9:50 on the morning of May 31, 1970, his death. Brad Park talks about Sawchuk's Ranger teammates hearing the news. They went to practice, carrying on as usual according to the hockey player's code, "as if Ukey had been traded away."

Following his stint in Chicago, Howie Morenz went to New York, another sad step down the staircase out of hockey, it looked like. But then the Canadiens brought him back in September of 1936. He was thirty-four. Cecil Hart, his old friend, was in again as the coach, and he reunited Morenz with Joliat and Gagnon. By Christmas the Canadiens were at the top of the league, with Morenz one of the leading scorers. "I'm going the limit right now," Morenz himself said. "I'm giving the fans everything I've got. The end may be in sight but the heart is still sound. You know what I mean."

If you were writing this as fiction, you'd never make it so starkly obvious. He's supposed to have told Frank Selke that he was quitting. "It's getting too tough."

On January 28, a Thursday, the Canadiens played Chicago at home. Morenz's knee was heavily bandaged. He was down at the south end of the Forum, closest to St. Catherine Street. Nowadays there's a rule to stipulate that the boards *shall be constructed* in such a manner that the surface facing the ice *shall be smooth* and free of any obstruction or *any object that could cause injury to players*. In those years, though, it was more of a tongue-in-groove design.

As Toe Blake saw it from the Montreal bench, Morenz went looping behind the Black Hawks' net, where he lost his balance and fell into the boards, then Chicago's Earl Seibert "kinda fell on him." Sportswriter Andy O'Brien saw one of Morenz's skates dig into the boards; when he rolled over, the leg snapped. Joliat watched it from the ice: Morenz lost his footing, went down, put his feet up as he slid into the boards, and the "heels" of his skates stuck in the boards. Somebody checked Earl Seibert, who fell on Morenz's legs, and broke the left one.

Clarence Campbell was the referee that night. The way he describes it, Seibert dove headlong at Morenz, knocking him down, skate stuck, buckety-buck-buck. There was a novelist in the house, too: Hugh MacLennan remembered (as a novelist might) a little smile on Morenz's lips. "But once too often he charged into the corner relying on his ability to turn on a dime and come out with the puck. The point of his skate impaled itself in the boards. A defenceman, big Earl Seibert, accidentally crashed over the extended leg and broke it." MacLennan adds a detail that no one else mentions: "Howie's head hit the ice with a sickening crack and he was carried out." Unless Joliat and Gagnon helped him up and off. That's another version in circulation.

In the dressing room, there was a scene so stylized that somebody should paint it to hang up alongside Benjamin West's *The Death of General Wolfe*. Morenz was, apparently, a little more lucid than the general. He lay on the rubbing table, smoking a cigarette. "I'm all through," he's supposed to have muttered, "all finished." Don't blame Seibert, he said. "It was an accident. My skate caught." Joliat thought it was his wonky right knee that had betrayed him. Johnny Gagnon had tears in his eyes. Babe Siebert kept saying, "Hang on, Howie, hang on." Small boys wept in the Forum corridor as they took Morenz out, and though he was crying, too, he gave a cheery wave on his way to the ambulance.

His ankle was cracked and he had four broken bones in the leg. Or it was a compound fracture with the bones shattered in two places slightly above the ankle and below the knee. The reports varied. When *La Patrie* published the hospital x-rays, in Montreal, the *malleolus* became a hockey-bone.

Six days later, from his bed in L'Hôpital Saint-Luc, Morenz wrote a letter home. A couple of years ago, if you'd been quick with your credit card, you could have winked at the auctioneer and bought this actual item. Or whatever the online equivalent of winking is. The bidding started at $1,500. "Hello Dad + all," it starts. Fate gave him quite a blow, he says. The x-rays show a vast improvement. "Enclosed you will find a little money. If you have not got enough let me know."

Two days after the crash, the team went to New York and Boston, where they won, which Howie appreciated. Gagnon and Joliat wrote to him every day they were away and went to visit when they got back. Dr. Hector Forgues, the Canadiens' doctor, was quite satisfied, Joliat reported in his newspaper column. "Howie is most enthusiastic," he wrote. He'd be back sooner than people thought. The fracture was nothing compared to the ache of not lining up as a Canadien. "This is the suffering," he told his friends. At the end of February, Joliat's column offered this little koan:

> Hockey temporarily leaves the mind of the player. His nervous system is calm and he can live more at ease. Plans of attacks, errors forgotten, the player returns to play, well-rested, physically and morally.

His cast was arabesqued with a hundred signatures.

There's a haze of suggestion around these visitations, more winking, drifting innuendo, a whiff of whiskey. Nurses muttered later about bottles hidden under the bed. Stan Fischler mentions the words *overwhelmed* and *well-intentioned friends*, and conjures a room filled with flowers, candy, books. The well-wishers took a *toll*, Morenz's biographer, Dean Robinson, says, and he suffered a nervous breakdown. Dr. Forgues said no more visitors. Then there was a guard at the door.

There are several photos of Morenz in hospital, one with his wife and his son, another from February 25, when Toronto's Charlie Conacher came to visit and examine the cast. Morenz looks good. He's wearing a warm-looking dressing gown, with a pipe in his mouth. I'd like to know the titles of the six books that are piled on the bedside table.

This is said to be his last photo. On Tuesday, March 9, Toronto's *Daily Star* reported the stunning news: "Like a tired child dropping softly to sleep, Howie Morenz died in a Montreal hospital last night."

The time of death was 11:30 PM. Myths and facts were already mixing together by morning. An immediate report said he had a light supper, smiled at his nurse, "then turned his head wearily on the pillow." One account added a "tired sigh." A "strange pallor" settled over his face and the nurse called in the doctor. Too late.

Another story was that he'd tried to get up—"took one faltering step," as Trent Frayne tells it, "then slowly crumpled to the floor." A Toronto newspaper said that those closest to him weren't surprised; the decline had been "appallingly rapid," his weight was down to under one hundred pounds. The *debonairly gay caballero* was, at the end, a *pitiful shadow*. "The frame of him was wasted. He didn't know his friends."

The death certificate gave the cause as, quote, cardiac deficiency and acute excitement. This is where the broken-heart stories got started. Newspapermen wrote,

> To those who knew the strong vein of sentimentality that surged in the make-up of this remarkable athlete, it was as if the fibre of the man slowly disintegrated as he faced the uncertainties of a hockeyless future.

Also, there was Aurèle Joliat to add, "He told me one time, he says, whenever I can't play hockey, he says, I'd just as soon be dead." And, yes, if you were writing a libretto, that's the end you'd write. Further facts that came out, years later, regarding blood clots? The blunt clarity they'd provide wouldn't be useful to the story of Howie Morenz. You'd have to lay them aside. Meanwhile, hockey hockeyed on. What else was it supposed to do? Three days after Morenz was buried, the Canadiens beat the New York Rangers.

Before the month was out, Dr. Forgues himself had died of a heart attack in the Canadiens' dressing room, on duty in Detroit during a playoff game.

In 2004, at another auction, Morenz's "death skates" sold for US$25,000.

THE CREEK BEGAN to rush. Overnight, its adjectives thawed from *burbling* to *torrentine*. The whole place was hurrying towards the spring, melting and gurgling, glistening in the bolder sunshine. In the pasture of snow in front of the house, the crisses and crosses of winter paths turned to green, and the snow that was still there revealed its mice trails, faint and blue as veins in your wrist. Then all the snow was gone, except for the ruins of our snow forts. The bats came out in the daylight, too soon, flinging around in front of the living room window as they tried to tune their radar. It was still too cold for them, and for a couple of days the long verandah was where the bats went to die.

Over at the pond, pucks kept turning up along the shore, as pleasing to discover as a crop of vegetables I'd planted myself. Early in March I was still skating but the ice was going soft—*sishy* they'd say in Newfoundland, according to the poet Randall Maggs. After that, during the week, whoever it was who'd been walking on my rink with big stegosaurus snowshoes left a looping trail at centre and the water rose up through the footprints. One of my nets got stuck, frozen in meltwater, and for the next few days I watched it sink. One Saturday morning I put on my boots and went over and stood on the shore and thought for a while before I didn't venture out. I'd like to tell you that I hook-checked the net to safety, but it was too far out. I didn't have to tell the dog to stay ashore. She knew.

I HAVEN'T READ *100 Things Sabres Fans Should Know & Do Before They Die* (2012), and probably won't, but could, and might. By leaving some of the hockey books unread, I don't rule out the possibility that there's a high shelf somewhere and on it, the volume that explains everything.

The ongoing challenge that all the hockey books present to a reader is that—well, they're so ongoing. I'm not complaining when I say that there are too many of them, even for me, they just keep coming and coming. Larry Robinson is out with his second autobiography in 2014 which, as Brad Park, Paul Henderson, and Gerry Cheevers will tell you, is the new norm.

Recently I've been doing my best to catch up on hockey's unwritten literature, in particular, the many rules and codes that govern the game. For instance: If you're challenged to a fight but you're injured, you're allowed to decline, respectfully. That's one, a clause in the legendary honour system that guards hockey's fighters from harm like a magic cloak. It's on page 65 of Ross Bernstein's *The Code: The Unwritten Rules of Fighting and Retaliation in the* NHL (2006), about one-third of the way through. I came across it while I was looking for some kind of explanation of who gets to transcribe the codes and under what circumstances. I couldn't figure it out, though. I always feel so guilty, reading about hockey's oral traditions, let alone writing about them, though nobody else seems to feel that way.

It's important to acknowledge the game's newest languages, which already have their own books, although I haven't learned to speak any of them yet, can't even say *Hello, how are you?* I'm talking here of Corsi and Fenwick, THoR and Zone Starts, and all the rest of the Advanced Stats, including those practised by tribes still living deep in the forests without having yet made contact with civilization.

Hockey's literature has reached the point where it's generating whole new genres. I don't know that the one I'm thinking about in particular has yet produced its own version of *The Game*, but there's surely time. Not sure how sales are going either, but the lawsuits filed by former players against the NHL contending that the league knew about the risks of head trauma inherent in the game long before it took steps to address them make for compelling reading. I have two of them on the corner of my desk, from early 2014, and I plan to get to them right after I find out what happens at the end of *The Continued Examination for Discovery of David Nonis, Volume II* from the Steve Moore lawsuit against Todd Bertuzzi and the Vancouver Canucks.

Books I would have read if they existed:

- Peter Gzowski's work on the Montreal Canadiens that he researched but never published.
- The inspirational poetry that Georges Vézina is supposed to have written when he tended the Habs' goal.
- All nine volumes on the "Books to Look For" page of Gordie Howe's autobiography *And . . . Howe!* (1995), including *On Frozen Pond*, "the personal, wondrous and intimate account of the pre-hockey, prairie boy years of Gordie Howe and the formation of his native intellect and survival instincts."

I'd like to read a Scotty Bowman memoir and a Milt Schmidt, also a Sprague Cleghorn biography and the hockey novel that Philip Roth is working on while he pretends to have given up fiction. I am looking forward, too, to the history someone writes when the fighting dwindles out of the game, which is how Gary Bettman says it's going to go. "We respect the history, the tradition, and the vibrancy of the game," the commissioner said in 2013. "You just don't throw a light switch and effectuate a major change."

Will hockey last long enough for that? Will there be sufficient winter? In 2007, Walter Gretzky told Roy MacGregor that if Wayne were growing up today in Brantford, he wouldn't be able to build a backyard rink for his boy, it just isn't cold enough. And the Nith River? "Winters are warmer now. There's no ice." A national study broadcast the alarm in 2012: global warming is endangering the very ice that makes our game and us. *Maclean's* was on the case, too: "The Year That Winter Died" was the cover story that March.

So maybe that's what happens: hockey just melts away. With many recent professional lockouts to help us, the dire warnings do open up just enough of a crack for our imaginations to slip through and conjure an altogether hockeyless Canada. Once you get going, hockey subtracts fairly easily from the equation.

To return a century's worth of sticks to their natural state would take some doing—every Northland and Bauer, all the Sher-Woods, CCMs, Coopers, Canadiens, Hespelers, Eastons, the Reeboks, the Warriors, every last Supreme Rogue and Stealth Reflex III, rock elm to rock elm forest, carbon fibre to certified recycling facility for thermal depolymerization. Skates to the incinerators—sorry, you ice dancers and short-track speedsters. Unvulcanizing all the pucks might take a while, and we'd want to get that rubber stockpiled away somewhere safe, where we can get at it come the next war. "Hockey never leaves the blood of a Canadian," Harry Sinden reminds us, but we'd have to figure it out. We now know that reading most of the hockey books doesn't work, so that's a start. Some kind of transfusion might do it, a procedure we'll call *hemahockeyamotiosis*. Sounds risky.

With no hockey, we'd be looking at a whole lot of real estate freed up downtown in Toronto and Montreal, Peterborough and Voskresensk. In Toronto's Leafless Gardens there's a model for what we could do with all of these sudden hulks of rinks: state-of-the-art supermarkets for all! Or better, big parks, filled with gardens, new urban forests with little lakes and many statues of famous and not-so-famous writers and their characters, and poets and scientists and doctors—no politicians. Maybe on Saturday nights in winter, without hockey to watch on our TVs, that's where we'd go, climbing aboard our bicycle skates, slicing down there in no time.

We'd have to think of other ways to sell our beer and our dough-
nuts. We'd need to be prepared for the spike in crime. Mordecai
Richler was writing in 1981 about the obvious correlation between
violence on the ice and the safety of Canadian streets. Why do muggers prowl Detroit, New York, and Boston, while nobody feels
threatened in Montreal, Toronto, or Calgary? "This is because we have
cunningly put our potential muggers into team sweaters, shoving
them out on the ice, paying then handsomely to spear, slash and
high stick or whatever."

If he's right, if hockey is the place where we channel the worst of
us, our self-loathing and base instincts, a national midden for
everything we're not too proud of, all the anger and poor sportsmanship and rudeness, we're going to have to find somewhere else
to stow all that, and soon, maybe with the help of the carbon seques-
tration people.

And what would all the hockey players do? On the evidence of
Eddie Shore and Max Bentley, we know that they can farm, given a
quarter section near Peace River, Alberta, or on the road to Vanscoy,
Saskatchewan. They drive beer trucks in Kitchener, Ontario (Bingo
Kampman); sell Bee-Hive Corn Syrup for the St. Lawrence Starch
Company (Bob Davidson); direct funerals (Alf Pike); tend ten mil-
lion bees (Butch Bouchard); cut toe rubbers at Merchants Rubber
Company (Frank Selke). There's no reason why they can't work in
wealth management (Derek Sanderson); run a billiard academy
(Hooley Smith); golf professionally (Bill Ezinicki); divide their time
between oil wells and orchards in California (Ching Johnson); be
elected band chief (Fred Sasakamoose); sell accident insurance (Nels
Stewart); serve in the upper house of Russia's Federal Assembly, representing Primorsky Krai (Viacheslav Fetisov); or deploy to the war
in Afghanistan with Princess Patricia's Canadian Light Infantry (Ed
Staniowski).

Some of us would be harder to disenthrall than others. There would be resistance, maybe some of us up in the hills with a left-handed Titan and a copy of *Dipsy-Doodle Dandy*.

But would it last? I don't think so. There's only so long we'd be able to go without inventing hockey all over again. Curling will never win us over, and lacrosse—lacrosse would present itself, shyly smiling, *what about me?* and we'd send it on its way, again.

The winter wouldn't have to be especially severe; just cold enough would do. In November of 1608, in Scotland, a *vehement frost* locked the tide at the Firth of Forth, and "The sea freized so farre as it ebbed, and sindrie went in to shippes upon yce, and played at chamiare a myle within the sea marke."

That would do it. Chamiare! How could we deny the stirring in our veins? We'd think at first, why go out in the cold when we can stay in? But pretty soon we'd be looking around for toques and life jackets. It wouldn't have to be in Canada. It could be anywhere. Maybe this time we'd decide on the rules—maybe even a preamble— before we got out there, to be sure there's a sense to it ahead of time. I'm just talking here, making it up as I go.

Actually, save the rules for later. When it's cold, with wind sweeping the snow for you, that's the time to rig up something like a skate, get out there. The ice can't wait forever. Its call is urgent. It's not a page, never was, that's going to write itself.

[Acknowledgements]

If you're going to read all the hockey books and then write about them, you're going to need an eminently enthusiastic and very patient publisher. I did, anyway, and I was lucky enough to find him in Rob Sanders. Without him and the wise and unfailingly encouraging Jan Walter, *Puckstruck* would be languishing still on my desk.

For meeting and talking, for answering questions both small and not-so small, and/or for their general willingness to help, my thanks go to: Dave Bidini, Craig Campbell, Lloyd Davis, Stan Fischler, Martin Levin, Roy MacGregor, Ron MacLean, Roy McMurtry, James Milks, Stephen Osborne, Phil Pritchard, Dr. Vern Stenlund, Dianna Symonds, and Jane Winton.

I met Bill Fitsell long ago in the newsroom of the *Kingston Whig-Standard* and he continues to inspire me with his good-humoured and tireless hockey scholarship. Thank you, Bill.

It's a pleasure to work with the dedicated team at Greystone: Jennifer Croll and Jessica Sullivan, Andrea Damiani, Lesley Cameron, Ingrid Paulson, Peter Norman, and Beverly Dunne.

Without George Powell, there would have been no rink at Indian Hill.

Thanks to Dr. Mike Evans and Steve Thuringer for picking me for their teams.

I'm grateful to Chris Dennis for his many years of watching my back, even if that's meant taking a penalty now and again, and to James Darling for his steadfast love of Habs.

Hail to Andy Heintzman, Mike McGowan, Miles Kronby, and Nick de Pencier for getting me down all those (terrifying) rapids and for the laughter and unwavering support. Also to Sarah Atkinson, Ian Spears, Roz Heintzman, Shelagh McNulty, Jennifer Baichwal, and Tammy Quinn: thank you.

Evan Solomon helped shape this book with his insight and literary instincts as much as with his wholehearted passionate self and unapologetic drop-passes.

Dawn and Denis Smith, Alastair and Andrea: *abrazos*.

Thank you, and love—all of it—to Sarah and Zac and Ruairi, who believe.

[Endnotes]

FIRST

1. Peter Mahovlich Sr., father of Frank and Peter Jr.
2. Doug Messier, father of Mark
3. Ben Conacher, father of Lionel
4. William Bentley, father of Max, Doug, Reg, et al.
5. Cal Gardner's father
6. Louis Sawchuk, father of Terry
7. Garnet Henderson, father of Paul
8. Vladimir Bure, father of Pavel and Valeri
9. Charlie Meeker Jr., father of Howie
10. Steve Barilko, father of Bill
11. Ted Baun, father of Bobby
12. Borden Bossy, father of Mike
13. George Mikita, father of Stan
14. Onésime Richard, father of Maurice and Henri
15. Jacques Vézina, father of Georges
16. Fred Armstrong, father of George
17. Gilbert Dionne, father of Marcel
18. Ted Donato's father
19. William Cleghorn, father of Sprague and Odie
20. Steve Patrick, father of James
21. Doug Messier, father of Mark
22. Tom Clancy, father of King
23. Borden Bossy, father of Mike

[Sources]

A complete list of sources cited and quoted for this book is available at puckstruck.com, along with notes and annotations.

[All the (Selected) Hockey Books]

Angus, Charlie. *Les Costello: Canada's Flying Father*. Toronto: Novalis, 2005.

Arnold, Ed. *Hockey Town: Life Before the Pros*. Toronto: McClelland & Stewart, 2004.

Atwood, Margaret. *Survival*. Toronto: House of Anansi, 1972.

Barbour, Ralph Henry. *Guarding His Goal*. New York: D. Appleton, 1926.

Batten, Jack. *The Leafs in Autumn*. Toronto: Macmillan, 1975.

Beardsley, Doug. *Country on Ice*. Winlaw: Polestar, 1988.

Beers, William. *Lacrosse: Canada's National Game*. Montreal, 1869.

Bernstein, Ross. *The Code: The Unwritten Rules of Fighting and Retaliation in the NHL*. Chicago: Triumph, 2006.

Bidini, Dave. *Tropic of Hockey*. Toronto: McClelland & Stewart, 2000.

———. *A Wild Stab for It: This Is Game Eight from Russia*. Toronto: ECW, 2012.

Birdwell, Cleo. *Amazons*. New York: Holt, Reinhart and Winston, 1980.

Bowlsby, Craig. *1913: The Year They Invented the Future of Hockey*. Vancouver: Knights of Winter, 2013.

Carrier, Roch (illustrated by Sheldon Cohen). *The Hockey Sweater*. Toronto: House of Anansi, 1979.

Cosentino, Frank. *Hockey Gods at the Summit: How the 1972 Team Canada-Soviet Series Became a September to Remember*. Renfrew: General Store, 2011.

Craig, John. *Power Play*. New York: Dodd, Mead, 1968.

Drackett, Phil. *Flashing Blades: The Story of British Ice Hockey*. Ramsbury: Crowood Press, 1987.

Dryden, Ken (with Mark Mulvoy). *Face-Off at the Summit*. Toronto: Little, Brown, 1973.

Dryden, Ken. *The Game: A Thoughtful and Provocative Look at a Life in Hockey*. Toronto: Macmillan, 1983.

Duplacey, James. *The Rules of Hockey*. Toronto: Dan Diamond, 1996.

Dutton, Meryvn. *Hockey: The Fastest Game on Earth*. New York: Funk & Wagnalls, 1938.

Eskenazi, Gerald. *A Thinking Man's Guide to Pro Hockey*. New York: E.P. Dutton, 1972.

Esposito, Phil (with Peter Golenbock). *Thunder and Lightning: A No-B.S. Hockey Memoir*. Toronto: McClelland & Stewart, 2003.

Farrell, Arthur. *Hockey: Canada's Royal Winter Game*. Montreal: C.R. Corneil, 1899.

Faulkner, William. *Essays, Speeches and Public Letters*. New York: Random House, 1965.

Ferguson, Donald. *The Chums of Scranton High at Ice Hockey*. Cleveland: World Syndicate, 1919.

Fischler, Stan. *Those Were the Days: The Lore of Hockey*. New York: Dodd, Mead, 1976.

Fitkin, Ed. *Max Bentley: Hockey's Dipsy-Doodle Dandy*. Toronto: Castle, 1951.

Fitsell, J.W. (Bill). *Hockey's Captains, Colonels & Kings*. Erin: Boston Mills Press, 1987.

———. *How Hockey Happened*. Kingston: Quarry Heritage, 2007.

Fitzsimmons, Cortland. *Crimson Ice: A Hockey Mystery*. New York: Grosset & Dunlap, 1935.

Frayne, Trent. *The Mad Men of Hockey*. Toronto: McClelland & Stewart, 1974.

Fyffe, Iain. *On His Side of the Puck: The Early History of Hockey Rules*. Fredericton: Blurb. 2014.

Gaston, Bill. *The Good Body*. Dunvegan: Cormorant, 2000.

Gidén, Carl, Patrick Houda, and Jean-Patrice Martel. *On The Origin of Hockey*. Stockholm and Chambly: Hockey Origin, 2014.

Gitler, Ira. *Blood On The Ice: Hockey's Most Violent Moments*. Chicago: Henry Regnery, 1974.

Gopnik, Adam. *Winter: Five Windows on the Season*. Toronto: House of Anansi, 2011.

Gzowski, Peter. *The Game of Our Lives*. Toronto: McClelland & Stewart, 1981.

Harper, Stephen J. *A Great Game: The Forgotten Leafs & The Rise of Professional Hockey*. Toronto: Simon & Schuster, 2013.

Harrison, Richard. *Hero of the Play*. Toronto: Wolsak and Wynn, 1994.

Hood, Hugh. *Strength Down Centre: The Jean Béliveau Story*. Scarborough: Prentice-Hall, 1970.

Howe, Gordie, and Colleen Howe (with Tom Delisle). *and . . . Howe!* Traverse City: Power Play, 1995.

Hull, Bobby. *Hockey Is My Game*. Don Mills: Longmans, 1968.

Jagr, Jaromir (with Jan Smid). *Jagr: An Autobiography*. Pittsburgh: 68 Productions, 1997.

Jarman, Mark Anthony. *Salvage King, Ya!* Vancouver, Anvil Press, 1997.

Johnston, Wayne. *The Divine Ryans*. Toronto: McClelland & Stewart, 1990.

Kidd, Bruce, and John Macfarlane. *The Death of Hockey*. Toronto: New Press, 1972.

Klein, Jeff Z., and Karl-Eric Reif. *The Death of Hockey: or, How a Bunch of Guys with Too Much Money and Too Little Sense Are Killing the Greatest Game on Earth*. Toronto: Macmillan, 1998.

Larionov, Igor (with Jim Taylor and Leonid Reizer). *Larionov*. Winnipeg: Codner, 1990.

Ludwig, Jack. *Hockey Night in Moscow*. Toronto: McClelland & Stewart, 1972.

MacGregor, Roy. *The Last Season*. Toronto: Macmillan, 1983.

MacSkimming, Roy. *Cold War*. Vancouver: Greystone, 1996.

Maggs, Randall. *Night Work: The Sawchuk Poems*. London: Brick Books, 2008.

Martin, Lawrence. *The Red Machine: The Soviet Quest to Dominate Canada's Game*. Toronto: Doubleday, 1990.

McCormack, Pete. *Understanding Ken*. Vancouver: Douglas & McIntyre, 1998.

McIlhone, Quinn. *Trade Rumours*. Toronto: McClelland & Stewart, 1985.

McMurtry, William R. *Investigation and Inquiry into Violence in Amateur Hockey*. Toronto: Ministry of Community and Social Services, 1974.

Meeker, Howie. *Howie Meeker's Hockey Basics*. Scarborough: Prentice-Hall, 1973.

Moffatt, James. *Blue Line Murder*. North Hollywood: Leisure, 1970.

Muller, Charles Geoffrey. *Puck Chasers Incorporated*. New York: Harper & Brothers, 1927.

Orr, Bobby (with Mark Mulvoy). *My Game*. Boston: Little, Brown, 1974.

Palmer, Bernard. *Danny Orlis Plays Hockey*. Chicago: Moody Press, 1957.

Plimpton, George. *Open Net*. New York: W.W. Norton, 1995.

Podnieks, Andrew. *The Complete Hockey Dictionary*. Toronto: Fenn, 2007.

Quarrington, Paul. *King Leary*. Toronto: Doubleday Canada, 1987.

Richards, David Adams. *Hockey Dreams: Memories of a Man Who Couldn't Play*. Toronto: Doubleday, 1996.

Robinson, Dean. *Howie Morenz*. Erin: The Boston Mills Press, 1982.

Roche, Bill. *The Hockey Book*. Toronto: McClelland & Stewart, 1953.

Ronberg, Gary. *The Ice Men*. New York: Crown, 1973.

———. *The Hockey Encyclopedia*. Toronto: Macmillan, 1974.

Roy, Guy. *Violence au Hockey*. Montreal: Les Éditions Sherbrooke, 1977.

Salming, Borje (with Gerhard Karlsson). *Blood, Sweat and Hockey*. Toronto: HarperCollins, 1991.

Salutin, Rick. *Les Canadiens*. Vancouver: Talonbooks, 1977.

Scherer, Karl Adolf. *1908-1978: 70 Years of LIHG/IIHF*. Munich: Edition Prosport, 1978.

Scanlan, Lawrence. *Grace Under Fire: The State of our Sweet and Savage Game*. Toronto: Penguin, 2002.

Segal, Seymour (images) and Hood, Hugh (text). *Scoring: The Art of Hockey*. Ottawa: Oberon, 1979.

Smith, Michael D. *Violence And Sport*. Toronto: Canadian Scholars' Press, 1988.

Sinden, Harry. *Showdown: The Canada-Russia Hockey Series*. Toronto: Doubleday, 1972.

Stenson, Fred. *Teeth*. Regina: Coteau, 1994.

Sterling, Chandler W. *The Icehouse Gang: My Year With The Black Hawks*. New York: Charles Scribner's Sons, 1972.

Tarasov, Anatoli. *Road To Olympus*. Toronto: Griffin House, 1969.

Tretiak, Vladislav. *The Art of Goaltending*. Edmonton: Plains Publishing, 1989.

Vaughan, Garth. *The Puck Starts Here*. Fredericton: Goose Lane Editions, 1996.

Young, Chip. *The Wild Canadians*. Toronto: Clarke, Irwin, 1975.

Young, Scott. *Scrubs on Skates*. Toronto: McClelland & Stewart, 1952.

———. *That Old Gang of Mine*. Markham: Fitzhenry & Whiteside, 1982.

Young, Scott (with George Robertson). *Face-Off*. Toronto: Macmillan, 1971.

[Permissions]

[Photo Credits]

[Index]

Madison Square Garden (New York), 43, 44,
57, 82, 169, 217, 229, 297, 306
Maggs, Randall, 393; *Night Work*, 362
Magnuson, Keith, 225, 243; *None Against!*,
348–9; pre-game routines, 54, 55
Mahovlich, Frank, 131, 234, 237, 286, 298, 304–
5; childhood, 27; on playing hockey, 53
Mahovlich, Peter Jr., 188, 284, 286; joy of
hockey, 56; medical problems, 13
Mahovlich, Peter Sr., father of Frank and
Peter Jr., 32 (401n1)
Maki, Chico, 130
Maki, Wayne, 337
Malarchuk, Clint, 243
Malone, Joe, 140
Maloney, Dan: assault charge, 363
Maltby, Kirk, 216
Manhattan Melodrama, 10
Manitoba Hockey: A History (Leah), 69
Mansbridge, Peter, 227–8
Mantha, Sylvio, 306
Maple Leaf Gardens, 63, 159, 205, 233, 277,
296, 297, 311, 396
Maple Leafs. *See* Toronto Maple Leafs
Marchand, Brad, 134
Mariucci, Johnny, 226
Markov, Andrei, 198
Maroon, Joseph, 228
Maroons. *See* Montreal Maroons
marriage, 249
Marsh, Lou, 176, 306, 307
Marsh, Mush: on cold, 42
Marshall (Inspector), 357
Marshall, Grant, 216
Martel, Jean-Patrice: *On the Origin of
Hockey*, 73; presentation, 74
Martin, Lawrence, 299; *The Red Machine*,
332
Massey, John, 69
Massey, Vincent, 314–5, 319; *On Being
Canadian*, 48

Masterton, Bill: death of, 337
May, Julian: *Hockey with a Grin*, 40
McAllister, Scottie, 110
McArthur, Dalton, 344
McCabe, Bryan, 131
McCool, Frank, 326
McCormack, Pete, 384; *Understanding Ken*,
52, 249, 328, 387
McDiarmid, Mac (artist), 144
McDonald, Wilfred, 335
McFadden, Fred: *Bobby Clarke*, 39–40
McFarlane, Leslie, 147–8
McGee, Frank, 266, 267
McGiffen, Minnie (Roy), 355–6
McGrath, Ben, 353
McGrath, Charles, 352
McGrath, James, 305
McGrattan, Brian, 254
McGuire, Pierre, 131
McIlhone, Quinn: *Trade Rumours*, 260
McIntyre, Alex, 113
McKee, Ann, 228
McLaughlin, Frederic, 167
McMaster, Jack, 295–6
McMurtry, Bill: inquiry into violence, 366–
75; "Investigation and Inquiry into
Violence in Amateur Hockey," 363
McMurtry, Roy, 283; 362–375; *Memories and
Reflections*, 362
McNamara, Howard, 356
McNeil, Gerry, 326
McNutt, Paul V., 273
McSorley, Marty, 224, 297; on change, 85
Meagher, George, 69
meanness, 277–85. *See also* anger; hate;
violence
medical problems, 13, 168–9. *See also*
deaths; injuries
Meeker, Charlie Jr., father of Howie, 32
(401n9)
Meeker, Howie, 26, 63, 101–2, 168;

· 422 ·

smoking, 7, 61–62, 159, 334, 386. *See also* conditioning; tobacco, chewing

Smolka, Martin: *Nagano*, 8

Smythe, Conn, 64, 140, 158, 159, 168, 174, 205, 233, 234, 249, 250, 301, 359, 361, 364; on change, 84. *See also* Conn Smythe Trophy

Smythe, Stafford, 360

Snow in America (Mergen), 65

soccer, 85, 193, 195, 206, 222, 262; ball, 75; Moscow Dynamo, 193, 194; Soccer War, 263

Society for International Hockey Research (SIHR). *See* SIHR

Society of North American Hockey Historians and Researchers. *See* SONAHHR

Solman, Lol, 355

Solzhenitsyn, Alexander, 213–4

SONAHHR (Society of North American Hockey Historians and Researchers), 72–73

Sonnenberg, Hendrika: *Hockey Fights/Fruit Bowls*, 8

Soul on Ice (Black Power manifesto) (Cleaver), 11

sounds: hockey, 126–7; fighting, 226. *See also* language

Sovsport, 195

Speaking Canadian English (Orkin), 133

speed, of the game, 29

spitting, 269

sports: rivals of hockey, 312–4 . *See also* baseball; basketball; boxing; golf; lacrosse; soccer

Sports Canada, 331

Sports College, 339

Sports Illustrated, 125, 249, 260; Faulkner essay in, 59, 62

St. Germain, Ralph, 177

St. Laurent, Dollard, 245

St. Pats, 58, 296

Staios, Steve, 216

Standish, Burt L. *See* Patten, Gilbert

Staniowski, Ed, 397

Stanley Cup, 9, 24, 25, 26, 40, 55, 56, 61, 81, 89, 90, 101, 128, 197–8, 200, 203, 217, 272, 305, 322, 327, 332, 347, 349, 379

Star. See Toronto Daily Star

Starkman, Randy, 287

Steckel, Dave, 135

Steel on Ice, 11

Stenson, Fred, 384; *Teeth*, 133, 261, 347

Stephenson, Wayne, 209

Sterling, Chandler W., 129–30; *The Icehouse Gang*, 50–51

Sterner, Ulf, 207, 209–11, 215

Stewart, Bill, 306

Stewart, Black Jack, 156, 226; eating, 7

Stewart, Gaye: childhood, 27

Stewart, Nels, 89, 157, 269, 397

Stewart, Ron, 388

stickfight, 82

sticks, hockey. *See under* equipment

stitches, 241–5. *See also* injuries

Stoner, Clayton, 134

Storey, Red, 269, 282, 298

Strength Down Centre (Hood), 49–50

Stromber, Arne, 209

Struthers, Betsy, 137

Summit Series. *See* 1972 Summit Series

Summit Series, The (Bendell), 189

Sunday hockey, 211

Sundin, Mats, 378

Survival (Atwood), 66

Sutter, Brian: on playing hockey, 53

Sutter, Duane: on cold, 42

Sutter, Louie, 34

swearing. *See* profanity and insults

Sweden: history of hockey, 206–11

Swedish books, 8